The Psychoanalysis Choice, Job Perform Satisfaction

Freud said that "love and work" are the central therapeutic goals of psychoanalysis: the twin pillars for a sound mind and for living the "good life." While psychoanalysis has masterfully contributed to understanding the experience of love, it has made only a modest contribution to understanding the psychology of work. This book is the first to explore fully the psychoanalysis of work, analyzing career choice, job performance and job satisfaction, with an eye toward helping people make wiser choices that bring out the best in themselves, their colleagues and their organization.

The book addresses the crucial questions concerning work: how does one choose the right career; what qualities contribute to excellence in performance; how best to implement and cope with organizational change; and what capacity and skills does one need to enjoy everyday work?

Drawing on psychoanalytic thinking, vocational counseling, organizational psychology and business studies, *The Psychoanalysis of Career Choice, Job Performance and Satisfaction* will be invaluable in clinical psychoanalytic work, as well as for mental health professionals, scholars, career counselors and psychologists looking for a deeper understanding of work-based issues.

Paul Marcus, PhD, is a training and supervisory analyst at the National Psychological Association for Psychoanalysis in New York City and the author/editor of eighteen books, including *Creating Heaven on Earth: The Psychology of Experiencing Immortality in Everyday Life* and *Sports as Soul-craft: How Playing and Watching Sports Enhances Life*. He can be reached at Tibs9@aol.com

It is not your responsibility to finish the work [of perfecting the world], but neither are you free to abstain from it.
—Rabbi Tarfon, *Sayings of the Fathers* (author's translation)

The Psychoanalysis of Career Choice, Job Performance, and Satisfaction

How To Flourish in the Workplace

Paul Marcus

Routledge
Taylor & Francis Group

LONDON AND NEW YORK

First published 2017
by Routledge
2 Park Square, Milton Park, Abingdon, Oxon OX14 4RN

and by Routledge
711 Third Avenue, New York, NY 10017

Routledge is an imprint of the Taylor & Francis Group, an informa business

© 2017 Paul Marcus

British Library Cataloguing in Publication Data
A catalogue record for this book is available from the British Library

Library of Congress Cataloging in Publication Data
Names: Marcus, Paul, 1953- author.
Title: The psychoanalysis of career choice, job performance, and satisfaction: how to flourish in the workplace / Paul Marcus.
Description: Abingdon, Oxon ; New York, NY : Routledge, 2017.
Identifiers: LCCN 2016022876| ISBN 9781138211643 (hardback) | ISBN 9781138211650 (pbk.) | ISBN 9781315452531 (ebook)
Subjects: LCSH: Vocational guidance–Psychological aspects. | Career development–Psychological aspects. | Psychology, Industrial. | Occupations–Psychological aspects. | Work–Psychological aspects. | Psychoanalysis.
Classification: LCC HF5381 .M3175 2017 | DDC 650.101/9–dc23
LC record available at https://lccn.loc.gov/2016022876

ISBN: 978-1-138-21164-3 (hbk)
ISBN: 978-1-138-21165-0 (pbk)
ISBN: 978-1-315-45253-1 (ebk)

Typeset in Times New Roman
by Cenveo Publisher Services

To my late psychoanalyst, Phillip M. Stone, who was still capably analyzing two weeks before his death at age 98.

Books by Paul Marcus

Sports as Soul-craft: How Playing and Watching Sports Enhances Life (Marquette University Press, 2015).

Creating Heaven on Earth: The Psychology of Experiencing Immortality in Everyday Life (Karnac, 2015).

They Shall Beat Their Swords Into Plowshares: Military Strategy, Psychoanalysis and The Art Of Living (Marquette University Press, 2014).

How to Laugh Your Way Through Life: A Psychoanalyst's Advice (Karnac, 2013).

In Search of the Spiritual: Gabriel Marcel, Psychoanalysis and the Sacred (Karnac, 2013).

Theater as Life: Psychological Insights Drawn from Great Acting Teachers, Actors and Actresses (Marquette University Press, 2011, with Gabriela Marcus).

In Search of the Good Life: Emmanuel Levinas, Psychoanalysis and the Art of Living (Karnac Publishers, 2010).

Warring Parents, Wounded Children, and the Wretched World of Child Custody: Cautionary Tales. Co-author J. Helmreich (Greenwood Publishers, 2008).

Being for the Other: Emmanuel Levinas, Ethical Living and Psychoanalysis (Marquette University Press, 2008).

Levinas and Psychoanalysis. Editor, A Special Issue of the Psychoanalytic Review (2007).

Ancient Religious Wisdom: Spirituality and Psychoanalysis (Praeger, 2003).

Autonomy in the Extreme Situation: Bruno Bettelheim, the Nazi Concentration Camps and the Mass Society (Praeger, 1999).

Blacks and Jews on the Coach: Psychoanalytic Reflections on Black-Jewish Conflict (Co-editor Alan Helmreich.) (Praeger, 1988).

Psychoanalytic Versions of the Human Condition: Philosophies of Life and Their Impact on Practice (Co-editor Alan Rosenberg) (New York University Press. 1998).

On the Death of My Father: A Psychoanalyst's Memoir (Edwin Mellen Press. 1995).

Bruno Bettelheim's Contribution to Psychoanalysis. Co-editor with Alan Rosenberg. A Special Issue of the Psychoanalytic Review (1994).

Into the Great Forest: A Story for Children Away from Parents for the First Time (Co-authored with Irene Wineman Marcus), (Brunner-Mazel, 1992).

Scary Night Visitors: A Story for Children with Bedtime Fears (Co-authored with Irene Wineman Marcus), (Brunner-Mazel, 1990).

Healing Their Wounds: Psychotherapy with Holocaust Survivors and Their Families (Co-edited with Alan Rosenberg), (Praeger, 1989).

Psychoanalytic Reflections on the Holocaust: Selected Essays (Co-edited with Steven A. Luel), (University of Denver and KTAV Publishers, 1984).

Contents

Chapter 1

Introduction

"Without work, all life goes rotten," said Albert Camus, "but when work is soulless, life stifles and dies" (www.oxfordreference.com).[1] Indeed, Camus' astute observation resonates with most people who seriously reflect on the problem of what it takes to fashion a work life that is joyful, or at least satisfying, over a sustained period of time.[2] To loathe one's work, or to experience it as barely tolerable, is a kind of personal horror that calls to mind a bad marriage or failed relationship with a significant other in which one feels utterly trapped. Regrettably, in western society this feeling of disenchantment with one's work life is fairly common; phrases like "I am burned out," "I am only working for the pay check," "I can't stand my job" punctuate ordinary conversations with adults who honestly convey their feelings about work life. In my activities as a psychoanalyst and psychologist I have been struck by how so many patients are distressed for one reason or another by their work life, the subject getting more talking time than their love lives. Indeed, it is a blessed soul who can affirm what Thomas A. Edison allegedly said: "I never did a day's work in my life. It was all fun" (www.inspirational-quotations.com). Edison's incredible confession may be rooted in the fact that he had an enviably healthy attitude towards failure as an inventor: "I have not failed. I've just found 10,000 ways that won't work" (Farrington, 2014, p. 75). As clinical research psychologist Ann Roe noted, "Occupation plays an immensely important role in the life of the individual," including of one's economic and social status, and "if one wishes to understand the total psychology of any person, it is at least as important to understand his occupational behavior as it is to understand his sexual behavior. (They are not unrelated)" (1956, pp. 24, vi). More recently, French psychoanalyst Christophe Dejours wrote that "the relation to work is intertwined with the sexual economy" (2015a, p. xv), that is, with the attitudes and behaviors in the personal realm, including body-ego, body-image and love relationships. Moreover, the psychodynamics of work are "always involved, both in the construction of mental health [i.e., psychological functioning] and in the genesis of [psychiatric] illness," such as in the worsening of a patient's health and their ability for recovery (ibid., p. xvii). Finally, Dejours notes that "the theoretical and clinical questions raised by the impact of the pressures of professional life ["the experience of work," especially its psychopathology] on mental health remain poorly understood by psychiatrists" (2015b, p. 1) and other mental health professionals (Thomas and Hersen, 2004).

For many years now I have been publishing books that deal with what is most important to the average person in terms of everyday existence: how to live the "good life."[3] By "good life" I mean a life that is characterized by deep and wide love and creative and productive work, one that is also guided by reason and ethics and is aesthetically pleasing. This book is a further contribution to delineating what constitutes the "nuts and bolts" of living a flourishing life, a way of being that blends practicality and passion as it pertains to what an adult spends most of his or her time doing, namely, working (Albion, 2006, p. xxiv). In particular, it focuses on what it takes to achieve excellence in work, that quality of having outstanding performance and productivity while also enjoying what one does. As Freud reflected, "I could not contemplate with any sort of comfort a life without work. Creative imagination and work go together with me; I take no delight in anything else" (1910 [1963], p. 35).[4]

While there is a huge so-called scientific literature on the psychology and sociology of work, as well as important contributions from vocational guidance, career education and career counseling (Savickas, 2011, p. 7), this study has a unique angle that is animated by a psychoanalytic sensibility. For example, while I strongly value the roles of such consciously embraced capacities as efficacy, hope, optimism and resiliency, the "stuff" of "positive" work and organizational psychology, the role of early childhood experience, such as parenting practices, family dynamics, trauma and perhaps most importantly, unconscious motivations, has been under-studied and under-appreciated in accounting for why a person chooses his particular career and how he adapts to work issues, as well as the idiosyncratic trajectory of his career journey. For example, Whiston and Keller's empirical review of the influences of the family of origin on career development concluded, "a significant limitation of this body of research is [a] lack of theoretical foundation that clearly defines how families positively or negatively influence career development" (2004, p. 559). Moreover, they noted, "It is disappointing that the period when individuals are probably most influenced by their parents (i.e. elementary school age) has been the least studied by researchers interested in the influence of families across the lifespan" (ibid., p. 560). Also of great importance to understanding work choice, career path and even everyday behavior on the job is how one was psychologically introduced in childhood to the concept of money, earning a living and the range of values associated with work, including attitudes towards authority and peers (symbolic parents and siblings psychoanalytically speaking), and what constitutes being "successful." Most of these topics have also been under-investigated in the mainstream vocational psychology and related literatures.[5] One review article noted, " the vocational development of children [i.e., the dynamics of the self within the work-world] has been inadequately addressed" (Hartung et al., 2005, p. 386), while Arnold and Cohen more recently noted in their fine review chapter on careers in organizations, "most empirical findings in careers do not appear to generalize especially strongly," hence the need "for more qualitative and case study research" (2013, p. 298). Likewise, those researchers studying the "meaning of work" have acknowledged that this important subject has been studied "from a bewildering array of angles," that the "literature remains splintered," and "the fragmented nature of the meaning of work literature has left this research difficult to interpret as a whole" (Rosso *et al.*, 2010, p. 93). In addition, twenty-first century organizations are significantly different than those of previous eras, generating new challenges for individual vocational identity (having a lucid and stable notion of one's goals, interests and abilities), career development and small group functioning. Today's "information age" and global organizations must be effective at negotiating and managing a complex situation typified more by change than by stability, organized around networks rather than rigid hierarchical arrangements, fashioned on fluctuating partnerships and shifting alliances rather than self-sufficiency, and built on technological savvy instead of "bricks and mortar" (Cascio, 2010, p. 22). Rosso and colleagues have also observed that organizational research approaches lodged in assumptions of earlier eras may not be as applicable to the social context of current work life. For example, job boundaries inside organizations have become considerably more fluid and employees are shifting jobs much more often.[6] In 2006, the average American changed jobs about ten times between ages of 18 and 42 and similar statistics were reported in Europe.[7] Moreover, organizations are using team-based work structures more frequently. Each one of these developments has changed the nature of one's relationships to colleagues and bosses (Rosso *et al.*, 2010, pp. 105–106; Berg *et al.*, 2010, p. 973).[8]

While there have been useful studies in vocational psychology that have dealt with some of these issues as they pertain to our century, the fact is that in the most recent *Handbook of Vocational Psychology* it is acknowledged by leaders in the field "that the field now requires a veritable renaissance of its foundational theories and application practices to respond to the challenge and reinvigorate itself for the twenty-first century" (Walsh *et al.*, 2013, p. xii). Indeed, Watkins and Savickas noted that "traditional [psychoanalytic career] theory and research seems dead in terms of what it has offered career counselors over the past couple of decades" (1990, pp. 83, 82). This calls to mind the famous statement by Mark Twain, "The reports of my death have been greatly exaggerated." For example, in the *Handbook* mentioned above, one of the chapter authors notes that the crucial vocational construct of "personality"—what, along with emotions, is the bailiwick of psychoanalysis, "has actually received little attention in vocational psychology" (Hartung *et al.*, 2013, p. xiii). This, despite the fact that "personality traits and trait-like characteristics have been consistently shown to have significant relationships with work-related outcomes" (Youssef and Luthans, 2010, p. 281). Moreover, it is common knowledge that in organizations, once one removes the "façade of rationality," which includes goals, purposes, tasks and objectives, one discovers "a veritable explosion of emotional tones" (Sekerka and Fredrickson,

2010, p. 81).[9] An organization has been characterized as "the seat of irrational life," of "people's unconscious hopes and fears, the dreams and myths they live by, and the history embedded in them" (Thomas, 1993, p. 191). This being said, one recent group of prominent "meaning of work" researchers noted, "There is a dearth of scholarship on the role of *affect*, either as a source or a mechanism of meaning or meaningfulness" (Rosso *et al.*, 2010, p. 99). Moreover, their suggestion for future research beautifully correlates with what psychoanalysis is so good at doing, namely investigating "the affective components of the self or affective responses to self-related cognitions" (ibid., p. 100). Thus, there is an important dynamic relationship between personality functioning and emotional states and the goals that one successfully pursues as forerunners to liking one's job (Rottinghaus and Miller, 2013, p. 117). Psychoanalytic theory and practice is at its best when it conceptualizes and intervenes in the individual's and group's often high-octane emotions that circulate beneath the surface and between the lines in the range of work contexts. This approach is especially applicable when one remembers that, in both clinical and non-clinical contexts, what a person thinks he knows may be quite different from what he actually feels "deep down," and these unacknowledged and/or disavowed feelings can have massive and decisive sway on his occupational choice, motivations and how he engages with his everyday work (Bruce and Borg, 2002, p. 71).

The strength of an "in-depth" psychoanalytic sensibility compared to the more "surface" approaches, such as those rooted in vocational guidance, career education and career counseling,[10] for understanding important aspects of the work experience is suggested when we juxtapose the pragmatic words of Benjamin Franklin with Freud on the issue of decision-making. Most people make everyday decisions of "minor" significance in a manner that is fairly straightforward and sensible, as Franklin aptly described his technique of "moral algebra":[11]

> My way is to divide half a sheet of paper by a line into two columns; writing over one Pro, and over the other Con. Then, during three or four days' consideration, I put down under the different heads short hints of the different motives, that at different times occur to me for or against the measure. When I have thus got them all together in one view, I endeavor to estimate the respective weights ... [to] find at length where the balance lies.
>
> (1840, p. 20)

Franklin offers careful examination of the pros and cons and costs and benefits of decisions of "minor" significance, while Freud comments on the process of making life-altering decisions involving love and work:

> When making a decision of minor importance, I have always found it advantageous to consider all the pros and cons. In vital matters, however, such as the choice of a mate or a profession, the decision should come from the

unconscious, from somewhere within ourselves. In the important decisions of personal life, we should be governed, I think, by the deep inner needs of our nature [i.e., the unconscious].

(Reik, 1983, p. vii)

Freud's point is that when you lay bare all the rational procedures of decision-making, such as the production of options and the careful evaluation of information, what remains at the "center" is strong emotion.[12] That is, emotionally infused questions animated by one's dearly held values, beliefs and desires, such as "What kind of person do I wish to be? What do I believe is in the long term best interests of my family?" And if you are a business leader or manager, "What kind of organization do I wish to preside over?" and "What is in the long term best interests of my team?" (Heath and Heath, 2013, p. 179).

Bearing in mind conventional psychological wisdom that all decision-making involves inextricably entwined conscious rational and unconscious intuitive processes, my point is that a psychoanalytically oriented outlook can help illuminate important aspects of the psychology and sociology of work that have been significantly neglected, especially as psychoanalysis is uniquely able to provide the "flesh and blood," the freshness of personal detail, to understanding the inner experience of the average person's work life, including from its originating intimate moments in childhood fantasy and unconscious assumptions to retirement. Even in retirement the love of one's work can decisively impact how one experiences life after retirement (Bordin, 1987, p. 367). As psychiatrist Peter D. Kramer noted, such psychoanalytically informed "storytelling," as exemplified in the vignette, provides a robust point of entry into "the texture of life in one of its forms," including the idiosyncratic trajectory of the career journey. That is, the psychoanalytically animated vignette "sets us in the clinical moment, it remind[s] us of the variety of human experience and enrich[es] our judgment" (2014, p. 7). A good vignette, one that provides a "reactional biography of the individual" (Bordin, 1987, p. 359) thus helps develop our empathy to others and thereby aids us in deepening and sharpening our professional reasoning and better connecting theory to practice (Blair, 2013, p. vii). Such a "way of seeing" that gives primacy to an individual's personal experience of his work has critical bearing on understanding many aspects of non-clinical populations in terms of vocational identity, career development and attainment, and behavior on the job.[13] Even Watkins and Savickas's rather critical review of psychodynamic career counseling noted that in contrast to commonly used so-called objective assessment methods such as interest inventories, ability tests and actuarial methods, "psychodynamic theory and method offer a way to operationalize the subjective perspective on career decision-making" (1990, p. 101). Moreover, they conclude that "some psychodynamic theories and concepts can be used to inform one's thinking about vocational behavior," and specific "techniques and methods can be effectively integrated in one's career counseling efforts" (ibid., p. 110).

I use a psychoanalytically informed lens that also draws from the findings of other relevant scholarly and popular literatures as well as experience from my work as a psychotherapist and court-appointed forensic evaluator in the most ethnically diverse borough in the United States—Queens, New York—where multicultural knowledge and skills are essential to effectively deal with the work lives of my patients. I focus on the following three questions and associated problems that serve as a backdrop to the specific topics I discuss:

1. What are the conscious and unconscious motivations, including the goals and life stories, that lead a person to decide on a particular kind of work? This is the problem of career choice.
2. What distinguishes the person who is really good at their work from the person who is mediocre or even a failure? This is the problem of job performance.
3. What psychological and contextual factors foster a person's love of their work as opposed to suffering through it? This is the problem of job satisfaction.

Although answering these questions for a particular person would involve a thorough study of the individual's life history, including important context-dependent and setting-specific considerations related to culture, age, socioeconomic background, family arrangement (Schultheiss *et al.*, 2001, p. 217) and work-related barriers and opportunities, I will be drawing from pertinent quotations, anecdotes and statistics from a diverse range of workers and sources, always with an eye to being able to make some thought-provoking general statements, formulations and conclusions about the meaning of the typical work experience for people in western culture. This approach is based on the admittedly bold assumption that it is reasonable to believe that there is at least some common psychological ground that can be delineated to account for how an orthopedic surgeon, a school crossing guard and a factory worker engage in their work in a manner that reflects performance excellence and personal satisfaction, even joyful life-affirmation. As one patient of mine, a building contractor who loved his work, told me, "it's like the fun I had building *Legos* when I was a kid." Indeed, this contractor is in very good company in realizing what the "trick" is to smart occupational choice and attainment, for as British historian Arnold J. Toynbee said, "The supreme accomplishment is to blur the line between work and play" (Tapio, 2014, n.p.).

Final word

In the remainder of this introductory chapter, I will briefly contextualize the gist of my focus and methodology by providing a few comments on what I mean by psychoanalysis and artful self-fashioning.

I conceive of psychoanalysis as a form of life, a resource for individuals who can appropriate the life- and identity-defining narrative of psychoanalysis when they seek to understand, endure and possibly conquer the problems that beset the human condition: despair, loss, tragedy, anxiety and conflict. In effect, they try to synthesize, come to grips with the emotionally painful experiences of life through a psychoanalytic outlook. Psychoanalysis can be viewed as what Michel Foucault called a "technology of the self": "an exercise of the self, by which one attempts to develop and transform oneself, and to attain a certain mode of being" (1989, p. 433). As philosopher Pierre Hadot notes about ancient Greek philosophy in another context, psychoanalysis can be understood as a "spiritual exercise," a tool for living life skillfully and wisely. The aim of a spiritual exercise is to foster a deep modification of an individual's way of "seeing and being," a decisive change in how one lives a practical, everyday life. The main objective of a spiritual exercise is "a total transformation of one's vision, life-style, and behavior" in the service of increased personal freedom and peace (Hadot, 1997, pp. 83, 103, 14). According to this view, as philosopher Emmanuel Levinas described "Jewish Humanism," psychoanalysis is "a difficult wisdom concerned with truths that correlate to virtues"—in other words, it is a "poetics to human existence,"[14] a powerful tool for the art of living a "good life," as one construes and fashions it (Levinas, 1989, p. 275; Ruti, 2008, p. 3).[15]

It is the contention of this book that the individual capacity to create a meaningful and productive work life is a core activity that partly constitutes living well, and this "project of the self" and "self-authorship of identity," as it has been called in the vocational psychology and career counseling literatures (Arnold and Cohen, 2013, p. 279; Savickas, 2011, p. 18), requires precisely the self-exploration, self-knowledge (e.g., of personal and familial history) and self-responsibility that psychoanalysis can help provide. Career choice, trajectory and attainment are to a large extent expressions of "personal development" (Bordin, 1987, p. 358), of one's autonomy, personality integration and humanity.[16] As is the received wisdom of psychoanalysis, the selection of a line of work is a symbolic expression of both internal and external conflicts and other dynamic emotionally-animated processes, and changing the obvious and superficial manifestations of these struggles will not significantly modify the deeper impulses, drives, the passion for the activity (Nicholls, 2007, p. 62). As Camus noted in *Solidarity and Solitude*, "A man's work is nothing but this slow trek to rediscover, through the detours of art [or one's occupation], those two or three great and simple images in whose presence his heart first opened" (lareviewofbooks.org).

Notes

1 This often quoted passage is actually an "attributed" one cited in Schumacher (1979).
2 I am aware that the claim that work should be self-fulfilling reflects a set of possibly elitist and ethnocentric values, especially since "the majority of people in contemporary societies do not do the kinds of work that could be a source of self-fulfillment" (Rosso *et al.*, 2010, p. 117).
3 See Marcus (2003, 2010, 2013a, 2013b, 2014) and Marcus, with Marcus (2011).

4 I am grateful to Patrick J. Mahony's essay, "Freud: Man At Work" (1997), for drawing my attention to this and some of the other Freud quotations used elsewhere throughout this book.

5 There have been some exceptions: for example, Blustein *et al.*'s (1995) study of career development draws from John Bowlby's attachment theory and observations rooted in psychoanalytically glossed object relational perspectives.

6 This is a debated claim in the organizational literature. For example, Inkson *et al.* cite a comprehensive 2010 review of mobility data drawn from the United States, Europe and Japan since 1992 that indicated "There is … no evidence of a significant increase in mobility across organizational boundaries" (2012, p. 7). This being said, the prominent sociologist, Zygmunt Bauman, noted that we live "in a world that no longer offers reliable career tracks and stable jobs." This condition, among other destabilizing social changes, exposes people "to an uncharacteristically high level of risk and a prolific source of anxiety and fear" (2003, p. 42). For example, the pervasive use of automation software like Kensho, "a real-time statistical computing systems and scalable analytics architecture," has led to many in the financial services being made redundant. Anthony Jenkins, the former chief executive of Barclays, a British multinational banking and financial services company, recently predicted "that the number of branches and people employed in the financial sector may decline by as much as 50 percent." About half of futurologists and technologists surveyed believe that machines are taking over the workplace, and jobs will "continue disappearing at a faster rate than they are created" (Popper, 2016, pp. 59, 62).

7 A 2009 US Bureau of Labor Statistics survey reported that Americans between the ages of 25 and 54 who are employed and reside in households with children under 18 spend about 8.8 hours working each day, 7.6 hours sleeping, 2.6 hours in leisure and sports, and about 1.3 hours engaged in caring for others, including children. For these Americans, it is work that is most consuming of their time (Carroll, 2013, p. 595).

8 One of the best writers on the negative and positive changes of globalization on the economy, on the challenges of the employment marketplace, and our working lives is Richard Sennett (1998, 2006).

9 Sekerka and Fredrickson are paraphrasing from Fineman (1993, p. 1).

10 What comes to mind is Frank Parsons's path-breaking, talent-matching approach to occupational selection, later called trait and factory theory of occupational choice, that is used in most career theories in some form. In his book based on his career counseling of Bostonian adolescents, *Choosing a Vocation* (1909), Parsons claims: "In the wise choice of vocation there are three broad factors: (1) a clear understanding of yourself, your aptitudes, abilities, interests, ambitions, resources, limitations, and their causes; (2) a knowledge of the requirements and conditions of success, advantages and disadvantages, compensation, opportunities, and prospects in different lines of work; (3) true reasoning on the relations of these two groups of facts" (p. 5). "True reasoning" means engaging in logical, reasonable and objective matching of the person's traits to the job that most "fits."

11 Franklin's remarks were contained in a letter written to Joseph Priestley (the discoverer of oxygen) who was troubled by a career decision and wanted Franklin's advice (Heath and Heath, 2013, pp. 8, 19).

12 Judith Butler made a similar point when she noted in another context that a person ideally needs to choose a profession that is both lodged in, and an expression of, a "primordial passionate attachment." Of course, this is not always so clear to the decision maker, in Lacanian terms it is as if "It was something in me more than myself which decided" (Zizek and Daly, 2004, pp. 24, 25).

13 Given the broad scope and wide ranging topics of this book, it is the psychoanalytic outlook or "way of seeing" that animates my methodology, though I have occasionally used quotes or an anecdote to illustrate important points.

14 By "poetics to human existence," Ruti means "an approach that is content to play with meaning without attempting to arrest it in unequivocal or transparent definitions." Such an approach emphasizes the "inventive, artistic usages of language" (2008, pp. 96, 109).

15 As John Lechte points out, the psychoanalyst, philosopher, literary critic and feminist Julia Kristeva has a similar view in which she criticizes the "atrophying of psychic space," in part rooted in the fact "that everything that used to be directly lived has moved into a representation" (in other words, the imaginary has become "thing-like"). With this so-called "society of spectacle" in which "standardized virtual forms" erode the individual's capacity to personally fantasize, that is, to fashion "a new self in the spirit of revolt," society becomes nihilistic since hardly anyone is interrogating taken-for-granted values, beliefs and "natural attitudes" towards the world (2003, p. 187). Moreover, as philosopher Slavoj Zizek noted, imaginative productions beget self-formations that tend to be alienating and repressive rather than autonomous and enabling (Elliott, 2003, p. 277).

16 This study does not focus on those whose occupational choice and work lives are driven or controlled primarily by external forces such as economic, cultural or geographical considerations that severely limit individual freedom of choice (Bordin *et al.*, 1963, p. 110). Of course, there is no absolute individual freedom of choice, that is, career choice, development and performance are constrained by external forces to varying degrees, reminding us that all behavior is best understood as context-dependent and setting-specific.

References

Albion, M. (2006). Foreword. In: L. Kang (Ed.), *Passion at Work: How to Find Work You Love and Live the Time of Your Life*. Upper Saddle River, NJ: Prentice Hall.

Arnold, J. and Cohen, L. (2013). Careers in Organizations. In: W. B. Walsh, M. L. Savickas and P. J. Hartung (Eds.), *Handbook of Vocational Psychology: Theory, Research, and Practice* (pp. 273–304). New York: Routledge.

Bauman, Z. (2003). *Liquid Love*. Cambridge, UK: Polity Press.

Berg, J. M., Grant, A. G. and Johnson, V. (2010). When Callings are Calling: Crafting Work and Leisure in Pursuit of Unanswered Occupational Callings. *Organization Science*, *21*:5, 973–994.

Blair, S. E. E. (2013). Foreword. In: L. Nicholls, J. C. Piergrossi, C. de Sena Gibertoni and M. A. Daniel (Eds.), *Psychoanalytic Thinking in Occupational Therapy: Symbolic, Relational and Transformational* (pp. ix–x). London: Wiley Blackwell.

Blustein, D. L., Prezioso, M. S. and Schultheiss, D. P. (1995). Attachment Theory and Career Development: Current Status and Future Directions. *The Counseling Psychologist*, *23*:3, 416–432.

Bordin, E. S. (1987). The 1986 Leona Tyler Award Address: Aim and Trajectory. *The Counseling Psychologist*, *15*, 358–367.

Bordin, E. S., Nachman, B. and Segal, S. J. (1963). An Articulated Framework for Vocational Development. *Journal of Counseling Psychology*, *10*:2, 107–116.

Bruce, M. A. G. and Borg, B. (2002). *Frames of Reference in Psychosocial Occupational Therapy*. Thorofare, NJ: Slack.

Carroll, S. T. (2013). Addressing Religion and Spirituality in the Workplace. In: K. I. Pergament (Ed.), *APA Handbook of Psychology, Religion, and Spirituality, Volume 2* (pp. 595–612). Washington, DC: American Psychological Association.

Cascio, W. F. (2010). The Changing World of Work. In: P. A. Linley, S. Harrington and N. Garcea (Eds.), *Oxford Handbook of Positive Psychology and Work* (pp. 13–23). Oxford: Oxford University Press.

Dejours, C. (2015a). Introduction. In: C. Dejours (Ed.), *Psychopathology of Work: Clinical Observations* (pp. xiii–xviii). C. Williamson (Trans.). London: Karnac.

Dejours, C. (2015b). Madness and Work: From Aetiological Analysis to Theoretical Contradictions (A Case of *Status Asthmaticus*). In: C. Dejours (Ed.), *Psychopathology of Work: Clinical Observations* (pp. 1–19). C. Williamson (Trans.). London: Karnac.

Elliott, A. (2003). Slavoj Zizek. In: A. Elliott and L. Ray (Eds.), *Key Contemporary Social Theorists* (pp. 273–378). Malden, MA: Blackwell Publishers.

Farrington, C. (2014). *Failing at School: Lessons for Redesigning Urban High Schools.* New York: Teachers College Press.

Fineman, S. (1993). *Emotion in Organizations.* Newbury Park, CA: Sage.

Foucault, M. (1989). The Ethics of the Concern for Self as a Practice of Freedom. In: S. Lotringer (Ed.), *Foucault Live: Collected Interviews, 1961–1984* (pp. 432–449). New York: Semiotexte.

Franklin, B. (1840). *The Works of Benjamin Franklin* (Vol. 8). J. Sparks (Ed.), Boston, MA: Hilliard Gray and Company.

Freud, S. (1910) [1963]. *Psychoanalysis and Faith: The Letters of Sigmund Freud and Oskar Pfister.* H. Meng and E. L. Feder (Eds.). E. Mosbacher (Trans.). London: Hogarth Press.

Hadot, P. (1997). *Philosophy as a Way of Life.* Oxford: Blackwell.

Hartung, P. J., Porfeli, E. J. and Vondracek, F. W. (2005). Child Vocational Development: A Review and Reconsideration. *Journal of Vocational Behavior, 66,* 385–419.

Hartung, P. J., Walsh, W. B. and Savickas, M. L. (2013). Introduction: Stability and Change in Vocational Psychology. In: W. B. Walsh, M. L. Savickas and P. J. Hartung (Eds.), *Handbook of Vocational Psychology: Theory, Research, and Practice* (pp. xi–xvi). New York: Routledge.

Heath, C. and Heath, D. (2013). *Decisive. How to Make Better Choices in Life and Work.* New York: Crown Business.

Inkson, K., Gunz, H., Ganesh, S. and Roper, J. (2012). Boundaryless Careers: Bringing Back Boundaries. *Organizational Studies, 33*:3, 323–340.

Kramer, P. D. (2014). Why Doctors Need Stories. *New York Times,* Sunday Review, 10/19/14, pp. 1, 7.

Lechte, J. (2003). Julia Kristeva. In: A. Elliott and L. Ray (Eds.), *Key Contemporary Social Theorists* (pp. 183–189). Malden, MA: Blackwell Publishers.

Levinas, E. (1989). *Difficult Freedom: Essays on Judaism.* S. Hand (Ed.). Baltimore, MD: The Johns Hopkins University Press.

Mahony, P. J. (1997). Freud: Man At Work. In: C. W. Socarides and S. Kramer (Eds.), *Work and Its Inhibitions: Psychoanalytic Essays* (pp. 79–98). Madison, CT: International Universities Press.

Marcus, P. (2003). *Ancient Religious Wisdom, Spirituality, and Psychoanalysis.* Westport, CT: Praeger.

Marcus, P. (2010). *In Search of the Good Life: Emmanuel Levinas, Psychoanalysis and the Art of Living.* London: Karnac.

Marcus, P., with Marcus, G. (2011). *Theater as Life: Practical Wisdom from Great Acting Teacher, Actors and Actresses.* Milwaukee, WI: Marquette University Press.

Marcus, P. (2013a). *How to Laugh Your Way Through Life: A Psychoanalyst's Advice*. London: Karnac.

Marcus, P. (2013b). *In Search of the Spiritual: Gabriel Marcel, Psychoanalysis, and the Sacred*. London: Karnac.

Marcus, P. (2014). *They Shall Beat Their Swords Into Plowshares: Military Strategy, Psychoanalysis and The Art of Living*. Milwaukee, WI: Marquette University Press.

Nicholls, L. (2007). A Psychoanalytic Discourse in Occupational Therapy. In: J. Creek and A. Lawson-Porter (Eds.), *Contemporary Issues in Occupational Therapy* (pp. 55–86). Chichester: John Wiley & Sons, Ltd.

Parsons, F. (1909). *Choosing a Vocation*. Boston: Houghton-Mifflin.

Popper, N. (2016). Stocks and Bots. *The New York Times Magazine*, 2/28/16, pp. 59, 62.

Reik, T. (1983). *Listening with the Third Ear*. New York: Farrar, Straus and Giroux.

Roe, A. (1956). *The Psychology of Occupations*. New York: John Wiley & Sons.

Rosso, B. D., Dekas, K. H. and Wrzesniewski, A. (2010). On the Meaning of Work: A Theoretical Integration and Review. *Research in Organizational Behavior*, *30*, 91–127.

Rottinghaus, P. J. and Miller, A. D. (2013). Convergence of Personality Frameworks Within Vocational Psychology. In: W. B. Walsh, M. L. Savickas and P. J. Hartung (Eds.), *Handbook of Vocational Psychology: Theory, Research, and Practice* (pp. 105–131). New York: Routledge.

Ruti, M. (2008). *A World of Fragile Things: Psychoanalysis and the Art of Living*. Albany, NY: State University of New York Press.

Savickas, M. L. (2011). *Career Counseling*. Washington, DC: American Psychological Association.

Schultheiss, D. E. P., Kress, H. M., Manzi, A. J. and Glassock, J. M. J. (2001). Relational Influences in Career Development: A Qualitative Inquiry. *The Counseling Psychologist*, *29*, 216–241.

Schumacher, E. F. (1979). *Good Work*. New York: Harper & Row.

Sekerka, L. E. and Frederickson, B. L. (2010). Working Positively Toward Transformative Cooperation. In: P. A. Linley, S. Harrington and N. Garcea (Eds.), *Oxford Handbook of Positive Psychology and Work* (pp. 81–94). Oxford: Oxford University Press.

Sennett, R. (1998). *The Corrosion of Character: The Personal Consequences of Work in the New Capitalism*. New York: Norton.

Sennett, R. (2006). *The Culture of the New Capitalism*. New Haven, CT: Yale University Press.

Tapio, R. (Ed.). (2014). *The Forbes Quote Bible: Inspiring, Eye-Opening and Motivational Words for Success*. Forbes Media (Kindle).

Thomas, D. A. (1993). Mentoring and Irrationality: The Role of Racial Tensions. In: L. Hirschhorn and C. K. Barnett (Eds.), *The Psychodynamics of Organizations* (pp. 191–202). Philadelphia: Temple University Press.

Thomas, J. C. and Hersen, M. (Eds.). (2004). *Psychopathology in the Workplace: Recognition and Adaptation*. New York: Brunner-Routledge.

Walsh, W. B., Savickas, M. L. and Hartung, P. J. (Eds.). (2013). *Handbook of Vocational Psychology: Theory, Research, and Practice*. New York: Routledge.

Watkins, E. C., Jr. and Savickas, M. L. (1990). Psychodynamic Career Counseling. In: W. B. Walsh and S. H. Osipow (Eds.), *Career Counseling: Contemporary Topics in Vocational Psychology* (pp. 79–116). Hillsdale, NJ: Lawrence Erlbaum Associates.

Whiston, S. C. and Keller, B. K. (2004). The Influences of the Family of Origin on Career Development: A Review and Analysis. *The Counseling Psychologist, 32,* 493–567.

Youssef, C. M. and Luthans, F. (2010). An Integrated Model of Psychological Capital in The Workplace. In P. A. Linley, S. Harrington and N. Garcea (Eds.), *Oxford Handbook of Positive Psychology and Work* (pp. 277–288). Oxford: Oxford University Press.

Zizek, S. and Daly, G. (2004). *Conversatons with Zizek.* Cambridge, UK: Polity.

Web sources

lareviewofbooks.org/review/a-man-apart, retrieved 10/27/14.

www.inspirational-quotations.com/success-quotes.html, retrieved 8/20/14.

www.oxfordreference.com/view/10.1093/acref/...001.../q-oro-00002544, retrieved 10/20/14.

Chapter 2

Choosing the "right" career

It was the great French nineteenth-century novelist and playwright, Honoré de Balzac, who reflected that after a night making love to a beautiful woman, there always was a novel left in between the sheets! Indeed, Balzac was emphasizing, long before Freud, that the realms of work and love are psychologically connected (Neff, 1965, p. 333). Many empirical studies have demonstrated that given we are social beings, "satisfaction in one domain is associated with satisfaction in the other," in other words, psychoanalytically speaking, "work and genital sexuality have a stimulating influence on each other" (Hazan and Shaver, 1990, p. 270; Lantos, 1943, p. 117). Moreover, unlike senseless destructiveness, aggressive impulses can be shaped and steered in a productive and satisfying direction through the influence of erotically tinged impulses such as in creative activity (Marcus, with Marcus, 2011; Menninger, 1942, p. 173). What is true about finding a satisfying life partner is also true about choosing a satisfying career. As Freud famously said, "all love is a re-finding": it tends to replicate emotional aspects of infantile templates, those impacting early experiences of satisfaction and frustration between parents and children. Psychoanalytic theory assumes that a person's choice of career is based on conscious and, most importantly, unconscious factors, and this is one of the reasons that choosing a suitable career and flourishing in it is so difficult. As Freud noted, "A man like me cannot live without a hobby-horse, without a consuming passion, without—in Schiller's words—a tyrant. I have found one ['working well, writing well']. In its service I know no limits" (1895 [1985], p. 129). Sounding similar to Freud who advocated choosing a career by listening to "the deep inner needs of our nature," the unconscious (Reik, 1983, p. 7), the great thirteenth-century Persian poet and Sufi mystic, Rumi, put it just right, "Everyone has been made for some particular work, and the desire for that work has been put in every heart. Let yourself be silently drawn by the stronger pull of what you really love" (https://resurrectionwaltz2013. wordpress.com).

Despite Freud and Rumi's wise counsel, researchers Heath and Heath have pointed out that career choices are frequently "abandoned or regretted." For example, an American Bar Association survey indicated "that 44% of lawyers would recommend that a young person not pursue a career in law." An investigation "of 20,000 executive searches found that 40% of senior-level hires 'are pushed out, fail or quit within 18 months.'" Even more troubling, over 50 per cent "of teachers quit their jobs within four years." One study in the Philadelphia school system reported that a teacher was nearly "two times more likely to drop out than a student" (2013, p. 3).

The gist of the psychoanalytic perspective on career choice has been aptly summarized by Malach-Pines and Yafe-Yanai:

> Childhood experiences (both positive and negative) and familial heritage have a major influence on vocational choices. People choose an occupation that enables them to replicate significant childhood experiences, satisfy needs that were unfulfilled in their childhood, and actualize dreams passed on to them by their familial heritage.
>
> (2001, p. 171)

While this summary of the general psychoanalytic perspective on career choice appears to be rather straightforward, the fact is that beginning with Freud, psychoanalytic theorists and clinicians have put forth a very complex and compelling array of interdependent, interrelated and interactive concepts that help to illuminate the range of conscious and unconscious motives and meanings associated with career choice and work behavior. In the remainder of this chapter I unpack some of these concepts mainly in regards to the feelings, thoughts and actions that tend to animate an individual's unique career choice, and secondarily, his career development, adjustment and attainment.

The meaning of work

Freud, Erik Erikson tells us, said that "to love and work" were the central therapeutic goals of psychoanalysis, these being the twin pillars of a sound mind and for living the "good life" (Erikson, 1959, p. 96).[1] Indeed, psychoanalysis is full of work metaphors, many first used by Freud, such as "analytic work, dream work, mourning work, joke work, working through" (and Ralph Greenson's notion of "working alliance"), reinforcing the notion that "adult maturity" involves a robust capacity to work effectively (Blum, 1997, p. 19).[2] Freud's views of work, however, were hardly clear and consistent, though his ambiguous and ambivalent formulations were the precursors to most psychoanalytic theorizing on work behavior.

As Neff notes (1965, p. 325), on the one hand, Freud claims that along with love, work is the great realm of human activity that helps us comprehend the nature of human society:

> the communal life of human beings had ... a twofold foundation: the compulsion to work, which was created by external necessity, and the power of love .... Eros and Ananke [Love and Necessity] have become the parents of human civilization ....
>
> (Freud, 1930 [1961], p. 101)

In Freud's view, work allowed humans to be "able to live together in a community" with a minimum of discord and hostility (ibid., p.101). Moreover, he said, there is an economic motivator for human society in that humanity "does not possess enough provisions to keep its members alive unless they work," so "it must restrict the number of its members and divert their energies from sexual activity to work" (1916–1917 [1961], p. 312). On the other hand, Freud did not view work as inherently pleasurable activity in which man wanted to engage, but rather a hardship, a burdensome, if not painful, obligation to be endured (Neff, 1965, p. 325). Said Freud, "men are not spontaneously fond of work" and therefore require a certain amount of societal "coercion and renunciation of instinct" (1927 [1961], p. 8). Indeed, Mark Twain affirmed Freud's observation when he famously quipped, "Work is a necessary evil to be avoided" (www.quoteworld. org). Freud explains why work is so objectionable in terms of his understanding of the human condition: "Human beings exhibit an inborn tendency to carelessness, irregularity and unreliability in their work ... a laborious training is needed before they learn to follow the example of their celestial models" (Freud, 1930 [1961], p. 93). What Freud is getting at here is now common knowledge— growing up requires relinquishing the childhood cast of mind, one that is geared toward maximizing pleasure and avoiding unpleasure, the "pleasure principle," in favor of living according to the "reality principle." The reality principle requires that one no longer lives according to the demands of immediate gratification of one's needs and wishes, but rather a reasonable and self-preserving evaluation of the external world governs decision-making in the service of pleasure attainment. Indeed, Freud was well aware that perhaps more than anything else humans do, it is work that lodges a human being in the totality of "real" things in the world— in "actual" being and existence: "No other technique for the conduct of life attaches the individual so firmly to reality as laying emphasis on work; for his work at least gives him a secure place in a portion of reality, in the human community" (ibid., p. 80).

Moreover, Freud continues, work can be gratifying, at least in terms of "the economics of the libido":

> The possibility that work offers of displacing a large amount of libidinal components, whether narcissistic, aggressive or even erotic, on to professional work and on to the human relations connected with it lends it a value by no means second to what it enjoys as something indispensable to the preservation and justification of existence in society. Professional activity is a source of special satisfaction if it is a freely chosen one if ... by means of sublimation, it makes possible the use of existing inclinations, of persisting or constitutionally reinforced instinctual impulses.

> (ibid.)

While Freud acknowledges above that work can provide a modicum of personal satisfaction (e.g., a sense of competence and mastery), he nevertheless concludes that for most people, it is hardly the "royal road" to the "good life":

> And yet, as a path to happiness, work is not highly prized by men. They do not strive after it as they do after other possibilities of satisfaction. The great majority of people only work under the stress of necessity, and this natural human aversion to work raises most difficult social problems.
>
> (ibid.)

What Freud is claiming regarding the function of work is in sync with his general view of the human condition—namely, that there is a painful dialectic between culture and desire, one in which most of the time the individual has to repudiate his instinctual life, his sexual and aggressive wishes, and adapt to living according to the reality principle, both for the sake of individual and collective survival. Perhaps this is most evident in terms of the parent/child relationship in which parents try to civilize their children, that is, tame their sexual and aggressive tendencies through a range of child-rearing strategies and tactics, including those that take advantage of the child's vulnerability, his need for love and support and his fear of losing it.

For Freud, then, broadly speaking, individuals work because they have to survive, and this self-preservation requires effectively managing those pressing demands emanating from external circumstances (e.g., society's rules and norms of permissible conduct) and internal sources (e.g., sexual and aggressive wishes). The great English playwright, Noel Coward, captured the main thrust of Freud's view in terms of everyday life: "Your motivation is your pay packet on Friday. Now get on with it" (Fadiman and Brand, 1985, p. 146).

Childhood experiences that influence career direction and occupational choice

For Freud and his followers, it is the experiences in childhood played out mainly within the nuclear family that significantly affect career direction and occupational choice. These childhood experiences have been conceptualized in terms of classical Freudian theory with its instinctual emphasis on oral, anal and phallic development and its impact on personality formation, sublimation, and in terms of Neo-Freudian thinking, most notably Erikson's ego-psychological human development stage theory which stresses later childhood and adolescent emotional experience such as identity development. In addition to these conceptualizations, objection-relational glossed versions of attachment theory, most notably English psychiatrist/psychoanalyst John Bowlby's insights, have been used to comprehend which childhood parenting experiences tend to shape personality development and propel a person in a particular career direction and occupational choice. Whatever psychoanalytic perspective one is using, all theorists agree that the reasons why a person chooses the career path he does, and the elements that provide gratification, are mainly unconscious and are connected to powerful emotional needs and wishes that are rooted in childhood experiences largely in the social unit of the nuclear family (Obholzer and Roberts, 1994, p. 106).

Classical theory

From a classical psychoanalytic perspective, roughly defined as one that is in sync with Freud's instinct-dominated outlook, "the work of an adult" emanates "from his work as a child." For example, the toddler's (ages one to three) curiosity, staying power, pride in expressing competence, capacity for cooperation and teamwork, and enthusiasm, foretell the fundamental attitudes that he will likely show during his school years that are further crystallized, especially in terms of likes and dislikes, through work experiences in adolescence (Pruyser, 1980, p. 63). Indeed, research findings (Hartung *et al.*, 2005) have shown that children between the ages of three and five have elementary knowledge regarding occupations, though psychoanalytically this knowledge is usually laden with distorting unconscious fantasy, often of an Oedipal nature. Moreover, these children understand the normative occupational status hierarchy and maintain clear attitudes about the fittingness of specific occupations for them, though most often these attitudes are lodged in stereotyped notions and incomplete information, also animated by unconscious Oedipal and other fantasy. Hartung and colleagues further note that children who are about seven or eight develop their notions and perceptions of adult work on a loose amalgamation "of fantasies and assumptions" in addition to a smattering of realistic observations of working adults. By about age 10 or 11, children have knowledge concerning occupations and about "self-in-occupations," and by 11 or so, they have a more realistic comprehension of the world of adult work, including in terms of job salaries and training requirements. By age 14, adolescents' attitudes about adult work are heavily influenced by their turbulent emotional lives, in particular the upsurge of genital sexual desire, though they are prone to seek out work in an effort to self-fashion a vocational identity. This vocational identity is a crucial aspect of their efforts to create a cohesive, stable, vigorous, harmonious and self-valuing sense of personhood. For instance, by 7th grade (ages 12 to 13) about 75 percent of children reported some regular or frequent extra-familial paid work experience such as child minding, yard work or other kinds of manual labor, while 33 percent indicated they had worked for an organization (ibid., pp. 391, 394, 389). In enlightened classical theory, while the evocative metaphors of Eros and Thanatos, the vicissitudes of the instincts— sexuality and aggression—are what matter most in terms of understanding and helping an analysand, any adequate understanding of a person, including his career journey, must occur within the context of the totality of circumstances of that person's internal and external life, such as the adolescent's forays into the world of work and what he makes of them.

Play versus work

The great American educator and TV host Fred Rogers perceptively observed, "Play is often talked about as if it were a relief from serious learning. But for children play is serious learning. Play is really the work of childhood" (www.fcs. txstate.edu). Classically oriented and other psychoanalytic writers make an important psychological distinction between play in childhood and adult work. Play has been defined as "activity engaged for its own sake, for the pleasure it gives without reference to serious aims and ends." This is in contrast to adult "work or the performance of other socially or biologically necessary acts" (Rycroft, 1995, p. 134). As Winnicott noted, it is free, non-purposive play, including non-rule governed games, that can be conceived as the equivalent of work in childhood, and for some analysts it is what constitutes psychoanalytic work, that is, psychotherapy at its creative best (Moore and Fine, 1990, p. 206). For example, psychoanalysis thrives on the play with words and thoughts that emanate from dream images to the analysand's free associations (Blum, 1997, p. 28). Erikson, in his efforts to broaden and expand, though, as he said, never to amend or replace Freudian theory, also notes that play in childhood is not leisure but is work: "The playing adult steps sideward into another reality; the playing child advances forward to new stages of mastery" (1950, p. 222). Elsewhere, Erikson suggests the connection between child's play and adult work:

> You see a child play, and it is so close to seeing an [adult] artist paint, for in play a child says things without uttering a word. You can see how he solves his problems. You can also see what's wrong. Young children, especially, have enormous creativity, and whatever's in them rises to the surface in free play.
>
> (www.nytimes.com)

Moreover, the psychoanalytic approach to play stresses that it is the unconscious symbolic meanings and ramifications of how a child plays that matter most, and these considerations are also evident in adult career choices and work behaviors. Where play focuses on things and actions that are symbolic, work, as Freud noted, is concerned with realistic results. Thus, deriving gratification from the process and attainment of working signifies the culminating point of an extremely complicated developmental line from play to work, one that includes the skillful integration of most elements of the fully structured personality which also impacts other aspects of personality adaptation and adjustment (Furman, 1997, p. 3).[3]

It is the capacity to experience aspects of work as a form of playfulness that is the basis for a high degree of job satisfaction, this being the telltale sign that there is a good "fit" between the person and chosen occupation. That is, while play and work are psychological opposites, in some instances the two of them may be "mutually facilitating and synergistic," a kind of "playful work" (Blum, 1997, p. 21). Indeed, organizational researchers have noted that as part of "job crafting," using one's personal agency to fashion a work context that feels in sync with one's goals, skills and values, "people strive to make their work meaningful by making it feel less like 'work' and more like 'play'"(Rosso *et al.*, 2010, pp. 101, 104). Studies have shown that adult playfulness is behaviorally manifested, including in work settings, by those who pursue delight in all its glorious forms, engage in affable, low-stakes rivalries, and deploy precious psychological and other resources in making themselves and others smile and laugh. Moreover, playfulness, conceived as a personality trait, has real-life positive ramifications: people who display high levels of playfulness—"those who are predisposed to being spontaneous, outgoing, creative, fun-loving, and lighthearted—appear to be better at coping with stress," including at work. They are "more likely to report leading active lifestyles, and more likely to succeed academically." Playfulness also tends to make both men and women more attractive to those of the opposite sex (www.bostonglobe.com). Indeed, one well-known clinical professor of leadership development and organizational change and a trained psychoanalyst, Manfred F. R. Kets de Vries, noted, "Executives have to discover or rediscover the ability to 'play,' learn how to use humor and how to engage in flights of fancy. It is from such characteristics that vision and adaptability derive," the core qualities of a successful organization (1993, pp. 214–215).

The cultivation of adult playfulness thus becomes an important consideration in terms of flourishing at work, a necessary but not sufficient basis for creating the "good life." Choosing a career direction and occupation thus requires that a person assess whether the work one does, and just as importantly, the work setting, fosters such adult playfulness. Indeed, the most successful businesses seem to be aware that a hospitable work setting, one that is more likely to facilitate innovation, in part emanates from allowing workers to intellectually play with ideas without worrying about failing. For example, Google has the 20 percent rule that encourages employees to use 20 percent of their time engaging in projects they conjure up that are likely to assist in the growth and development of the company. Google's leadership has the conviction that for employees to be creative and innovative they require positive enablers like having free time to explore and experiment with their interests. Moreover, employees are more productive when they are working on projects they view as significant, feel passionate toward or have invented. The 20 percent rule creates the conditions of possibility for the upsurge of bottom-up innovation (Wooten and Cameron, 2010, p. 60). As Carl Jung noted, "The creation of something new is not accomplished by the intellect but by the play instinct acting from inner necessity. The creative mind plays with the objects it loves" (www.jungseattle.org). Thus, while intellectual and scholarly work may be very demanding, in the mind of such a person it is experienced as the "playful cultivation of one's intellectual faculties" in the service of attaining a desired and achievable result. In this way, it is experienced with a similar pleasure associated with playing a game of tennis or poker (Gedo, 1997, p. 135).

"In every real man a child is hidden that wants to play," wrote Nietzsche (www.notable-quotes.com). Indeed, most adults, at least in Western culture, are too bound, tied and gagged by societal and personal restrictions, if not neuroses, to live playfully in their everyday lives. Instead, what is called adult play is mainly restricted to watching and participating in competitive games like basketball and baseball, and sports competitions like the Olympics. Such activities are pleasurable sublimations of childhood play and have important cultural functions. However, what is needed is a re-finding of the aliveness and joy associated with play activities engaged in for their own sake, for the pleasure they provide, most often without any serious goal or end-point and without much conscious anxiety, inhibition and/or guilt (Rycroft, 1995, p. 134). In contrast to adult work, such non-purposive play is not easily achieved, for most adults are overly concerned with their presentation of self, the negative judgment of others and a wide range of other inhibitions. Perhaps it is for this reason that Winnicott famously argued that the goal of psychoanalysis at its best is to transform "the patient from a state of not being able to play into a state of being able to play…. It is in playing and only in playing that the individual child or adult is able to be creative and to use the whole personality, and it is only in being creative that the individual discovers the self" (1971, p. 10). To be able to play is thus a sign of "mental health," an expression of autonomy, integration and humanity. It is also self-healing and therapeutic. Yet, sadly, for most people in our society it is regarded more as a luxury than a necessity. Through play one can learn an awful lot about people if one knows for what to look. Sounding more like a psychoanalyst than the wise philosopher he was, Plato noted, "You can discover more about a person in an hour of play than in a year of conversation" (www.seattleplaytherapy.com).

The particular aspect of adult play that I briefly focus on is how certain individuals have the capacity to take the spirit of childhood playfulness and use it to animate their adult way of being in the world, including in their work lives. Such rare people are often striking in their comportment and are often described as "charming." That is, they have an uncanny capacity to actualize the inconceivable, to delight and attract others, often gaining their admiration without coming across as narcissistic or self-serving. As nineteenth-century philosopher, poet and critic Henri-Frédéric Amiel said, "Charm is the quality in others that makes us more satisfied with ourselves" (www.izquotes.com). It is this capacity to be charming when fully integrated into one's mode of being in the world that gives a person that lightness of being, that beauty and grace, that most people desire. The psychological elements of this charming comportment are precisely the qualities that make for enhanced living, especially in the work context where it is so rare. In this view, psychological health is roughly equivalent to being dramatically accomplished, to having the kind of intense, gripping and/or humorous excitement, startling suddenness or larger than life impressiveness associated with the theater. The self-fashioning goal is to increase one's capacity to enter a playful state at will and to broaden the capacity to think, feel and act beyond habitual ways of being in the world. This requires the cultivation of spontaneity, creativity, producing and co-producing new realities, sensory/physical/emotional expressiveness and interpersonal trust, among other qualities of mind and heart. However, as Erikson notes, this self-fashioning can be a most challenging task, especially in adolescence when experimenting with manifold identities is in ascendance. Drawing from theatrical metaphors, Erikson says that to be dramatically accomplished as described above requires that whatever identity and role experimentation is chosen that role must not become more "real" than the actor's core identity: "Even an actor is convincing in many roles only if and when there is in him an actor's core identity—and craftsmanship" (1974, p. 107). Erikson's cautionary note calls to mind Kata Levy's (1949) description of the character type she calls "eternal dilettante" that is more common among delinquents. Such a person is characterized by an inability to crystallize an occupational identity, and he is a perennial drifter in terms of his interests and work behavior. While he superficially experiments in various contradictory occupational interests, he is never able to comfortably and passionately settle into one. From the classical, Freudian point of view, in order to psychically accomplish such positive self-fashioning an individual has to have the robust capacity for sublimation.

Sublimation

Sublimation is Freud's technical term for the way a relatively healthy individual resolves intra-psychic conflict among the id (roughly the sexual and aggressive drives), ego (the "I" or "Me") and super-ego (the conscience), this being the basis for experiencing the modicum of happiness that the pessimistic Freud thought was possible. The purpose of psychoanalysis, Freud famously said in *Studies on Hysteria*, was to "transform neurotic misery into common unhappiness." Sublimation involves "changing the sexual or aggressive aim of an urge and finding a substitute gratification," one "that implies a constructive or socially admirable outcome that is satisfying and flexible" (Person *et al.*, 2005, p. 560). All sublimation relies on symbolization, so that, for instance, gardening, an activity that is infused with erotic impulse and is a long-standing metaphor in literature and the arts for sexuality, requires just such instinctual redirection and refashioning, that is, engaging in adaptive "desexualized" and "deaggressified" psychic processes. It is not by chance that horticultural metaphors are often used by people as creative visualizations regarding their career journey, using such terms as "growing, flowering and blossoming," as well as when the going gets tough as in "being pruned and cut back" (El-Sawad, 2005, p. 27). Likewise, voyeuristic wishes are satisfied by becoming a psychoanalyst or photographer; the wish to hurt or kill is satisfied by becoming a surgeon or butcher; or exhibitionistic wishes are satisfied by becoming an actor or lifeguard. In other words, work represents one very good venue for the individual to negotiate the conflicting demands between desires, that is, instinctual gratifications, and culture, the requirements of normative social reality. As psychoanalyst and Freud translator A. A. Brill noted, from a classical point of view, "Every activity or vocation not directed to sex in the broadest sense, no matter under what guise, is a form of sublimation ... in the service of hunger and love ... guided by the individual's unconscious motives" (1949, p. 266).

As I said, for Freud, work is in itself not pleasurable, but rather, it is a necessary evil—"we must work in order to live" (Menninger, 1942, p. 171). However, Freud did acknowledge that under certain circumstances work could be somewhat pleasurable, at least derivatively speaking, depending on particular external and internal circumstances. If work is skillfully animated by erotically and aggressively tinged impulses, though allowing for some conflict-free satisfaction and mastery, chances are the individual will enjoy his work. Hendrik has gone further and argued for what he called the "work principle," that is "the principle that primary pleasure is sought by efficient use of the central nervous system ['the muscular and intellectual tools'] for the performance of well-integrated ego functions which enabled the individual to control or alter his environment." In this view, work can be ego satisfying on its own terms, and sexual and aggressive satisfactions are secondary outgrowths of this work principle (Hendrik, 1943, p. 311). Such activities can be viewed self-psychologically as motivated by the self's powerful need for affirming response from the human and non-human environments (Wolf, 1997, p. 105).

Thus, choosing the right work involves understanding how one's sexual and aggressive drives have played out in one's life, transforming them to a "higher" level of expression, and finding the appropriate venue to satisfy those desires in ways that are free of conflict. Freud noted that artistic creation of the painter, sculptor or—my particular interest—the actor (Marcus, with Marcus, 2011) was an especially good example of how sublimation works in that the artist is able to create something beautiful amidst the harshness of life by using his sexual and aggressive drives, guided by the ego, in the service of that socially praiseworthy, reparative goal.

Sublimation by definition involves a socially approved result that is gratifying, supple, and judged to be personally and socially beneficial. For example, an actor may have had a childhood in which he was rarely genuinely listened to, appreciated or otherwise validated by his parents; his need to be heard and admired gets sublimated in his choice of an acting career, of playing to an adoring audience. In authentic sublimation, the original strong desire always comes through in the substitute activity. Meryl Streep and Marlon Brando have superbly described sublimation, the former with a pinch of humor, the latter acerbically: "Let's face it, we were all once 3-year-olds who stood in the middle of the living room and everybody thought we were so adorable. Only some of us grow up and get paid for it"; "Acting is the expression of a neurotic impulse. It is a bum's life. The principal benefit acting has afforded me is the money to pay for my psychoanalysis." Paul Newman and Al Pacino, respectively, have also regarded their acting careers as a kind of sublimation: "To be an actor you have to be a child"; "My first language was shy. It's only by having been thrust into the limelight that I have learned to cope." And finally, the immortal Russian actor and theater director Constantin Stanislavski perceptively noted in his autobiography, "Actors often use the stage to receive what they cannot get in real life" (Marcus, with Marcus, 2011, pp. 238–239). Psychoanalytically speaking, what is true for the actor is also true for other types of work—meaning, career choice is intimately tied to unconscious childhood experiences of satisfaction and frustration that still have a strong interpretive grip on how one views oneself and others.

While sublimation is an enormously complex subject in psychoanalytic theory, I want to focus on one underappreciated aspect of it that most critically applies to the issues of occupational choice, development, adjustment and attainment— namely, that the best sublimations are those that "fuse" the erotic with the aggressive. As Menninger points out, "If the erotic impulse sufficiently dominates, the result is constructive behavior; if the aggressive impulses dominate, the result is more or less destructive behavior" (1942, p. 170). The point is that in civilized society an individual's aggression cannot have full expression; it cannot find a direct outlet. Therefore it has to turn inward, and by doing so it becomes used by the super-ego. The super-ego in turn forces the ego to use its executive functions to submit to the reality of work with all of its adversity, drudgery and boredom. As Lantos further notes, "This internalized aggression [i.e., the ego submitting to the super-ego] is the ultimate guarantee for the maintenance of work and therefore, of self-preservation" (1952, p. 442). In this view, instinctual pleasure is not the ultimate driving force of work. Rather, the need for self-preservation is mediated by reason and intellect and reinforced by the voice of conscience. Thus, from a classically based perspective, the pleasure connected with work is the relief from the tension between the super-ego and ego as suggested above, that is, the harmonization of conscience and reason, and this process allows the person to transform instinctually driven play actions rooted in one's childhood into reality-driven adult work ones. As Lantos concludes, "it is not the object or the skill of the activities which makes the difference between work and play, but the participation of the super ego, which changes play-activities into work-activities" (ibid.). In short, at its best adult work is a pleasurable form of purposive play that is judged to be creative and productive. As Mark Twain quipped, "Work and play are words used to describe the same thing under differing conditions" (www.bancroft.berkeley.edu). That is, "Work consists of whatever a body is obliged to do. Play consists of whatever a body is not obliged to do" (www.pbs.org).

In sum, following Freud, classical-based theory regards work as sublimation, as a symbolic expression of the sexual and aggressive drives, ultimately mediated by the ego (including being acceptable to the super-ego, that is, engaging in work without guilt and anxiety, unlike, for example, workaholics who use work as a drug to get them through their lives), and thus a unique form of defense. By viewing work as a sublimation/defense means that the chosen occupation is socially acceptable, maybe even useful (which is always a value-laden judgment call), consciously gratifying, adaptive and flexible, as opposed to rigid and compulsive (Moore and Fine, 1990, p. 188). Indeed, fashioning a work life that is a good sublimation is no easy achievement. As British philosopher/interpreter of Eastern thought Alan Watts noted, "No work or love will flourish out of guilt, fear, or hollowness of heart, just as no valid plans for the future [including pertaining to one's career journey] can be made by those who have no capacity for living now" (www.quoteauthors.com). From the classical point of view, at its best work is erotically tinged, if not infused, by love. It is Eros made manifest.[4]

Personality organization and career choice

The great Victorian-era English author, Samuel Butler, wisely observed in *The Way of All Flesh* that "Every man's work, whether it be literature, or music or pictures or architecture or anything else, is always a portrait of himself and the more he tries to conceal himself the more clear his character will appear in spite of him" (1903 [2004], p. 91). Indeed, what Butler intuited has been a longstanding preoccupation in both the psychoanalytic and vocational literatures, namely, connecting different occupational roles and career choices to personality organization or character type. The claim here is that personality/character organization/type accounts for work behavior across the board of contexts and settings. Super (1990), for example, suggested that an individual attempts to put into practice his evolving self-concept (e.g., interests, values and skills) by selecting an occupation that he views as most probable to allow self-expression and self-actualization. In fact, research has shown that personality traits predict occupational success (Roberts, 2009, p. 137). This being said, the fact is that the vocational psychology literature on personality frameworks and work behavior "has not been consistent," and has hardly come together into what can be reasonably described as a "received" view that favors one theoretical perspective or set of findings. As Rottinghaus and Miller have further noted in a recent review article:

> Personality researchers from differing perspectives acknowledge that the concept of personality is much more extensive than traits alone [e.g. the "Big Five," the five factor model of neuroticism, extraversion, openness to experience, agreeableness and conscientiousness], including biological factors, needs, motives, objective biography, the role of culture, and how transactions between these factors coalesce into a coherent, though somewhat malleable, personality system.
>
> (2013, p. 105)

Thus, a considerable amount of "career insight" as it is called in vocational psychology—the reflective capacity to understand one's personality needs and wishes in terms of the relationship between career aspirations and making sensible career decisions—is very important in order to get things right (De Vos and Sorens, 2008, p. 450).

In light of the rather fluid and contested state of the vocational psychology and related work literatures, psychoanalytic theory and practice has contributed some important concepts to the conversation that have not been adequately appropriated by mainstream career counselors and other professionals interested in helping people make better career choices. As Osipow (1983, p. 42) and Watkins and Savickas (1990, p. 81) correctly note, probably the best systematic psychoanalytic study of vocational development and personality organization was done by Bordin *et al.* (1963), though Silver and Spilerman's (1990) is also very thought-provoking. While I will briefly summarize some of their interesting findings, what these somewhat dated studies more importantly put forth is a way of understanding and "seeing" what may be some of the deeper unconscious needs and wishes that animate a person's career choice. While it is crucial to be ever-mindful that the process of career choice, development, adjustment and attainment is extremely complicated and many-sided, and that no theory alone, not even psychoanalysis, is the "master key" to helping people make good career decisions, the fact is that psychoanalysis (and its offshoot, psychodynamic career counseling) has put forth much "food for thought" that is illuminating beyond the mere historical interest as Watkins and Savickas have debatably concluded in 1990: that between about 1970 and 1990 mainstream psychoanalytic career theory, practice and investigation appeared to be "dead," or at least dying with regards to what it has usefully provided to career counselors (1990, pp. 83, 82).[5] Indeed, career counselors could greatly benefit by taking a fresh look at earlier psychoanalytic contributions to their specialty as well as more current ones (Kets de Vries, 2010).

Classically based and other psychoanalytic approaches have applied two especially important notions to help illuminate occupational choice and work behavior, namely, character structure (roughly equivalent to personality structure) and defense mechanism (Silver and Spilerman, 1990, p. 181). Character structure can be simply defined as a system of more-or-less permanent traits that are exhibited in the specific ways that an individual relates and reacts to others, to different kinds of stimuli, and to the environment. Defense mechanism refers to the way an individual manages anxiety and other threatening feelings. The underlying assumptions of using these concepts are that different character structures choose, and flourish in, occupations that are favorable to their particular personality type. In addition, Silver and Spilerman claim that certain "mature" defenses, even "neurotic" ones, actually promote success in a number of occupations. For instance, obsessive-compulsive traits are likely to lead to success as, say, an accountant, engineer or draftsman: "Concentration, logical thinking, and *neurotic symptoms*—such as limited affect, narrow mindedness, obsessive doubting, and driven activities—contribute to the successful performance of many systematic tasks" (italics in original; ibid.). The same qualities in an actor, however, are lethal; for anyone in the performing arts, being more emotionally free, flowing and unrestrained is necessary to convincingly inhabit the internal world of a character.

Thus, a good occupational choice is mindful of one's character structure and way of dealing with anxiety and how such a way of being "fits" with the selected occupation and work setting. The latter includes assessing the underlying anxieties and defenses that are operative in any organization or institution. "Social defenses," those rituals that use splitting, projection and introjection to bring about thoughtlessness (i.e., being on "automatic pilot"), are particularly important to be mindful of. By not engaging in critical thinking, employees avoid feeling anxiety. The way hospital protocol is used to depersonalize a nurse's affiliation with very ill patients (Hirschhorn, 1988, p. 2) is one example of a social defense. The problem with this is that most people are clueless about their character structure and the way they cope with anxiety and other disturbing affects, as these mechanisms are mainly unconscious. This is one of the "deeper" reasons why employees find themselves so unhappy in their chosen work.

Likewise, to adequately understand the "culture" of an organization, including its anxieties and defenses, requires being embedded in it for a substantial period of time that is not typically permitted before one accepts a job offer. For example, many people complain about having difficulties with their boss or supervisor, those judgmental parental-like authority substitutes that have to be effectively managed to feel safe and secure, let alone to be able to flourish on the job. This can be extremely challenging, if not debilitating, for consciously and/or unconsciously employees often feel child-based fear and anxiety toward these parental-like overseers. As psychoanalyst Hanna Segal noted, "In the same way in which fear of an external authority can make us afraid to speak, the fear of internal authority can make us afraid to think" (1977, p. 219).

What follows is a simplified and brief description of three psychoanalytically conceived character types rooted in psychosexual theory—oral, anal, phallic—to give the reader a "feel" of how character structure and their correlated defenses, conceived as a way of being in the world, can really matter in terms of career choice and work behavior. The idea here is that these basic character types, originally brilliantly formulated by the early pioneers of psychoanalysis and elaborated by others as psychoanalysis has evolved, are evocative phenomenological descriptions, powerful conceptual metaphors that point to the unconscious motives that animate a person's overall psychology and comportment, including choice of occupation and career trajectory. This being said, one should always be mindful of the fact that in psychoanalytic theory all behavior is over-determined. That is, it is motivated by simultaneous activity of the drives and conflicts at several different levels of the personality, and therefore has more than one meaning and behavioral ramification (Rycroft, 1995, p. 123). Thus, fashioning a compelling meaning-giving, affect-integrating and action-guiding self-narrative is extremely important to reasonably function in work and love. Such self-knowledge about one's drives and conflicts, the "stuff" of any convincing self-narrative, can be the lynchpin to job satisfaction and good job performance. As Erikson noted,

"A man's conflicts represent what he 'really' is" (1970, p. 65), and therefore, without a high degree of self-knowledge about these internal matters, one is bound to get career choice wrong or at least not as right as one could if one had greater self-awareness. This being said, as Freud and his followers have observed, having the "right" knowledge does not necessarily guarantee the "right" action, for there are contrapuntal psychic forces of ambivalence and ambiguity at play that can sway one's decision-making. As Carl Jung noted, "You are what you do, not what you say you'll do" (Roberts and Creary, 2012, p. 79).

The "oral character" is fixated at the oral stage, the first stage of libidinal and ego development, roughly from birth to weaning, in which the mouth is the main basis of pleasure and the focus of the infant's psychological experience. Oral eroticism refers to sensuous pleasure emanating from the mouth like in sucking and eating, while oral sadism is the pleasure in hurting by biting, as in biting the breast and "biting" remarks. Oral characters tend to be discernible by their optimism, self-confidence and carefree generosity, this being a reflection of the pleasurable aspects of the stage. Such people may be drawn to teaching, social work, non-profit work or the performing arts. Oral characters may also be characterized by pessimism, futility, anxiety and sadism, these being expressions of frustrations or conflicts occurring during this phase of psychosexual development. Such people tend to experience their occupation in dark, nasty terms and they are, often correctly, perceived as needy, dependent and moody, these being their main defensive ways of managing their anxiety and emptiness. The overweight, lazy, oblivious and rather selfish Homer Simpson character from the *Simpsons* animated sitcom is a good example of an oral character: "Son, if you really want something in this life, you have to work for it. Now quiet! They're about to announce the lottery numbers" (www.snpp.com).

The hysterical personality style has been conceptually linked to problems in the oral stage. Such people, for example, have an inordinate fear of loss and disappointment (of the symbolic breast, one might say), and they can become explosively attacking (like a hungry and furious infant) when their needs for immediate satisfaction are frustrated. Artists, comedians, writers, fashion design-ers and musicians are some of the occupations where such a personality style may serve such people well (Silver and Spilerman, 1990, p. 193).

The "anal character" is a particular kind of neurosis in which the person is fixated at the anal stage of development (i.e., roughly the toilet training period). Anal eroticism describes the sensuous pleasure originating from anal sensations related to evacuation and the like. Moreover, the parent and child's concern with toileting and staying clean points to the psychodynamic link between bodily self-care and working, as in the phrase parents often say to their young children, "doing one's job" (Furman, 1997, p. 11). Anal sadism refers to the sadistic infan-tile fantasies that are assumed to emanate from the anal stage. The term "anal character" is usually used to refer to reaction formations (i.e., the tendency of a repressed wish or feeling to be expressed at a conscious level in a contrasting

form) against anal eroticism, such as compulsive obstinacy, orderliness and parsimony, but they can also apply to their opposites, such as compulsive flexibility,
untidiness and generosity. Typically, the obsessive-compulsive personality has an
"anal character." Felix Ungar, the tidy, tense, fussy, hyper-critical, hypochon-
driacal and anhedonic news writer whose marriage is ending, from Neil Simon's
play *The Odd Couple*, is a good example of an anal character. Such a person has
an emotionally constricted comportment that is overly rigid, stubborn, perfectionistic and stingy, with preoccupation with trivial details and over-concern with
having everything done one's own way, and he displays excessive devotion to
work, productivity and conscientiousness. These personality types tend to
perform well and are happy in occupations that emphasize technical details,
which demand concentrated, logical, methodical ways of thinking and continuous
attention to their practical tasks. Moreover, they do well where social interaction
is not primary to the work requirements, where decision-making is limited to their
narrow technical expertise and where emotional expressiveness is not highly
valued. Such personality types perform well on the job in work circumstances
where they can control the parameters of work and in occupations that emphasize
objectivity and detachment. One only has to call to mind the typical computer
analyst, programmer, scientist, accountant, surveyor and lithographer to have an
intuitive understanding of why an obsessive-compulsive personality would likely
"fit" well in these occupations (ibid., pp. 190–191).

Finally, we come to the "phallic character," those men who are fixated at the
phallic phase of psychosexual development when the child is preoccupied with
his penis, its function and its potency. In adulthood such a person compulsively
displays sexual behavior (usually in derivative forms) as an expression of
masculine will, effectiveness and potency. The licentious and libertine fictional
character Don Juan is a good example of the phallic character. The phallic
character is different than the "genital character" in that the latter conceives of
sexuality in terms of a mutual loving relationship. Phallic characters often express
inordinate degrees of narcissistic behavior such as vanity, undue self-assurance,
swagger, compulsive sexual behavior and in some contexts, primitive
exhibitionistic and violent behavior. Indeed, more recently, such phallic
characters are typically described as phallic-narcissistic characters. Political,
religious and academic occupations permit such people to take advantage of their
personality organization and defenses in which they satisfy their needs and
wishes for adulation, self-aggrandizement and dependency attachments in a fairly
shielded set of circumstances (ibid., p. 196).

Drawing on the pioneering work of early psychoanalysts, Bordin and
colleagues (1963) apply the above-described psychoanalytical way of thinking
about character/personality to vocational behavior, though they take it somewhat
further. Using the occupations of accounting, social work and plumbing to illustrate their theory, they put forth a series of dimensions (i.e., needs, impulses,
and unconscious motivations), "traceable to infantile physiological functions"
(i.e., body zones), which they claimed accounted "for all of the gratifications

which work can provide" (ibid.). In this view, the personal meanings of work are connected to the early childhood cast of mind, to infantile understandings, imaginings and inquisitiveness pertaining to "the contents, products, and functions of his body" (Levine, 1997, p. 144).

The authors described ten dimensions that were critically important for understanding vocational behavior, such as *nurturing* (feeding and fostering), *oral* (aggressive, biting), *manipulative* (physical, interpersonal), *sensual* (sight, sound, touch) and *anal* (acquiring, timing-order, hoarding, smearing). Bordin and colleagues also discussed the extent to which a dimension was relevant in an occupation, the way an impulse was typically expressed, and in what way the occupational behavior was geared toward people or objects. Not surprisingly, social workers were inclined to be very nurturing (feeding and fostering) as their job requires tending to their needy clients, in some instances giving them literal food like in a homeless shelter; plumbers were engaged in physical manipulation of pipes and valves and needed to use exploratory dimensions such as finding leaks as well as flowing-quenching dimensions, such as arranging pipes and valves. Accountants mainly required manipulation of an interpersonal kind via providing counsel and proposals as well as anal dimensions such as obtaining investments, time-ordering systems and audits.

While there have been other interesting studies of personality and vocational choice and behavior using, to varying degrees, a similar classically glossed psychoanalytic approach, for example, Roe (1956), Nachman (1960), Galinsky (1962) and Segal and Szabo (1964), my main "take home" point in presenting the above formulations and findings is that they strongly suggest how an enlightened Freudian outlook can be an illuminating and useful tool to help a person sort out what career choice is likely to be most satisfying. Classically based psychoanalysis provides a number of compelling notions—for example, sublimation, character, defense and identification (the process of internalizing role-oriented elements of significant others, a subject I will take up shortly). These conceptual metaphors that can help a person put into words the feelings and thoughts that are hard to pin down and to more aptly express experiences and affects which might otherwise stay unsaid, but in fact are extremely relevant in terms of career choice, development, adjustment and attainment.

Individuals use a variety of evocative metaphors to talk about their careers. I earlier mentioned the horticultural one, but there are many other erotically and/or aggressively tinged ones that are referred to in the vocational literature: spatial and existential journey, competition, imprisonment, military, school-like surveillance, life in the Wild West and nautical metaphors (El-Sawad, 2005). While all of these metaphors can be useful depending on the person and context, the Freudian perspective provides what I believe is a unique angle for the problem of career choice. It boldly puts forth the notion that what perhaps matters most in terms of occupational choice is to view it as a practical expression of character/ personality development rooted in early childhood experiences of satisfaction and frustration, always within the context of the totality of evolving circumstances of a person's internal and external life. The validity of this audacious assertion is affirmed when we consider the experiences of late adolescents and emerging adults whose main developmental task is "establishing and integrating character modes into a unified pattern of functioning." That is, to fashion from their many earlier identifications and role experiences a viable identity (Galinsky and Fast, 1966, p. 89), for, as Erikson noted, "In the social jungle of human existence, there is no feeling of being alive without a sense of identity" (Muller, 1995, p. 81).

Erikson's theory of identity and career choice

"There is only one thing harder than being an adolescent," said Anna Freud, "and that is being the parent of one."[6] Indeed, much of the struggle between parents and their adolescent children focuses on preparing them for the adult work world and this requires the adolescent to fashion a feasible identity, a sense of relative continuity of self despite being in flux. Says Erikson, "the term identity ... connotes both a persistent sameness within oneself ... and a persistent sharing of some kind of essential character with others" (1956, p. 57).[7] This sense of continuity and sameness of self amidst flux and change is the basis for a robust "ego-identity," as Erikson calls it (which he later calls simply "identity," partly in deference to Heinz Hartmann's insistence that the ego and self were different) (Akhtar, 2009, p. 140). As with all other personality theories, Erikson's formulations never adequately resolve the knotty problem of how personality traits or identity show both continuity and change (Roberts, 2009, p.139).

In his famous eight-stage theory of human development, Erikson states the central ego-psychological conflict of adolescence, roughly correlated with Freud's early genital stage of libidinal development, including the popular notion of "identity-crisis," that period of uncertainty and confusion in which the adolescent's sense of identity becomes insecure due to a change in their expected aims or role in society. Needless to say, both of these notions are relevant to the problem of career choice as well as job performance and job satisfaction.

The "identity crisis," when there is an upsurge of the key existential questions—Who am I and whom do I want to become? (Monte, 1980, p. 237)—occurs during the adolescent phase of the life cycle. Erikson described it as a time "[w]hen each youth must forge for himself some central perspective and direction, some working unity, out of the effective remnants of his childhood and the hopes of his anticipated adulthood" (1962, p. 4). Adolescence thus signifies an awesome internal emotional upheaval, a struggle between the powerful yearning to stay lodged in the past, to desperately cling to one's childhood cast of mind and home world, and the equally powerful yearning to boldly move into the future equipped with a sense of autonomy and integration (Kaplan, 1995). It is within this high-conflict context when 17- and 18-year-old high school seniors have to begin to seriously consider, at least to some degree, what they may want to do with their lives in terms of their adult careers. As Erikson noted, work provides the "ego a vital setting for the exercise of its activity in regard to the definition of a sense of self and the regulation of self-esteem" (Socarides and Kramer, 1997, p. xv). While some teenagers are pretty clear about what they want to do in terms of work, most are not, and they are sometimes coaxed by external and internal forces, like parents, teachers, peers and/or other imagoes, those idealized mental images of another person or the self, to prematurely make important career decisions. From my experience working with late teens and young adults in psychotherapy, these ill-conceived decisions are often ill-fated, sometimes with dire psychosocial consequences especially when they go to college or enter into the adult work world and feel "stuck" and angry about their fate. Such adolescents are prone to move into one of the various forms of absolutism, which in its extreme can mean joining a gang or radical politics of the Left or Right, or becoming part of a cultish "alternative" lifestyle, what Erikson calls "totalism." Totalism is "a fanatic and exclusive preoccupation with what seems unquestionably ideal within a tight system of ideas." This is opposed to having "solidarity of conviction," a sense that one's generation is different, if not better than the former one, ideally leading to creative and productive affirmations (1977, p. 107).

It is fairly obvious that to the extent that one is relatively "at one with oneself," that is, has fashioned a robust sense of identity (Erikson, 1974, p. 27), or a "real" and "true self" as Winnicott called it, the chances of being able to choose a viable career that one can flourish in is much more likely. However, what is often over-looked in discussions of Erikson's identity theory is that with a sense of positive identity (and this is a value-laden judgment call), there is inevitably a negative component also animating one's self-narrative. This negative identity reflects the residual high-conflict identifications and other unresolved intra-psychic conflicts with parents and siblings from childhood that were "presented to the individual [by his parents] as most undesirable or dangerous, and yet also as most real" (1959, p. 131). For Erikson, what matters most is the preponderance of positive identity over negative identity, for rarely is one cluster of identity processes completely dominating in terms of personality functioning and behavior. In more extreme cases, this negative identity can become highly problematic for those who have close contact with the adolescent, such as parents and teachers.

> The loss of a sense of identity often is expressed in a scornful and snobbish hostility toward the roles offered as proper and desirable in one's family or immediate community. Any part or aspect of the required role, or all parts, be it masculinity or femininity, nationality or class membership, can become the main focus of the young person's acid disdain.
>
> (ibid., p. 129)

When adolescents are in the grip of these aggressive feelings, they not only vindictively lash out at the people closest to them, they tend to choose massively ill-conceived and ill-fated roles, including in the career realm, that are meant to provide them with at least a modicum of a sense of control over their turbulent, anxiety-ridden and angry lives. Erikson calls this stage of late adolescence and early manhood "role confusion": "to keep themselves together [youth] temporarily over-identify, to the point of apparent complete loss of identity, with the heroes of cliques and crowds" (1950, p. 228). In short, says Erikson, an adolescent in the midst of longstanding role confusions would "rather be nobody or somebody bad, or indeed, dead—and this totally, and by free choice—than be not-quite some-body" (1959, p. 132). For adolescents who are amidst "role confusion," not only are they susceptible to the bad influences of cliques and crowds, prone to delin-quency and even vulnerable to psychotic manifestations, they are unwilling and unable to make a vocational choice. In the adult work context, if such individuals have not consolidated a viable authentic identity they can resemble in their way of being what Erich Fromm called the "marketing orientation," a form of think-ing, feeling and acting that Fromm believed was common in contemporary capi-talistic life. The marketing orientation is characterized by someone having an unstable and insecure sense of identity; he is inordinately surface-oriented and shallow, and markedly variable in his outlook. For such an individual identity appears to be a chameleon-like performance of changing one's opinions, behav-ior and appearance according to the role he self-servingly believes he is supposed to play. As Fromm puts it in *Man for Himself: An Inquiry into the Psychiatry of Ethics*, "the premise of the marketing orientation is emptiness, the lack of any specific quality to which would not be subject to change, since any persistent trait of character might conflict someday with the requirements of the market" (1947, p. 85).

It is worth noting that prominent analysts like Otto Kernberg and Salman Akhtar have distinguished those Eriksonian-formulated identity crises that are more typical in adolescence with their trials and tribulations associated with inte-grating early childhood-based identifications into a harmonious psychosocial identity, from the severe pathology emanating from high levels of frustration associated with chronically inadequate childhood parenting. Where Erikson was describing the normative "role confusion," Kernberg and Akhtar have distin-guished this experience from the more severe condition of "identity diffusion." As a consequence, says Kernberg, in the more severe conditions, splitting prevails over repression, and the self continues to hold on to poorly or uninte-grated introjections and identifications that often become the basis for a full-blown personality disorder. Where the adolescent's "identity confusion"—for example, his idealizations and devaluations of his heroes—tends to be more defensive in nature, the person amidst "identity diffusion" often shows symptoms that ripple through the whole of their self-experience, such as marked gender identity problems and profound emptiness (Akhtar, 2009, p. 140).

While the risks of role diffusions in adolescence remain real, for the most part, the majority of adolescents move through this phase of development without too much "drama" and extremist behavior or self-injury. These adolescents who have fashioned a reasonably consolidated ego-identity acquire a sense of mastery in a domain of their personal and social life, what Erikson calls an ego-strength or moral "virtue": "fidelity," the "virtue" associated with a successful resolution of this phase of development, "is the ability to sustain loyalties freely pledged in spite of the inevitable contradictions of value systems" (Erikson, 1964, p. 125). Young people who live according to the heartfelt value of "fidelity" are true to themselves and have a set of life-guiding and life-affirming moral values. As it is called in personality theory, "self-concordance"—the extent to which individuals "believe they are behaving consistently with their interests and values"—leads to a feeling of enlivening authenticity (Rosso et al., 2010, p. 109). That is, their outer appearance, such as the roles that constitute their self-presentation, and their inner reality, their nuclear sense of self, are the same. Such young people are impressive when you encounter them, for one can sense there is no marked discrepancy between what they seem to be and what they are.

Erikson's formulations about adolescent role confusion and identity formation as well as his overall theory of human development have a number of ramifications for how one understands the difficulties of career choice and commitment. Most importantly, when you skillfully combine the ego-psychological insights of Erikson with Freud's classical outlook (this was always Erikson's focus, his Freudian legacy), what emerges is a powerful psychoanalytic "angle of vision" on a wide range of issues pertinent to career behavior, including the way that social and cultural factors interact with individual psychology (e.g., drives, conflicts, sublimations and the like), and profoundly influence career choice and work behavior. Indeed, Erikson's ego-psychological viewpoint correlates well with Freud's theory of psychosexual development, so, for example, an enduring sense of ego identity "cannot begin to exist without the trust of the first oral stage; it cannot be completed without a promise of fulfillment which from the dominant image of adulthood reaches down into the baby's beginnings and which creates at every step an accruing sense of ego strength" (Erikson, 1959, p. 91). Likewise, the autonomy versus shame and doubt stage is dynamically connected to the anal stage, the initiative versus guilt stage to the phallic one, and industry versus inferiority to the latency stage of psychosexual development. Thus, Erikson's life span theory, especially when combined with Freud's instinctual-based insights, offers "a broad overview of human development" (Munley, 1977, p. 263) which may act as a powerful frame of orientation for the complex and personally challenging process of fashioning a career, including career choice, development, adjustment and attainment.

While I have not discussed the other stages of Erikson's theory, the fact is that these formulations also have important applicability to the problem of career choice and development. For example, an individual's sense of basic trust versus mistrust can contribute to his degree of self-confidence and self-efficacy as well as his sense of trust of colleagues and bosses and his overall attitude toward the viability of work as a plausible and enduring meaning structure. Career commitment problems so common in youth of late are often linked to unresolved childhood issues of trust. Without the fashioning of a sense of autonomy in contrast to shame and doubt, a person may have a reduced sense of self-control, self-governance, as well as the truncated capacity to freely choose what he wants to do in the adult work world (e.g., the common problem of career choice indecisiveness that is especially prominent in late adolescence and young adulthood). Developing a sense of initiative versus guilt can impact to what degree a person can create a realistic basis for his aspirations, focus and work-related decisions, including exploring what one might want to do in the adult work world. A lack of initiative often leads to choosing unsatisfying career paths. Acquiring a sense of industry versus inferiority can impact a sense of self-assurance, productivity and that all-important sense of being an agent in the world that can make things work: "I am what I can learn to make work," said Erikson (ibid., pp. 263, 265). From a psychoanalytic point of view, the ability to actualize one's creative visualizations and projections in real life is a sign of psychological "health" (Lapierre, 1993, p. 28) as well as a necessary constituent aspect of living the "good life."

A simple example of how unresolved developmental issues in late adolescence and emerging adulthood can negatively impact career choice pertains to what in vocational psychology is called "career" or "vocational exploration." Vocational exploration refers to the exploration of self and the work world "broadly and deeply" to determine the global aspects of the self and to learn about possible career options that strongly suggest to the individual that there is likely a good "fit" with those aspects (Porfeli et al., 2013, p. 136). This in-breadth and in-depth distinction has been recast in terms of "diversive" career exploration, "learning broadly about the work world and the self," while "specific career exploration" refers to "an in-depth investigation focused on aligning one's perceptions of self and career prospects" (Porfeli and Skorikov, 2010, p. 46). The capacity to engage in these forms of career exploration is lodged in early childhood experiences that facilitated curiosity and exploratory activity, especially during unstructured play that led to satisfying feelings rooted in successful consequences and results. Indeed, research suggests that children tend to scan novel surroundings (in-breadth) prior to centering their attention on specific aspects (in-depth) (Porfeli et al., 2013, p. 137).

While curiosity can be defined as "the recognition, pursuit, and intense desire to explore novel, challenging, and uncertain events" (Kashdan and Silva, 2009, p. 368), it is a complex psychological phenomenon worthy of additional research as it relates to career choice and behavior. Psychoanalytically speaking, curiosity is often based in childhood "sexual curiosity," that is inquisitiveness about the body and about interpersonal relations, for example, "what things do parents do that the child does not understand and has difficulty finding out about" (Galinsky, 1962, p. 299). As Freud noted, it is a child's inquisitiveness and troubled wondering about sexuality that "becomes the prototype of all later intellectual work directed towards the solution of problems" (1908 [1959], p. 219). As a child grows up there are at least three options in terms of his experiences: he may be exposed to circumstances which maintain and further spotlight his interest in the realm of interpersonal relationships; he may have his curiosity re-directed into other domains via displacement, or he may have experiences which lead him to relinquish all efforts at having his curiosity satisfied. So, for example, someone who becomes a clinical psychologist (or psychoanalyst) probably has a strong interest in interpersonal relationships going back to childhood, especially his parents' attitudes and styles of discipline, while, say, physicists usually have a different form of childhood-rooted curiosity, one that focuses on "the structure of and relationships among elements of the physical world" (ibid., p. 305). The point is that one has to have some sense of the relationships between one's current personality make-up, including one's most urgent needs and desires, and developmental experiences, especially how one has internalized parenting attitudes toward curiosity, in order to make a more prudent career choice.

Erikson's identity theory thus puts forward the powerful claim that the career one chooses reflects the individual's deepest needs, wishes and values. It's an important way that a youth deploys and instantiates his identity. Put differently, from a psychoanalytic point of view, career choice is like a living Rorschach inkblot. To the extent that an emerging adult has a coalesced identity, one that is experienced as definite and clear, he is more likely to be able to engage in effective career exploration and, therefore, to access useful career information to make sounder career decisions. Likewise, such an individual is more likely to choose a career or job that is more in sync with who he is, one that is more fitting to his self-conception as he is more self-aware and self-knowledgeable. By having fashioned a positive identity an individual is more likely to have "career maturity," the willingness and ability to make educational and vocational choices pertinent to one's career journey.[8] Such people are less likely to procrastinate and be indecisive about their career choices since they have a greater sense of self-confidence and self-efficacy about the likely results and consequences of their decision. In having fashioned a positive identity one also has a more reality-based outlook that does not generate unrealistic expectations about what a career can offer or unrealistic self-expectations that are built on unrealizable, grandiose and idealizing notions of self. Rather, the individual with a positive identity has what in self-psychology is called a robust "self," one that is cohesive, stable, vigorous, harmonious and appreciated. In contrast to Freud who saw the self as what is contained inside the ego, self-psychologists view the "self" as "the initiating center of the person" that is characterized by "healthy expression of grandiosity and mature goals." Individuals with a firm sense of self or positive identity are able to accurately and more deeply empathize with others, to take constructive criticism, to separate and to metabolize the range of losses that are common in the realms of work and love. In addition, with a firm sense of self or positive identity such people are more capable of creating reasonable life plans, including in terms of their career, and maintain the energy, focus and the go-getting attitude necessary to actualize their plans (Robbins and Patton, 1985, pp. 221, 222). Perhaps most importantly, a firm sense of self is a prerequisite for a high degree of "career adaptability"—that is, the ability to creatively, realistically and effectively improvise to the often unanticipated, changing demands of the totality of work circumstances.[9] Similar to "reality adaptation" in psychoanalytic theory, it is important to be able to effectively adapt to the realistic "facts" that constitute the external world. This means being governed by the reality principle, by consciously perceived external percepts, as opposed to the pleasure principle, by internal mental images and phantasies that frequently lead to poor decision-making (Rycroft, 1995, p. 153).

Attachment theory and career choice and trajectory

A life-affirming frame of reference characterized by openness to the future, lived in the here-and-now and mindful of the past (Hartung *et al.*, 2005, p. 477) is a hugely important sensibility that personifies the art of living the "good life." Such an outlook at its best animates career choice and work behavior, though it has its roots in early attachment relationships. Attachment theory is a number of notions that illuminate the development of the close, lasting emotional bond between the infant and primary caregiver mainly in terms of the infant's innate requirement for proximity and protection, and the diverse ways that this bond impacts the child's psychosocial development into adulthood and throughout the life cycle.

Following Freud and Erikson, I have suggested that there is a theoretical and real-life link between a parent's attitude toward a child's curiosity and the child's later ability to engage in effective career exploration and decision-making. Blustein and colleagues (1995, p. 420) report what is common knowledge among those psychotherapists who work with older adolescents—namely, that those older adolescents who are more closely emotionally tied to their parents while being less ambivalent and conflictually dependent on them are less likely to prematurely settle on their ill-conceived career choice and are more inclined to progress further in their commitment to their choice of careers. In other words, an adolescent amidst his heightened struggle to fashion a viable identity and who feels a high degree of safety and security in his relationship with his responsive and responsible parents is more inclined to engage in career exploration, sensible risk-taking and other level-headed behavior related to career choice and development. One only has to consider the typically pained trajectory of an adolescent whose parents are divorcing, especially in those families in which there is a high-conflict "custody war" raging and the children are caught in the "cross fire." In these situations there is often a "telescoping" of adolescent developmental tasks (Scott and Church, 2001, p. 330), an erosion of the emotionally "secure home base" that leads to serious personality/character and behavior problems that to some degree taint the teenager for the rest of his life (Helmreich and Marcus, 2008).

It was Bowlby who famously pioneered attachment theory. In contrast to Freud who viewed the instincts as the key to motivation, Bowlby thought human beings were driven to fashion strong "affectional bonds" to specific others beginning in early childhood. Moreover, these attachments, conceived as an "internal working model" of the self and other, as Bowlby called it, not only animates later adult behavior, but contributes to adult manifestations of psychological distress and personality problems, such as "anxiety, anger, depression and emotional detach-ment," especially when unwilling and/or unanticipated separation and traumatic loss are involved (Rycroft, 1995, p. 10; Lopez, 2009, p. 406). There is considerable research on how early and later attachments impact career choice and behavior and a summary of these key findings is worth reflecting on.

Attachment theorists (Ainsworth and Bowlby, 1965) have described three basic paradigms of early attachments conceived as unconscious stimulus-response patterns that create a "readiness to respond," as Bowlby puts it (Roberts, 2009, p. 142): 1) the "secure" paradigm, in which the infant responds to the "good enough" primary caregiver with effortlessness and comfort and is able to continue to zestfully engage in exploratory activity; 2) the "anxious-ambivalent" paradigm, where an infant becomes anxiety-ridden and conflicted as a consequence of inconsistent and unreliable caregiving; and 3) the "avoidant" paradigm, where the infant pays no attention to or dismisses as inadequate the care that the caregiver offers. As a result of these encrypted caregiver/infant patterns, adult career behavior is often impacted. For example, secure attachment relationships tend to foster self-exploration and the exploration of educational and occupational envi-ronments. There is a correlation between secure attachment and career planning, making progress in commitment to career choices, environmental exploration, career self-efficacy, orientation and congruence of choice of career, and positive moral values in terms of career pursuits (Schultheiss et al., 2001, pp. 218–219). Likewise, infants and children who have anxious/ambivalent attachments are more inclined to work mainly to satisfy their inordinate needs for approval and affirmation. This often leads to choosing to work with others (where working alone might actually be better for them), a propensity to become over-committed and guilty about not meeting obligations at a high level, feeling under-recognized and under-appreciated by colleagues and bosses, feeling high levels of perfor-mance anxiety, fear of failure and anxiety about the reduction of self-esteem. In short, such people are generally anxious about their work, job performance, and their relationships with colleagues. Moreover, such people have poorer job performance (Hardy and Barkham, 1994, p. 267; Hazan and Shaver, 1990). An adult lodged in an avoidant attachment pattern is deactivated as a person. In the work context such a way of being usually manifests itself in emotional remote-ness and disconnection to colleagues, bosses and the organization. There is an unwillingness and inability to support colleagues, especially under stress, and paradoxically such people are often workaholics who use work to avoid close and intimate relationships in their personal lives. Researchers have found that those individuals who are lodged in avoidance patterns tend to be less satisfied with their job. They conflict more with their colleagues and have more troubling concerns pertaining to relationships outside of work (Blustein et al., 1995, p. 422).

Thus, attachment theory puts into sharp focus the fact that child attachment paradigms tend to thread themselves through an adult's work and love life. There is "generative and self-organizing power" and its opposite, which respectively are rooted in attachment security and insecurity (Lopez, 2009, p. 406). Studies have shown that there is a correlation between satisfaction and two crucial realms of adult experience—love life and work life—that constitute the main thrust for living the "good life": lasting gratification in one realm, for example, a happy marriage, is linked to gratification in the other realm, having an enjoyable job (Hazan and Shaver, 1990, p. 270). As Hazan and Shaver have suggested following Bowlby, adult attachment (the love realm) supports work activity in a manner that calls to mind how infant attachment supports "exploration" of the environment, as Bowlby calls it. Most importantly, the equilibrium between attachment and exploration linked to good psychological functioning in childhood is, significantly, similar to the love/work equilibrium that characterizes good psychological functioning in adulthood (ibid.). So, for example, in a similar way to how children play and explore as a source and expression of feelings of competence and mastery, adults explore and master their environment through creative and productive work. The point is, in a comparable manner to how attachments in one's love life can be secure and healthy, anxious/ambivalent, or avoidant (and there are additional types and combinations cited in the literature), an adult can engage in their work. Indeed, research supports the connection between adult attachment types and certain types of work behavior (Hardy and Barkham, 1994, p. 263), though there are still a number of unanswered questions about the relationship between childhood attachment paradigms, adult interpersonal relationships and work attitudes, difficulties and behavior. No doubt it is highly plausible to view career choice, development and attainment, that is, one's whole career journey, to be significantly related to early attachment patterns and needs (ibid., p. 278). Most importantly, as Bowlby and his followers have shown, acquiring and internalizing a secure adult attachment orientation serves a vital function in being able to choose a suitable career and flourish at work (Lopez, 2009, p. 411).

Final reflections on how to make a sensible career choice

While researchers have estimated that "genetic factors" probably "explain as much as 40 or 50% of the variance in vocational interest" (Savickas, 2001, p. 307), psychoanalytic theory and practice has considered the psychology of work, in particular the problem of career choice, mainly from three intriguing psychological perspectives: from the instinct-dominated views of Freud, from the ego-psychological views of Erikson and from the object-relational view of Bowlby. Self-psychology has also made an important contribution with its description of the development of a "cohesive self," a stable sense of identity, one that is rooted in two lines of healthy psychological development, grandiosity and idealization. Grandiosity refers to the progression from infantile exhibitionism to assertiveness and culminates in mature work ambitions and career plans. Idealization refers to the progression from infantile wishes to merge with one's parents' omnipotence, through admiration of others, and culminating in a mature system of reasonable goal-setting notions (Robbins and Patton, 1985, p. 222). Likewise, Kleinian thought has put into sharp focus the role of unconscious phantasy in career choice, and the defensive, restorative and reparative meanings that particular occupations can provide. "Working for a living," said Elliot Jacques, is "a fundamental activity in a person's testing and strengthening of his sanity," that is, it is a way of defending against early depressive and paranoid psychotic anxieties (1960, p. 365). All of these perspectives emphasize the important role of early childhood experience on later adult work life, and whether one is focused on the pleasure-seeking, meaning-seeking or object-seeking aspects of work behavior, they have provided crucial insights to what is important when trying to choose a career as well as other issues pertinent to one's career journey.

Undoubtedly, what a psychoanalytic angle of vision has to offer someone trying to make a career choice is that it provides an illuminating way of thinking about the problem, one that might just give a thoughtful person a meaning-giving, affect-integrating and action-guiding "lever" for making a sensible career decision. That is, psychoanalysis of any theoretical persuasion stresses the need for robust self-awareness rooted in critical self-knowledge (i.e., the capacity for reasonable self-scrutiny, self-searching and self-analysis [Blum, 1997, p. 27]), a kind of practical wisdom that considers the totality of "inner" and "outer," personal and contextual circumstances (e.g., occupational knowledge)[10] that constitute a person's life in "real time." While the "right" self-knowledge does not assure the "right" decision (and this is always a context-dependent, setting-specific judgment), for there are so many known and unknown, shifting, ambiguous and inconsistent variables at play in any decisional field, it is nevertheless reasonable to assume that critical self-knowledge tends to tilt the scale in terms of making a decision that is less likely to be ill-fated. Moreover, while personality/character traits are, for the most part, "stable in adulthood" (Rounds and Tracey, 1990, p. 14), personality/character traits are not completely static entities, and therefore career decisions are not simply straightforward "matching" procedures (Bordin et al., 1963, p. 67). Rather, if anything, career choice is a much more complex intuition-guided, creative "mix and match" decision-making process (including dialoging with one's "internal objects" [Bergmann, 1997, p. 205] and thinking about why one did not choose a particular career), in part geared to better "manage" if not eradicate primal and other anxieties and ego-dystonic aspects of one's personality/character. For example, dentists have to sublimate their aggression, as in the retributive principle of an "eye for an eye, a tooth for a tooth," while lawyers need to sublimate their oral exhibitionism/ aggression (Nachman, 1960, p. 243). Sometimes, the choice of work can even stand for a person's "love object [e.g., a parent or paramour] and his potent self" (Blum, 1997, p. 33). To make matters even more challenging, as one analyst noted, "diverse [work-related] motives operate in concert, each at its own level of awareness; they co-exist without canceling each other's particular feeling tones or affects" (Pruyser, 1980, p. 62). Thus, it is within the context of an evolving, often opaque reciprocal interplay between the "inner" and "outer" worlds, and in which happenstance can also play an important role (I will take this issue up in another chapter), that an individual must make a reasonable career choice. Most importantly, a sensible career choice must be heartfelt; it must at least feel "right." As philosopher John Dewey so aptly said, "To find out what one is fitted to do and to secure an opportunity to do it is the key to happiness. Nothing is more tragic than failure to discover one's true business in life, or to find that one has drifted or been forced by circumstances into an uncongenial calling" (1916, p. 358).

Indeed, for an individual to arrive at a moment where a choice feels "right" points to that blessed "unified sense of individuality," as one career constructionist, "life design" scholar called it, he must have engaged in an "inner journey" that "traces an emotional odyssey shaped by a central conflict with its associated needs and longing." In other words, feeling a career choice decision is "right" requires struggling with and attempting to overcome "the fear, limitation, block, or wound" that prevents a person from feeling more "whole and complete," this being the psychological aftermath of having made the "right" career choice decision (Savickas, 2012, p. 16).[11] Moreover, such people are not in that wretched state of quasi-mourning about the career options that were not followed, this taking the form of nagging regret that is personified by an individual ruminating about "the road not taken."

While I have discussed a number of technical psychoanalytic concepts to account for work behavior, especially choice of career, the fact is that for the average person the optimal psychological and contextual conditions of possibility for making a reasonable decision are not necessarily in play. In many instances, an emerging adult feels riddled with ambivalence, ambiguity and other muddling psychological and real-life considerations. In such circumstances, there are at least two psychoanalytically based insights that form the practical wisdom that a person can draw from when he has to make a decision about career direction. Let's recast these insights in terms of "thought experiments," that is, creative visualizations, imaginative exercises meant to facilitate reasonable decision-making processes.

First, recall that to the extent that one is able to experience one's work as play, as a pleasurable activity, as an instinctual satisfaction engaged in for its own sake, without serving any other function (Lantos, 1943, p. 116), like a child intensely engaged in organizing the furniture and people in a doll house, the better the chances are that one will experience a high degree of job satisfaction. As Alan Watts noted, "This is the real secret of life—to be completely engaged with what you are doing in the here and now. And instead of calling it work, realize it is play." Plato had a similar view: "What then is the right way to live? Life should be lived as play" (www.riverbankoftruth.com; www.careerwisdom.net.au). In other words, a sensible career decision should involve the creative visualization that wonders if the career one is considering can for the most part be experienced as if it were a playful childhood activity in which one felt most engaged and alive. The American singer and songwriter Lady Gaga put the point just right, even highlighting the delicate art of residing in the transitional space where the division between the real and unreal, true and the untrue and the actual and imaginary

(Akhtar, 2009, p. 104) are beautifully mingled: "I'm half living my life between reality and fantasy at all times. It is best not to ask questions and just enjoy … I am focused on the work. I am constantly creating. I am a busy girl. I live and breathe my work. I love what I do. I believe in the message. There's no stopping. I didn't create the fame, the fame created me" (www.theguardian.com; www. examiner.com).

The critical point is simply that if you can't imagine yourself at the end of a long workday feeling energized and grateful that you have been able to dwell part of your day in play, metaphor and creativity (Akhtar, 2009, p. 104), saying to yourself what Dr. Seuss famously wrote, "Today was good. Today was fun. Tomorrow is another one," chances are the proposed career choice is not a good one (www.centria.wordpress.com).

Secondly, following Freud, I have stressed that the chances of making a good career choice are related to whether what one chooses emanates from "the deep inner needs of our nature" (i.e., the unconscious). Another way of thinking about choosing a career is to conceive of it like falling in love. While practical considerations are always involved in successfully choosing a long-term significant other, these considerations cannot reasonably take psychological precedence over the mysteriously deeper emotional state that has to feel enduringly and profoundly "right." Too much reliance on rationally assessing realistic qualities of the love object can be love's executioner. It is also fundamentally ill-conceived to use reason as the only, or even the primary, methodology for decision-making, especially about deeply significant issues. As cognitive psychologists have shown, "most processing performed by the human mind for decision-making and behavior initiation is not performed at the conscious level" and "introspective access to cognitive processes is limited" (Krieshok et al., 2009, p. 278). Within the work context, the legendary Steve Jobs made this connection between work and love rather well, calling to mind Khalil Gibran's beautiful formulation that "work is love made visible" (www.nytimes.com). Jobs' words of practical wisdom are the perfect bridge between this chapter on career choice and the following chapter that provides some insights into people from diverse careers who chose well as emerging adults and who still love their work after many years:

> You've got to find what you love and that is as true for work as it is for lovers. Your work is going to fill a large part of your life and the only way to be truly satisfied is to do what you believe is great work. And the only way to do great work is to love what you do. If you haven't found it yet, keep looking and don't settle. As with all matters of the heart, you'll know when you've found it. And, like any great relationship, it just gets better and better as the years roll on. So keep looking until you find it. Don't settle.

(www.news.stanford.edu)

The "take-home" point quite simply is that the art of living the "good life" includes conceiving of one's choice of work as a way to actualize personal autonomy and transcendence (Guindon and Hanna, 2002, p. 205), as a "calling," and therefore, don't choose a career that is too small for your spirit, but rather, let your choice of work be your ultimate seduction.[12]

Notes

1 Gedo believed that Freud was "excessively careerist" in his viewpoint. Gedo claims that Freud would have been less tied to his bourgeois socioeconomic values and more psychologically right if he simply put forth the notion that mental health required the "freedom from any incapacity" to love and work. Indeed, there are normative circumstances where it is not unhealthy to work, such as in retirement (1997, pp. 134, 133).

2 As Freud noted in his *Introductory Lectures on Psychoanalysis*, "The distinction between nervous health and neurosis is thus reduced to a practical question and is decided by the outcome—by whether the subject is left with a sufficient amount of capacity for enjoyment and efficiency" (1916–1917 [1961], p. 457).

3 Anna Freud has a developmental line she calls from play to work.

4 I am paraphrasing from the great Lebanese artist, poet and writer, Khalil Gibran.

5 Other evidence suggests that the situation more recently can be characterized similarly, for example a leading textbook on career counseling published by the American Counseling Association in 2009 (third edition) has no entries for psychoanalysis, psychoanalytic theory or Freud in the index (Gysbers *et al.*, 2009).

6 This was related to me by my wife, Irene Wineman Marcus, a child and adult psychoanalyst who trained with Anna Freud when the Anna Freud Center, as it is now named, was called the Hampstead Clinic.

7 I have liberally drawn from Monte's (1980) excellent overview of Erikson's theory in this section.

8 "Career maturity" is a term that is no longer in vogue in vocational psychology; it has been replaced by "career adaptability."

9 According to Super and Knasel there are five aspects to "career adaptability": 1) adequate preparation with regards to important life events; 2) career exploration or information gathering; 3) the capacity to exploit such information in the service of career adaptability; 4) mindfulness of career decision-making principles; 5) a reality orientation to the demands of work (Krieshok *et al.*, 2009, p. 276).

10 Bright and colleagues described some of the contextual variables that have bearing on career choice: "interests; direct exposure to work-relevant activities; vicarious exposure to work-relevant activities; work conditions or reinforcers; thinking one is good at an activity; and leisure experiences." Family, friends and teachers are also important influences (2005, p. 21).

11 "Constructionist counseling," as Savickas calls it, "is a relationship in which career," including career choice, "is coconstructed through narration," through compelling stories. "Stories serve as the construction tools for building narrative identity [a convincing story about the self] and highlighting career themes in complex social interactions." As in psychoanalytic storytelling, constructionist storytelling "crystallizes what clients think of themselves …. [N]arrating the self increases comprehension, coherence, and continuity" (Savickas, 2011, pp. 38, 39). While I find much of constructionism as a meta-theory useful and appealing, my sense is that constructionist career counseling, at least Savickas's version of it, does not give nearly enough attention to unconscious processes and phantasy, the enormously complex ways that

early childhood conflicts and deficits animate one's storytelling, decision-making and behavior, and the powerful resistances people have to changing their status quo, including replaying again and again earlier self-destructive patterns.

12 I am paraphrasing Studs Terkel and Pablo Picasso.

References

Ainsworth, M. D. and Bowlby, J. (1965). *Child Care and the Growth of Love*. London: Penguin Books.

Akhtar, S. (2009). *Comprehensive Dictionary of Psychoanalysis*. London: Karnac.

Bergmann, M. V. (1997). Creative Work, Work Inhibitions and their Relation to Internal Objects. In: C. W. Socarides and S. Kramer (Eds.), *Work and Its Inhibitions: Psychoanalytic Essays* (pp. 191–207). Madison, CT: International Universities Press.

Blum, H. P. (1997). Psychoanalysis and Playful Work. In: C. W. Socarides and S. Kramer (Eds.), *Work and Its Inhibitions: Psychoanalytic Essays* (pp. 19–34). Madison, CT: International Universities Press.

Blustein, D. L., Prezioso, M. S. and Schultheiss, D. P. (1995). Attachment Theory and Career Development: Current Status and Future Directions. *The Counseling Psychologist, 23*:3, 416–432.

Bordin, E. S., Nachman, B. and Segal, S. J. (1963). An Articulated Framework for Vocational Development. *Journal of Counseling Psychology, 10*:2, 107–116.

Bright, J. E. H., Pryor, R. G. L., Wilkenfeld, S. and Earl, J. (2005). The Role of Social Context and Serendipitous Events in Career Decision Making. *Journal for Educational and Vocational Guidance, 5*, 19–36.

Brill, A. A. (1949). *Basic Principles of Psychoanalysis*. Garden City, NY: Garden City Books.

Butler, S. (1903) [2004]. *The Way of All Flesh*. Garden City, NY: Dover.

De Vos, A. and Sorens, N. (2008). Protean attitude and career success: The mediating role of self-management. *Journal of Vocational Behavior, 73*, 449–456.

Dewey, J. (1916). *Democracy and Education: An Introduction to the Philosophy of Education*. New York: Macmillan.

El-Sawad, A. (2005). Becoming a "Lifer"? Unlocking Career through Metaphor. *Journal of Occupational and Organizational Psychology, 78*, 23–41.

Erikson, E. H. (1950). *Childhood and Society*. New York: Norton.

Erikson, E. H. (1956). The Problem of Ego Identity. *Journal of the American Psychoanalytical Association, 4*, 56–121.

Erikson, E. H. (1959). *Identity and the Life Cycle: Selected Papers* (Psychological Issues, Vol. 1, No. 1, Monograph 1). New York: International Universities Press.

Erikson, E. H. (1962). *Young Man Luther: A Study in Psychoanalysis and History*. New York: W.W. Norton.

Erikson, E. H. (1964). *Insight and Responsibility*. New York: W.W. Norton.

Erikson, E. H. (1970). *Gandhi's Truth: On the Origins of Militant Nonviolence*. New York: W.W. Norton.

Erikson, E. H. (1974). *Dimensions of a New Identity: Jefferson Lectures, 1973*. New York: W.W. Norton.

Erikson, E. H. (1977). *Toys and Reasons*. New York: W.W. Norton.

Fadiman, C. and Brand, A. (Eds.). (1985). *Bartlett's Book of Anecdotes*. New York: Little, Brown & Co.

Freud, S. (1895) [1985]. *The Complete Letters of Sigmund Freud to Wilhelm Fliess: 1887–1904*. J. Masson (Ed.). Cambridge, MA: Harvard University Press.

Freud, S. (1908) [1959]. On the Sexual Theories of Children. In: J. Strachey (Ed. and Trans.), *The Standard Edition of the Complete Psychological Works of Sigmund Freud*, Vol. 9 (pp. 205–226). London: Hogarth Press.

Freud, S. (1916–1917) [1961]. Introductory Lectures on Psycho-Analysis. In: J. Strachey (Ed. and Trans.), *The Standard Edition of the Complete Psychological Works of Sigmund Freud*, Vol. 15 and 16. London: Hogarth Press.

Freud, S. (1927) [1961]. The Future of Illusion. In: J. Strachey (Ed. and Trans.), *The Standard Edition of the Complete Psychological Works of Sigmund Freud*, Vol. 21 (pp. 5–56). London: Hogarth Press.

Freud, S. (1930) [1961]. *Civilization and Its Discontents*. In: J. Strachey (Ed. and Trans.), *The Standard Edition of the Complete Psychological Works of Sigmund Freud*, Vol. 21 (pp. 57–145). London: Hogarth Press.

Fromm, E. (1947). *Man for Himself: An Inquiry into the Psychiatry of Ethics*. New York: Fawcett.

Furman, E. (1997). Child's Work: Developmental Aspects of the Capacity to Work and Enjoy It. In: C. W. Socarides and S. Kramer (Eds.), *Work and Its Inhibitions: Psychoanalytic Essays* (pp. 3–17). Madison, CT: International Universities Press.

Galinsky, M. D. (1962). Personality Development and Vocational Choice of Clinical Psychologists and Physicists. *Journal of Counseling Psychology*, *13*, 89–92.

Galinsky, M. D. and Fast, I. (1966). Vocational Choice as a Focus of the Identity Search. *Journal of Counseling Psychology*, *13*:1, 89–92.

Gedo, J. E. (1997). In Praise of Leisure. In: C. W. Socarides and S. Kramer (Eds.), *Work and Its Inhibitions: Psychoanalytic Essays* (pp. 133–141). Madison, CT: International Universities Press.

Guindon, M. and Hanna, F. (2002). Coincidence, Happenstance, Serendipity, Fate, or the Hand of God: Case Studies in Synchronicity. *The Career Development Quarterly*, *50*, 195–208.

Gysbers, N. C. and Heppner, M. J. and Johnston, J. A. (2009). *Career Counseling. Contexts, Processes, and Techniques*. Alexandria, VA: American Counseling Association.

Hardy, G. E. and Barkham, M. (1994). The Relationship between Interpersonal Attachment Styles and Work Difficulties. *Human Relations*, *47*:3, 263–281.

Hartung, P. J., Porfeli, E. J. and Vondracek, F. W. (2005). Child Vocational Development: A Review and Reconsideration. *Journal of Vocational Behavior*, *66*, 385–419.

Hazan, C. and Shaver, P. R. (1990). Love and Work: An Attachment Theory Perspective. *Journal of Personality and Social Psychology*, *19*:2, 270–280.

Heath, C. and Heath, D. (2013). *Decisive. How to Make Better Choices in Life and Work*. New York: Crown Business.

Helmreich, J. and Marcus, P. (2008). *Warring Parents, Wounded Children and the Wretched World of Child Custody: Cautionary Tales*. Westport, CT: Praeger.

Hendrik, I. (1943). Work and the Pleasure Principle. *Psychoanalytic Quarterly*, *12*, 311–329.

Hirschhorn, L. (1988). *The Workplace Within: Psychodynamics of Organizational Life*. Cambridge, MA: The MIT Press.

Jacques, E. (1960). Disturbances in the Capacity to Work. *International Journal of Psycho-Analysis, 41*, 357–367.

Kaplan, L. J. (1995). *Adolescence: The Farewell to Childhood*. New York: Touchstone Books.

Kashdan, T. B. and Silva, P. J. (2009). Curiosity and Interest: The Benefits of Thriving on Novelty and Challenge. In S. J. Lopez and C. R. Snyder (Eds.), *Oxford Handbook of Positive Psychology* (2nd ed., pp. 367–374). Oxford: Oxford University Press.

Kets de Vries, M. F. R. (1993). Alexithymia in Organizational Life: The Organizational Man Revisited. In: L. Hirschhorn and C. K. Barnett (Eds.), *The Psychodynamics of Organizations* (pp. 203–218). Philadelphia: Temple University Press.

Kets de Vries, M. F. R. (2010) *Reflections on Leadership and Career Development: On the Couch with Manfred Kets de Vries*. West Sussex, UK: Jossey-Bass.

Krieshok, T. S., Black, M. D. and McKay, R. A. (2009). Career Decision Making: The Limits of Rationality and the Abundance of Non-Conscious Processes. *Journal of Vocational Behavior, 75*, 275–290.

Lantos, B. (1943). Work and the Instincts. *International Journal of Psychoanalysis, 24*, 114–119.

Lantos, B. (1952). Metapsychological Consideration on the Concept of Work. *International Journal of Psychoanalysis, 33*, 439–443.

Lapierre, L. (1993). Mourning, Potency, and Power in Management. In: L. Hirschhorn and C. K. Barnett (Eds.), *The Psychodynamics of Organizations* (pp. 19–32). Philadelphia: Temple University Press.

Levine, H. (1997). Men at Work: Work, Ego and Identity in the Analysis of Adult Men. In: C. W. Socarides and S. Kramer (Eds.), *Work and Its Inhibitions: Psychoanalytic Essays* (pp. 143–157). Madison, CT: International Universities Press.

Levy, K. (1949). The Eternal Dilettante. In. K. R. Eissler (Ed.), *Searchlights on Delinquency* (pp. 65–76). New York: International Universities Press.

Lopez, F. G. (2009). Adult Attachment Security: The Relational Scaffolding of Positive Psychology. In S. J. Lopez and C. R. Snyder (Eds.), *Oxford Handbook of Positive Psychology* (2nd ed., pp. 405–415). Oxford: Oxford University Press.

Malach-Pines, A. and Yalfe-Yanai, O. (2001). Unconscious Determinants of Career Choice and Burnout: Theoretical Model and Counseling Strategy. *Journal of Employment Counseling, 38*, 170–184.

Marcus, P. with Marcus, G. (2011). *Theater as Life: Practical Wisdom from Great Acting Teaches, Actors and Actresses*. Milwaukee, WI: Marquette University Press.

Menninger, K. A. (1942). Work as Sublimation. *Bulletin of the Menninger Foundation, 6*:6, 170–182.

Monte, C. F. (1980). *Beneath the Mask: An Introduction to Theories of Personality* (2nd ed.). New York: Holt, Rinehart and Winston.

Moore, B. E. and Fine, V. D. (Eds.) (1990). *Psychoanalytic Terms & Concepts*. New Haven, CT: American Psychoanalytic Association and Yale University Press.

Muller, J. P. (1995). *Beyond the Psychoanalytic Dyad: Developmental Semiotics in Freud, Peirce and Lacan*. New York: Routledge.

Munley, P. M. (1977). Erikson's Theory of Psychosocial Development and Career Development. *Journal of Vocational Behavior, 10*, 261–269.

Nachman, B. (1960). Childhood Experiences and Vocational Choice in Law, Dentistry and Social Work. *Journal of Counseling Psychology, 7*, 243–250.

Neff, W. S. (1965). Psychoanalytic Conceptions of the Meaning of Work. *Psychiatry, 28*:4, 324–333.

Obholzer, A. and Roberts, V. Z. (Eds.). (1994). *The Unconscious at Work: Individual and Organizational Stress in the Human Services*. East Sussex, UK: Routledge.

Osipow, S. H. (1983). *Theories of Career Development* (3rd ed.). Englewood Cliffs, NJ: Prentice-Hall.

Person, E. S., Cooper, A. M. and Gabbard, G. O. (Eds.). (2005). *Textbook of Psychoanalysis*. Washington, DC: American Psychiatric Publishing.

Porfeli, E. J. and Skorikov, V. B. (2010). Specific and Diverse Career Exploration During Late Adolescence. *Journal of Career Assessment, 18*:1, 46–58.

Porfeli, E. J., Lee, B. and Vondracek, F. W. (2013). Identity Development and Careers in Adolescents and Emerging Adults: Content, Process, and Structure. In: E. E. Watkins, M. L. Savickas and P. J. Hartung (Eds.), *Handbook of Vocational Psychology: Theory, Research, and Practice* (pp. 133–153). New York: Routledge.

Pruyser, P. W. (1980). Work: Curse or Blessing. *Bulletin of the Menninger Clinic, 44*:1, 59–73.

Reik, T. (1983). *Listening with the Third Ear*. New York: Farrar, Straus and Giroux.

Robbins, S. B. and Patton, M. J. (1985). Self-Psychology and Career Development: Construction of the Superiority and Gold Instability Scales. *Journal of Counseling Psychology, 32*:2, 221–231.

Roberts, B. W. (2009). Back to the Future: Personality and Assessment and Personality Development. *Journal of Research in Personality, 43*, 137–145.

Roberts, L. M. and Creary, S. J. (2012). Positive Identity Construction: Insight from Classical and Contemporary Theoretical Perspectives. In K. S. Cameron and G. M. Spreitzer (Eds.), *The Oxford Handbook of Positive Organizational Scholarship* (pp. 70–83). Oxford: Oxford University Press.

Roe, A. (1956). *The Psychology of Occupations*. New York: John Wiley & Sons.

Rosso, B. D., Dekas, K. H. and Wrzesniewski, A. (2010). On the Meaning of Work: A Theoretical Integration and Review. *Research in Organizational Behavior, 30*, 91–127.

Rottinghaus, P. J. and Miller, A. D. (2013). Convergence of Personality Frameworks Within Vocational Psychology. In: E. E. Watkins, M. L. Savickas and P. J. Hartung (Eds.), *Handbook of Vocational Psychology: Theory, Research, and Practice* (pp. 105–131). New York: Routledge.

Rounds, J. B. and Tracey, T. J. (1990). From Trait-and-Factor to Person-Environment Fit Counseling: Theory and Process. In: W. B. Walsh and S. H. Osipow (Eds.), *Career Counseling: Contemporary Topics in Vocational Psychology* (pp. 1–44). Hillsdale, NJ: Lawrence Erlbaum Associates.

Rycroft, C. (1995). *A Critical Dictionary of Psychoanalysis* (2nd ed.). London: Penguin.

Savickas, M. L. (2001). Toward a Comprehensive Theory of Career Development: Dispositions, Concerns, and Narratives. In F. T. L. Leon and A. Barak (Eds.), *Contemporary Modes in Vocational Psychology: A Volume in Honor of Samuel H. Osipow* (pp. 295–320). Mahwah, NJ: Lawrence Erlbaum.

Savickas, M. L. (2011). *Career Counseling*. Washington, DC: American Psychological Association.

Savickas, M. L. (2012). Life Design: A Paradigm for Career Intervention in the 21st Century. *Journal of Counseling and Development, 90*, 13–18.

Schultheiss, D. E. P., Kress, H. M., Manzi, A. J. and Glassock, J. M. J. (2001). Relational Influences in Career Development: A Qualitative Inquiry. *The Counseling Psychologist, 29*, 216–241.

Scott, D. J. and Church, T. (2001). Separation/Attachment Theory and Career Decidedness and Commitment: Effects of Parental Divorce. *Journal of Vocational Behavior, 58*, 328–347.

Segal, H. (1977). *The Work of Hanna Segal: A Kleinian Approach to Clinical Practice.* London: Free Association Books/Maresfield Library.

Segal, S. and Szabo, R. (1964). Identification in Two Vocations: Accountants and Creative Writers. *Personnel and Guidance Journal, 43,* 252–255.

Silver, C. B. and Spilerman, S. (1990). Psychoanalytic Perspectives on Occupational Choice and Attainment. *Research in Social Stratification and Mobility, 9,* 181–214.

Socarides, C. W. and Kramer, S. (Eds.). (1997). Editor's Introduction and Overview. In: C. W. Socarides and S. Kramer (Eds.), *Work and Its Inhibitions: Psychoanalytic Essays* (pp. xiii–xxii). Madison, CT: International Universities Press.

Super, D. E. (1990). A Life-Span, Life-Space Approach to Career Development. In D. Brown and L. Brooks (Eds.), *Career Choice and Development: Applying Contemporary Approaches to Practice* (2nd ed., pp. 197–261). San Francisco, CA: Jossey-Bass.

Watkins, E. C., Jr. and Savickas, M. L. (1990). Psychodynamic Career Counseling. In: W. B. Walsh and S. H. Osipow (Eds.), *Career Counseling: Contemporary Topics in Vocational Psychology* (pp. 79–116). Hillsdale, NJ: Lawrence Erlbaum Associates.

Winnicott, D. (1971). *Playing and Reality.* London: Tavistock.

Wolf, E. (1997). A Self Psychological Perspective of Work and Its Inhibitions. In: C. W. Socarides and S. Kramer (Eds.), *Work and Its Inhibitions: Psychoanalytic Essays* (pp. 99–114). Madison, CT: International Universities Press.

Wooten, P. and Cameron, K. S. (2010). Enablers of a Positive Strategy: Positively Deviant Leadership. In: P. A. Linley, S. Harrington and N. Garcea (Eds.), *Oxford Handbook of Positive Psychology and Work* (pp. 53–65). Oxford: Oxford University Press.

Web sources

https://resurrectionwaltz2013.wordpress.com/category/r-m.../page/24/, retrieved 10/29/14.

www.bancroft.berkeley.edu/.../mtatplay/wor..., retrieved 11/28/14.

www.bostonglobe.com/ideas/...playfulness.../story.html, retrieved 11/28/14.

www.careerwisdom.net.au/career-quotes/, retrieved 12/2/14.

www.centria.wordpress.com/2009/11/16/dr-seuss-today, retrieved 12/10/14.

www.examiner.com/.../lady-gaga-quotes-outrageous-witty-intelligent-ins..., retrieved 12/2/14.

www.fcs.txstate.edu/cdc/, retrieved 12/2/14.

www.izquotes.com/quote/4378, retrieved 12/9/14.

www.jungseattle.org/f10/f10long.html, retrieved 12/9/14.

www.news.stanford.edu/news/2005/june15/jobs-061505.html, retrieved 12/2/14.

www.notable-quotes.com/n/nietzsche_friedrich.html, retrieved 12/9/14.

www.nytimes.com/books/98/.../gibran-secrets.html, retrieved 12/3/14.

www.nytimes.com/learning/.../onthisday/.../0615.ht..., retrieved 11/26/14.

www.pbs.org/marktwain/learnmore/writings_tom.html, retrieved 11/28/14.

www.quoteauthors.com/quotes/alan-watts-quotes.html, retrieved 12/26/14.

www.quoteworld.org › Mark Twain, retrieved 11/2/14.

www.riverbankoftruth.com/2013/03/14/leave-it-alone-by-alan-watts, retrieved 12/2/14.

www.seattleplaytherapy.com/play-therapy, retrieved 12/9/14.

www.snpp.com/episodes/8F24.html, retrieved 12/10/14.

www.theguardian.com › Arts › Music › Lady Gaga, retrieved 12/2/14.

Chapter 3

Flourishing on the job

The legendary track and field athlete and four-time Olympic Gold Medalist Jesse Owens could have been mistaken for a seasoned psychoanalyst when he said, "The battles that count aren't the ones for gold medals. The struggles within yourself—the invisible battles inside all of us—that's where it's at" (www.forbes.com). Indeed, from a psychoanalytic point of view, the capacity to flourish in work (and love) mainly depends on what kind of person one is. That is, while there are organizational practices and other contextual factors that both positively and negatively impact how one feels, thinks and acts on the job, psychoanalysis most values the art of self-fashioning—creating an autonomous, integrated and humane personal identity—as the lynchpin to being able to flourish in work. Such inventive self-fashioning is rooted in liberating self-knowledge about one's character, power, limitations and the like. Rather than looking outward to discover the value that tells you how to proceed when faced with "on a par" work-related choices, it is wiser to look inward "to what you stand behind, commit to, resolve to throw yourself behind." In dedicating yourself to an alternative, you not only bestow value on it and project meaning into it, you also engage in a process of re-fashioning yourself (Chang, 2015, p. 7). As Freud said, "Analysis does not set out to make pathological reactions impossible, but to give the patient's ego freedom to decide one way or another" (Meissner, 2003, p. 96).

Hearing the call within a call

The capacity to flourish at work begins with taking heed of Freud's wise counsel that when it comes to deciding on a career direction, one should be guided by the "deep inner needs of our nature" (i.e., the unconscious) (Reik, 1983, p. vii). As Freud noted, "But she [Nature] endowed me with a dauntless love of truth, the keen eye of an investigator, a rightful sense of the values of life, and the gift of working hard and finding pleasure in doing so" (Jones, 1953–1957, p. 118). Drawing from the vocational and organizational psychology literatures, a very useful way of applying Freud's advice is to conceive of choosing a career direction in terms of a "calling," as opposed to a "job" or "career." As sociologists Bellah and colleagues (1986) first pointed out in their bestselling book, *Habits of the Heart: Individualism and Commitment in American Life*, a person with a "job" orientation to work is geared toward earning a living for him and his family to prosper and to maximize their amount of leisure time. In other words, work is viewed strictly as a practical means to a financial end. Moreover, his sense of self is mainly defined by financial success, security "and all that money can buy" (p. 66). A "career" is a way to advance oneself in terms of accomplishment, status and prestige. Such people mainly work in order to move up the hierarchical ladder, to be promoted, a competitive process they very much enjoy. The sense of self that is associated with a career is characterized by a broader kind of success than a job in that by attaining a degree of expanding power and competency, work itself becomes a way of sustaining self-esteem (ibid.). Individuals who have a "job" and "career" orientation toward work tend to have personal identities that do not significantly overlap with the actual work they do; to a large extent they view what they do at work as distinct from the rest of their life (Berg *et al.*, 2010, p. 974). They narrate their lives in terms of having a "work self" and a "non-work self," and rarely do they feel they are a "whole" or "complete self."

In contrast, a "calling" is a work orientation in which a person views their work as deeply satisfying and socially beneficial. That is, an individual chooses an occupation that he "feels drawn to pursue," often powerfully. He anticipates it to be "intrinsically enjoyable and meaningful," especially as a socially useful endeavor, and he views it "as a central part of his identity" (ibid., p. 973). As Bellah and colleagues noted, such work "constitutes a practical ideal of activity and character that makes a person's work morally inseparable from his or her life," and it links the person not only more intensely to his co-workers but to the larger community (ibid.). The highly regarded television special hosted by anchorman Anderson Cooper, *CNN Heroes: An All-Star Tribute*, that honors everyday people who make remarkable contributions to humanitarian aid and make profoundly positive difference in their communities, is a wonderful example of the psychology of "callings." In 2014 the group was made up of individuals who protected lions, taught music to injured soldiers, opened new worlds to autistic youth, and helped children who are fighting cancer, poverty and a lack of opportunity (www.cnn.com).

Perhaps surprisingly to some, research has demonstrated that about "one-third of workers, across a whole range of different occupations, view their job or career as a 'calling.'" For example, a public toilet cleaner or garbage collector is just as capable of experiencing their work as meaningful, if not as a "calling," as, say, a doctor or member of the clergy. In other words, such a positive effect cuts across all socioeconomic levels (Hall and Chandler, 2005, p. 167; Stairs and Galpin, 2010, p. 161). The important point here in terms of the art of living the "good life," including its constituent realm of work, was aptly captured by Einstein who advised, "Try not to become a man of success, but a man of value" (www. quoteworld.org). Einstein was emphasizing the importance of being able to justify one's existence not in terms of how others evaluate you in relation to surface material success, but in terms of self-judgment based on living a life of personal integrity and decency. This being said, it is rather troubling if the way that one of the most prominent researchers on "callings," Amy Wrzesniewski, in part defines the phenomenon, as "an enactment of personally significant beliefs through work," is accepted without critical moral reflection (2012, p. 46). For such a definition would mean that an "ISIS" warrior engaged in violent *jihad* is also viewing his work as a "calling." Without acknowledging the moral values that are centrally contained in any definition of "calling," including how it is instantiated in "real" life, we are losing hold, at our peril, of the fact that every psychological construct is heavily value laden and must be qualified and judged accordingly. Moreover, it is precisely a "lack of human values in depth," both professional and personal, that is often correlated with pathological behavior on the job, such as with narcissistic leaders who foster horrid relations throughout an organization. Such people are largely incapable of relating to others using reasonable ego-ideal criteria (a person's notion of ideal behavior developed from parental and social values) and super-ego standards, including "the inability to judge people in depth" (Kernberg, 1979, pp. 35, 33).

While the "job," "career" and "calling" work orientations represent distinct paradigmatic types, the fact is that for many people their work can be experienced at different times and in different contexts as being any one of these orientations or a combination of them. For example, a young, passionate congregational Rabbi analysand of mine spoke in one session about his work as a way to make a good living so he could afford to send his five children to a first class *yeshiva* high school ("job"), about his wish to enlarge the membership and vitality of his small congregation as a way of showing his colleagues that he was made of the "right stuff" to be voted into a prestigious leadership position in a rabbinical association ("career"), and about his sacred duty and life commitment to significantly contribute to Jewish survival, continuity and enhancement ("calling"). Indeed, research has shown that people who, for the most part, view their work as a "calling" fare better on the job, and for that matter, in the rest of life. Such people have higher levels of work, life and health satisfaction, lower work absenteeism (and these findings remain constant when controlling for one's income, education, and type of occupation). They have higher levels of intrinsic work motivation, spend more time at work, even if they are not paid or in other ways compensated, report higher levels of passion for and pleasure in their work, feel stronger identification and engagement with their work, and they perform at higher levels compared to their peers. Those with a "calling" orientation also are less inclined to suffer from stress, depression, and psychic conflict between the work and non-work realms of their lives (Wrzesniewski, 2012, p. 51).

In terms of flourishing on the job what is most important about "callings" is "that *any* kind of work ['lofty to lowly'] can be a calling" (ibid., p. 47). That is, experiencing what one does as a "calling" largely depends on how one creatively conceives of the activity that one labels work. Put differently, when it comes to personal truth, it is a product of the imagination, that wonderful human capacity to form novel images and ideas in the mind:

> Three workers [were] breaking up rocks. When the first was asked what he was doing, he replied, 'Making little ones out of big ones'; the second said, 'Making a living'; and the third, "Building a cathedral."
>
> (Dik and Duffy, 2009, p. 424)

What this story highlights is the fact that what constitutes a "calling" depends on the individual's ability to project transcendent meaning, whether described in religious or secular language, into what he is doing. This involves a complicated deployment of matters connected to self-efficacy and agency in the psychic economy (Meissner, 1997, p. 37). As Heinrich Heine said, "The grandeur of the universe is commensurate with the soul that surveys it" (Gilbert, 1981, p. 131). In some situations, "hearing the call" is fairly straightforward though extraordinary, as in the case of the legendary Mother Teresa:

> On 10 September 1946 during the train ride from Calcutta to Darjeeling for her annual retreat, Mother Teresa received her "inspiration," her "call within a call." On that day, in a way she would never explain, Jesus' thirst for love and for souls took hold of her heart and the desire to satiate His thirst became the driving force of her life. Over the course of the next weeks and months, by means of interior locutions and visions, Jesus revealed to her the desire of His heart for "victims of love" who would "radiate His love on souls." "Come be My light," He begged her. "I cannot go alone." He revealed His pain at the neglect of the poor, His sorrow at their ignorance of Him and His longing for their love. He asked Mother Teresa to establish a religious community, Missionaries of Charity, dedicated to the service of the poorest of the poor. Nearly two years of testing and discernment passed before Mother Teresa received permission to begin. On August 17, 1948, she dressed for the first time in a white, blue-bordered sari and passed through the gates of her beloved Loreto convent to enter the world of the poor.
>
> (www.vatican.va)

Most people who feel their work is a "calling" are not blessed with such a powerful experience of insight and conviction that is perceived to emanate from the outside world, from a glorious realm that is utterly beyond one's ordinary self-experience, such as from God or another sacred or spiritual source. Indeed, researchers have noted that in general, the path to a calling is often not as easily discernible as was Mother Teresa's "transcendent summons" (Dik and Duffy, 2009, p. 427); rather, it is full of psychological and real-life "swings and roundabouts," and it thus requires considerable exploration of one's "inner" and "outer" world. In fact, research has suggested that searching for callings is linked to "feelings of discomfort, indecision, and identity confusion" (Berg *et al.*, 2010, p. 973). That is, the path to "callings" involves conceiving of it as a creative challenge of making everyday work "the birthplace of the transcendent," as Christian-Socratic philosopher Gabriel Marcel beautifully put it (Marcus, 2013, p. 19).[1] Such alive and enlivening creation involves projecting the deepest feelings and conflicts externally into a work of art or other equivalent work task, which is reflected in the art or task, but in addition, back to the self (Inman, 1997, p. 116). Making everyday work "the birthplace of the transcendent" also involves a number of related capacities, skills and emotional/cognitive forms of attunement.

For example, callings have been viewed as both discovered or created depending on the assumptions underlying one's angle of vision (Wrzesniewski, 2012, p. 49). If callings are regarded as discovered then one would be inclined to participate in deep introspection and critical reflection in order to better "hear" the call that is emanating from a sacred or spiritual source. The immortal words of Martin Luther King, Jr. come to mind: "I just want to do God's will. And he's allowed me to go to the mountain. And I've looked over, and I've seen the promised land! I may not get there with you, but I want you to know tonight that we as a people will get to the promised land" (www.africanamericanquotes.org).

If one views a calling as something that has been told to him by a career counselor based on a battery of occupational or career tests then one would be prone to deeply introspect, critically reflect and most importantly, vigorously search out confirmatory data that points one in the direction of the kind of job that is most likely to be experienced as suffused with transcendent meaning. These people progress in the work world by looking for the situations they deeply desire, and, if they can't discover them, they create the potentiating circumstances. The words of Picasso illustrate this approach: "My mother said to me, If you become a soldier, you'll be a general, if you become a monk you'll end up as the pope. Instead, I became a painter and wound up as Picasso" (www.quoteworld.org).

Finally, there are people who choose the best job option available at a particular time but do not at first experience their formal work role as a calling. However, they engage in "crafting techniques," active steps to alter their job role that tend to foster the sense of transcendent meaning associated with experiencing their work as a calling. Such people imaginatively re-frame their job role responsibilities: they actively modify "the behavioral, relational and cognitive boundaries of their jobs" to favorably change the meaning of their experiences and felt identity at work. Most often they do so in a direction that makes their work feel socially beneficial. They craft a work life "to align their experiences with their motivations to pursue their unanswered callings" (Berg *et al.*, 2010, pp. 978, 979). This effort, one that can be viewed as an aesthetically animated attempt at self-fashioning, leads to an increased sense of control on the job, a more favorable self-image, and intensified connection to others (Wrzesniewski and Dutton, 2001, p. 181). The words of a sanitation cleaner come to mind: "You can go your whole life without ever having to call a cop. And you can also go your whole life without ever calling a fireman. But you need a sanitation worker every single day" (www. nytimes.com).

With the exception of Mother Teresa's type of heard callings, for most people the path of a career calling is a continuing, reciprocal and cyclical process which includes deep exploration of personal needs, wishes and goals, trial and error efforts, and critical reflection on failure and success, all of which constitute thoughtful career self-exploration, judgment and decision-making. As Hall and Chandler note, most importantly in this formulation is the "feedback loop," as it "completes the success process and makes it self-reinforcing as a cycle" (2005, pp. 165, 166). Thus, given that unconscious meanings are in significant play with regards to the individual's trajectory of a career calling, from a psychoanalytic point of view it is best to view a calling as *both* discovered and created, encountered and imposed, and found and made (Shafer, 1984, p. 404). Regardless of how one comes to one's sense of having found/created one's "calling," the fact is that it is based on the heartfelt assumption that no kind of work is insignificant if it uplifts humanity, if it enhances individual dignity and significance. Therefore, whatever work one does it should be engaged in with painstaking excellence.[2] As Mark Twain aptly quipped, "The two most important days in your life are the day you are born and the day you find out why" (Kotb, 2014, p. 30).

What is psychoanalytically striking about people who regard their work as a "calling" is that they passionately feel an extreme sense of urgent responsibility to the other, whether that other is a person, animal or thing. This other is a "stranger," meaning the individual does not have any pre-existing personal connection or ego-investment to the person, animal or thing, which makes the sense of urgent responsibility to the other that much more extraordinary. Responsibility for the other, says ethical philosopher Emmanuel Levinas, occurs when a person regards the needs and sufferings of the other to matter more than one's own, or, to put it less severely, the other's needs and sufferings matter at least as much as one's own.

For Freud and his followers, usually when an individual feels such a compelling responsibility it has childhood origins and represents a sublimated version of a powerful unconscious need that has been transformed into a conscious wish. That is, there is an unconscious moral basis to callings that has its roots in early reparative wishes to make things better. Reparation, a term most associated with Melanie Klein, refers to the defense mechanism of diminishing guilt and anxiety by engaging in actions that are meant "to make good the harm" fantasized to have been done to an ambivalently regarded object (e.g., a significant other). The goal of reparation is to creatively restore an internal object that has been imagined as obliterated (Rycroft, 1995, p. 156). In adulthood, such unconscious reparative needs and wishes can become the moral basis for how one consciously lives one's life in both the work and love realms. Martin Luther King, Jr. has characterized the gist of this existential choice just right when he noted, "Every man must decide whether he will walk in the light of creative altruism or in the darkness of destructive selfishness" (www.civilrightsdefence.org.nz).

It was Klein who brilliantly formulated a plausible account for the development of strong reparative wishes. Reparative wishes emanate from the infant's experience of the "depressive position" that is postulated to take place at about four to six months. In that position that infant begins to internalize some of his imagined violent aggression rather than project all of it into the external world, an experience that is linked to him beginning to view his primary caregiver (the "mother"), as neither a fragmented "good" nor "bad" other, a "part" object, but rather as an integrated representation, a "whole" object that is "good" and "bad." With the "all good" mother representation no longer possible, the infant generates painful imaginings and feels terrible sorrow at what he has, in aggressive fantasy done, to the "all good" mother. In other words, the child begins to feel regretful and guilty for his destructive fantasies, his imagined violent attacks against a mother that has not nearly always been bad; in fact she has been the child's psychological parent, the one who has provided him life-sustaining nurturance and stability. It is out of this psychological matrix that the infant begins to feels concern and a proclivity toward reparation and genuine love. The qualities of humility and gratitude are the gradually acquired psychological outcomes of the depressive position, and though these acquisitions are never permanently secured, they must be protected and fortified throughout life against undermining internalized imaginings (Akhtar, 2009, p. 75).

While Klein discusses three types of reparation: manic, obsessional[3] and creative, it is the lattermost one that has greatest applicability to the issue of experiencing one's work as a "calling." For it is through creative reparation by which the individual reduces his guilt and anxiety in a manner that reflects profundity of character and respect for the needs, wishes and feelings of others (Rycroft, 1995, p. 98). Creative reparation has been defined as "where genuine concern for love objects [i.e., any instinctually invested person, animal or thing] is evident and the transformation of guilt into repair finds sublimated and artistic pathways." What distinguishes the love emanating from creative reparation versus, say, the more romantic, idealized love is that in the former the guiding value is one's strong commitment to ameliorate the suffering of the other (Akhtar, 2009, p. 245). This being said, how does one actually go about instantiating such creative reparation in the context of work so it is experienced as the "birthplace of the transcendent," that is, as a "calling"?

Work as the created birthplace of the transcendent

Drawing from Marcel's path-breaking formulations, I view creativity as having a central role in fashioning the "good life." By this I refer to the individual's quest for what Marcel called "spiritual reality" and "spiritual illumination" (Marcel, 2001a, pp. 1, 13), a life that is characterized by "novelty, freshness, revelation," that intends the transcendent and, perhaps most importantly, often leads to radical perspective-shifting, life-affirming self-transformation, a "renewal of being" (Gallagher, 1962, pp. 84, 95). While a life that is narrated in terms of "spiritual reality" and "spiritual illumination" can be psychoanalytically viewed as merely a regressive manifestation of infantile wishes pertaining to mother/infant merging, or an indication of defensive idealization against aggressive wishes, I will instead mainly view such experiences as phenomenological, that is, as creative expressions that are authentically transcendent, certainly in the mind and heart of the person experiencing them (Akhtar, 2009, pp. 269–270). Most importantly, perhaps, it is the capacity for what Averill calls "emotional creativity," the psychological bedrock for a "renewal of being," that Marcel insinuates gives us access to the best of what is both "inside" and "outside" of ourselves, namely, Beauty, Truth and Goodness, which includes the workplace. Simply stated, emotional creativity refers to the capacity for "novel, effective and authentic" receptiveness, responsiveness and responsibility, an openness, curiosity and imagination that leads to a process of "spiritualization of the passions," to quote Nietzsche, that is, to "self-realization and expansion" and an increased "vitality, connectedness and meaningfulness" (Averill, 2009, p. 255). In short, I am talking about self-fashioning or self-creating, which, as Marcel sees it, always includes an other-directed, other-regarding and other-serving thrust to it. Like Freud, for Marcel the fine arts are explicitly creative, but the creative impulse is also expressed in what can be broadly called the ethical sphere, in acts of hospitality, admiration, generosity, love, friendship, prayer, religion, contemplation and metaphysics. Such ethically animated creative impulses can also be enacted in the workplace, whether one is a volunteer doctor working with Ebola patients in West Africa, a policeman or fireman, or a graciously helpful clerk or doorman. In all such creative experiences of deep communion, of "being-with," of "self-donation to the thou, the spirit of encounter, co-presence, *engagement*" (italics in original; Miceli, 1965, p. 20) in Marcel's nomenclature, and more simply, the feeling of emotional and spiritual closeness, "*We do not belong to ourselves*: this is certainly the sum and substance, if not of wisdom, at least of any spirituality worthy of the name"(Marcel, "Foreword," in Gallagher, 1962, p. xiv).

In the vocational and organizational psychology literatures, the role of this kind of other-directed, other-regarding and other-serving spirituality in the workplace has been conceptualized in terms of "the spiritualization of work," in which work is geared to "broader life fulfillment" rooted in promoting care and concern for family, colleagues and the wider community. These include organizational strategies that demand ethical leadership, enhance employee well-being, facilitate sustainability and are socially responsible, while they also uphold profits and revenue growth (Carroll, 2013, pp. 595, 597, 604). Prosocial practices, as they have been called (Dutton *et al.*, 2011, p. 159), are meant to shield and/or support the best interests of other people and provide a medium for employees to partake in routine helping and giving in the work context. Research has clearly shown that those employees who engage in regularly helping others and giving to a cause that transcends themselves are more likely to flourish in terms of job performance and job satisfaction. Moreover, engaging in prosocial practices in the work setting "often increases psychological and social functioning, as indicated by greater persistence, performance and citizenship behaviors on the job" (ibid.). Indeed, such a "for the other" comportment in the work setting also has its psychoanalytically conceived, exquisitely sublimatory and self-reparative benefits, for it can stand for or replace a loved and loving internal object that enhances personality integration (Levine, 1997, p. 155). As English novelist George Eliot wrote in *Silas Marner*, "Everyman's work, pursued steadily, tends to become an end in itself, and so to bridge over the loveless chasms of his life" (1882, p. 121).

Defining Marcellian creativity

Marcel notes in his magnum opus, *The Mystery of Being*, that there is an intimate connection between creativity and existence, a clarification that provides a helpful context for getting a better sense of how he defines the notion of creativity, including as it applies to work behavior:

> A really alive person is not merely someone who has a taste for life, but somebody who spreads that taste, showering it, as it were, around him; and a person who is really alive in this way has, quite apart from any tangible achievements of his, something essentially creative about him; it is from this perspective that we can most easily grasp the nexus which, in principle at least, links creativity to existence, even though existence can always decay, can become sloth, glum repetition, killing routine. [Think of work "burnout" or bureaucratically induced alienation.]
>
> (2001a, p. 139)

To be a "really alive" person is to be one who strongly feels, this being Marcel's main indicator of authentic participation in the mystery of being (roughly, being fully engaged in the experience of the here-and-now).[4] Authenticity, says Marcel, is the opposite of "indifference"—it is responsiveness (1973, p. 121). Such a person experiences his mind, body and soul, his "self" in psychological language, deeply and joyfully, including those times when he feels threatened by the sham, drudgery and broken dreams of his daily life. He exudes what Marcel calls "presence," that experience "of the immediate 'witness' of real being" (Cain, 1979, p. 28). Presence, says Marcel is the:

> sudden emergence, unforeseeable, salvific, of a form that is not simply traced, but wedded, that is to say, to and re-created from within and in which the entire experience, instead of being lost, instead of being scattered like sand and dust, concentrates itself, affirms itself, proclaims itself
>
> (2005, p. 113)

Elsewhere, Marcel points out, presence "reveals itself immediately and unmistakably," for example, "in a look, a smile, and intonation or a handshake" (1995, p. 40). In addition to engaging in such novel, spontaneous self-creation, a "really alive" person is also willing and able to be self-consecrating and self-sacrificing (Cain, 1995, p. 104). He feels internally compelled to share this deep and joyful self-experience with others as a "being-among-beings" (http://www. lep.utm.edu). The creative impulse, then, is best conceptualized as a relational moment, as being both self-affirming and other-directed, other-regarding and other-serving: "the true artist" [in the broader sense we all can be artists], says Marcel, "does not create for himself alone but for everyone; he is satisfied only if that condition is fulfilled" (1964, p. 47). Indeed, the great Emerson concurred with Marcel's view, "The purpose of life is not to be happy. It is to be useful, to be honorable, to be compassionate, to have it make some difference that you have lived and lived well" (www.keepinspiring.me).

For Marcel, creativity is always a relational dynamic, whether conceived as "real," as in an act of love directed toward a significant other, or "imagined," as in an artistic vision that leads to the production of a work of art. In fact, any kind of work that has a reparative, healing or in other ways uplifting ripple effect on others can be said to be creative, in part because it involves the persistent ethically animated deployment of thought, imagination, discernment and decision-making (Levine, 1997, p. 152). Thus, to create in whatever form is to refuse reducing the self and the other to the level of abstractions and objectifications (Marcel, 1964, p. 47). As Marcel says, such an alienating moment amounts to "the denial of the more than human by the less than human" (ibid., p. 10). Indeed, Primo Levi has made a similar observation as it pertains to work: "I am persuaded that normal human beings are biologically built for an activity that is aimed toward a goal and that idleness, or aimless work (like Auschwitz *Arbeit*), gives rise to suffering and to atrophy" (1996, p. 179).

What are some of the key general characteristics of creativity, characteristics that Marcel suggests make the notion so summoning and enlivening even when we simply hear the word "creativity"? Creativity is associated with "novelty, freshness, revelation," as Gallagher has aptly summarized it (1962, pp. 84–85). Creativity is novel in the sense that it points to that which is unique, original and different, always in a thrilling, self-renewing way. It is fresh in the sense that it calls to mind that which is eternal, that is, the creative experience is unaffected by the passage of time, like creating or encountering a great piece of music or art. Finally, creation gives one the feeling that one is in a "beholding," looking at or hearing something that is amazing and exciting, and the sense that one has been given an irresistible, magical "gift" that makes the person feel "anew and beyond beginnings" (ibid., p. 85). As Mother Teresa said about her work with the poor, "The miracle is not that we do this work, but that we are happy to do it" (www.catholicbible101.com). Indeed, any act of kindness in the everyday workplace reflects a similarly praiseworthy sentiment.

In creation, whether one is the creator or the person who witnesses creation and its product, the experience is that one has engaged "the source, the beginning, which is also the end." As Gallagher further notes, "one who stands in the source transcends time," however paradoxically "we need time to stand in the source" (1962, p. 85). Put somewhat differently, in creativity, the creator surrenders himself to something other; he puts himself at the service of something, a source that transcends while at the same time depends on him (Cain, 1995, p. 104). Marcel notes, for example, that for the artist there is an encounter with "the original mystery, the 'dawning of reality' at its unfathomable source." Moreover, he says, "the artist [or any vocation that is experienced as a "calling"] seems to be nourished by the very thing he seeks to incarnate; hence the identification of receiving and giving is ultimately realized in him" (1964, p. 92).

In the act of creation, ironically, one does not feel as though one is giving up anything vital of the self, even as there is hard work and output that is required to create. As Michelangelo noted, "If people knew how hard I had to work to gain my mastery, it would not seem so wonderful at all" (www.movemequotes.com). Rather, the act of creation makes one feel as though one has become more bountiful, has a more plentiful supply of something that is judged by the creator as good and feels significantly healing. Calling to mind Klein's description of the depressive position and the reparative capacities that emanate from it, in Marcel's language we could say that such a creative person, conceived as a *homo viator*, a spiritual wanderer or wayfarer, has decisively moved further along his internal journey from "existential brokenness," from experiencing his life as having "lost its inner unity and its living center" (Marcel, 1963, p. 91) to a greater "ontological fullness" (Cain, 1995, p. 84). As the great Irish playwright George Bernard Shaw remarked, "I am of the opinion that my life belongs to the community, and as long as I live, it is my privilege to do for it what I can. I want to be thoroughly used when I die. For the harder I work the more I live. I rejoice in life for its own sake" (www.rebellesociety.com).

As I suggested earlier, Marcel notes that the creative experience fundamentally changes the experience of time during the creative act and its witnessing. Creativity does not take place in time as conventionally conceived, as a dimension that enables two identical events occurring at the same point in space to be distinguished, measured by the interval between the events. Rather, time tends to feel without beginning or end, being bathed in the eternity of the creative activity and its result. Such an experience of immediate, present time is the opposite of the way that time is experienced in ordinary life, especially in an overly routinized activity where one feels bored, predictable, monotonous and unchanging, e.g., as when a schoolchild waits for the recess bell or a clerk or assembly line worker waits for the end of the day. "Bureaucracy is the death of all sound work," said Einstein (www.izquotes.com). The point is that creation renews, replenishes and enlivens, while routine atrophies, empties and deadens.[5] As Gallagher aptly puts it, all creative activities—in the fine arts, in contemplation, in love or in encountering a beautiful sunset—"are absolute beginnings which thrust me into the plenitude [a palpable sense of "fullness" or completion] which is beyond beginnings … wherever there is joy, there is being: for wherever there is joy, there is creation" (1962, p. 87).

In the workplace, this experience of time has been formulated by scholars in terms of "flow" (or being in the "zone"), that condition of heightened focus, concentration, and immersion that also takes place in play and art. As the originator of this notion, Mihaly Csikszentmihalyi pointed out, it is precisely the total absorption with an activity and the situation one is in that is the basis for optimal performance, learning and the experience of joy and other positive affects (Nakamura and Csikszentmihalyi, 2009). Marcel's observations about how time is experienced during creativity also resonates with the construct of a psychological state called "work engagement." This concept is roughly defined as "a psychological presence in a role," or "being there," and refers to the degree to which workers are "attentive, connected, integrated, and focused on their role performances." Greater work engagement is associated with better job performance and increased job satisfaction (Rothbard and Patil, 2012, pp. 56, 57). As Marcel's observations suggest, during the creative act and its witnessing, one is more of a "visionary" in time perspective, as it has been called in the psychology of work literature. That is, such a person resides in a different dimension of the spirit, in a deeper form of attunement, and thus is able to intuit things that have not yet come into being. This is different than the "realist," who is bound only to the present and who cautiously proceeds as required, or those individuals who mainly dwell in the past to animate their way of engaging the present (Marianetti and Passmore, 2010, p. 193).

Another important aspect of all creativity, as Marcel construes it, is that the division of giving and receiving is overcome. Marcel makes this point in reference to hospitality, providing a friendly welcome and kind, generous treatment offered to a guest or stranger, or for that matter, a co-worker, colleague or boss:

> If we devote our attention to the act of hospitality, we will see at once that to receive is not to fill up a void with an alien presence but to make the other person participate in a certain plenitude. Thus the ambiguous term, "receptivity," has a wide range of meanings extending from suffering or undergoing to the gift of self; for hospitality is a gift of what is one's own, i.e. of oneself. … To provide hospitality is truly to communicate something of oneself to the other.
>
> (1964, pp. 28, 90)

What Marcel is getting at in this excerpt is that to be hospitable, to "receive" someone, is to open oneself to the other, to let the other into one's inner reality, that is, to literally and symbolically let the other into one's "home," that place where one finds refuge and feels most safe and secure. To "receive" a visitor I must unlock the door and allow him in, clutch his hand and openly and responsively give myself to him (Cain, 1979, p. 27). Feelings of vitality and generosity spontaneously emerge. In other words, hospitality is both a moment of receiving and giving, of being receptive and responsive, but also of being responsible to, and for, the other. At this juncture, receiving and giving are impossible to tell apart. Marcel puts this point succinctly:

> I can only grasp myself as being—on condition that I feel; and it can also be conceded that to feel is to receive; but it must be pointed out at once that to receive in this context is to open myself to, hence to give myself, rather than undergo an external action.
>
> (1964, p. 91)

Thus, it is a psychological paradox that to give the best of oneself is the surest way one can receive. Research inspired by Frederickson's "broaden and build" theory has found that, in the workplace, institutionalized care-giving and supportive attachments and other pro-social behaviors that are rooted in heartfelt collective values that reflect "organizational virtuousness" generate upward emotion spirals, so compassion begets compassion among employees (Lilius *et al.*, 2012, pp. 276, 278).

Marcel further elaborates this crucial fusion between giving and receiving when he discusses the example *par excellence* of work, namely, the artistic process, that "mysterious gestation" that makes the creation of an artistic work possible (1965, p. 25). According to Marcel,

> That which is essential in the creator is the act by which he places himself at the disposal of something which, no doubt in one sense depends upon him for its existence, but which at the same time appears to him to be beyond what he is and what he judged himself capable of drawing directly and immediately from himself [i.e., from his personality].
>
> (ibid.)

Marcel notes that while the creative act involves what he calls "the personality" of the artist, his inner resources broadly described, at the same time, as all artists will tell you, "creation depends in some way upon a superior order" (ibid.), a transcendent realm, perhaps God, as Michelangelo and Bach thought and felt, or the unconscious or collective unconscious, as Freud and Jung might have called it. According to Marcel,

> it will seem to the person that sometimes he invents the order ["giving"], sometimes he discovers it ["receiving"], and reflection will moreover show that there is always a continuity between invention and discovery [what "callings" researcher Wrzesniewski referred to as discovering and creating], and that no line of demarcation as definite as that ordinarily accepted by commonsense can be established between the one and the other.
>
> (ibid.)

The point is that in such ultimate domains of being such as creativity, the crea-tor simultaneously and indistinguishably receives and gives as he fully engages the creative process, right up to the last brush stroke, note, word or prosocial act in the workplace. Put somewhat differently, the creative "action is neither auton-omous nor heteronomous" (Gallagher, 1962, p. 88). Artistic creation feels as if it is not simply one's own possession, "it testifies to a gift from transcendence, even though the reception of the inspiration is itself an act of the artist" (ibid.). The great German psychiatrist/philosopher Karl Jaspers made a similar observation when he wrote, "There where I am myself I am no longer only myself" (ibid., p. 91). Transcendence, in other words, particularly in the creative realm broadly described (including in the workplace), refers to "that which is not myself but which can never be external to myself" (ibid., p. 93). Extrapolating from this point, we could say, as Marcel wrote, that the most receptive and responsive person, the one who is able to engage life openly with the fullness of his whole being, is also the most creative (1965, p. 264). It is within this context that the creator enters the realm of "creative testimony" or "creative attestation," that existential place "where the human person bears witness to the presence of being" (Cain, 1979, p. 75).

Finally, for Marcel, creativity, especially in the ethical realm, emanates from and is intimately involved in cultural beliefs and values. While an extensive discussion of the complex and murky subject of beliefs and values is well beyond the scope of this chapter, by cultural belief I simply mean any statement that attempts "to describe some aspect of collective reality," beliefs largely being the basis for our social construction of everyday reality, including its less common aspects such as spirituality or cosmology (Johnson, 1995, p. 24). By cultural values I mean those "shared ideas about how something is ranked in terms of its relative social desirability, worth or goodness" (ibid., p. 309). Most importantly, for Marcel, values, which he closely links to being and creativity, can be psychologically viewed as the core components of a clustering of beliefs that direct behavior on a long-range basis toward a particular goal. A value, says sociologist Barry Barnes, is "a cluster of accepted modes of action" (1983, pp. 29–30), while Richard Rorty notes that beliefs are "successful rules for action" (1990, p. 65). For Marcel, the domain of being, of "fullness" and transcendence, of which creativity is one of its most exquisite points of entry and expression, is always embedded in and animated by values. In fact, for Marcel values are the same as, or at least strongly point to, being and transcendent reality. "Being cannot be separated from the exigence of being … the impossibility of severing being from value" (Marcel, 2001b, p. 61). And elsewhere he notes, "For what we call values are perhaps only a kind of refraction of reality, like the rainbow colors that emerge from a prism when white light is passed through it" (2008, p. 122). In other words, creativity, whether in the artistic or ethical realms—and this includes everyday life in the workplace—is always intimately connected to such concrete values as Beauty, Truth and Goodness, those sacred values being the basis for living with a sense of transcendent meaning and purpose.

For Marcel, the process of integrating these higher values into one's artistic endeavors and inter-subjective relations, as Bach did in his music, Jesus did in his relationships, and Mother Teresa did in her tireless work with the poor, involves both actively inventing usable truths and discovering universal Truths, a fundamentally active, dynamic, creative process that is both self- and other-affirming.

Creative testimony

Creative testimony, says Marcel, is a "witness to the spiritual" (1965, p. 213). It is "the fundamental vocation of man" (1967, p. 17). It is Marcel's discussion of creative testimony in its many forms, especially in terms of the ethical realm, that best reveals his most original contribution to understanding the experience of creativity as the birthplace of the transcendent, both inside and outside the workplace.

According to Marcel, in creative testimony, "[t]he witness, of course, is not just he who observes or makes a statement; that is not what he really is, but he is one who testifies and his testimony is not a mere echo, it is a participation and a confirmation; to bear witness is to contribute to the growth or coming of that for which one testifies" (1965, p. 213).

What Marcel is pointing to is a mode of being that is perhaps best clarified when we consider the word creation not simply in terms of its common usage and application as in creating a work of art. In addition, for example, "a great love is a creation as well as a poem or a statue; a great love is creative participation in what, in order to simplify, I shall call ... the divine life" (ibid., p. 220). Thus, Marcel uses such terms as "creative fidelity," "creative generosity," "creative receptivity" and "creative belonging" or fraternity, to help the reader expand his conception of creativity into the ethical realm of what he calls intersubjectivity. Intersubjectivity, as Marcel and I use the term, is the "realm of existence to which the preposition *with* properly applies," a relation that "really does bind" and brings "us together at the ontological level, that is *qua* beings" (Marcel, 2001a, pp. 180, 181, 178). Marcel thus mainly understands and describes being in terms of intersubjectivity, the opposite of self-centeredness, such as in love, fidelity, faith, hope (Cain, 1995, p. 172), the capacity for "openness to others" and "to welcome them without being effaced by them" (Marcel, 1973, p. 39). In his view, intersubjectivity is the pre-requisite of human awareness, while communion, that mode of engagement that facilitates a sense of deep emotional and spiritual closeness, which is also profoundly creative as it transforms and enhances both people, is the form that an authentic life takes (Keen, 1967, pp. 28–29). For example, sacrifice, being for the other before oneself, is fundamentally a creative act of self-donation, "radiating out into intersubjectivity, expressing our ontological rootedness and togetherness" (Cain, 1995, p. 173). Finally, it should be noted that for Marcel, intersubjectivity, receptiveness, responsiveness and responsibility to and for the other, are not secure states; rather, they are "perpetually threatened" (as is Klein's reparation), largely because of the pull of such intruding narcissistic urges as excessive self-centeredness and self-admiration. According to Marcel, the self is always in danger of closing "itself again" and becoming "a prisoner of itself, no longer considering the other except in relation to itself" (1973, pp. 253–254). While the "welcoming" of the other can only be done with an open and loving heart, the demands of the selfish ego almost always demand a hearing. In the context of the workplace, what this means is that work that is done without love is a form of imprisonment, if not slavery. Moreover, all manifestations of prosocial behavior and "organizational virtuousness" as described above are expressions of creative testimony. Indeed, Freud had a similar sentiment when he wrote, "Sincerity is the source of all genius [i.e., creative work] and man would be more intelligent were he only better" (Socarides and Kramer, 1997, p. xviii).

Two everyday examples of creative testimony will help illuminate Marcel's innovative notion of creativity as it applies to the ethical realm within the workplace.

Admiration of colleagues, managers and leaders

Admiration, that feeling of pleasure, approval and, often, wonder and reverence that we have from time to time is usually viewed in psychoanalytic circles in terms of the dynamics of the admirer's "ego ideal," that is, the self's image of how he wishes to ideally be. For Freud, the ego ideal emanates from the fusion of narcissism and early identifications with one's caregivers: "What man projects before him as his ideal is the substitute for the lost narcissism of his childhood in which he was his own ideal" (1914 [1957], p. 94). As the American humorist Evan Esar aptly quipped, admiration is "Our feeling of delight that another person resembles us" (www.zimbio.com). Self-psychologist Heinz Kohut viewed admiration as stemming from experiences with idealized "selfobjects," that is, from those compelling experiences of merging with calm, powerful, wise and good others (Moore and Fine, 1990, p. 178). Marcel, however, had discussed the phenomenology of admiration and pointed to its exquisitely creative nature and to the dismal inner life of those who are not able to admire, long before "positive psychology," "the 'scientific' study of what makes life most worth living," became a prominent psychological sub-discipline (Peterson, 2009, p. xxiii). In the context of the workplace, the capacity to admire one's colleagues, managers and leaders is an important quality of mind and heart to have if one is to be able to flourish on the job. For example, compared to faultfinders, grumblers and others who cannot give respect and warm approval, admiration is a powerful motivator; it facilitates trust and confidence and it makes people feel valued, needed, appreciated and special. Of course, as Nietzsche noted, too much admiration can inhibit our own striving for excellence and achieving admiration.

The following two quotations clearly illustrate Marcel's perceptive views about admiration:

> Do not let us ever forget, indeed, that to admire is already, in a certain degree, to create, since to admire is to be receptive in an active, alert manner ....

Experience, indeed, proves to us in the most irrefutable fashion that beings incapable of admiration are always at bottom sterile beings, perhaps sterile because exhausted, because the springs of life are dried or choked in them.

(Marcel, 2001a, p. 136)

I have always said that I experience a kind of horror in the presence of people who are incapable of admiration. Admiration is a form of readiness. I remember being shocked when a playwright remarked, "I do not like to admire at all, because I feel that if I admire, I am humiliating myself." This seems to me the most scandalous untruth that could possibly be uttered. I have always felt that in admiring I am not increasing my stature (one cannot speak of it in that sense), but rather opening myself up. I would say that admiration broadens us.

(Marcel, 1984, p. 202)

For Marcel, admiration has a special effect of "lifting" us in a way that is obvious when, for example, a fellow spectator does not share our enthusiasm for a musical or theatrical performance: "It not only seems that the other person is earth-bound while we are soaring, but we also have a painful impression that he is dragging or weighing us down; the violence with which we protest against his attitude is in a sense a measure of the effort with which we resist him" (1964, p. 47). We resist such people who drag us down because we sense the aggressive criticalness that often underlies their lack of enthusiasm. What Marcel is getting at is that the function of admiration is to reduce our excessive self-centeredness, "to tear us away from ourselves and from the thoughts we have of ourselves" (ibid.).

Admiration, says Marcel, is not only an "élan" but it is an "irruption" that can only take place in a person who is radically open and "available." In a certain sense, it is as if something is "revealed to us" (ibid., p. 48), but only if we are receptive and responsive to the other's unique and compelling otherness. This point is clearer when we consider those people, too many these days, who either *refuse* to or are *unable* to admire, who are, in Marcel's language, "unavailable." As Klein has best clarified, psychoanalytically speaking, such people are often under the psychological sway of jealousy, or even worse, envy. Jealousy is a triadic relationship with "whole" objects that intends the possession of the love object and elimination of the rival. Jealousy emanates in one's early triangular relationships with one's siblings and parents during the Oedipal phase. As Iago famously said in Shakespeare's *Othello*, "O! beware, my lord, of jealousy; It is the green-eyed monster which doth mock the meat it feeds on." Envy, a dyadic relationship with "part" objects, is aimed at the love object itself and greedily desires to obtain all of its "good" qualities. For Klein, envy is rooted in the infant's inherent envy of the mother's breast and its wish to have all of its creative "goodness." As Carl Jung noted in *The Psychology of the Unconscious*, envy, like jealousy, is a horrid emotion to be in the grip of: "Envy does not allow humanity to sleep" (1917, p. 38).

Some people experience the urge to admire as a moment of radical diminishment. To admire someone else's intelligence, work product, good character or looks, for example, is experienced as humiliating and, hence, is vigorously resisted. Such people are extremely suspicious of any act of recognition of some-one else's superiority in any domain. In fact, they resent such acknowledgment of another's superiority. For such people there is "a burning preoccupation with self at the bottom of this suspicion, a 'but what about me, what becomes of me in that case?'" (Marcel, 1964, p. 48). According to Marcel, what people who cannot admire hate is the awareness that the acknowledgment of superiority is an "absolute" judgment at the time it is given: "it [the judgment] admirably indicates that this new light can make me pale into insignificance in my own eyes or in those of others whose judgment I must consider since that judgment directly influences the judgment I tend to have of myself" (ibid.). Such people experience the admired other as having power over them, while further fostering their beleaguered sense of self-control; hence, they often feel resentment, jealousy or envy. Where the jealous person feels bitter and unhappy because of another's perceived advantages, possession or luck, the envious person, in addition, wants to aggressively "steal" somebody else's success, good fortune, qualities or possessions, take it all for himself, and leave the "victim" with nothing. Perhaps what the person who cannot admire most profoundly resents and is jealous of is that both the admiring and admired other lack the "inner inertia," as Marcel calls it, the self-enclosure, low self-esteem and poor self-concept that the person who cannot admire feels. Thus, for the person who *refuses* to admire, the main self-deficit is that he will feel that his own dignity and pride are irrevocably damaged if he admires; he will experience a profound and lasting narcissistic injury that becomes fertile breeding ground for narcissistic rage; for the person who is *unable* to admire, the main self-deficit is that he is self-enclosed, hermetically sealed from allowing the unique otherness of the other inside himself. To do so would be too disruptive, disorienting or over-stimulating for him to let the other enter him; thus he pretends to himself that he does not notice the admirable qualities in others. In real life these two types of people who do not admire are inextricably related and often blended. However, they share at least two important negative characteristics. Firstly, in both types of persons there is an enfeebled self that consciously and/or unconsciously feels under siege from the condemning self-judgment that is evoked in the presence of someone or some-thing who they believe is superior to them. Secondly, in both types the greater plenitude that one feels and derives in the presence of someone or something that transcends us is denied and they are less of a person as a result.

The capacity to admire a creative act requires one to be free, flowing and unrestrained enough, open and available enough, to be able to give oneself up to, and be for, the other, without feeling self-diminishment or other related toxic emotions. Admiration, in other words, while mainly other-directed, other-regarding and other-serving also involves the creative use of the self in a manner that is self-actualizing and self-affirming. "To admire is already, in a certain degree, to create, since to admire is to be receptive in an active, alert manner" (Marcel, 2001a, p. 136). For example, we are often stirred by the virtue, qualities or skillfulness of admired others to improve ourselves; people with low self-esteem can view themselves more favorably by being associated with people they admire. This latter dynamic need not be manipulative and exploitatively narcissistic, but, rather, such people can creatively participate in these relationships to feel closer to the real and symbolic beliefs and values they dearly hold. Sounding like Marcel, the poet Wordsworth put it just right: "We live by Admiration, Hope and Love;/ And, even as these are well and wisely fixed,/ In dignity of being we ascend" (1888, ll. 763–765).

Generosity in the workplace

Generosity, simply defined, is having or showing the willingness to give money, help or time freely, perform acts of kindness that are almost always judged as reflecting what can be called a nobility of character. Generosity, says Marcel, is an important virtue, to be distinguished from prodigality, that is, being a spend-thrift or extravagant to a degree that borders on recklessness. Generosity is defined by Marcel as "*a light whose joy is in giving light, in being light?*" (italics in original; 2001b, p. 119). Light, says Marcel, denotes the common bond between people, "what we can only define as the identity at their upper limit of Love and Truth" (2008, p. 197). It is the relationship between generosity and the metaphor of light that is crucial to understanding what Marcel is getting at. According to Marcel,

> The property peculiar to light is that of being illuminating, illuminating for others—it goes beyond the boundaries which contemporary philosophy attempts to fix or lay down between the *for self* and the *for the other*. One might even say that this distinction does not exist for light, but that if its joy is in being light, it can only wish to be always more so. It knows itself, then, as illuminating; as far from this knowledge being comparable to an enfeebling waste of self, it helps, on the contrary, to increase its power. Like fire, generosity feeds on itself. There is a possibility, however, of a certain perversion, and we must be careful of this. If generosity enjoys its own self it degenerates into complacent self-satisfaction [it becomes mainly narcissistic and self-aggrandizing in its motive and meaning]. This enjoyment of self is not joy, for joy is not a satisfaction but an exaltation. It is only in so far as it is introverted [self-centric] that joy becomes enjoyment.
>
> (2001b, p. 119)

The metaphor of light thus helps us to understand the creative aspect of generos-ity, including, says Marcel, the generosity of the saint, the artist and the hero, and I would add, the prosocial motivated employee and "spiritual" and "ethical" organizational leader (Carroll, 2013, p. 605). In each of these and other forms of generosity a kind of "radiance" of spirit, a joy and energy is involved, a light that comes from "being itself" in its work, act or example (Marcel, 2001b, p. 120).

As Marcel further notes, "light can be recognized only through the medium of that which it illuminates—for in itself it is blinding and I cannot look straight at it—so generosity can be discerned only through the gifts it lavishes" (ibid., p. 121). For example, openhandedness that does not emanate from a loving heart but is motivated by self-interest such as to look charitable in the eyes of others, to win someone over or to make the receiver beholden, is not properly to be called generosity. The soul of gift-giving and "the soul of service" to others is unquestionably generosity (ibid., p. 120, 2008, p. 143).

What is creative about generosity is dramatically illustrated when we compare what Jean-Paul Sartre says about "giving" and generosity in his masterpiece, *Being and Nothingness*, with Marcel's interpretation of the same. According to Sartre,

> Gift is a primitive form of destruction .... Generosity is, above all, a destructive function. The frenzy of giving which comes over certain people at certain times is, above all, a frenzy of destruction; but this frenzy of destruction, which assumes the guise of generosity is in reality, nothing other than a frenzy of possession. All that which I destroy, all that which I give, I enjoy the more through the gift I make of it .... To give is a form of destruction enjoyment, of destructive appropriation. But the gift also casts a spell over the one who receives; it forces him to re-create and continually to maintain in being that self which I no longer want, which I have enjoyed to the point of annihilation, and of which nothing remains but an image. To give is to enslave. It is to appropriate by destroying and to use the destruction to enslave another.
>
> (Marcel, 1995, p. 100)

While Sartre is putting his finger on certain pathologies of giving in which the person "chooses to appropriate himself through destruction rather than through creation" (ibid.)—what psychoanalysts Seelig and Rosof (2001) describe as conflicted, pseudo or psychotic altruism—he is describing distortions and corruptions of what he and others may mistakenly call generosity. He seems, says Marcel, unable to comprehend the "genuine reality of what is meant by *we* or of what governs that reality," namely, "our capacity to open ourselves to others" (Marcel, 1995, p.100). What Sartre does not grasp is that to give oneself as in gift-giving is the opposite of servitude, it is "to devote or consecrate oneself to another," it is an act of creative testimony, of "creative receptivity." To give a gift, to be a giving self, in other words, is a way of being for the other before oneself, as it is mainly motivated by the wish to give pleasure and usually involves a modicum of sacrifice, such as spending the money to purchase a bouquet of flowers for one's friend or work colleague on her birthday. This is hardly the pathological or narcissistic maneuver that Sartre is describing; rather, such generous gestures emanate from another dimension of the spirit.

In the vocational and organizational psychology literatures, generosity is usually subsumed under the subject of prosocial motivation, the wish to have a favorable effect on other people or social collectives (Grant and Berg, 2011, p. 29). Research in prosocial motivation has been shown to have a positive influence on employee work behavior and performance on the job. Employees who have a generosity of spirit and are in other ways prosocial are more prone to take initiative, assist others, persevere in meaningful tasks, metabolize constructive criticism, and are better able to embrace more credit for proactive behaviors such as helping, voice, issue-selling, and taking charge. They are more effective at stopping employees with positive self-concepts from becoming self-satisfied and complacent, they direct the activities of employees who are concerned about impression management toward becoming improved citizens, and they are more prone to direct intrinsically motivated employees toward increased task perseverance, performance and productivity. Finally, employees who are animated by generosity and a prosocial outlook are inclined to focus intrinsically motivated employees on generating ideas that are not only innovative, but also useful, thus promoting greater creativity (ibid.).

What Marcel's account is putting forth strongly resonates with contemporary psychoanalytic views of "normal" altruism, of what has been called by Seelig and Rosof "generative altruism," an inborn psychological capacity that is, in part, rooted in the ability to be accurately empathic. Generative altruism "is the ability to experience conflict-free pleasure in fostering the success and/or pleasure of another." Following Heinz Hartmann, it can be viewed as an "autonomous ego function," that is, it is functionally autonomous behavior that is not interfered with by instinctually driven conflict. In contrast to pathological forms of altruism that are rooted in sadomasochism, intense aggression, envy and super-ego motives to suffer and be the victim, such generative altruistic behavior is highly adaptive and reflects a robust capacity for sublimation (Seelig and Rosof, 2001, pp. 946, 947, 934, 952).

Final remarks: emotional creativity as the "royal road" to flourishing on the job

Following Marcel, I have suggested that creativity, conceived as "creative testimony," especially but not only in the ethical realm, is the dimension of the spirit from which one is most likely to experience the "exigency of transcendence," including in the workplace. Such experiences of radical self-overcoming, self-mastery and self-transformation, of the "renewal of being," emanate from genuine experiences of intersubjectivity, ultra-meaningful relational experiences that point to the "eternal and absolute thou [God] that is the heart of all communion" (Gallagher, 1962, p. 95), that is, communion as the emotional and spiritual closeness that is evoked in any relationship that is characterized by other-directed, other-regarding and other-serving forms of fellowship. In more straightforward psychological terms, I am referring to the important role of emotional creativity in generating the psychological conditions of possibility for entering into the dimension of the spirit that tends to potentiate the experience of a for the other transcendence. By way of concluding this chapter, I want to briefly suggest a few ways that emotional creativity, the spiritualizing of the passions, as Nietzsche called it, is an important precursor, if not psychological prerequisite, for the experience of Marcellian-conceived transcendence, or, for flourishing in the workplace.

Emotional creativity, as I am using the term,[6] refers to the human capacity for using one's emotions, both positive and negative, to fashion more aesthetically pleasing, meaningful, coherent and inspired contexts for inventive everyday living. Emotional creativity—for example, transforming one's anger, grief or sexual desire into something original, imaginative and life-affirming such as assertiveness, joy and love, respectively, is a form of sublimation that psychoanalysts have aptly described. As Averill points out, for emotions to be conceived as creative products they must express three interrelated qualities: they must be novel, something new or different; they must be effective, have a desired or intended result; and they must be authentic, animated by one's dearly held beliefs and values (2009, pp. 251–253). Needless to say, there are a wide range of individual differences to emotional creativity, from those who suffer from alexithymia (extreme difficulty in feeling, describing and expressing emotions such as the Holocaust survivor in the book *The Pawnbroker*), inhibitions and other forms of neurosis, to the persons capable of expressing and actualizing deep and wide love (think of the great writer/poet, Goethe, who was also a humane person in his everyday life). Likewise, there are a wide range of individual differences in terms of the childhood experiences and developmental influences that account for a particular person's capacity for emotional creativity.

The capacity for emotional creativity and creative testimony come together when we postulate that it is the cultivation of a kind of "intra-worldly mysticism," as ancient Taoist philosopher Chuang Tzu described such a mode of being, that is, most likely to evoke the everyday experience of Marcellian transcendence in the workplace. Such a spiritual outlook and sensibility tends to cultivate in ordinary life an upsurge of vitality and aliveness, of connectedness, of feelings of union and harmony, and of being part of an all-embracing, overarching meaningfulness, that sense of deep personal significance that is so important to living a spiritualized life.

According to Yearley (1983, pp. 130–131), intra-worldly mysticism is a way of being that encompasses a person focusing intensely on the perceptions that are directly and immediately before him, only moving on to another perception when a new perception enters consciousness or the old one diminishes and vanishes, a kind of mindfulness, as Buddhists call it. This "hold and let go" approach sees everyday life as a movie, a series of changing frames. Unlike other forms of mysticism in which union with an absolute reality or higher being is mainly sought, intra-worldly mysticism primarily aims to see the world in a new way, to create "a way through the world." As Yearley further points out, "One neither attains union with some higher being, nor unification with a single reality. Rather, one goes through a discipline and has experiences that allow one to view the world in a new way." In other words, Chuang Tzu suggests that we ought to deal with everything the way we deal with esthetic objects. For example, when we look at a beautiful rose, we stare at it, note its loveliness and, when satisfied, move on to the next perception without clinging to the memory of the rose or trying to interfere with it. We simply engage the rose on its own terms with the fullness of our entire being. We then move on and become temporarily attached to another beautiful object of perception. "Life, in other words," says Yearley, "is a series of esthetically pleasing new beginnings, and all such beginnings should be grasped and then surrendered as change proceeds" (ibid., p. 186).

Like Marcel, Chuang Tzu emphasizes the need to heighten our sensitivity in order to experience reality more directly, immediately and presently, to experience a greater openness and availability to the mystery of being. The best way to go through the world, including in the workplace, is to experience life as it is lived, on its own terms, at least as one construes it, without trying to hold on, direct and/or control the experience. With this kind of moment-to-moment awareness, the mind is less likely to be ensnared by an experience, but instead can move effortlessly and continuously, seeing the world as a series of movie frames, some more pleasing than others but always changing, just as Nature does. The trick is to be able to become a person in whom the "Tao acts without impediment" (Tzu, 1965, p. 25). In Marcellian language, this means to be receptive, responsive and responsible to the animate and inanimate other in everyday life.

Such intra-worldly mysticism offers a new way to understand, experience and manage our emotions, a way that enhances our freedom to respond to situations very differently, with less unhelpful reactivity and with more immediacy and directness, less wishfully and more realistically and reasonably, and less nervously and frantically and in a more relaxed fashion. In other words, both Chuang Tzu and Marcel point to the disadvantages of misplaced emotion and, in particular, to the inordinately narcissistically driven subjectivity that is its underpinning. Instead, they advocate cultivating a different outlook, a way of being in which one sees and respects things as they are, as "thou," without the undue interference of our narcissistically driven strivings. By "thou," Marcel means "that which I can invoke rather than that which I judge to be able to answer me" (1952, p. 200). It is from this psychological and existential context that one is better able to engage in "creative testimony," in other words, to recognize, honor and serve the other and the otherness of life, in love, faith and hope, the very basis and expression of felt and lived transcendence. As Marcel noted, "the term transcendence taken in its full metaphysical sense seems essentially to denote an otherness, and even an absolute otherness" (2001a, p. 48). Most importantly, following Marcel, I have argued that creation as we have been discussing it, as "creative testimony," does not inevitably refer to something external to the person; it is not mainly to produce an object like a work of art. What Marcel is affirming is that a most worthwhile goal for each of us is to be a creator, to bear witness to a creation especially through our "for the other" relationships, what is called prosocial motivation in vocational psychology and "generative altruism" in psychoanalytic theory. Such people, few as they may be, observes Marcel, stand out "by the radiance of charity and love shining from their being." It is through their numinous and creative presence that they add a most "positive contribution to the invisible work which gives the human adventure the only meaning which can justify it" (2001a, p. 48). In short, whether inside or outside the workplace, Gandhi's penetrating psychological advice about how to live the "good life" equally applies: "The best way to find yourself is to lose yourself in the service of others" (www.forbes.com).

Notes

1   Marcel's description of "vocation" emphasizes that it is a "response to a call": "It comes both from me and outside me at one and the same time or rather, in it we become aware of that most intimate connection between what comes from me and what comes from outside the connection, which is nourishing or constructive and cannot be relinquished without the ego wasting or tending toward death" (Marcel, 1965, p. 23).
2   I am paraphrasing from Martin Luther King, Jr.
3   Manic reparation or defense has been defined as the tendency to de-emphasize the power of the object, to scorn it, while simultaneously upholding maximum control over it. Manic defenses are characterized by three emotions: control, triumph, contempt (www.encyclopedia.com › ... › International Dictionary of Psychoanalysis, retrieved 12/22/14). Obsessional reparation involves repetitious actions of "undoing" (magically causing something to be negated) that are intended to reverse the unconscious aggression that is aimed at an object (Akhtar, 2009, p. 245).
4   A mystery, says Marcel, "is something in which I am myself involved, and it can therefore only be thought of as a sphere where the distinction between what is in me and what is before me loses its meaning and its initial validity" (Marcus, 2013, p. 205).
5   I am aware that not all routine is detrimental, for without certain routines we would not be able to function in our everyday life (e.g., imagine what one's morning would feel like if we always put our toothbrush in a different place the night before and had to remember where we put it!), nor would we feel the crucial sense of ontological security that, as sociologist Anthony Giddens noted, routine helps us feel.
6   I am largely drawing from Averill's (2009, pp. 294–257) work on emotional creativity in this section.

References

Akhtar, S. (2009). *Comprehensive Dictionary of Psychoanalysis*. London: Karnac.
Averill, J. R. (2009). Emotional Creativity: Toward "Spiritualizing the Passions." In: S. L. Lopez and C. R. Snyder (Eds.), *Oxford Handbook of Positive Psychology* (pp. 249–258). Oxford: Oxford University Press.
Barnes, B. (1983). *T.S. Kuhn and Social Sciences*. New York: Columbia University Press.
Bellah, R. N., Madsen, R. Sullivan, W. M., Swidler, A. and Tipton, S. M. (1986). *Habits of the Heart: Individualism and Commitment in American Life Paperback*. New York: Harper & Row.
Berg, J. M., Grant, A. G. and Johnson, V. (2010). When Callings are Calling: Crafting Work and Leisure in Pursuit of Unanswered Occupational Callings. *Organization Science, 21*:5, 973–994.
Cain, S. (1979). *Gabriel Marcel*. South Bend, IN: Regnery/Gateway.

Cain, S. (1995). *Gabriel Marcel's Theory of Religious Experience*. New York: Peter Lang.

Carroll, S. T. (2013). Addressing Religion and Spirituality in the Workplace. In: K. I. Pergament (Ed.), *APA Handbook of Psychology, Religion, and Spirituality, Volume 2* (pp. 595–612). Washington, DC: American Psychological Association.

Chang, R. (2015). Resolving to Create a New You. *New York Times Sunday Review*, 1/4/15, p. 7.

Dik, B. J. and Duffy, R. D. (2009). Calling and Vocation at Work: Definitions and Prospects for Research and Practice. *The Counseling Psychologist*, *37*:3, 424–450.

Dutton, J. E., Roberts, L. M. and Bednar, J. (2011). Prosocial Practices, Positive Identity, and Flourishing at Work. In: S. I. Donaldson, M. Csikszentmihalyi and J. Nakamura (Eds.), *Applied Positive Psychology: Improving Everyday Life, Health, Schools, Work, and Society* (pp. 155–170). New York: Routledge.

Eliot, G. (1882). *Wit and Wisdom of George Eliot*. Boston, MA: Roberts Brothers.

Freud, S. (1914) [1957]. On Narcissism: An Introduction. In: J. Strachey (Ed. and Trans.), *The Standard Edition of the Complete Psychological Works of Sigmund Freud*, Vol. 14 (pp. 67–102). London: Hogarth Press.

Gallagher, K.T. (1962). *The Philosophy of Gabriel Marcel*. New York: Fordham University Press.

Gilbert, D. L. (1981). *Oxygen and Living Processes: An Interdisciplinary Approach*. Berlin: Springer-Verlag.

Grant, A. M. and Berg, J. M. (2011). Prosocial Motivation At Work: When, Why, and How Making a Difference Makes a Difference. In: K. Cameron and G. Spreitzer (Eds.), *Oxford Handbook of Positive Organizational Scholarship* (pp. 28–44). New York: Oxford University Press.

Hall, D. T. and Chandler, D. E. (2005). Psychological Success: When the Career is a Calling. *Journal of Organizational Behavior*, *26*, 155–176.

Inman, L. D. (1997). A Room of One's Own Revisited. In: C. W. Socarides and S. Kramer (Eds.), *Work and Its Inhibitions: Psychoanalytic Essays* (pp. 115–131). Madison, WI: International Universities Press.

Johnson, A. G. (1995). *The Blackwell Dictionary of Sociology: A User's Guide to Sociological Language*. Oxford: Oxford University Press.

Jones, E. (1953–1957). *The Life and Work of Sigmund Freud* (3 vols.). New York: Basic Books.

Jung, G. C. (1917). *The Psychology of the Unconscious*. B. M. Hinkle (Trans.). New York: Moffat, Yard and Company.

Keen, S. (1967). *Gabriel Marcel*. Richmond, VA: John Knox Press.

Kernberg, O. (1979). Regression in Organizational Leadership. *Psychiatry*, *42*, 24–39.

Kotb, H. (2014). *Ten Years Later: Six People Who Faced Adversity and Transformed Their Lives*. New York: Simon and Schuster.

Levi, P. (1996). *Survival in Auschwitz*. New York: Touchstone.

Levine, H. (1997). Men at Work: Work, Ego and Identity in the Analysis of Adult Men. In: C. W. Socarides and S. Kramer (Eds.), *Work and Its Inhibitions: Psychoanalytic Essays* (pp. 143–157). Madison, CT: International Universities Press.

Lilius, J. M., Kanov, J., Dutton, J. E., Warline, M. C. and Maitlis, S. (2012). Compassion Revealed: What We Know About Compassion at Work (and Where We Need to Know More). In: K. S. Cameron and G. M. Spreitzer (Eds.), *The Oxford Handbook of Positive Organizational Scholarship* (pp. 273–287). Oxford: Oxford University Press.

Marcel, G. (1952). *Metaphysical Journal*. B. Wall (Trans.). Chicago, IL: Henry Regnery Company.

Marcel, G. (1963). *The Existential Background of Human Dignity*. Cambridge, MA: Harvard University Press.

Marcel, G. (1964). *Creative Fidelity*. R. Rosthal (Trans.). New York: Farrar, Straus and Girous.

Marcel, G. (1965). *Homo Viator: Introduction to a Metaphysic of Hope*. E. Crauford (Trans.). New York: Harper & Row.

Marcel, G. (1967). *Searchings*. New York: Newman Press.

Marcel, G. (1973). *Tragic Wisdom and Beyond*. Evanston, IL: Northwestern University Press.

Marcel, G. (1984). Reply to Otto Friedrich Bollnow. In A. Schilpp and L. E. Hahn (Eds.), *The Philosophy of Gabriel Marcel* (pp. 200–203). La Salle, IL: Open Court.

Marcel, G. (1995). *The Philosophy of Existentialism*. New York: Carol Publishing Group.

Marcel, G. (2001a). *The Mystery of Being: Volume I: Reflection and Mystery*. South Bend, IN: St. Augustine Press.

Marcel, G. (2001b). *The Mystery of Being: Volume 2: Faith and Reality*. South Bend, IN: St. Augustine Press.

Marcel, G. (2005). *Music and Philosophy*. S. Maddux and R. E. Wood (Trans.). Milwaukee, WI: Marquette University Press.

Marcel, G. (2008). *Man Against Mass Society*. South Bend, IN: St. Augustine Press.

Marcus, P. (2013). *In Search of the Spiritual: Gabriel Marcel, Psychoanalysis, and the Sacred*. London: Karnac.

Marianetti, O. and Passmore, J. (2010). Mindfulness at Work: Paying Attention to Enhance Well-Being and Performance. In: P. A. Linley, S. Harrington and N. Garcea (Eds.), *Oxford Handbook of Positive Psychology and Work* (pp. 189–200). Oxford: Oxford University Press.

Meissner, W. W. (1997). The Self and the Principle of Work. In: C. W. Socarides and S. Kramer (Eds.), *Work and Its Inhibitions: Psychoanalytic Essays* (pp. 35–60). Madison, WI: International Universities Press.

Meissner, W. W. (2003). *The Ethical Dimension to Psychoanalysis: A Dialogue*. Albany, NY: State University of New York Press.

Miceli, V. P. (1965). *Ascent to Being: Gabriel Marcel's Philosophy of Communion*. New York: Desclee.

Moore, B. E. and Fine, V. D. (Eds.) (1990). *Psychoanalytic Terms & Concepts*. New Haven, CT: American Psychoanalytic Association and Yale University Press.

Nakamura, J. and Csikszentmihalyi, M. (2009). Flow Theory and Research. In: S. L. Lopez and C. R. Snyder (Eds.), *Oxford Handbook of Positive Psychology* (pp. 195–206). Oxford: Oxford University Press.

Peterson, C. (2009). Foreword. In: S. L. Lopez and C. R. Snyder (Eds.), *Oxford Handbook of Positive Psychology* (pp. xiii–xiv). Oxford: Oxford University Press.

Reik, T. (1983). *Listening with the Third Ear*. New York: Farrar, Straus and Giroux.

Rothbard, N. P. and Patil, S. V. (2012). Being There: Work Engagement and Positive Organizational Scholarship. In K. S. Cameron and G. M. Spreitzer (Eds.), *The Oxford Handbook of Positive Organizational Scholarship* (pp. 56–68). Oxford: Oxford University Press.

Rorty, R. (1990). *Objectivity, Relativism, and Truth*. New York: Cambridge University Press.

Rycroft, C. (1995). *A Critical Dictionary of Psychoanalysis* (2nd ed.). London: Penguin.

Seelig, B. J. and Rosof, L. S. (2001). Normal and Pathological Altruism. *Journal of the American Psychoanalytic Association, 49*, 933–959.

Shafer, R. (1984). The Pursuit of Failure and the Idealization of Unhappiness. *American Psychologist, 39*:4, 398–405.

Socarides, C. W. and Kramer, S. (1997). Editors' Introduction. In: C. W. Socarides and S. Kramer (Eds.), *Work and Its Inhibitions: Psychoanalytic Essays* (pp. xiii–xxii). Madison, WI: International Universities Press.

Stairs, M. and Galpin, M. (2010). Positive Engagement: From Employee Engagement to Workplace Happiness. In: P. A. Linley, S. Harrington and N. Garcea (Eds.), *Oxford Handbook of Positive Psychology and Work* (pp. 155–172). Oxford: Oxford University Press.

Tzu, C. (1965). *The Way of Chuang Tzu*. T. Merton (Trans.). New York: New Directions.

Wordsworth, W. (1888). *The Complete Poetical Works*. London: Macmillan and Co.; Bartleby.com, 1999. www.bartleby.com/145/.

Wrzesniewski, A. (2012). Callings. In K. S. Cameron and G. M. Spreitzer (Eds.), *The Oxford Handbook of Positive Organizational Scholarship* (pp. 45–55). Oxford: Oxford University Press.

Wrzesniewski, A. and Dutton, J. E. (2001). Crafting a Job: Revisioning Employees As Active Crafters of Their Work. *Academy of Management Review, 25*:2, 179–201.

Yearley, L. (1983). The Perfected Person in the Radical Chuang Tzu. In: V. H. Mair (Ed.), *Experimental Essays in Chuang Tzu* (pp. 125–139). Honolulu, HI: University of Honolulu Press.

Web sources

www.africanamericanquotes.org/martin-luther-king-jr.html, retrieved 12/19/14.
www.catholicbible101.com/motherteresaquotes.htm, retrieved 12/23/14.
www.civilrightsdefence.org.nz/tuhoe/mlk.html, retrieved 12/21/14.
www.cnn.com/2014/10/02/world/heroes-reveal/, retrieved 12/21/14.
www.encyclopedia.com › ... › International Dictionary of Psychoanalysis, retrieved 12/22/14.
www.forbes.com/.../12-great-quotes-from-gandhi-on-his-birthday…, retrieved 12/25/14.
www.forbes.com/.../2013/05/28/inspirational-quotes/5, retrieved 12/14/14.
www.izquotes.com/quote/226584, retrieved 12/24/14.
www.keepinspiring.me/helping-others-quotes/, retrieved 12/29/14.
www.lep.utm.edu/marcel/, retrieved 12/29/14.
www.movemequotes.com/top-25-work-ethic-quotes/, retrieved 12/29/14.
www.nytimes.com/.../in-picking-up-an-inside-view, retrieved 12/20/14.
www.quoteworld.org › Pablo Picasso, retrieved 12/20/14.
www.quoteworld.org/quotes/4132, retrieved 12/14/14.
www.rebellesociety.com › troublemakers, retrieved 12/24/14.
www.vatican.va/.../ns_lit_doc_20031019_madre-teresa_en.html, retrieved 12/18/14.
www.zimbio.com/Evan+Esar+Quotes, retrieved 12/24/14.

Chapter 4

Psychopathology I: the individual

At age 60, after over 45 years of brilliantly performing and being regarded as one of the greatest actors of the twentieth century, Sir Laurence Olivier reported in a 1983 *60 Minutes* television interview that he was suddenly overwhelmed with an unbearable case of stage fright that occurred on and off for many years. Olivier vividly described his first panic attack, especially his constricted throat and feeling like he was being asphyxiated while performing. He was playing *Othello* and every night he beseeched Frank Finlay, who was playing Iago, not to abandon him on the stage. Like an infant who anxiously needs to see his comforting mother, he pleaded with Finlay to be in continuous eye contact with him. In fact, Olivier's abandonment anxiety was so intense, he even threatened Finlay that if he left him alone in front of the audience (against whom he had already positioned himself to avoid facing), he would run off the stage. "My courage sank, and with each succeeding minute it became less possible to resist the horror" (Aaron, 1986, p. 61). Needless to say, Olivier reported feeling utter shame about his infantile abandonment anxiety (Gabbard, 1997, p. 211).

As the above Olivier quotation indicates, geniuses, too, can be afflicted with neurosis in their work life. In Freud's case, while his suffering had its masochistic texturing if not satisfaction, it ultimately became part of the conditions of possibility for his tremendous creativity as a thinker and writer: "I returned to a sense of too much well-being and have since then been very lazy because the modicum of misery essential for intensive work will not come back" (1896 [1985], pp. 180–181). Freud further elaborates: "During an industrious night last week, when I was suffering from that degree of pain which brings about the optimal condition for my mental activities, the barriers suddenly lifted, the veils dropped, and everything became transparent—from the details of the neuroses to the determinants of consciousness" (1895 [1985], p. 146).[1]

In contrast to Freud, for Olivier his neurosis was extremely destructive to his capacity to effectively perform his craft. Moreover, his prohibitive stage fright cut deeply into his personal identity, making an incredibly capable and talented person feel helpless, hopeless and hapless. This stage fright was especially undermining to his very sense of personhood, including its ability to degrade his self-concept and diminish his self-esteem, when we consider that it was his work which most mattered to him: "Work is life for me, it is the only point of life—and with it there is almost religious belief that service is everything" (m.imdb.com).

While being mindful of the fact that the individual is best psychologically understood as always residing in a social context, that is, he works within a web of relations, a force field composed of other people's interrelated and interdependent actions and reactions (Hirschhorn, 1988, p. 90) such as a unique environmental setting and organizational culture, in this chapter I want to discuss some of the common problems on the job mainly from the point of view of individual psycho-dynamics.[2] In the next chapter I will take up problems on the job that can be usefully looked at from the point of view of the psychopathology of organiza-tions. While there are many different kinds of individual psychopathologies that are manifested and "played out" in the workplace, I discuss three of the more common inhibitions that make one's work life a misery.

Generally speaking, a psychological inhibition exists when there is extreme uncertainty and hesitation or blockage of forward movement and action, a state that has been regarded as the opposite of facilitation. I will be focusing on one inhibition in which there is a clearly perceived debilitating anxiety, that is, "stage fright" (also called "performance anxiety"), mainly on the theatrical stage, but also on the lecturer's podium, while presenting in the boardroom or to a small work group, or even in conversation with a colleague. Next, I will discuss an inhibi-tion in which the anxiety is usually more unconscious, as in "writer's block," the condition of being unable to think of what to write or how to proceed with writing. While I will be focusing on creative writing as with the professional author, the challenge of completing a piece of writing in a timely and effective manner is a problem that manifests itself in many work settings. Finally, I will discuss what I regard as another form of inhibition as reflected in a person who compulsively works hard and long hours. Such "workaholics," as they are called, are engaged in an extreme idealization of work rooted in unconscious psychic conflicts at the expense of crafting a sensible "work/life" balance.[3] This inhibition can be concep-tualized as a lack of willingness and ability to listen to one's self-modulating and ultimately self-preserving "voice of reason." Often very "successful" in work, these people are prone to high levels of stress and personal/familial problems, often with lousy marriages and "messed up" children, in part because they have not been mean-ingfully engaged and emotionally "present" in their spouse and children's lives.

By way of contextualizing my discussion of inhibitions in the workplace, I want to first briefly discuss "success neurosis" as Sandor Lorand (1950) first called it, that is, people whom Freud described as "those wrecked by success" (1925) [1957]. Individuals with work inhibitions frequently have the unconscious conviction that they cannot endure the happiness connected to accomplishment and success. This group of people should be distinguished from what is probably a much larger group of pathologically inhibited people, that is, those individuals who do not let themselves succeed; instead, they avoid or disguise success (Levy et al., 1995, p. 639).

The wrecking impact of success

Freud succinctly lays out the intriguing psychological problem that caught his clinical eye:

> So much the more surprising, and indeed bewildering, must it appear when as a doctor one makes the discovery that people occasionally falling ill precisely when a deeply-rooted and long-cherished wish has come to fulfillment. It seems then as though they were not able to tolerate their happiness; for there can be no question that there is a causal connection between their success and their falling ill.
>
> (1925 [1957], p. 316)

Drawing from Shakespeare's *Macbeth* and Ibsen's Rebecca in *Rosmersholm*, Freud explains success neurosis in terms of the "forces of conscience [later to be called the super-ego by Freud[4]] which forbid the subject to gain the long hoped for advantage from the fortunate change in reality" (ibid., p. 318). That is, "these judging and punishing trends" are "closely connected to the Oedipus complex, the relation to father and mother—as perhaps, indeed is our sense of guilt in general" (ibid., p. 331). What Freud is claiming is that in the individual's mind, success is equated with sinful and "criminal intentions" (ibid., p. 333), with incest and murder, these being common phantasies associated with the Oedipal phase of development, in particular, with "Oedipal victory" or "triumph." Such an Oedipal victory typically occurs when the rival father in the case of a boy, or mother in the case of a girl, has crumbled or collapsed, has been jettisoned from his or her role of power and authority and "defeated." This sense of Oedipal victory can occur if the same sexed parent coincidentally dies, or is not in the child's life due to divorce or abandonment. In other instances, an opposite sex parent can be both seductive to the child and belittling of the other parent, causing a similar sense of Oedipal victory. Children who have experienced an Oedipal victory tend to become adults who are "cocky, irreverent, hurried and unable to abide by the incest barrier" (e.g., they might have affairs with their boss or a married colleague or violate normative generational boundaries). Whatever the circumstances that contribute to a child's sense of Oedipal victory, such an experience of triumph evokes intense guilt and self-flagellation as Freud noted (Akhtar, 2009, p. 196). Most importantly, in the child's mind, where there is guilt, there must be punishment. It is this internal demand that accounts for the adult who, while under the psychological sway of this regressive caste of mind, engages in self-undermining and self-defeating behavior following a work success, like a promotion that provides advancement in salary, prestige, power and responsibility.

There have been other formulations about the nature of the anxiety that inhibits individuals from enjoying happiness following their accomplishment and success. For example, in some instances, the successful individual may feel unconscious homosexual anxiety rooted in a fantasy about being loved by their adversarial father (in the case of a girl, her mother), this reflecting both the positive and negative aspects of the Oedipus complex and its powerful emotional link to the meaning of success (Moore and Fine, 1990, p. 189). Other formulations have theorized gender differences, such as the girl "Oedipal victor" feeling that the affirmation she receives from her father may not be the "real thing," and may be had only at the expense of her not developing an autonomous sense of self. Advancement in a career may be equated with losing her father's admiration and idealization that is acquired through her faithful service to him as his mirroring "selfobject." That is, in the eyes of the father, his daughter who is regarded as a "selfobject" has no autonomous needs or wishes, and she is strictly used to strengthen his self-cohesion and vitality. Career success for a girl may thus be an anxiety-ridden experience that requires punishment, avoidance or disguise (Kieffer, 2004, p. 77). Whatever the particular content of the anxiety, it is quite likely that "there is something of being wrecked by success that is inherent in every case of neurosis." That is, all neurotics are engaged in diverse types of self-undermining behavior that usually have some important emotional connection to unresolved Oedipal issues (Levy *et al.*, 1995, p. 642).

The larger group of people who have work inhibitions are those who unconsciously equate success with serious danger (Szekely, 1950, p. 49), most often of an Oedipal nature. In other instances, pre-Oedipal, "archaic meanings" may be in play, such as the fear that one's grandiose notions about the self may become conscious which causes real and imagined internal and external havoc, such as the deeply troubling "sense of merging with the grandiose imagos [unconscious object relations] of the parents of very early childhood." Such persons are especially prone to problems in reality testing and anxiety management when they impressively exercise their unique talents and become aware of their resultant attainments (Shafer, 1984, p. 399). Whatever the combination of Oedipal and pre-Oedipal factors, what is most important is that such people avoid what they unconsciously conceive as hugely dangerous, namely, accomplishment and success, for it is unconsciously connected to early child/parent attachment patterns, a sense of loss, seduction, being vanquished or damaged (ibid., p. 402). Even worse, they may actively seek out failure. Typically, they are marked underachievers and live their dreary, non-descript lives in terms of "neurotic mediocrity" (Levy *et al.*, 1995, p. 643), and/or they engage in the "idealization of unhappiness" (Shafer, 1984, p. 398).

Understanding why people avoid happiness linked to accomplishment and success in the workplace is perhaps made clearer when we consider what Freud said about the "negative therapeutic reaction," "repetition compulsion" or "fate neurosis" (also called "fate compulsion"). These clinically based concepts point to the fact that, paradoxically for some, what normatively speaking is conceived as a cause for happiness is unconsciously imagined as its opposite and is therefore avoided or disguised at all costs.

Negative therapeutic reaction is said to occur when a seemingly "correct" and helpful interpretation to an analysand does not reduce their neurotic suffering but intensifies it. As Freud succinctly put it, "Every partial solution that ought to result, and in other people does result, in an improvement or a temporary suspension of symptoms produces in them for the time being an exacerbation of their illness" (1923 [1955], p. 49). While some analysts have suggested that there may be a "primary" masochistic aspect to such a reaction, that is, these individuals have powerful inborn unconscious needs to suffer and be punished, others argue that more likely is the fact that these individuals feel unconscious guilt that their achieved health comes about "on the backs" of some other person, possibly one's Oedipal father or mother (Rycroft, 1995, p. 108). For example, some actors (and other types of performers) unconsciously believe that to possess something good requires that someone else will be deprived. The actor is persuaded that in inhabiting center stage and effectively displaying his talents he is preventing someone else from having a comparable chance of success. As a result, he imagines that the audience will experience intense envy toward him as they feel deprived and angry that he is successful rather than them (Gabbard, 1983, pp. 434–435). Other explanations for a negative therapeutic reaction relate to early identification with a masochistic parent who seems to "enjoy" a life of anguish. In this scenario, getting healthy is equated with being disloyal to the anguished parent. In other instances, an individual may be guilty for his self-assertiveness and his wish to be independent from an enveloping, needy and/or seductive mother. Fashioning a separate identity that does not revolve around "serving" his mother may be unconsciously viewed as having a detrimental, if not lethal, impact on the loved and still needed mother. It is this powerful fear of abandonment, of getting healthy and not needing the analyst/mother, that is defended against via the negative therapeutic reaction. In other instances a patient may be in the grips of intense envy of the analyst who can be comforting, helpful and inventive, and the analysand resists getting healthy as an expression of his resentment toward the analyst (Akhtar, 2009, p. 186).

In all these contexts the person aggressively avoids success as a way of pursuing failure coupled with the unhappiness that usually goes with it. Such a way of being calls to mind those patients Theodore Reik described who engage in self-punitive behavior that gives them an unconscious sense of "victory through defeat," that is, success through failure. As a Kafka parable aptly puts it, "The master beats the horse, then the horse takes the whip and beats himself, so that he can be the master" (Kaplan, 1969, p. 75). The self-lacerating and provocative behavior of these patients expresses what they unconsciously view to be their moral fortitude and superiority while making others feel guilty for their self-choreographed victimization.

The gist of this compulsion to repeat (named the repetition-compulsion), at least from the point of view of individual psychopathology, is the individual engages in ungovernable behavior that emanates from his unconscious. As a consequence of this unconscious process, the individual purposely lodges himself in upsetting situations, thereby repeating a troubling, painful or traumatic childhood experience, but he does not recollect this old template. In fact, the individual is utterly emotionally disconnected from the old template and he vigorously makes the claim that the upsetting situation that he is in is strictly a result of the "real life" circumstances of the here-and-now, rather than emanating from his personality, character and way of comporting himself (Laplanche and Pontalis, 1973, p. 78). This tendency to repeat is an important reason why patients resist therapeutically induced change—it is an unconsciously gratifying way that they enact (as opposed to remember) their forgotten troubling, painful and traumatic memories, a process that is duplicated in the transference. Freud accounted for this strange phenomenon as an example *par excellence* of the conservative and regressive nature of instinct, that is, as one of those psychological processes that are animated by the more biologically primitive aspects of the human psyche. As Freud said, "the manifestation of a compulsion to repeat ... exhibit[s] to a high degree an instinctual character and, when they act in opposition to the pleasure principle, give[s] the appearance of some 'daemonic' force at work" (1920 [1964], p. 35). Ultimately, Freud applied this notion of "'daemonic' force,'" the repetition-compulsion, to bolster his speculative concept of the Death Instinct, the inborn tendency for the animate to return to the inanimate. In other words, the repetition-compulsion is "beyond the pleasure principle" (ibid., p. 33), that is, it cannot be regarded as a mere expression of a conflict between the pleasure and reality principles.

While Freud and others have pointed out that the repetition-compulsion occurs in non-therapeutic contexts—such as during a child's play in which the repetition helps the child master his sense of loss, abandonment, or other passively experienced traumas, and in nightmares that follow traumatic experiences in which there is an attempt at mastery—it has most importantly been linked to understanding those individuals who consistently engage in self-undermining and self-devaluing behavior as suggested above (Moore and Fine, 1990, p. 165).[5] In the context of the workplace, especially when one works in an organizational setting, one can easily understand that someone in the grip of the repetition-compulsion can find one way or another to engineer his own demise.

"Fate neurosis" is another way that Freud described the repetition-compulsion, the slight difference being that this sub-species of people do not have any obvious neurotic symptoms that betray a neurotic conflict (Freud, 1920 [1964], p. 22):

> What psycho-analysis reveals in the transference phenomena of neurotics can also be observed in the lives of some normal people. The impression they give is of being pursued by a malignant fate or possessed by some "daemonic" power; but psychoanalysis has always taken the view that their fate is for the most part arranged by themselves and determined by early infantile influences.
>
> (ibid., p. 21)

Freud gives a few examples of the fate neurosis that we can all easily relate to, including in the workplace: "The man who time after time in the course of his life raises someone else into a position of great private or public authority and then, after a certain interval, himself upsets that authority and replaces him by a new one." Or, "The benefactor who is abandoned in anger after a time by each of his protégés ... doomed to taste all the bitterness of ingratitude." Freud also mentions "the man whose friendships all end in betrayal by his friend" and "the lover each of whose love affairs with a woman passes through the same phases and reaches the same conclusion." The point is that in all of these instances, there is "perpetual recurrence of the same things" which appears to be part of a pattern of life (ibid., p. 22). What is most noteworthy, says Freud, is that the person who choreographs his life this way is entirely oblivious to the unconscious wish to suffer. Rather, he experiences this wish as boomeranging from the outside world and persecuting him, this being precisely what Freud meant when he described fate neurosis as having a "daemonic power," a radically self-destructive interpretive grip on the person's outlook and behavior (Laplanche and Pontalis, 1973, p. 162).

Stage fright

The best-selling female music artist in recording history, Barbra Streisand, once forgot the words while performing on stage. She noted,

> It was shocking to me to forget the words ... You know, I didn't make up words ... some performers really do well when they forget the words. They forget the words all the time ... but they somehow have humor about it. I remember I didn't have a sense of humor about it. I was quite shocked.

Indeed, Streisand further noted, "I couldn't come out of it," and she phobically avoided going on the stage for several years following her traumatic forgetfulness (www.panicattacktreatmentreviews.com). Indeed, there are many accomplished performers who have admitted to varying degrees of stage fright in their workplace, including, for example, actors Helen Mirren and Michael Douglas, and singers Carly Simon and Andrea Bocelli. Luciano Pavarotti, in fact, noted, "I would not want even an enemy to suffer those terrible moments," while another famous actress who routinely vomited before she went on stage had throw-up buckets located by each of her entrance positions (Aaron, 1986, pp. 59, 60). A 2011 California-based doctoral study indicated that over 80 percent of professional actors have experienced stage fright at least in one instance in their careers (www.backstage.com). One of the most prominent and celebrated classical pianists of the twentieth century, Canadian Glen Gould, probably best expressed what all performers prone to stage fright sometimes feel: "I detest audiences. I think they are a force of evil." In fact, in 1964 Gould abandoned a hugely successful concert career and returned to his native Toronto, holed up in what he described as "a kind of Howard Hughesian secrecy" (www.nytimes.com).[6]

While being a stage performer is phenomenologically different than other more common types of "performance" on the job, that is, for example, the nature of the audience being performed in front of tends to generate different anxious fantasies, it does plausibly put into sharp focus many of the psychodynamics that are likely to be operative in other work contexts to a lesser degree. We all have to "play" to an audience of one type or another in our workplace and face the real and imagined judgments of others, especially those that stir up infantile fears and archaic anxieties. As Gabbard (1983, p. 424) noted, stage fright emanates from crucial developmental experiences that we all have, ones that are of a "universal nature." Indeed, stage fright calls to mind an experience that is all too human, namely, the ego's inability to use "signal anxiety," our early warning system that tells us there is an incoming danger, to effectively implement protective defenses (Aaron, 1986, p. 81). Thus, given the limited scope of this section, I will focus on stage fright among creative performing artists, mainly actors, as unlike other kinds of stage performers they have to deal with the archaic anxieties associated with inhabiting another person, their character role. Through enormous internal work on himself, the actor must believably transform himself to be someone else, a process that demands extraordinary ego capacities and narcissistic reorganizations (ibid., p. 131). I will also make passing reference to performance anxieties in other work contexts that reasonably have a "family resemblance" to actors and other stage performers.

The experience of stage fright

"But I never was happy, never could make a good impromptu speech without several hours to prepare it," quipped the incomparable Mark Twain (www. quoteinvestigator.com). Or to put it a bit differently, "There are always three speeches, for every one you actually gave. The one you practiced, the one you gave, and the one you wish you gave" (www.trainingindustry.com). Indeed, Twain is pointing to the fact that public speaking, and I would add, any performance before an audience, is a potential venue for the experience of high anxiety which includes stressful cardiovascular reactions like elevated blood pressure and rapid breathing. Some of the typical distresses that people who are inclined to stage fright experience include the fear that one's mind will go utterly blank, of trembling, shaking or demonstrating other indications of intense anxiety, of doing something extremely embarrassing or shameful, of suddenly being incapable of continuing to speak, and saying something incredibly stupid or unintelligible (www. psychologytoday.com). It is important to understand that such signs of stage fright can occur many weeks prior to performing, not only immediately before or during a performance. There have been many psychoanalytically based hypotheses to account for stage fright, all of which strike me as plausible depending on the unique history of a person's psychological suffering and idiosyncratic career trajectory. A review of some of the more illuminating formulations is instructive.[7]

British psychoanalyst J. C. Flugel's 1938 paper on stage fright and its relation to anal eroticism, the sensual pleasure associated with the anus and sometimes the rectum, and toileting activities, put forth the claim that the underlying internalized conflict in such performers (two musicians he analyzed) focused on the fact that "real or symbolical faeces had to be produced at a given time and place." That is, "the precious material was forcibly demanded, whereas the gift should have remained a matter for the patient's own discretion and control" (Flugel, 1938, p. 195). Like any compromise formation, Flugel is suggesting that stage fright represents both erotically tinged satisfactions, in his cases, being willing and able to retain their faeces as they wished, and the fear of punishment by parental and/or other equivalently fantasized disapproving figures for doing so. Moreover, stage fright conceived as rooted in anal conflict manifests itself in the fantasized "aggressive combat between the performer and the audience" (ibid., p. 189). For example, one prominent actor sadistically wants "to fuck the audience up the ass," and felt that he had them "by the balls," another used the battle cry before going on the stage, "Go out there and maim them," while Olivier used to repetitively mutter behind the curtain to the audience, "You bastards" (Aaron, 1986, pp. 73, 125, 123). With all of this sadistic gratification going on, it is no wonder that actors get a "performance high" (ibid., p. 123) though there are other reasons for why actors find performing narcissistically exhilarating.

The Austrian-born American psychoanalyst Edmund Bergler (1949) stressed that it was repressed, childish voyeuristic dread that was the basis for the emergence of stage fright in the 12 actors he treated. Drawing from Freud's hypothesis that voyeurism is always coupled with its opposite, exhibitionism, meaning that voyeurism is the active expression of exhibitionism while exhibitionism is the passive expression of voyeurism (Rycroft, 1995, p. 194), Bergler speculated that voyeurism is in fact a more powerful repressed urge than exhibitionism, the latter being a defense against the former. The person under the sway of stage fright embraces his guilt for his less "criminal" exhibitionistic desire, rather than the more dangerous and frightening voyeuristic one. As Gabbard further elaborates, for Bergler the ultimate basis for this sense of danger are frightful primitive oral fantasies of being eaten up, of being deprived of food, and of having something aggressively stuck down one's throat, all of this as retribution for his infantile voyeuristic satisfaction of gazing at his parents' body parts and delighting in viewing them having sex. In this primal scene-based formulation, the actor is trying to relocate his guilt onto the audience—"Others, not I, peep"—however, the guilt is not entirely eradicated, because the actor empathically identifies with the audience and is in effect "peeping" at himself (Gabbard, 1979, p. 384). The great apprehension and fear associated with stage fright is the punitive result.

In a barely two-page reflection, Ferenczi intriguingly puts forth the view that stage fright is related to extreme "narcissistic self-observation," for example, performers "hear their own voices" and "note every movement of their limbs."

It is this splitting of attention between the objective interest in the thing being done and the subjective experience of doing it that markedly interferes with their ability to effectively perform. In this view, the performer is not shy or modest as the casual onlooker may surmise, but rather, it is his inordinate narcissism that undermines his performance. In addition to the hyper-vigilant, severely self-critical observation of their own performance, they are also "intoxicated by their own voices and doings, and forget to bring about an accomplishment with these." This "doubling" dynamic or defensive splitting of the ego may indicate that the performer feels that what they are saying or doing reflects their phoniness, or even worse, that they are an imposter through and through (1919 [1980], pp. 421–422). Needless to say, in general, actors want the audience to experience only their performance self, not what is "really" going on inside. Consider that actors who have performed naked do not experience any more anxiety than when clothed, suggesting that exposing one's deeper feelings and conflicted wishes in a role is the crux of stage fright (Aaron, 1986, p. 89).[8] As is so common with socially anxious people in general, such performers often suffer from two related narcissistically animated cognitive biases, the "spotlight effect," the inclination to exaggerate the degree to which their behavior and appearance are in fact perceived and appraised by others, and the "illusion of transparency," an inclination to misjudge the degree to which their internal states overflow and are noticed by others (Gilovich and Savitsky, 1999, p. 165).

Otto Fenichel (1945) has put forth what is probably the more familiar view of the internalized conflict driving stage fright, namely, that the performer gets extremely fretful when he senses that his exhibitionistic wishes are threatening to break through into consciousness and become noticeable to the audience. The performer fears that the audience will respond with severe censure when it detects his "true" motivations, to manipulate the audience into admiring and adoring him, a moment of imagined seduction, and to satisfy his fantasized Oedipal wishes of incest and murder. As the highly accomplished American actor Burgess Meredith inadvertently described his aggressive Oedipal wish, "the audience is the dragon to be slain, the woman to be raped" (Aaron, 1986, p. 68). In the mind of the performer, not only will the audience be angry at him for hoodwinking them, they will also want to punish him for his shameful narcissistic and Oedipal desires. To make matters even worse, the performer's intense anxiety is related to the fact that he actually feels disgracefully inferior because he unconsciously believes he has been castrated for his Oedipal wishes, and he is attempting to camouflage this awful fact via his exhibitionistic behavior on the stage. Once he is exposed for being the shameful impostor he is, the performer feels utterly humiliated.

There have been a few other notable contributions to the stage fright literature. For example, Safirstein's (1962) analysis of one musician suggests her stage fright was related to her internalized conflicts over her dependency needs, her resignation and inertia, versus her wish to be expansive and self-assertive, while Freundlich (1968) put forth the view that stage fright was rooted in a performer's fear of punishment for his archaic fantasies of omnipotence and boundless narcissistic gratification.

In a thoughtful review of the literature, Donald Kaplan (1969) suggested that the root cause of stage fright is strong feelings of fraudulence and the dread of exposure that leads to an erosion of poise, that wonderful feeling that calls to mind the supportive/comforting mother/child dyad, combined with "blocking" and "depersonalization." Blocking, says Kaplan, is not inhibition, rather it is "the momentary experience of complete loss of perception and rehearsed function," a kind of numbness, whereas "inhibition has a volitional element and constrains only certain but not all functioning" (p. 64). Moreover, blocking eliminates all sense of control over what is happening and targets the total eradication of impulse by de-linking the self from all types of functioning, including speech, the use of the postural system to self-comfort, or other impairments in soothing muscular control. Indeed, this is what gives the performer the terrible feeling of being inescapably trapped. Once the performer is onstage, blocking morphs into depersonalization, a split between a functioning and observing self, with marked spatial disorientation. That is, the observing self discerns the functioning self as off afar and operating mechanically in front of an audience that is also viewed as fairly distant. In other words, stage fright is the feeling of catastrophic loss originally associated with one's supportive, comforting, collaborative mother, displaced onto the director and audience (actors will tell you that even worse than a condemning audience is a non-responsive or indifferent one). Kaplan also makes the important point, one that Gabbard (1997) picks up on, that stage fright is not simply a performer's disability equivalent to getting a bad flu, but rather it is a creative difficulty that the performer tries to solve along with other difficulties of artistic performance. As the American theater producer David Balasco noted, "I wouldn't give a nickel for an actor who isn't nervous" (Aaron, 1986, p. 80). Most importantly, as I have said, stage fright in one form or another is frequently operative to varying degrees in everyday life. In fact, says Kaplan, it is best regarded as a "phenomenon" that "mainly resides ... beyond the clinical" (1969, p. 60). Likewise, coming from a Jungian perspective, Hayes suggests that the unwarranted anxiety that performers and non-performers have in speaking in a group context is related to the universal racial "imprint of the victim, the outcast, the stoned man that bedevils us." That is, stage fright is the archetypal fear of self-assertion that leads to standing out from the anonymous mass and becoming the vulnerable victim (Hayes, 1975, p. 280).

Gabbard (1997) emphasizes that the anxiety that a performer feels before an audience can be best conceptualized as happening on a range from "normal" worries that one may not be able to perform at one's absolute best, to much more severe inhibitions that interfere with one's career trajectory. In his analytic work with many different types of performers, and to some extent recapitulating and elaborating the earlier stage fright literature, Gabbard has described a number of psychodynamic themes that appear to be operative in this condition separately and/or in combination, depending on the internal and external circumstances of the person: 1) The role of shame, that painful feeling of humiliation or distress caused by the consciousness of wrong or foolish behavior. Shame is rooted in severely negative parental reactions to common childhood failures in psychomotor and social realms and in other contexts where the child displays a loss of control. In the context of the adult performer with stage fright, shame is related to one's "genital inadequacy or loss of bowel or bladder control" (ibid., p. 209); 2) The connection between stage fright and unconscious aggressive wishes that evoke guilty feelings that one is vanquishing Oedipal and sibling rivals in the act of performing successfully; 3) The role of separation anxiety, which is connected to the rapprochement sub-phase of Margaret Mahler's separation-individuation (age 16 to 24 months, the "terrible twos") in which the child reckons that his autonomy and psychomotor freedom is not limitless and that the outside world is considerably more challenging than he thought. This narcissistic wounding leads to regression back to the symbiotic relation to the mother and the development of "ambitendency" which reflects both his symbiotic and autonomous wishes, such as when a child clutches onto his mother and then suddenly dashes away from her. This dynamic is enacted in the adult performer suffering from stage fright when he feels utterly alone and isolated on the stage (recall Olivier). In other instances, the performer may fear that the audience will get up and leave because his performance is so bad; 4) The fear that one's narcissistic needs for affirmation and approval will not be satisfied, leading to "annihilation" or "disintegration anxiety," that catastrophic sense of threat to one's very psychic survival. Such a primal feeling of loss of self, of course, goes beyond mere signal anxiety and can reach psychotic levels of intensity in an otherwise non-symptomatic person. Many believe that the primal anxiety of annihilation or disintegration is probably the ultimate existential basis of stage fright; and 5) The role of greed, a kind of unquenchable hunger rooted in an inadequate early oral connection to the mother, can be manifested in a performance. That is, the successful performer can be conflicted that he has devoured all the adoration and approval for himself. In addition, such greediness may evoke anxiety that the audience will turn its envious anger on the performer. Thus, says Gabbard, both the fear of failure and success may be embodied in stage fright (ibid., p. 210).

As Mark Twain noted, "There are only two types of speakers [performers] in the world. 1. The nervous and 2. Liars" (www.forbes.com). Indeed, even Freud was prone to extreme anxiety when he had to publicly speak, whether to an unfamiliar or familiar audience. He reassured himself and reduced his anxiety using many strategies, including saying to Jung, "When my turn comes [to lecture] I shall comfort myself with the thought that at least you and [Sándor] Ferenczi will be listening" (Freud, 1974, letter of July 19, 1909, p. 243). While I have discussed many interesting psychoanalytic formulations of what accounts for the debilitating aspects of stage fright, the question that needs to be asked and at least tentatively answered is what can be done by the average person in terms of self-fashioning a way of being that creatively uses stage fright as an advantage?

While there are hundreds of useful self-help books and other materials on managing the "nuts and bolts" of stage fright and related performance anxieties, I want to end this section by mentioning two psychoanalytically based suggestions, in lieu of seeking out analytic treatment for a serious case of the condition, that not only speak to the difficulties of reckoning with one's irrational fear of performing in front of others in the workplace but also point to how to creatively overcome this state of mind. They are the cultivation of an enhanced capacity for spontaneity and the downsizing of one's selfish ego. Such a sublimatory capacity is what partially constitutes the art of living the "good life." As Freud wrote to the Austrian novelist and playwright Stefan Zweig, the basic strategic and tactical task of psychoanalysis is to "struggle with the demon [that is, with irrationality], in a sober way" (Gay, 1988, p. xvii).

One way to begin to "master" one's stage fright is to reflect upon and learn from one of its emotional opposites, namely, spontaneity, the capacity to perform as a result of a sudden inner impulse or inclination and without premeditation or external stimulus.[9] As Australian feminist social theorist Germaine Greer noted, "the essence of pleasure is spontaneity" (www.cbn. com). Moreover, for Freud, the art of living the "good life" in part means mindfully living according to the notion that man is fundamentally pleasure-seeking in an erotically-tinged universe, so when one's hedonic capacity is truncated as in stage fright, it is no laughing matter. Why truncated ties to spontaneous pleasure are so self-destructive in everyday life, so indicative of neurotic misery, becomes obvious when we compare the subjective experience of stage fright and spontaneity.

Where spontaneity includes the capacity "to be natural and passionate," stage fright feels like one is bound, tied and gagged by terror. Where spontaneity fosters "the joy of living life impulsively, without too many constraints," stage fright reduces existence to one narrow theme, to a stereotyped and structure-bound psychic cage. Spontaneity values "the adventure of ending up somewhere unexpected and discovering something new," but stage fright feels Kafkaesque, as if one is trapped in a maze of grotesque happenings (www.katherinepreston. com). In short, spontaneity is free, flowing and unrestrained, it is life-affirming, a derivative of Eros, while stage fright is its opposite: life-denying, a derivative of Thanatos. In the former condition, one feels like the world is a gate; in the latter, the world feels like a wall.

While a robust capacity for spontaneity is needed in all performing arts, the one art form where spontaneity is perhaps most needed is in theater improvisation, or as insiders call it, "improv" or "impro." The way that skillful improv performers manage their curtailment of spontaneity, another way of describing stage fright, is instructive. As Marlon Brando quipped in a 1976 interview in *Playboy*, "If an actor can't improvise, perhaps the producer's wife cast him in that part" (www.theatromathia.gr). The capacity to effectively improvise works against stage fright in that it increases the actor's belief in the play and his conviction about its artistic truthfulness, and it shores up his feeling that he adequately comprehends the character, that is, that he and the character have merged with each other or are radically in sync (Aaron, 1986, p. 33).[10] It was Viola Spolin, "the high priestess" of improv, the developer of hundreds of theater games meant to release spontaneity, creativity, playfulness, and other qualities of mind and heart necessary to be a great actor and fully engaged person in ordinary life, who taught a way of overcoming, or at least better managing stage fright both on and off the stage.[11]

Theater games like "Swat Tag," "Mirror," Playball," and "Gibberish," and exercises with such titles as "Space Walk" and "Feeling Self with Self" are each "accepted group activit[ies] which [are] limited by rules and group agreement" and tend to be lots of fun. They evoke naturalness, passion and delight and are comparable to the theater experience as well as real life contexts. The goal of these games and exercises is "to almost fool spontaneity into being" (Marcus, with Marcus, 2011, p. 79). Unlike the detached intellectualizing, discursive reasoning and obsessive cerebral doings that are rooted in the empiricisms and rationalism of the Western mindset, improv cultivates a different cast of mind. It aims to fully engage the immediacy of the real-life human situation in its essential fluidity and changeability. This form of attunement glimpses unrehearsed perfection and is the opposite of the paralyzing anxiety and panic associated with stage fright.

Spolin defines spontaneity as "a moment of explosion; a free moment of self-expression; an off-balance moment; the gateway to your intuition; the moment when, in full sensory attention, you don't think, you act!" (1999, p. 370). What is important to grasp in Spolin's definition of spontaneity is the relationship between spontaneity and intuition, the latter being the way the player can evoke that exquisite moment when one is creatively being in the world as an organic whole, when "we are re-formed into ourselves." Spolin notes, "intuition bypasses the intellect, the mind, the memory, the known. Using intuition cannot be taught. One must be tripped into it" (1986, p. 4). In other words, intuition requires transcendence of the familiar categories of thought, feeling and action, and "to enter courageously the area of the unknown, and to experience the release of momentary genius within themselves" (ibid.). As William James remarked, "Genius means little more than the faculty of perceiving in an unhabitual way" (www.quotes.net). This is the opposite of stage fright, which is more analogous to the narrowing of perception and action that we see in depressive and obsessive-compulsive disorders (Becker, 1969, p. 83). Most importantly, continues Spolin, "the intuitive can only be felt in the moment of spontaneity, the moment when we are freed to relate and act, involving ourselves in the moving, changing world around us … [intuition] comes bearing its gifts in the moment of spontaneity" (Spolin, 1986, p. 4). The goal of this combustible mixture of spontaneity and intuition, argues Spolin, is what she calls "transformation"—"the heart of improvisation is transformation" (ibid.). And the heart of transformation is creativity, not rearranging what is already known as most of us usually opt for in our ordinary lives, but a radical change in one's way of being in the world, at least during the theater game. Spolin aptly defines transformation in her teacher's handbook for theater games for kids using the cast of mind I am trying to delineate that is on the way to "mastering" stage fright on the job:

> The effects of game playing are not only social and cognitive. When players are deeply focused on a game, they are capable of transforming objects or creating them. Whole environments arise spontaneously out of thin air. Impossible to capture fully in words, transformation seems to arise out of heightened physical movement and of exchange of this moving energy between players. Change occurs not once but over and over again. Transformations are theater magic and an intrinsic part of most theater games ... [In transformation,] [c]reation momentarily breaks through isolation, and actors and audience alike receive (ahhh!) the appearance of a new reality (theater magic).
>
> (Spolin, 1999, p. 372)

It is crucial to understand that each of Spolin's theater games presents a problem that needs to be solved within the context of the rules of the game. All the player's efforts, his or her focus—"directing and concentrating attention on a specific person, object or event with the stage reality ... the point of concentration of a theater game that keeps the players in process"—must be intensely directed toward playing the game (ibid., p. 360). Paradoxically, it is within the context of the structure of the game that such a focus, to which every action must be directed, facilitates spontaneity: "In this spontaneity, personal freedom is released, and the total person physically, intellectually, and intuitively is awakened" (ibid., p. 6). Moreover, and this is one of the implications of theater games for everyday life, such excitement and boldness often leads the player to transcend many of his or her anxieties and inhibitions, his stage fright—call it a transformative liberating moment—and thus, the player is better able to go out into the "real" world, "to explore, adventure, and face all dangers unafraid" (ibid.). The great German philosopher Walter Benjamin made a similar point in a different context, "These are days when no one should rely unduly on his 'competence.' Strength lies in improvisation. All the decisive blows are struck left-handed" (www.values.com). Indeed, there are many adults in psychoanalysis who have told me about childhood moments of personal fearlessness and triumph while playing a game or sport, an experience that became a radically transforming, deeply positive metaphor for their lives.

Of course, the liberation of one's spontaneity, intuition and creativity via the theater game probably comes easier to kids who are less shackled by restrictions in self-expression. However, a deep point about the art of living the "good life" and better managing one's stage fright can be garnered from Spolin; namely, it is the cultivation of spontaneity in one's everyday life that is essential to the maximal enjoyment of one's life, including moving beyond one's stage fright. For Spolin, the way into spontaneity/intuition/liberation is via the theater game, though the qualities it requires and evokes in the players are transferable in other contexts in which the theater game is the learning paradigm. For this release of one's personality to occur requires the overcoming of the major stumbling block to great improv and living the "good life": fear. It is fear of how one is coming across to others and of one's own irreverent and hidden impulses that leads improv players to expurgate and edit their responses, such as getting stuck in the future (by planning their actions in advance), or in the past (by doing the safe and familiar)—the antithesis to being in the moment. Keith Johnstone, one of the great theorists on theater improv, pointed out its socially threatening nature in that it reveals the "real" self as opposed to the choreographed one (hence, one must be "tripped" into the intuitive, says Spolin). Whatever the specific nature of the fear one has doing improv, or in any type of performance in front of an audience, Spolin caught its essential thrust when she wrote, "the fear is not of the unknown, but of not knowing" (Spolin, 1999, p. xiv), which is probably rooted in the childhood fear of being amiss. It is the tension associated with fear that blocks "free open thought" (Hodgson and Richards, 1974, pp. 56, 57), the foundation of all improv and creative living. As Henry Miller wrote, "all growth is a leap in the dark, a spontaneous, unpremeditated act without benefit of experience" (www. zquotes.com).

If we conceptualize stage fright fundamentally as a fear of internal freedom, as an avenue of flight from oneself, from the "dark" side of one's unconscious wishes so vividly described by psychoanalytic writers, then it becomes quite plausible that the antidote to stage fright is courageous and compassionate self-acceptance. As Benjamin further noted, "To be happy is to be able to become aware of oneself without fright" (www.worldofquotes.com).

However, courageous and compassionate self-acceptance is not the whole story to mastering stage fright, as any great actor or improv performer will tell you. In addition, one needs to conceptualize one's craft, one's performance differently, to create a new "retelling" or "metaphorical redescription" as Shafer and Hess noted. That is, stage fright tends to go away when one's conscious and/ or unconscious view of one's performance is that it is not mainly an infantile, self-serving, narcissistic activity meant to gain love or a perverse gratification from the audience and others. To be able to tell a great story in the improv context requires a feeling of emotional and spiritual closeness to one's fellow players, to the audience and toward oneself (e.g., openness to one's otherness). Indeed, Spolin made this point when she wrote, "that improvisation is not exchange of information between players; it is communion" (1999, p. 45). That is "individual freedom (expressing self) while respecting community responsibility (group agreement) is our goal" (ibid., p. 44). These insights derived from the world of improv have their obvious correlations to ordinary life, including managing stage fright, namely, in order to produce and co-produce new realities, "story making" not merely "story telling," realities that are spontaneously creative and enhancing, requires one to obtain a high degree of "openness to contact with the environment and each other and willingness to play" (ibid., p. 25). To achieve this kind of openness to the otherness of one's players, the audience, the material and oneself requires a diminution of one's narcissism, one's need for infantile self-aggrandizement, emotional "hunger" gratification, and the like. As Spolin noted, to fill a pail full of apples requires an empty pail, a kind of "unselving or transelving," a jettison of the selfish ego. It is only then, when one has generated a less self-centric subjectivity, that one is properly receptive to the other broadly described. Moreover, this inner state is a kind of waiting, an openness and accessibility that is different than ordinary waiting for something to happen: "the improviser is in waiting, not waiting for," says Spolin (ibid., p. xiv). As with a queen who has "ladies in waiting" to attend to her needs as they arise, so the improviser must attend to the other, in service.

The upshot of this for the problem of "mastering" or better managing stage fright is to better reckon with its morbid narcissistic structure. As Gabbard notes, it is precisely the commonness of narcissistic preoccupations that is the bedrock of "all the dynamics" of stage fright. As I have noted earlier, such individuals have serious problems with psychological themes intimately connected to their feeble sense of self-regard and impoverished self-conception, such as: "self-esteem regulation, self-validation from the response of the audience as a mirroring or idealizing object, around envy, around fears that one's greed will damage others and one's self, around separation as a narcissistic extension of mother, and around shame connected with exhibitionism" (Gabbard, 1983, p. 426). In other words, as one recent study of performers with stage fright suggested, it was the performers' relationship to their performance troupe that mattered most in terms of coping with their stage fright, such as "teamwork, bonding, support, humor, emotionality," and probably most of all, "responsibility to others" (Simmonds and Southcott, 2012, p. 326). When one views performance—on or off the stage—the preferred way of being that is most likely to avoid or creatively use stage fright is one that is other-directed, other-regarding and other-serving. Freedom of expression is radically enhanced when one views one's performance as an "act of giving" to others; in other words, "fright fades away when fellowship is established" (Hayes, 1975, pp. 279, 280).

Writer's block

Stephen King, the author of modern-day horror, supernatural fiction, science fiction, and fantasy, whose books have sold roughly 350 million copies, noted during what sounds like a bout of writer's block, "I gradually realized that I was seeing another example of creative ebb, another step by another art on the road that may indeed end in extinction" (www.inkorkeys.wordpress.com). Indeed, writer's block, most often a temporary psychological incapability to begin or carry on working on a piece of writing, is a common difficulty that the average person can have on the job. While writer's block may not always manifest itself in its most extreme form and with the dire career consequences it has for the professional writer, just about everyone recognizes the hesitations, procrastinations and postponements, the blocked creativity, associated with many forms of writing. Ernest Hemingway replied when asked how he went about his writing, "First I defrost the refrigerator" (Olinick, 1997, p. 183). Whether called writer's block, "publication anxiety," "writer's cramp," or a "writing inhibition," and whether fleeting, recurring or lasting, the experience of writing as a failure to launch and deliver a completed and "good enough" piece of work is "ubiquitous and natural" (Britton, 1994, p. 1213; Olinick, 1997, p. 185). In the workplace, the failure to produce a piece of writing in a timely and competent manner can make one's everyday life very hard going, not only in terms of the tension one feels related to one's sense of personal failure, but also in terms of the negative ramifications on colleagues and bosses who can be irritated if not angry for having to wait for the work to be properly completed. This is especially the case when members of a work group have put significant effort and sacrifice of personal life into successfully completing the work task on time and may feel disrespected by their colleague who appears to feel that he or she is "special" and should not have to comply with the requirements that everyone else must meet.

In this section I review some of the important psychoanalytic renderings of why professional writers develop writer's block and how it impairs their work life. Such self-knowledge can help facilitate the resolution of at least some of the neurotic misery associated with this very common experience among both professional and non-professional writers, the latter operating in varying work contexts. I then provide one psychoanalytically informed suggestion for how the average person can begin to "master" writer's block, another troubling example of a work inhibition that can make one's existence in the workplace one of considerable unhappiness.

Why do people write?

The great English author of *Animal Farm*, George Orwell, aptly described why professional writers engage in their challenging craft. Having a sense of what makes a professional writer tick is critical to better understand the unconscious dynamics of writer's block. In his 1946 essay "Why I Write," Orwell commented:

> Writing a book is a horrible, exhausting struggle, like a long bout of some painful illness. One would never undertake such a thing if one were not driven on by some demon whom one can neither resist nor understand. For all one knows that demon is the same instinct that makes a baby squall for attention. And yet it is also true that one can write nothing readable unless one constantly struggles to efface one's own personality.
>
> (orwell.ru › Library › Essays › Wiw › English, retrieved 2/9/15)

While it is beyond the scope of this section to review the vast literature on why people professionally write, what is striking about Orwell's self-observations is that they are perfectly in sync with a psychoanalytic outlook on both the unconscious motivations and psychological functions of writing and our current focus, its opposite, writer's block. Whatever "demons" are motivating Orwell to write are irrepressible and have the compelling force of an infantile instinct. One of the greatest English novelists of the twentieth century, Graham Greene suggests how these demons may feel, at least to him: "Writing is a form of therapy; sometimes I wonder how all those who do not write, compose or paint can manage to escape the madness, melancholia, the panic and fear which is inherent in a human situation" (www.nytimes.com).

As we shall soon discuss, while all such writing that Orwell and Greene describe has a narcissistic motive, meaning that it is intimately tied to self-esteem and self-concept enhancement, it also involves a degree of self-obliteration, or to put it less starkly, self-struggle and self-overcoming. For example, good writing demands coming to terms with what one really believes matters and this means relinquishing much of the protective, often delusional nonsense that we all tell ourselves mimics honest and productive thought.[12] The popular tongue-in-cheek saying among professional writers goes, "Writing is easy. You just open a vein and bleed." Indeed, as another great English writer, Virginia Woolf, noted, to make matters even more challenging, this bloodletting is a public one: "Every secret of a writer's soul, every experience of his life, every quality of his mind, is written large in his works" (2007, p. 499). Playing off Woolf's astute observation, while we can plausibly say that all such creative writing, and probably other types of writing as well, can be an author's attempt to improve his biography, a writing block represents a defense against self-confrontation with one's "demons" and is a way of not revealing them to the real or imagined disapproving audience. It is to this subject that I now turn.

Psychoanalytic reflections on writer's block

Bergler (1950, 1955) made one of the first important contributions to understanding the psychology of the creative writer and writer's block (he claims to have coined the term). To some extent, Bergler formulated the main psychological themes that set the stage for most other psychoanalytically informed reflections on these subjects.[13] While some of Bergler's formulations may seem far-fetched or at least dated, the main thrust of his work is still quite pertinent for understanding the creative writer and writer's block in the workplace.

As Bergler boldly and lyrically put it:

> Every writer, without exception, is a masochist, a sadist, a peeping Tom, an exhibitionist, a narcissist, an "injustice collector" and a depressed person constantly haunted by fears of unproductivity.
>
> (wheelercentre.com/dailies/post/a0cf1a03c5e2/, retrieved 2/15/15)

Moreover, wrote Bergler,

> Writers are fortunate in that they are able to treat their neuroses every day by writing and as soon as a writer is blocked, this was catastrophic because the writer would start to go to pieces.

(www.goodreads.com)

Bergler is certainly not mincing words in these quotations. In his view, the writer is "chock full" of neurotic motivations and he uses writing as a form of indispensable though painful self-healing.[14] Both Philip Roth and Kurt Vonnegut have implied the truth of Bergler's observations when they quipped, respectively, "The road to hell is paved with works-in-progress"; "Who is more to be pitied, a writer bound and gagged by policemen or one living in perfect freedom who has nothing more to say?" (www.poemhunter.com; www.ivcc.edu).

Bergler begins his account of writer's block by locating the problem in the broader context of the psychology of the creative writer. The writer's main conflict, he says, is "psychic masochism"; further, "the inner situation of the writer is desperate loneliness, masochistically elaborated" (Bergler, 1950, pp. 258, 113). At the time that Bergler was writing, masochism was a popular topic in psychoanalytic circles and was viewed as a fundamental human striving (it was "primary," Freud said). Bergler came up with an interesting three-tier formulation to explain masochism that still makes sense in the clinical context: the person organizes a refusal of his needs, that is, he unconsciously orchestrates rejection; he then works himself up into a fine lather of moral indignation and pseudo-fury at the refusing person, mainly in order to deny his role in the rejection and his pleasure in being mistreated; and finally, he derives great unconscious pleasure from being vanquished and delights in the self-pity and wound-licking that accompanies it (Akhtar, 2009, pp. 199, 166).

For Bergler, creative writing is a way of overcoming a "lifelong 'battle of the conscience,'" that is, with a severe super-ego (1955, p. 160). By this he means the writer's attempt at sublimation is a "a self-curative alibi sickness" (ibid.), one that has three distinct elements absent in other sublimations: 1) It is temporary and probationary and the writer, as the above Vonnegut quote indicates, is haunted by the dread of "drying up"; 2) Such a painful and depressive fight with himself, one that continues even when effectively writing, is defended against by a kind of "megalomaniacal self-elevation" (ibid.) that he has created beautiful and/or brilliant original words that will be vigorously affirmed by others; 3) His sublimation is an isolated element in his personality, meaning that he is enveloped by neuroticism in his personal life.

In Bergler's account, the creative writer is a "perpetual defendant" (ibid., p. 161) to a prosecutorial and accusatory conscience that has two aspects: 1) The unconscious conscience shouts: "You still want to enjoy, masochistically, the end result of your infantile conflict—to be refused by the images of the pre-Oedipal mother." That is, the writer does not want to consciously know that he has strong oral-masochistic wishes towards his milk/love/kindness-denying early childhood mother; 2) The conscience continues its diatribe: "You are still an infantile Peeping Tom," that is, he derives pleasure at imagining his parents having sex, the so-called primal scene (ibid., p. 161) For Bergler, all writers fight "a never-ending battle with his peeping (voyeuristic) tendencies." Imagination, the key to being a good writer "is the 'purified' successor to infantile peeping." Moreover, voyeurism is oral in nature, in that it is "ocular intake" (1950, pp. 90–91, 125).

In defense of these merciless super-ego accusations, the creative writer unconsciously says four things: 1) "I am not guilty of being a masochistic glutton for punishment, simply because the alleged provider of disappointments [the milk/love/kindness-denying mother] does not even exist." Rather, he tells himself, "I myself out of myself and for myself, give myself beautiful words and ideas" (milk/love/kindness). The writer has killed off the frustrating, milk/love/kindness-denying, pre-Oedipal mother, and has himself become "the giving mother and the recipient child." Therefore, continues the unconscious inner voice, "There can be no indictment for murder without a *corpus delicti*?" Moreover, "I am autoarchic [having absolute sovereignty] and live on the basis of the unification theory" (ibid., p. 161). That is, the unification tendency expresses the unconscious conviction that the desired disappointment experienced at the hands of the milk/love/kindness-denying mother is gratified by setting up the "mother-child shop" in himself, and thus unconsciously denies that there was any disappointment in the first place, as his "mother does not exist "(1950, p. 258); 2) Next, says Bergler, the writer unconsciously says to himself, "If I am guilty at all, at best I am guilty, not of psychic masochism," but rather, "the opposite crime—I am frequently aggressive" (in effect taking the rap for a lesser crime) (1955, p. 161); 3) Carrying on in his defense, the inner voice declares, "I'm not guilty because the whole of humanity is my accomplice" (ibid.). The fact that people approve of his writing means they approve of the content, too, and any guilt he feels is shared with them and therefore reduced, if not vacated; and finally 4) The placating conscience concludes, "I am not guilty of being a voyeur. On the contrary, I am an exhibitionist: by publishing, I exhibit" (ibid.). Psychic exhibitionism is used as a defense against psychic peeping (1950, p. 92).

Finally, it is within this incredibly complex, multi-determined psychodynamic context that writer's block occurs the instant the conscience no longer accepts the elaborated internal alibis and defenses for his "crimes," mainly his oral-masochistic wishes, as described above. As Bion noted, "good writers make ... a demolition of the breast," meaning they unconsciously kill off the disappointing milk/love/kindness-denying mother (Tuch, 1995, p. 244). In effect, the writer's inhibition is the internally obligatory self-induced punishment for imagined perverse and malevolent desires and behavior. Thus, if successful creative writing is a way of vanquishing the condemning conscience, then "writer's block represents a defeat in the battle," one that is not only debilitating in terms of the writer not performing his craft, but important in a number of other destructive ways for the individual's personal life (Bergler, 1955, p. 163).

Approaching writer's block from an object relations, Kleinian point of view, Britton (1994) claims that the origins of "publication anxiety," in particular among psychoanalysts who want to publish, is rooted in a "fear of rejection by the primary intended listener." This fear leads to an "inability to conceptualize or, in lesser states of inhibition, produces an inability to write." In other words, says Britton, publication anxiety stems from the fantasized negative judgment of authority figures, such as one's teachers, and a fear of being discredited by them and by colleagues to whom the author wants to be intimately connected and by whom the author wishes to be accepted. Such anxiety about not belonging may lead to not publishing a written work and to not speaking in a public forum. If this inhibition is not so severe the writer may publish but distort and deviate inside the text in the process of publishing his work. In other words, he will narratively "smooth" and "sanitize" the text with an eye to making it read more acceptably to his imagined audience whose acceptance, if not love, he craves. As Britton succinctly puts it, "The conflict" in publication anxiety "is between the urge to communicate a novel idea to a receptive audience, thus winning their allegiance, and the conflicting wish to say something to bind the author to his affiliates and ancestors by the utterance, in a shared language, of shared beliefs—the recital of a creed as means of unification." Such "unification," with its triangular character—the passionately driven writer, his beloved written words, and the receptive audience—has profoundly troubling Oedipal meanings (1994, pp. 1214, 1215). That is, to publish a work "is to know and possess a subject" with the heartfelt goal of pleasing and winning over one's readers. However, this can also generate distance from one's teachers and estrangement from one's colleagues, which leads to an intense fear of retaliation that becomes the basis for one's dread of writing and publishing (Akhtar, 2009, p. 235).

Tuch (1995) provides a self-psychological account of writer's block based on his three-year analysis of a man in his late twenties who could not finish his novel. He makes the interesting point that while Bergler was correct in emphasizing that writing can be a defense against many unacceptable infantile wishes, writer's block can also be a defense against other developmentally emanating impulses that Bergler tends to de-emphasize. For example, if writing symbolizes anal productions, then writer's block, which is analogous to stubborn and determined constipation, may evolve as a defense against one's anal aggressive, if not sadistic, wishes to smear. When writing becomes a sexualized expression and assumes a phallic meaning, as Freud said, "making a liquid flow out of a tube onto a piece of white paper," it may then become inhibited by a censuring superego. Writing, says Tuch, can also be a defense against the anxiety often associated with the necessary immersion into fantasy that creative writing entails (as does acting), as in Kris's "regression in the service of the ego." Lastly, writing block can be a defense against one's aggression toward significant others, say a beloved parent or spouse, especially if one is writing something that has an important emotional connection to an ambivalently related to other. This is even more the case when writing is a way of individuating or defining one's unique identity, which inevitably involves a modicum of real and imagined psychic violence toward significant others. In this sense, no writing is "innocent." As Sartre said, "Words are loaded pistols" (www.articles.chicagotribune.com), and writer's block may be a way of protecting one's real or imagined significant other from one's real or imagined aggression (Tuch, 1995, pp. 244, 245). In fact, the Pulitzer Prize-winning author Alice Walker put this point just right, "Writing saved me from the sin and inconvenience of violence" (1994, p. 108).

Finally, and most importantly, following Kohut who noted that writing expresses an "aim inhibited, socially acceptable way to fulfill the elements of one's grandiose/exhibitionistic strivings," Tuch believes that writer's block is often rooted in conflict that is generated as a result of the childhood fear that one's wishes to be affirmed, that is, mirrored, will again be distressingly frustrated. In his analyzed case with Mr. L, Tuch concludes by saying that this young man's writer's block "developed around a conflicted wish for shared experience, one that could lead the patient to feel that his affective life was understandable and acceptable to others." Once Mr. L worked through how he was unconsciously substituting writing to compensate for or undo the unresponsiveness, criticism and negativity associated with his relationship with his father, and that he had transposed onto his writing his childhood wishes and meanings for paternal acceptance and affirmation that he again imagined would be withheld, he was able to complete his novel (Tuch, 1995, pp. 256–257).

As with stage fright, there have been many "how to" books written on how to conquer writing block. Rather than review these materials, by way of concluding this discussion of writer's block in the workplace I want to offer one psychoanalytically glossed idea about how one can "think differently" about one's writer's block and its creative overcoming, short of seeking out psychoanalytic or another form of professional help.[15]

From my clinical experience working with a variety of professional and non-professional writers suffering from writer's block in the workplace, I have noticed that these people appear to be especially prone to what Ferenczi (1919) [1980] famously called "Sunday neurosis." Sunday neurosis refers to the intensification of neurotic manifestations like grouchiness, moodiness, and sub-clinical malaise, and psychosomatic symptoms like stomach conditions and head and muscle aches, which prevent enjoying one's day off, including with one's family and friends. Moreover, the "long sleep" and "overeating" that is associated with Sunday, or with religious Jews on the Saturday Sabbath, do not alone account for the upsurge of debilitating neurotic and psychosomatic symptoms. Existential psychiatrist Viktor E. Frankl noted, "Sunday neurosis [is] that kind of depression which afflicts people who become aware of the lack of content in their lives when the rush of the busy week is over and the void within themselves becomes manifest." Such troubling feelings as emptiness, boredom, apathy, cynicism, and a sense of being without meaningful direction are common manifestations of Sunday neurosis (1963, p. 169).

According to Ferenczi, some people are prone to Sunday neurosis because they experience an "inner liberation" of "repressed instincts," that is, what comes to mind are deeply troubling memories and distressing unsavory wishes (and, Frankl would add, a feeling of existential meaninglessness). Without the externally imposed structure, controls and demands of ordinary work, without such "external censorship," the person inclined to Sunday neurosis, especially with their "hypersensitive conscience," feels guilty for his dangerous impulses and wishes. He therefore defends against this awareness via the mobilization of self-punishment fantasies. The neurotic and psychosomatic symptoms described above are the psychological expression of, and physiologically anchoring to, this self-punishment (Ferenczi, 1919 [1980], p. 76).

The person with writer's block is roughly analogous to someone suffering from an extreme version of Sunday neurosis, meaning that he too erects an elaborate defensive regime against feeling the disturbing power and truth of his troubling memories and distressing unsavory wishes (and vacuous life, as Frankl would view it). By fashioning a kind of "character armor," symbolically his writer's block, to protect himself from his sense of vulnerability and weakness and upsetting illicit desires, he quite literally arms himself so that he can effectively navigate the threatening inner and outer world that he has constructed. As with Sunday neurosis, the person with writer's block closes himself off from the world. He circles the wagons, as it were, "in the very process of his own growth and organization." As a result, he truncates his creativity and effectiveness as a writer as an attempt at self-preservation from his phantasmagoric imaginings (Becker, 1969, p. 83). Through such self-protective maneuverings he establishes a degree of control over his feelings, thoughts and actions, albeit with a psychic price paid in his dramatically reduced creativity and productivity. Without such self-protective constraints, as in Sunday neurosis, the person with writer's block feels he would be swamped by dangerous feelings, including those that would generate intense guilt and the need for punishment. As bad as the punishment of blocked creativity feels, the blocked person believes that it is still preferred to his worst punitive imaginings.

Thus, writer's block is usefully conceptualized as a process of what Ernest Becker called "fetishization," "the organization of perception and action, by the personality, around a very striking and compelling—but narrow theme" (ibid., p. 85). Rather than face his disturbing memories and insalubrious wishes (and angst), the person artificially inflates the meaning of his writer's block, giving it a higher value of significance in the horizon of his perception and actions. The reason he does this, says Becker, is because the writing block itself symbolizes an area that he can firmly hold on to, that he can skillfully manipulate, that allows him to justify himself, his actions, his sense of self, and his choices in the world. In other words, the writer's block as a fetish "is an arbitrary focus for" the "derivation of self-value" (ibid.). Moreover, by serving such a function, the person with writer's block does not have to contend with the more threatening "demons" that he is fleeing from as described above. Nor does he have to engage in the "heavy lifting" of fashioning a more robust self-identity, including creating a free, flowing and unrestrained way of engaging his inner and outer world. Indeed, it is precisely this self-fashioning of a more open, expansive and receptive self, one that has adequately reckoned with one's soul-destroying, life-denying "demons," that is the lynchpin of overcoming one's writer's block.

Workaholism

The brilliantly irreverent singer, Madonna, could have been describing the typical inner experience of the person whose involvement in work is quite simply "over the top": "I'm anal retentive. I'm a workaholic. I have insomnia. And I'm a control freak. That's why I'm not married. Who could stand me?" (www.forbes.com). Indeed, Madonna is pointing to some of the salient aspects of those people who feel a compulsive and unrelenting need to work. While Wayne E. Oates first coined the term "workaholic" in his landmark book, *Confessions of a Workaholic: The Facts about Work Addiction* (1971), "there is still no widely accepted definition of workaholism" in the scholarly vocational and organizational literatures. That is, "there is no consensus regarding which set of dimensions provides the most accurate and complete definition" of the phenomenon (Ng *et al.*, 2007, p. 112). Moreover, "there has been little research on personality traits associated with being a workaholic" (Clark *et al.*, 2010, p. 786). This being said, for my purposes a serviceable definition of workaholism is "an individual difference characteristic referring to self-imposed demands, compulsive overworking, an inability to regulate work habits, and an overindulgence in work to the exclusion of most other life activities" (Bakker *et al.*, 2009, p. 24).

Causes of workaholism

There are three main psychological accounts for workaholism in the vocational and organizational scholarly literatures (Bonebright *et al.*, 2000, p. 470), all of which are plausible and worth reflecting on when trying to understand and help someone whose work life has become "out of control," at least in the eyes of one's family and friends.

The first account of workaholism claims that people become workaholics because they thoroughly enjoy working—think of the achievement-driven, goal-oriented, and competitive employee who derives great psychic income from working and describes what he does as "fun," "creative" and "stimulating" (ibid.). While most workaholics consciously enjoy their work, the so-called "nonenthusiastic workaholics" do not (ibid., p. 471), such as those who are close to "burn out," but see no way of changing their habituated behavior that has become thoroughly enmeshed with their organizational identity.

The main problem with this account of workaholism is that it strictly relies on conscious reasons that workaholics give to explain their over-working; however, it does not address possible unconscious motives, such as the masochistic need for punishment and the like. It is also worth noting that like all psychological constructs, workaholism is value-laden in that one man's workaholism is another man's passion, and often it is others, like one's family and friends, who ascribe the pejorative term to the so-called workaholic, not the workaholic himself. The clinician also makes such value-laden judgments regarding work/life balance. The vocational and organizational literatures acknowledge the distinctions between "happy versus dysfunctional" and "fulfilled versus unfulfilled" types of workaholics (Porter, 1996, p. 70), and among "work enthusiasts, work addicts, enthusiastic addicts" (Burke and Matthiesen, 2004, p. 301). Moreover, what constitutes workaholism is always context-dependent and setting-specific, that is, it relies on the culture of the workplace (and more broadly, the culture one is lodged in), as well as the degree of identification with one's job and occupation, with one's family and non-work life, and other situational demands (Ng and Feldman, 2008, p. 875). Lastly, it is undeniable that certain characteristics associated with workaholism can have positive implications for the worker and the organization, such as job satisfaction and career success and high levels of work quality and productivity (ibid., pp. 858, 855).

The second account of workaholism is one that conceptualizes the workaholic as suffering from an obsessive-compulsive disorder. These theorists focus on the fact that many workaholics don't actually like over-working, the "nonenthusiastic" ones, but they cannot adequately control themselves. Such workaholics have been found to have "more work-life conflict, less life satisfaction, and less purpose in life" (Bonebright *et al.*, 2000, p. 476). From my clinical experience with a wide range of workaholics, their character structure tends to be obsessive-compulsive in that they often have the telltale signs of this condition, what Freud famously described as orderliness, parsimony and obstinacy. They have additional qualities associated with this character type, such as an inability to reasonably cope with dirt and/or disorder, a need to keep exacting records, and they are annoyingly punctual, over-controlling and perfectionist in their outlook and behavior (Akhtar, 2009, p. 195).

Finally, the third perspective on workaholism uses an alcohol addiction model, similar to Oates's original formulation. The idea here is that as with alcoholics (or other kinds of addicts), the workaholic has what amounts to an understimulated nervous system, one that craves "high-octane" experiences, especially the "rush" associated with affirmations from hard work, such as organizational recognition for achievement, verbal praise from colleagues and bosses, and financial rewards and promotions. Researchers using this model have found that there are dysfunctional aspects of how workaholics behave that are analogous to alcoholics which have a markedly negative impact on effective organizational operations. For example, like alcoholics, workaholics display serious identity issues (e.g., they work to bolster a feeble self, to self-numb or to avoid), rigid thinking (e.g., they are perfectionistic and controlling, they can't work well in groups or delegate), withdrawal (e.g., they get anxious/depressed if they are not working), progressive involvement (e.g., they need to work more and more to bolster their feeble self), and they frequently use the primitive defense of denial (e.g., they rationalize their over-work using societal or work-related arguments). These factors negatively influence decision-making and the goals that the workaholic generates. Moreover, such a way of being interferes with the establishment of good interpersonal relations with colleagues, bosses and customers along with other organizational problems (Porter, 1996, pp. 70, 72).

The main problem with this addiction model of workaholism is that the condition is seen in many workaholics who do not significantly present with the typical problems of most alcoholics, at least psychoanalytically speaking, such as their oral dependency and tendency to regress from a genital orientation to a masturbatory one (classical view); the expression of primitive emotions and an inclination to use regressive modes of defense like denial, over-reliance on others who are conceived as strictly need-satisfying objects, and other hugely ill-conceived and ill-fated pseudo-solutions to their problems in living (ego-psychological view); the borderline personality orientation (object-relational view), especially the lack of self-regulation that is typical of most alcoholics (self-psychological view). Indeed, many workaholics do not have the pre-oedipal traumatic histories and the ego deficits associated with most alcoholics, making the addiction model of workaholism a questionable one (ibid., p. 5). Moreover, as I have said, there are workaholics whose behavior is ego-syntonic and not necessarily problematic to family and friends, the "enthusiastic," "happy" and "fulfilled" workaholics mentioned above.

Psychoanalysts have not done much with workaholism, conceived as a unique clinical or proto-clinical condition in the vocational and organizational literatures. Most analysts would probably agree that the typical workaholic can at least, in part, be comprehended in terms of the above three models, that is, by understanding the nature of the pleasure and ego-gratification that work provides to the workaholic, by showing him that his relation to work has some obsessive-compulsive aspects to it, and that he has some of the personality features and behaviors associated with alcoholism and other addictions (Bonebright et al., 2000, p. 470).

It is worth noting that it is often the case that workaholics derive less pleasure from the particular work they are doing than from the act of working itself, an important observation that has been described as the difference between "enjoyment of work and enjoyment of working" (Ng et al., 2007, p. 112). The point is that whatever is motivating the workaholic to so heavily invest in working can be conceived as a powerful cluster of feelings, thoughts and behaviors that appears to have an irrational thrust to it, at least in terms of generating a sensible work/life balance in the eyes of family, friends and concerned others. From a psychoanalytic point of view, when a person's way of being is irrational and it seriously negatively impacts his love and work life, it usually is motivated by unconscious infantile impulses, fears and the like. In the remainder of this section, I want to briefly mention two of what I regard as underappreciated motives that may animate many forms of workaholism, followed by one suggestion on how to begin to put things right.

As is often reported by workaholics and their family and friends, it is typical of a workaholic to feel unsettled if not anxious, troubled or guilty if he is not working. These emotional reactions are an illuminating point of entry to understand what the workaholic may be psychologically seeking in his compulsive working.

The workaholic's anxiety appears to be another example of "fetishization" as described above, the defensive constriction of one's life to one salient emotional/behavioral theme in order to bolster one's shaky self-esteem and sense of self-efficacy. Self-efficacy, says Albert Bandura, the originator of the concept, is that all-important "belief about" a person's "capabilities to produce designated levels of performance that exercise influence over events that affect their lives" (www.uky.edu). The main anxiety that the workaholic seems to be unconsciously experiencing relates to his fear of dying; thus, working is a way of protecting himself from his sense of mortality by fashioning the fantasy that by working, by affirming his power to make things effectively and successfully happen in the workplace, he has guaranteed his immortality. What the workaholic cannot consciously tolerate is awareness that he is radically vulnerable to the same "outrageous fortunes," as Shakespeare put it, as everyone else, the same lack of control over important matters in one's life, including how and when one will die. Robert Jay Lifton has described the positive side of this process as striving for "symbolic immortality," an "experiential transcendence," that intense feeling when "time and death disappear." Such experiences of being enamored with existence centrally involve "losing oneself" and can occur in a number of enthralling contexts: in religious and secular forms of mysticism, "in song, dance, battle, sexual love, childbirth, athletic effort, mechanical flight, or in contemplating works of artistic or intellectual creation" (1976, pp. 33–34). In the case of the workaholic, however, this drive for symbolic immortality has gone terribly awry and has assumed a malignant character in that the workaholic spends enormous amounts of time and effort controlling and perfecting the minutiae of his existence in the workplace rather than the main sources of his anxiety and guilt. It is not surprising that the typical workaholic has an obsessive-compulsive character structure in which the theme of control over oneself and one's environment is the central concern of one's life (Schwartz, 1982, pp. 429, 430). The workaholic's lack of reasonable self-care as reflected in his out of whack work/life balance is rooted in his unwillingness and inability to mourn his lack of control over important matters, specifically, letting go of his omnipotence and magical thinking (Lapierre, 1993, p. 31). As Melanie Klein noted in her insightful discussion of the "depressive position," the workaholic has not come to terms with the fact that the world was not fashioned with him in mind, with satisfying his needs and wishes and the only place he has in it is small and fleeting (Schwartz, 1993, p. 238), and even then, his existence is characterized by frequent struggle, frustration and pain. The well-known American singer and songwriter, Moby, put this point just right in saying, "What fascinates me about addiction and obsessive behavior is that people would choose an altered state of consciousness that's toxic and ostensibly destroys most aspects of your normal life, because for a brief moment you feel okay" (Allen, 2014, p. xxv).

The workaholic is not only prone to anxiety when not working, but he also has that gnawing feeling of having done something wrong, a vague feeling that is usually accompanied by a sense of shame and regret. Sometimes this is manifested in a maudlin presentation, that is, a self-pityingly or tearfully sentimental way of being that is often brought about through drunkenness. The workaholic feels guilty because he has radically failed his family and other significant others, in terms of being mainly for himself rather than for them, and being emotionally remote or "AWOL." While the workaholic will frequently rationalize his over-work as motivated by his wish to give his family a better life, he unconsciously knows this is a lie and that he is mainly motivated by his inordinate narcissistic needs and wishes, such as for greater power and a sense of self-importance. In this sense, his workaholism also has a punitive dimension to it as if the workaholic is saying to himself, "See I am blameless. I have done all that I could, even working to the edge of total exhaustion" for the sake of my family (Rhoads, 1977, p. 2618). The only problem with this affirmation is that the workaholic's guilty conscience is not in the least bit convinced by his own self-serving rhetoric, for it knows that he has committed the "sin" and "crime" of extreme selfishness and relentless power-seeking at the expense of hurting others, especially those who are dear to him. As Jung noted, "Where love reigns, there is no will to power; and where the will to power is paramount, love is lacking. The one is but the shadow of the other" (1966, p. 53).

Freud said in his *The Question of Lay Analysis* that neurotics, similar to work-aholics, "complain of their illness [or their troubling work circumstances], but they make the most of it, and when it comes to taking it away from them they will defend it like a lioness her young" (1926 [1959], p. 222). Indeed, giving up one's workaholism is no easy matter, nor is it easy for a therapist to help transform such people who unconsciously fight change every inch of the way. While there are no quick solutions to the complex and multidimensional problem of workaholism, for it is the lynchpin of the totality of circumstances that constitute a person's way of being in the world, one thing that the average person trying to fashion the "good life" can do is embrace without reserve the ancient moral virtue of moderation, the very opposite of extremism and excess that characterize the workaholic's outlook and lifestyle. Indeed, ancient religious and secular wisdom and spirituality, like Buddha's "middle path" and Aristotle's "golden mean," have always advocated that such a moderate and balanced way of living was the "royal road" to happiness. Freud, too, felt this way: "Just as a cautious business-man avoids investing all his capital in one concern, so wisdom would probably admonish us also not to anticipate all our happiness from one quarter alone" (www.glass-quotes.com). The workaholic unconsciously does exactly what

Freud says is a mistaken way to live in that he puts all of his psychic eggs in one basket. By concentrating all of his resources and prospect in working, he runs the risk that he could lose everything.

Final comment

No man dies but by his own hand. Indeed, while we have focused our discussion on those wrecked by success, stage fright, writer's block and workaholism, there are infinite ways that people can make their work lives into an experience of neurotic misery. Moreover, once one has created such a wretched and appalling work life, it is extremely hard to find a way out of it, as there are no quick or perfect solutions to these problems. While I have suggested some helpful ways that one can begin to "think differently" to better manage these conditions without getting professional help, in many instances, the latter is the most effective way to navigate oneself out of the ordeal one has inadvertently gotten oneself into. This being said, I want to conclude this chapter by reminding the reader that it is often one's inordinate narcissism, frequently expressed in extreme perfectionism, that plays a huge part in one's neurotic work misery. Perfectionists make their work lives torture by the unreasonable, impractical goals that they generate by viewing their errors as a moral indictment, as evidence of their terrible personal flaws. They create high anxiety about possible failure which in their minds is an ever-present background of "unsafety." While the psychology of perfectionism is a topic worthy of a book-length study in itself, one would be prudent to keep in mind, especially in the workplace, the practical wisdom of Vonnegut: "If you can do a half-assed job of anything, you're a one-eyed man in a kingdom of the blind" (www.zquotes.com).

Notes

1 Both of the Freud quotes in this chapter were taken from Mahony (1997).
2 Axelrod (1999) has written a good book on the work life and career of the individual from the point of view of psychoanalytic psychotherapy.
3 More recently, "work/life" balance has been re-named "work-life fit" to put into sharp focus the way workers attempt to cobble together the disparate pieces of their lives (Dominus, 2016, p. 48).
4 It is noteworthy that Freud's conjecture regarding the etiology of "success neurosis," namely, the "forces of conscience," was written seven years prior to the notion of the super-ego becoming part of psychoanalytic vocabulary (Akhtar, 2009, p. 287).
5 There have been notable post-Freudian elaborations of the repetition-compulsion such as Bibring (1941), Loewald (1971) and Casement (1991).
6 Hughes (1905–1976) was a prominent American business tycoon, one of the richest men of his time, who became a mentally ill recluse toward his later years.
7 I have liberally drawn from Glen O. Gabbard (1979, 1983, 1997) in my review of the literature on stage fright, for he has done some of the best work on this subject.
8 For more benign reasons, actors want the audience to suspend their disbelief that what they are viewing is make-believe, and so they do not want them to know that the actor

is strategically and tactically choreographing every word and movement to have its maximum effect on them in maintaining the believability of the make-believe taking place before them.

9 Aaron notes in his study, "by far the most common attempt at coping with the emerging anxiety" associated with stage fright "is to try to immerse oneself in the given circumstances of the play as the first step in the transformation from actor to character." He claims that "this preparation must be done alone" (1986, p. 75).

10 Stage fright can be brought on when the actor senses that he is becoming the character in a manner that is no longer make-believe, as if he is in reality the character, and that the play is not make-believe but is "real" (Aaron, 1986, p. 91).

11 For a detailed discussion of Spolin's version of theater improv, see Marcus, with Marcus (2011, pp. 77–98).

12 Ernest Hemingway described this self-obliteration quite literally: "I learned never to empty the well of my writing, but always to stop when there was still something there in the deep part of the well, and let it refill at night from the springs that fed it" (www.thewritepractice.com/hemingway-quotes/, retrieved 2/11/15).

13 Two other illuminating psychoanalytic studies of writer's block have been written by Zachary Leader (1991) and Joyce McDougall (1989).

14 Bergler's approach to understanding the motivations of writers (indeed, the general psychoanalytic approach has embraced his view for the most part) is that "the writer does not express directly his unconscious wishes, but rather, expresses his secondary unconscious defense against these wishes" (1950, p. 103; 1955, p. 161).

15 If you have writer's block, perhaps you should take the simple advice of American writer Maya Angelou: "What I try to do is write. I may write for two weeks 'the cat sat on the mat, that is that, not a rat.' And it might be just the most boring and awful stuff. But I try. When I'm writing, I write. And then it's as if the muse is convinced that I'm serious and says, 'Okay. Okay. I'll come'" (www.huffingtonpost.com/.../famous-writers-share-h…, retrieved 2/16/15).

References

Aaron, S. (1986). *Stage Fright: Its Role in Acting*. Chicago, IL: The University of Chicago Press.

Akhtar, S. (2009). *Comprehensive Dictionary of Psychoanalysis*. London: Karnac.

Allen, D. A. (2014). *How to Quit Anything in 5 Simple Steps: Break the Chains that Bind You*. Bloomington, IN: Balboa Press.

Axelrod, Steven D. (1999). *Work and the Evolving Self. Theoretical and Clinical Considerations*. Hillsdale, NJ: The Analytic Press.

Bakker, A. B., Demerouti, E. and Burke, R. (2009). Workaholism and Relationship Quality: A Spillover-Crossover Perspective. *Journal of Occupational Health Psychology*, *14*:1, 23–33.

Becker, E. (1969). *Angel in Armor: Post Freudian Perspectives on the Nature of Man*. New York: George Braziller.

Bergler, E. (1949). On Acting and Stage Fright. *Psychiatric Quarterly Supplement*, *23*, 313–319.

Bergler, E. (1950). *The Writer and Psychoanalysis*. Garden City, NY: Doubleday & Company.

Bergler, E. (1955). Unconscious Mechanisms in "Writer's Block." *Psychoanalytic Review*, *42*, 160–167.

Bibring, E. (1941). The Conception of the Repletion Compulsion. *Psychoanalytic Quarterly*, *12*, 486–519.

Bonebright, C. A., Clay, D. and Ankenmann, R. D. (2000). The Relationship of Workaholism with Work-Life Conflict, Life Satisfaction, and Purpose of Life. *Journal of Counseling Psychology*, *47*:4, 469–477.

Britton, R. (1994). Publication Anxiety: Conflict Between Communication and Affiliation. *International Journal of Psychoanalysis*, *75*, 1213–1224.

Burke, R. J. and Matthiesen, S. (2004). Short communication: Workaholicism among Norwegian Journalists: Antecedents and Consequences. *Stress and Health*, *20*, 301–308.

Casement, P. (1991). *Learning from the Patient*. New York: Guilford.

Clark, M. A., Lelchook, A. M. and Taylor, M. L. (2010). Beyond the Big Five: How Narcissism, Perfectionism, and Dispositional Affect Relate to Workaholism. *Personality and Individual Differences*, *48*, 786–791.

Dominus, S. (2016) Parent Companies. In: *The New York Times Magazine*, 2/28/16, p. 48.

Fenichel, O. (1945). *The Psychoanalytic Theory of Neurosis*. New York: W.W. Norton.

Ferenczi, S. (1919) [1980]. *Sunday Neurosis: Further Contributions to the Theory and Technique of Psychoanalysis* (pp. 174–177). J. I. Suttie (Trans.). New York: Bruner/Mazel.

Flugel, J. C. (1938). Stage Fright and Anal Eroticism. *British Journal of Medical Psychology*, *17*, 189–196.

Frankl, V. E. (1963). *Man's Search for Meaning. An Introduction to Logotherapy*. I. Lasch (Trans.). New York: Pocket Books.

Freud, S. (1895) [1985] *The Complete Letters of Sigmund Freud to Wilhelm Fliess*: 1887–1904. J. Masson (Ed.). Cambridge, MA: Harvard University Press.

Freud, S. (1896) [1985]. *The Complete Letters of Sigmund Freud to Wilhelm Fliess*: 1887–1904. J. Masson (Ed.). Cambridge, MA: Harvard University Press.

Freud, S. (1920) [1964]. *Beyond the Pleasure Principle*. In: J. Strachey (Ed. and Trans.), *The Standard Edition of the Complete Psychological Works of Sigmund Freud*, Vol. 18 (pp. 3–66). London: Hogarth Press.

Freud, S. (1923) [1955]. The Ego and the Id. In: J. Strachey (Ed. and Trans.), *The Standard Edition of the Complete Psychological Works of Sigmund Freud*, Vol. 17 (pp. 3–68). London: Hogarth Press.

Freud, S. (1925) [1957]. Some Character-Types Met with in Psycho-analytic Work. In: J. Strachey (Ed. and Trans.), *The Standard Edition of the Complete Psychological Works of Sigmund Freud*, Vol. 14 (pp. 311–333). London: Hogarth Press.

Freud, S. (1926) [1959]. *The Question of Lay Analysis*. In: J. Strachey (Ed. and Trans.), *The Standard Edition of the Complete Psychological Works of Sigmund Freud*, Vol. 20 (pp. 179–249). London: Hogarth Press.

Freud, S. (1974). *The Freud/Jung Letters*. W. McGuire (Ed.). Princeton, NJ: Princeton University Press.

Freundlich, D. (1968). Narcissism and Exhibitionism in the Performance of Classical Music. *Psychiatric Quarterly Supplement*, *42*, 1–13.

Gabbard, G. O. (1979). Stage Fright. *The International Journal of Psychoanalysis*, *60*, 383–392.

Gabbard, G. O. (1983). Further Contributions to the Understanding of Stage Fright: Narcissistic Issues. *Journal of the American Psychoanalytic Association*, *31*, 423–441.

Gabbard, G. O. (1997). The Vicissitudes of Shame in Stage Fright. In: C. W. Socarides and S. Kramer (Eds.), *Work and Its Inhibitions: Psychoanalytic Essays* (pp. 209–220). Madison, CT: International Universities Press.

Gay, P. (1988). *Freud: A Life for Our Time*. New York: Norton.

Gilovich, T. and Savitsky, K. (1999). The Spotlight Effect and the Illusion of Transparency: Egocentric Assessments of How We Are Seen by Others. *Current Directions in Psychological Science*, *8*, 165–168.

Hayes, D. (1975). The Archetypal Nature of Stage Fright. *Art Psychotherapy*, *2*, 279–291.

Hesse, M. (1980). The Exploratory Function of Metaphor. In: M. Hesse, *Revolutions and Reconstructions in Philosophy of Science*. Bloomington: Indiana University Press. Quoted in R. Rorty (1989), *Contingency, Irony, and Solidarity*. New York: Cambridge University Press.

Hirschhorn, L. (1988). *The Workplace Within: Psychodynamics of Organizational Life*. Cambridge, MA: The MIT Press.

Hodgson, J. and Richards, E. (1974). *Improvisation*. New York: Grove Weidenfeld.

Jung, C. G. (1966). *Two Essays on Analytical Psychology*. London: Routledge & Keegan Paul.

Kaplan, D. M. (1969). On Stage Fright. *The Drama Review*, *14*:1, 60–83.

Kieffer, C. C. (2004). Selfobjects, Oedipal Objects, and Mutual Recognition: A Self-Psychological Reappraisal of the Female "Oedipal Victory." *Annual of Psychoanalysis*, *32*, 69–80.

Lapierre, L. (1993). Mourning, Potency, and Power in Management. In: L. Hirschhorn and C. K. Barnett (Eds.), *The Psychodynamics of Organizations* (pp. 19–32). Philadelphia: Temple University Press.

Laplanche, J. and Pontalis, J.-B. (1973). *The Language of Psycho-Analysis*. D. Nicholson-Smith (Trans.). New York: Norton.

Leader, Z. (1991). *Writer's Block*. Baltimore, MD: Johns Hopkins University Press.

Levy, S. T., Seelig, B. J. and Inderbitzin, L. B. (1995). On Those Wrecked by Success: A Clinical Inquiry. *The Psychoanalytic Quarterly*, *64*, 639–657.

Lifton, R. J. (1976). *The Life of the Self: Toward a New Psychology*. New York: Basic Books.

Loewald, H. W. (1971). Some Considerations on Repetition and Repletion Compulsion. *International Journal of Psychoanalysis*, *52*, 59–65.

Lorand, S. (1950). *Clinical Studies in Psychoanalysis*. New York: International Universities Press.

Mahony, P. J. (1997). Freud: Man at Work. In: C. W. Socarides and S. Kramer (Eds.), *Work and Its Inhibitions: Psychoanalytic Essays* (pp. 79–98). Madison, CT: International Universities Press.

Marcus, P., with Marcus, G. (2011). *Theater as Life: Practical Wisdom from Great Acting Teachers, Actors and Actresses*. Milwaukee, WI: Marquette University Press.

McDougall, J. (1989). The Dead Father: Early Psychic Trauma and Its Relationship in Sexual Functioning and Creative Activity. *International Journal of Psychoanalysis*, *70*, 205–219.

Moore, B. E. and Fine, V. D. (Eds.) (1990). *Psychoanalytic Terms & Concepts*. New Haven, CT: American Psychoanalytic Association and Yale University Press.

Ng, T. W. H. and Feldman, D. C. (2008). Long Work Hours: A Social Identity Perspective on Meta-Analysis Data. *Journal of Organizational Behavior*, 29, 850–880.

Ng, T. W. H., Sorensen, K. L. and Feldman, D. C. (2007). Dimensions, Antecedents and Consequences of Workaholism: A Conceptual Integration and Extension. *Journal of Organizational Behavior*, *28*, 111–136.

Oates, W. E. (1971). *Confessions of a Workaholic: The Facts about Work Addiction*. New York: World Pub. Co.

Olinick, S. L. (1997). On Writer's Block: For Whom Does One Write or Not Write? In: C. W. Socarides and S. Kramer (Eds.), *Work and Its Inhibitions: Psychoanalytic Essays* (pp. 183–190). Madison, CT: International Universities Press.

Porter, G. (1996). Organizational Impact of Workaholism: Suggestions for Researching the Negative Outcomes of Excessive Work. *Journal of Organizational Health Psychology, 1*:1, 70–84.

Rhoads, J. M. (1977). Overwork. *Journal of the American Medical Association, 237*:24, 2615–2618.

Rycroft, C. (1995). *A Critical Dictionary of Psychoanalysis* (2nd ed.). London: Penguin.

Safirstein, S. L. (1962). Stage Fright in a Musician. *American Journal of Psychoanalysis, 22*, 15–42.

Schafer, R. (1983). *The Analytic Attitude*. New York: Basic Books.

Schwartz, H. S. (1982). Job Involvement as Obsession-Compulsion. *Academy of Management Review, 7*:3, 429–432.

Schwartz, H. S. (1993). On the Psychodynamics of Organizational Totalitarianism. In: L. Hirschhorn and C. K. Barnett (Eds.), *The Psychodynamics of Organizations* (pp. 237–250). Philadelphia, PA: Temple University Press.

Shafer, R. (1984). The Pursuit of Failure and the Idealization of Unhappiness. *American Psychologist, 39*:4, 398–405.

Simmonds, J. G. and Southcott, J. E. (2012). Stage Fright and Joy: Performers in Relations to the Troupe, Audience and Beyond. *International Journal of Applied Psychoanalytic Studies, 9*:4, 318–329.

Spolin, V. (1986). *Theater Games for the Classroom: A Teacher's Handbook*. Evanston, IL: Northwestern University Press.

Spolin, V. (1999). *Improvisation for the Theater: A Handbook of Teaching and Directing Techniques* (3rd ed.). Evanston, IL: Northwestern University Press.

Szekely, L. (1950). Success, Success Neurosis and the Self. *British Journal of Medical Psychology, 33*, 45–51.

Tuch, R. H. (1995). On the Capacity to be Creative: A Psychoanalytic Exploration of Writer's Block. *Progress in Self Psychology, 11*, 243–257.

Walker, A. (1994). *Everyday Use*. B. T. Christian (ed.). New Brunswick, NJ: Rutgers University Press.

Woolf, V. (2007). *Selected Works of Virginia Woolf*. Hertfordshire, UK: Wordsworth Editions.

Web sources

m.imdb.com/name/nm0000059/quotes, retrieved 1/5/15.

www.articles.chicagotribune.com/.../9001210747_1_humpty-..., retrieved 2/9/15.

www.backstage.com/.../study-shows-stage-fright-is-common..., retrieved 1/23/15.

www.cbn.com/.../spontaneous-50-ways-t..., retrieved 1/28/15.

www.forbes.com/.../another-humorous-view-on-the-fear-of-publi..., retrieved 1/26/15.

www.forbes.com/.../quotes-sayings-proverbs-thoughts-about-wom..., retrieved 2/13/15.

www.glass-quotes.com/quote/24185.html, retrieved 2/18/15.

www.goodreads.com/author/show/1143744.Edmund_Bergler, retrieved 2/15/15.

www.huffingtonpost.com/.../famous-writers-share-h..., retrieved 2/16/15.

www.inkorkeys.wordpress.com/2014/.../what-authors-say-about-writers-block/, retrieved 2/4/15.

www.ivcc.edu/jbeyer/.../Vonnegut.ht...izquotes.com/quote/191292, retrieved 2/6/15.

www.katherinepreston.com/the-importance-spontaniety/#sthash.Hj4dRKcW.dpuf, retrieved 1/28/15.

www.nytimes.com/.../books-of-the-times-books-of-..., retrieved 2/11/15.

www.nytimes.com/2006/10/20/arts/.../20goul.html?..., retrieved 1/22/15.

www.orwell.ru › Library › Essays › Wiw › English, retrieved 2/4/15.

www.panicattacktreatmentreviews.com/celebrities-social-anxiety-disorder-agor...,
    retrieved 1/20/15.

www.poemhunter.com/quotations/famous.asp?people..., retrieved 2/6/15.

www.psychologytoday.com/.../fighting-stage-fright, retrieved 1/22/15.

www.quoteinvestigator.com/2010/06/09/twain-speech/, retrieved 1/23/15.

www.quotes.net/quote/1914, retrieved 2/19/15.

www.theatromathia.gr/theaterland/impro_en.html, retrieved 2/19/15.

www.thewritepractice.com/hemingway-quotes/, retrieved 2/11/15.

www.trainingindustry.com/.../does-today's-market-dictate-your-need-for..., retrieved
    2/14/15.

www.uky.edu/~eushe2/Bandura/BanEncy.html, retrieved 2/18/15.

www.values.com/.../3113-these-are-days-when-no-one-should-rely-undu..., retrieved
    2/2/15.

www.wheelercentre.com/dailies/post/a0cf1a03c5e2/, retrieved 2/15/15.

www.worldofquotes.com/author/Walter+Benjamin/1/index.html, retrieved 2/2/15.

www.zquotes.com/quote/127300, retrieved 2/19/15.

www.zquotes.com/quote/191277, retrieved 2/19/15.

Chapter 5

Psychopathology II: the organization

"Hell is other people," wrote Jean Paul Sartre in his one act masterpiece, *No Exit*. While Sartre was not describing everyday existence in the workplace, he could have been if you believe Gallup's 2013 survey statistics about job satisfaction in the United States: only 30 percent of those employed report feeling engaged and inspired at work, 52 percent have a chronic case of the Monday blues; they're present, but not excited about their job, while the remaining 18 percent are actively disengaged (www.gallup.com). While problems related to job design such as boredom and extrinsic rewards such as low salary contribute to employee unhappiness, explicitly interpersonal factors related to organizational health such as job stress and managerial quality such as overbearing supervision are also key factors. Interestingly, after salary, workplace culture—the character and personality of an organization, its unique values, traditions, beliefs, interactions, behaviors, and attitudes—was the most cited reason for job satisfaction. The better the "fit" between the employee and workplace culture, the happier an employee tends to be (www.usatoday.com; Miller, 2016, p. 36).

Indeed, just about every workplace setting requires near continuous social interaction, whether it is with colleagues, supervisors, managers or leaders (and of course, with the public, such as customers, clients, patients, etc.). For example, a supervisor (and in a different way, any employee) must be able to provide constructive feedback, effectively manage emotional eruptions and complaints, mediate disputes, appropriately respond to criticism, make and deny requests, and assist staff to generate sensible solutions to work-related interpersonal difficulties. A supervisor must also be capable of wisely delegating responsibility, holding fast in the face of resistance to change, convincing others to do things differently, building consensus, presiding over effective meetings, foreseeing and eliminating impediments to communication, dealing with troublesome people, and providing unambiguous instructions. In the context of small groups or teams, a range of social skills for effective collaboration are required, such as providing helpful criticism and positive suggestions and giving encouragement for creative and innovative ideas (Gambrill, 2004, p. 243). Thus, given the extent of social interaction at a typical workplace, it is not surprising that distressing interpersonal conflicts are a common experience. For example, there are conflicts regarding the perception of unfair treatment by a boss such as not receiving a promotion or not getting a salary raise or bonus, a poor "fit" between the employee and the content of a job, dysfunctional team or group dynamics that exclude or snub an employee, and a poor "fit" between the employee and the organizational culture (Frew, 2004, p. 299).

In this chapter I delineate why so many employees (and bosses, for that matter) complain, "this job is driving me crazy." I explore some of the more troubling interpersonal, group and organizational processes that contribute to intense, often longstanding worker unhappiness. While the subjects of job stress and job satisfaction are well-researched in the vocational and organizational literatures, I focus on problems that emerge due to the continuing interaction between the worker and some pathological aspect of his work setting that are particularly receptive to psychoanalytic understanding, such as coping with an irrational boss, small group, or organization. By "pathological" I mean emotions that occur regularly, are powerful, unreasonable, and incapable of being controlled. Moreover, rather than view the distress associated with coping with such irrationality as mainly rooted in individual psychodynamics, I view these illustrative problems in the workplace as the consequence of a dynamic interaction between the individual and the work setting (ibid., p. 295). Put simply, while work can provide a sense of positive identity and meaning and enhance self-esteem and improve self-concept, it can also be the opposite—that is, it can be a deeply destructive experience due to the irrationality that pervades all groups and organizations, irrationality that every employee must continuously struggle with to keep from feeling that his job is driving him "crazy." Most importantly, once work, the activity that a person typically spends the most time doing during a weekday, becomes something one dreads or doesn't look forward to at least a little bit, it robs one of that all-important feeling associated with living the "good life;" namely, that one's everyday existence is justifiable. Without such an overarching meaning structure to fall back on when one faces challenges, difficulties and pathological processes in the work setting, a person is vulnerable to depression and anxiety and other severely undermining psychological problems. The great American writer, reporter, and political commentator Walter Lippman put this point just right: "Man must be at peace with the sources of his life. If he is ashamed of them, if he is at war with them, they will haunt him forever. They will rob him of his basis of assurance, and will leave him an interloper in the world" (Gould, 1993, p. 49).

The irrational boss

"And I particularly like the whole thing of being boss," quipped Golden Globe-winning English actor and producer Hugh Grant, "Boss and employee ... It's the slave quality that I find very alluring" (www.heightcelebs.com). Grant is putting into sharp focus one of the important conscious and/or unconscious motivations that propels a person to passionately want to be a boss, manager or leader;[1] namely, the crude or subtle sadistic pleasure in being a person in charge. Simply put, a person's private need to dominate is gratified in the public setting of the workplace. To some degree such a perverse motivation is probably always operative, depending on the instinctual make-up, defenses, childhood history and other psychological factors of the person. While power is a constituent aspect of human experience and is the "life-blood of organizational life," it also has its "darker" side that workers have to contend with if they are to survive, let alone flourish, on the job (Kets de Vries, 1991, pp. 123, 121). This is an old story, as Emmy Award-winning television journalist Judd Rose noted, "With power comes the abuse of power, and where there are bosses, there are crazy bosses. It's nothing new" (izquotes.com). This being said, if you have to endure a "crazy" boss, your work life can become an utter misery and understanding the psychodynamics can be helpful in better coping with the person, unless the situation becomes so intolerable that finding a new job is the only realistic solution.

There are many different types of "crazy" bosses that emerge in the psychological space on the interface of the person and organization. Researchers have suggested that in general, the most difficult personality types to work with have "high needs for control, perfection, approval and attention" (Aamodt, 2007, p. 501). One study recently found that of 261 senior executives in US companies, about "1 in 5 fits the psychological profile of a psychopath, the same ratio found among prison inmates". Such people generate considerable "chaos and tend to play people off each other" (*The Week*, 9/23/16, p. 6). The most troubling personality/organizational "type" is the extreme narcissist, especially in terms of the regressive, destructive processes that animate their behavior. I focus on the more malignant type of narcissistic boss to put into sharp focus the pathological features that are operative to varying degrees in the less pathological bosses that are more frequently encountered in the workplace.[2] I will describe these psychodynamics from both sides of the pathological relationship: from the mode of the narcissistic boss and from the employee who is ill-fated to be a "satellite in his orbit," as they are in dynamic interplay within the context of an organization that often facilitates and perpetuates such dysfunctional leader/follower relations. Intra-psychic and social conflicts always potentiate and strengthen each other (Kernberg, 1998, p. 13). All work organizations "select and mold character," and they can bring out psychopathology in their employees that was not necessarily there in the first place (Maccoby, 1984, p. 99). Thus, psychopathology, like any kind of behavior, is best phenomenologically conveyed and de-constructed, in terms of individual psychology that is indissolubly context-dependent and setting-specific.

Otto Kernberg, one of the great psychoanalytic theoreticians on the narcissistic personality, has described this kind of character structure, which includes manifestation in leaders in the workplace:

> [Such person's] interpersonal relations are characterized by excessive self-reference and self-centeredness; whose grandiosity and overvaluation of themselves exist together with feelings of inferiority; who are over-dependent on external admiration, emotionally shallow, intensely envious, and both depreciatory and exploitive in their relations with others.
>
> (1979, p. 33)[3]

By way of giving an everyday work context to this clinical definition, in the world of popular culture much of Kernberg's description calls to mind the comedy-drama film based on the novel about a demanding, unempathic fashion magazine editor, Miranda Priestly (played by Meryl Streep), in *The Devil Wears Prada*, or in a much more troubling manner, the Italian-American Mafia "boss" Tony Soprano (played by James Gandolfini) in the T.V. drama series *The Sopranos*. In both of these characters we sense a fragile and feeble sense of self beneath their outward façade of self-confidence and effectiveness. Indeed, such narcissistic bosses, managers and leaders are prone to extreme anger, if not rage, when their self-esteem and self-worth are threatened. In this context, rage is best understood as "love outraged," that is, their fury is a response to what they intensely experience as narcissistic wounding. Such bosses unconsciously construe threats to their self-esteem and self-worth as a violent attack on their delusional feeling that they are totally lovable and perfect. Their rage and power strivings are magical solutions to their profound sense of vulnerability and helplessness (Labier, 1984, p. 15). An unpacking of some of the other salient characteristics of a narcissist boss is provided below.

While the typical narcissistic boss is both extremely self-centered and grandiose, he is also powerfully resentful of others' success, qualities, possessions and luck. Such envy, as Melanie Klein noted, is rooted in the wish to appropriate what is perceived as "good" in the other. The psychological basis of envy is the infant's experience with his mother's gratifying "good breast," the "part-object" symbol of abundant nurturance and unshakeable stability, and his wish to be the ultimate source of such "goodness." Under conditions of frustration, especially of a lack of attunement and understanding to the infant's painful affects by the mother, the infant's envious wishes of the "good breast" become more extreme and morph into a wish to completely exhaust the "good breast," not simply to possess all of its "goodness," but in addition, to intentionally deplete it so that it no longer contains any contents that will evoke envy. While certain forms of envy can spark reasonable ambition, when it is pathological it can lead to intense anguish and paralysis of will (Akhtar, 2009, p. 96), though in the case of the narcissist, most often it turns into hatred. While in the adult, envy is perhaps a more psychologically passive dislike of the other, hatred is its active expression.[4] As Victor Hugo noted in his autobiography, "The wicked envy and hate; it is their [perverse] way of admiring" (Hugo, 1901 [1907], p. 359).

Precisely what the envious person hates in the other varies; however, almost always it has to do with some aspect of the other's capacity for loving, for joyfully being other-directed, other-regarding and other-serving in comportment. Kernberg makes this point rather well, saying "Envious of what they could not themselves enjoy, they had to 'spoil, depreciate and degrade' the capacity others had to find emotional gratification in love" (Lunbeck, 2014, p. 109). As Freud remarked, the envy-driven narcissist lives in a loveless hell because the very act of loving requires an "unselving" or "transelving" that is out of his reach:

"Whoever loves becomes humble [unlike the puffed up narcissist]. Those who love have, so to speak, pawned a part of their narcissism" (www.refspace.com).

Within the context of the workplace, the envious boss will find anyone threatening and highly suspect who displays prosocial behavior and attitudes such as altruism, trust and reflexivity (Richardson and West, 2010, p. 236), or courteousness, being a good sport, or being willing and able to go above and beyond the call of duty for the sake of the greater good (Judge *et al.*, 2006, p. 765), unless it is helping him achieve his own self-serving goals. The narcissistic boss always sees the bad and never the good in what others do, in part due to his competitive nature that cannot tolerate another appearing to be better than him, including in the ethical realm, when derivative behavior related to love is at play as they are when helping a colleague with no expectation of reward. What the narcissistic boss finds so horrifying about "for the other" behavior of a subordinate is that such a person can "lose himself" in others by assisting them to effectively manage the same challenges he may have had to manage himself, which avoids the hazard of becoming inordinately narcissistic like his boss (Kets de Vries, 1991, p. 133). This is one of the important reasons why narcissists can easily work themselves up into a fine lather of moral indignation over something that they believe a subordinate has done wrong (but actually right in the eyes of most others) according to their warped perception. As Erich Fromm aptly pointed out, "There is perhaps no phenomenon which contains so much destructive feeling as moral indignation, which permits envy or hatred to be acted out under the guise of virtue" (1947, p. 235). Such a person has the perverse gratification associated with feeling contemptuous of someone else perceived as threatening and altogether "bad."

When the meaning, direction and purpose of work is only self-glorification, competition and conflict (Huntley, 1997, p. 128), it is not surprising that narcissists are typically unwilling and unable to evaluate their own motives and behavior in detail and depth (e.g., they rely on social clichés and trivialities; Kernberg, 1998, p. 28), and as a result they are not able to make reasonable judgments about what is "good" or "bad" about themselves or others, nor implement ethically animated self-corrections. Thus, narcissists typically have truncated ties to empathy, they are not able to "feel" their way into another person, to engage his deeper needs and wishes, while maintaining a sense of themselves in the process. Since identification and attunement with another person's emotional life is beyond their interest and reach; they focus on superficial markers of a person like status and political expediency as their evaluative touchstones (Rycroft, 1995, p. 47). This is not surprising when we consider what is psychologically entailed in empathic listening. According to Daniel Stern, empathy has four interrelated, interdependent and interactive aspects to it: first, one must be mindful of feeling the other's "inner" state, such as hurt or anger (i.e., the other's feeling must emotionally resonate); second, one must have the intellectual acumen to cognitively conceptualize the hurt or anger as, in fact, hurt or anger, that is, to abstract this empathically derived knowledge from the other's experienced feelings; third, one must be able to use the empathically derived knowledge as the basis for an empathic response to, and for, the other; and last, one must be capable of a fleeting role identification, of putting one's feet in the other's shoes (Akhtar, 2009, p. 93). Thus, without the well-developed capacity to understand and appreciate the other qua other, that is, firstly for his sake rather than with a self-serving agenda, the narcissist who is a boss, manager or leader will not be able to compassionately and effectively interact with subordinates.[5] In short, he has the mindset of any close-minded fundamentalist who is "stuck in one truth," that he is the only one who matters (Friedman, 2015, p. A23).

To make matters even more challenging and unpleasant for subordinates, when narcissistic bosses have been frustrated in actualizing wishes for power and prestige, they may not become briefly depressed or feel a sense of personal failure as with ordinary reasonable people, but rather assume a more paranoid way of being, and this can make organizational life that much more dysfunctional and unbearable for subordinates. Not only do narcissistic leaders ignore and disregard their realistic functions as leader and administrator in an organization, including being properly responsive to the human needs, wishes and values of those they are leading, but they are entirely unaware that they are doing so, and most often they are unconscious that they have created a constellation of pathological relationships of people, tactics and ideas that negatively ripple throughout the organizational culture and create a highly toxic emotional environment (Kernberg, 1979, p. 33; Zaleznik, 1984, p. 309). This observation should not be surprising given the fact that empirical researchers like Penney and Spector (2002, p. 126) found that narcissism was positively correlated with deviant or counterproductive work behaviors (CWB). CWB are actions intended to harm the organization or its members, such as stealing, sabotage, relational aggression, work slowdowns, wasting time and/or materials, and disseminating rumors. Narcissists are also more at ease with ethically dubious sales practices because they feel less obligated to organizational rules, guidelines and property (Judge et al., 2006, p. 76). Destructive narcissists express their narcissistic rage via deviant and CWB (Penney and Spector, 2002, p. 133). Such "emotional contagion," as social psychologists call this tendency to feel and express emotions similar to and influenced by those of others, when animated by the perverse needs, wishes and behavior of a narcissistic boss, are near lethal in terms of its negative impact on the subordinates' moods, motivations and productivity.

Ironically, not only do narcissistic managers and leaders demand the psychological subjugation of their subordinates, they paradoxically also want to be loved and admired by them. Thus, those who interact with them recognize that the only way for them to stay out of the "line of fire," as it were, to feel relatively psychologically safe as an employee, is to approach the boss in a submissive manner that makes him feel thoroughly adulated. In other words, what subordinates learn fairly quickly on the job is to "lay it on like a trowel," that "flattery will get you everywhere" when it comes to interacting with a narcissistic superior. Indeed, Spinoza put this point just right, "None are more taken in by flattery than the proud who wish to be the first and are not" (www.unitedearth. com.au). As a result of this self-aggrandizing outlook, the narcissist only promotes the careers of junior staff and administration to the extent that it is self-serving, and when the juniors want to become more professionally independent and autonomous, and/or they appear to be edging close to the narcissistic boss's level of success, he can become ruthless in his efforts to put the juniors down and undermine their successful career trajectory. For example, a narcissistic manager who envies a more qualified co-worker may seriously overstate and broadcast the co-worker's inconsequential failings, while simultaneously greatly playing down important accomplishments. Even more pathetic, while the narcissist may envy the junior colleagues for their deep inner convictions and professional and human values (his envy being partially a consequence of the above-mentioned superficial moral outlook), his resentment undermines any fragments of those convictions and values that he himself may have (Kernberg, 1979, pp. 34, 35), leaving him feeling even more empty, enraged and retaliatory. An anonymous saying highlights this point: "Resentment is like drinking poison and waiting for the other person to die."

As a consequence of the narcissist's need for continuous ego "stroking" and to feel safe and secure within the organization, the narcissist tends to surround himself with a staff of weak people who always agree with him. This is because the narcissistic boss tends to envelop himself with people he unconsciously regards as reflected images of himself drawn from infantile experiences (Zaleznik, 1984, p. 236). Such sycophants have learned to "play" their boss in a way that satisfies his narcissistic needs while also subtly promoting the manipulative underlings' personal "agenda" for advancement. In a sense, the narcissist surrounds himself with other narcissists operating on a lower register, with people who can happily dwell in such a noxious emotional climate as they share similar psychological characteristics, and this can ironically include a self-promoting propensity for betrayal. As the great Taoist philosopher Chaung Tzu noted, "I have heard that those who are fond of praising men to their faces are also fond of damning them behind their backs" (www.reformtaoism.org). As a result of surrounding himself by those who agree with him, staff members and administrators who would provide more truthful, constructively critical and helpful feedback to enhance the organization are relegated to the margins and can become a disenfranchised "fifth column" that, in a variety of unconscious ways, tends to undermine the healthy and wholesome aspects of the organizational culture. Usually, the narcissistic boss senses there are rebellious forces at work in the organization and this can bring out paranoid tendencies and mean-spirited behavior that further create a poisonous emotional environment for everyone. In such instances, the narcissistic boss may fall into a dire state of mind, as he cannot discern constructive criticism from often-imagined menacing rumblings. As Emerson noted in his journal, "Let me never fall into the vulgar mistake of dreaming that I am persecuted whenever I am contradicted" (1984, p. 206). Paradoxically, the resentment that the narcissist boss feels when criticized is experienced unconsciously as proof that he deserved the criticism, further fueling his hurt and outrage. Needless to say, having to work with and for such an obsessively anxious, unreasonably suspicious boss is nothing short of nightmarish.

Kernberg makes the important point that the more the administrative structure of an organization becomes corrupted by the narcissist's perverse leadership needs and typical defenses, such as his use of splitting, primitive dissociation of the ego[6] and projective identification, "the more compensating mechanisms may develop in the form of breakdown of boundary control and boundary negotiations so that the institutional functions may actually go 'underground'" (1979, p. 35). In other words, the organization begins to unconsciously re-make itself in the image of narcissistic leaders' "crazy" internal object worlds and their accumulated perceptions get disseminated (Kets de Vries and Miller, 1985, p. 590) such that the separation between self and other becomes very fuzzy. Narcissists mainly relate to others as extensions of themselves, so what they want and expect from others must be satisfied; if not, the other does not exist, reasonable boundaries and limits that define us from others and foster a modicum of personal integrity and wholesome organizational culture tend to give way to warped emotions and reactions, distorted perceptions, questionable moral values, dubious goals and concerns and alienating and destructive social roles. Gone is the sense of psychological safety that is correlated with having a relatively clear self-definition.[7] Social order within the organization tends to become eroded, which causes confusion about one's relationships to others, and that all-important sense of empowerment that we derive from reasonable boundaries regarding how we will be treated by others becomes seriously compromised (www.glassmanpsyd.com). In such an amorphously "sick" emotional environment where behavior that causes individual and collective harm is commonplace, it is nearly impossible for an individual or organization to function properly, especially when most of what emotionally and practically "really matters" to the individual and organization is clandestine.

Take, for example, the narcissistic boss's use of defensive splitting, most basically defined as "the separating of positive feelings and perceptions, either toward the self or toward others, from negative feelings and perceptions so that the self and object is seen as either 'all good' or 'all bad'" (Person *et al.*, 2005, p. 560). While there are many subtleties to the various formulations of the confusing concept of splitting in the psychoanalytic literature, Kernberg notes the "defensive division of the ego, in which what was at first [in the infantile ego] a simple defect in integration [of distinguishing the pleasurable and unpleasurable] is then used actively for other purposes [like managing anxiety and maintaining self-esteem], is in essence the mechanism of splitting" (Akhtar, 2009, p. 270). Consider how horrible it would be to have to work with a boss where the defensive use of splitting is a common occurrence. The narcissistic boss has an inability to relate to you with any ambivalence or ambiguity; he cannot reside in the "gray zone," the psychic space of half-tints where most of us as fallible and flawed humans live the majority of the time. Rather, you are judged as either "all good," such as supportive and kind, or "all bad," such as rejecting and mean-spirited. The narcissist runs his interpersonal world demanding loyalty and devotion; "Are you with me, or against me?" is his watchword, as winning is all that matters. Such a boss has major fluctuations in his confidence in his own worth or abilities; his self-esteem and self-respect are insecurely anchored in any robust narrative of self-identity and dearly held beliefs and values. Narcissistic bosses are prone to intense expression of feelings, both negative and positive, which are hard for subordinates to metabolize and reasonably manage. Narcissistic bosses tend to make decisions without adequate consequential thinking because their sense of omnipotence leads them to believe that they will always get it right. Rather than focusing on working through the details of a work project, they are only interested in the grand scheme that prevents projects from coming to fruition (Lubit, 2002, p. 130). Moreover, their lack of impulse control in relations with others does not register as something problematic, let alone guilt-inducing *vis-à-vis* the other when they get things wrong (ibid.). To make matters worse, most of the time narcissists are unconscious of how they use splitting in a myriad destructively self-regulative ways. That is, they do not realize that their self-referential perceptions are gross distortions of social reality, which leaves the subordinate with no reasonable person with whom concerns may be expressed or conflicts resolved. In such a context, for the sake of self-preservation, the underling tends to frequently behave fraudulently, if not becoming something of an imposter in his overall way of relating to his boss, co-workers, and worst of all, to himself, eroding his sense of self-respect and personal dignity.

The narcissistic boss's use of projective identification makes organizational life feel even more "crazy" for the subordinate than his use of "splitting." Similar to splitting, projective identification is a confusing and complex notion in the psychoanalytic literature, though a serviceable definition for our purposes could be, "a fantasy in which one inserts oneself, or part of oneself, into an instinctual object [i.e., a person invested with powerful emotional significance] in order to possess it, control it, or harm it" (Colman, 2009, p. 607). Most importantly perhaps, projective identification always commences with the denial and rejection of troubling emotions lodged in a person's unconscious fantasy of a situation (Krantz and Gilmore, 1991, p. 309). While projective identification can have its positive role in child and adult development (e.g., it can be a mode of communication and the basis of empathy), it has its important defensive functions in that it shields the projector from an unpleasant feature of his own self-experience, including fusing with an external object (i.e., with a real person, place or thing that he has invested with considerable psychic energy and suffused with important emotional significance) in order to avoid painful separation; control of the destructive "bad object" (i.e., the split-off, frustrating and hated part of the self that has been projected onto the object, the other) which is experienced as a menacing, persecutory threat to the person's survival; and the safeguarding of "good," gratifying and loved aspects of the self by splitting them off and projectively depositing and identifying them in the sheltering other for "safe keeping" (Moore and Fine, 1990, p. 109).

The most troubling relational aspect of projective identification for the target is that powerful feelings are evoked, giving him the unsettling sense that he has been inhabited by the projective element, which most often in the narcissist's case is a "bad" feeling that needs to be jettisoned, like envy or hatred. It is as if the target has been taken over by something like a "dybbuk," which in Jewish folklore is a malevolent spirit of a dead person, a demon believed capable of taking over a living person's body and controlling his behavior unless exorcised by a religious ceremony. As I have indicated, in projective identification the projector identifies with the target person and thus can control the target while also unconsciously pressuring the target to play out the designated role to gratify the projector's infantile wishes and/or sinister needs. For example, a dependent boss may insinuate that he needs assistance, even though he does not actually require it, and the target complies with his subtle demand, thus manipulated by the control of the "dependent" boss. An angry or depressed boss may accuse the target of being angry or depressed to such a degree that he actually becomes angry or depressed. A boss who feels "crazy" may relentlessly accuse the target of being "crazy" (he projects his "crazy" thoughts and feelings into the other), with the aim of making the target believe that he is in fact "crazy." Such manipulation of a person by psychological tactics into doubting their own sanity is famously called "gaslighting." Likewise, the narcissist's lack of moral scruples and impressive "street smarts," the shrewd ability to survive hostile situations, allow him to engage in various forms of scapegoat behavior (Lubit, 2002, p. 129). Finally, Kets de Vries cites another good example of projective identification involving a high-level group of business executives in a department. First, they deny or reject (and thus downwardly modify) a painful experience to their self-concept and self-esteem by fantasizing that it belongs to another group of executives. The other group, the recipients of the projection, are then drawn into the situation and induced by subtle pressure from the first group to feel, think, and act in accordance with the received projection (Kets de Vries, 2011, p. 38).

It is worth noting that one of the appealingly seductive qualities of the narcissist, at least initially, is that he often exudes great powers of charm and influence. While the digital revolution has undeniably "sped up, flattened out and depersonalized communication," and the capacity for charm, the power or quality of giving delight or arousing admiration, has for the most part "become a lost language and forgotten skill," the narcissist has honed his ability "to entrance/allure/captivate" someone else in order to manipulatively win them over (Doonan, 2015, p. 10). Such charisma can have a short-term positive impact on subordinates and organizations since the heightened personal expansiveness, if not grandiosity, of the narcissist can stimulate excitement and prompt an upsurge of fleeting productivity in employees and organizations. However, such temporary individual and collective enhancement gives way to the pathological aspects of the narcissist's way of being with others, a mode of comportment that demands dependency, compliance and agreement. In such a subjugating emotional environment, there is little motivation and opportunity for worker creativity, innovation or other kinds of autonomously driven change. In fact, in part due to the prevalence of the narcissist's powerful conscious and unconscious envy, his tendency to diminish and denigrate others, his lack of "deep" moral values, and his insatiable need for novelty and high-octane excitement that is a defense against affective self-awareness, he is not able to satisfy the reasonable dependency needs of those around him, such as for compassionate listening, responsibly helping workers with their realistic problems and concerns, and affirming the subordinates' wishes for approval and warm relations with an authority figure. Moreover, from the organizational point of view, when employees feel unsupported the collective tends to split into two groups, "the submissive and dependent ingroup and the depressed and angry outgroup" (Kernberg, 1979, p. 36). When there is an ingroup, an extremely cohesive and closed social unit that fosters preferential treatment for its members and emphasizes loyalty among them and to their narcissistic boss, and an outgroup, one that is different from one's own that is most often an object of hostility or abhorrence, something unconsciously resembling a psychological "war zone" has been co-produced, and the integrity, functionality and creativity of an organization becomes seriously compromised.

Before I discuss the difficult problem of how one can individually "manage" and organizationally "contain" a destructive narcissistic boss, manager or leader, or for that matter, a co-worker (Lubit, 2002), I want to round out my portrait of a narcissist by mentioning some of these different narcissistic "subtypes." While there are many similarities to how a "destructive narcissist" (ibid.) behaves, there are some subtle differences in their way of being that are worth distinguishing.

Kets de Vries and Lapierre characterize the unconscious fantasies that animate three types of narcissistic leaders, each with a different experience of their early parenting. The most severe kind and the most difficult leader to work with is the "reactive narcissist." He fantasizes, "I was let down and I deserve to be compensated; I have special rights." Such a leader comes into being mainly as a result of parenting that consistently lacked attunement, meaning his parental caregivers were emotionally unresponsive and rejecting. The "self-deceptive" narcissist fantasizes, "I was so favored that I must be (or I am) perfect." This sort of person was encouraged by their delusional parents to believe that they were totally lovable and perfect, regardless of their contrary behavior and lack of supportive evidence of their child's alleged god-like state. The "constructive narcissist" that is equated with "normal" or "healthy" narcissism, has the fantasy, "I have special talents that allow me to make an impression on the world, but I have to deal with my personal limitations and those imposed by external reality" (Kets de Vries and Miller, 1985, pp. 591, 592, 593; Lapierre, 1991, p. 73). Such a person is blessed with a "good enough mother" (that is, an effective parental caregiver). As Winnicott described it, such a mother calls to mind a master gardener: "The good-enough mother ... starts off with an almost complete adaptation to her infant's needs, and as time proceeds she adapts less and less completely, gradually, according to the infant's growing ability to deal with her failure." Moreover, "this active adaptation demands an easy and unresented preoccupation with the one infant; in fact, success in infant-care depends on the fact of devotion, not on cleverness or intellectual enlightenment." As a result of such parental attunement, understanding and support, the child develops a robust sense of self-esteem and self-confidence (Winnicott, 1953, p. 94). It is precisely such "structural cohesiveness, temporal stability, and positive affective coloring of the self-representation" that are the hallmarks of the "constructive narcissist" (Stolorow, 1975, p. 198).

Kernberg (1979, p. 36) further elaborates some of the narcissistic subtypes. He mentions the psychological scenario in which the narcissistic leader's powerful wish to be successful and achieve great things in his job has not been realized due to external impediments beyond his control, often leading to a depressive reaction [in fact, narcissists take individual credit when they are successful while privately blaming situational factors and others for their failures (Campbell *et al.*, 2005, p. 1359)]. In such contexts, "inner circle" subordinates become roughly the "parental caregivers" to the deflated boss, spending inordinate amounts of time and effort in propping up his self-esteem and protecting his fragile emotional equipoise. Moreover, such subordinates' behavior may reinforce restitutive fantasies that are unconsciously exploited as rationalizations for their self-serving association to the narcissistic boss in the first place (Zaleznik, 1984, p. 237). With so much effort on the part of subordinates to shore up and shield the narcissistic boss from further distress, taking effective care of the organization is often sacrificed, which leads to a range of organizational problems.

Another "type" of narcissistic leader is the one whose infantile need to be unconditionally loved combines with his need for complete control of important decision-making without considering the moral context in terms of what is "right" and "wrong," and/or what are the realistic needs for the organization to flourish. Rather than being mindful of what is improper or immoral, the narcissistic boss is animated only by what is self-servingly convenient and practical. Moreover, this is done with considerable interpersonal finesse and without any guilt or anxiety. One could say that the narcissistic boss embraces a moral outlook well summarized by British playwright and novelist W. Somerset Maugham, "You can't learn too soon that the most useful thing about a principle is that it can always be sacrificed to expediency" (Ratcliffe, 2011, p. 300). Kernberg gives a good description of such a narcissistic type of leader:

> [He] is a 'nice guy' with no enemies, who seems slightly insecure and easily changeable, and who at the time is extremely expert in turning all conflicts among his staff into fights that do not involve himself. The general narcissistic qualities of shallowness, inability to judge people sensitively, inability to commit oneself to any values, are dramatically evident in his case, but what seems to be missing is the direct expression of grandiosity and the need to obtain immediate gratification from other people's admiration. At times this

kind of leader obtains the gratification from his position by using it as a source of power and prestige beyond the organization itself. He may let the organization run its own course trying to keep things smooth, so long as his power base is stable.

(Kernberg, 1979, p. 37)

Another variation on the above type of narcissistic leader that has a similarly dismal consequence for an organization pertains to those leaders whose repressed sadistic wishes and feelings are expressed at a conscious level in a radically contrasting form. Such reaction formation is evident in a leader who treats his immediate administrative subordinates in a welcoming and solicitous manner, but his way of behaving to the next level of subordinates is characterized by mean and nasty high-conflict. A final type of narcissistic leader is one who has become the head of an organization due to high-level professional accomplishments, but while he willingly becomes the organizational leader rather than actively assume the hands-on responsibilities, he ignores and avoids his designated leadership role and focuses on other personal interests that he finds more satisfying and self-promoting. This is not simply a matter of decentralized leadership; it is an example of an opportunistic leader who enjoys the trappings of being the head person while actually relinquishing individual responsibility for the everyday running of the organization. Rather than emotionally and practically engaging in the "nuts and bolts" of organizational life, especially making the tough decisions that are necessary to effectively lead an organization, the narcissist pursues his own pet interests and allows the organization to go adrift with no concern for how his irresponsible behavior negatively impacts others (ibid., p. 37).

Despite the troubled and troubling personality and behavior of the typical narcissistic boss, manager and leader, such individuals are actually quite adept at getting into positions of authority in many organizations. This is in part because they are incredibly good at pitching themselves in a way that is seductively impressive. With such intense drive and honed powers of manipulation they rise to the top of the hierarchy. For example, as Lubit (2002, pp. 134–135) aptly notes, while destructive narcissists have almost always had problems in previous jobs, those making decisions about hiring and transfer rely on testimonials from people they know or give too much weight to their favorable impression from a one-off interview rather than engage in the due diligence of sufficiently performing and using in-depth background checks. Destructive narcissists often know influential people who endorse their job application and they perform well in superficial interviews, re-writing their work history and concealing mistakes and failures while exuding self-confidence that masks the discrepancy between what they seem to be and what they are. In the case of managerial transfers, destructive narcissists have typically moved around a lot within an organization in an attempt to hide their mistakes before anyone notices.

Another reason why destructive narcissists are successful in an organization is because the organizational culture approves of such leaders. The wise statement, "you get the life you deserve," also applies to organizational culture. For instance, rather than emphasize a "balance scorecard," organizations mainly focus on short-term profits, and they thus pay little heed to the human cost of how managers facilitate these good short-term results. The higher-ups may not be mindful of or care how underlings and employees have been poorly treated as long as the "bottom line" has been accomplished: subordinates have not been professionally developed and enhanced, and there is lack of teamwork, *esprit de corps* and morale. In fact, as Lubit further points out, most organizations do not have "360 degree feedback[8] or do not make significant use of it in promotion and compensation decisions," rather they only rely on short-term profits or sales to give financial rewards to subordinates. Likewise, with their need and skillfulness to self-promote and self-glorify, destructive narcissists tend not to do well in organizations that mainly use teams, because the ability to work effectively and efficiently in these group contexts is notably limited (ibid.). That such individuals regard competition as more important than cooperating and that they are frequently interpersonally dismissive, abrasive and distrustful makes them unwilling and unable to be good team players (Judge *et al.*, 2006, p. 772).

Thus, the capacity of a subordinate to effectively cope with such a wretched and appalling character as a narcissist boss, manager or leader is no easy task, though in many instances being able to do it is necessary to survive at a job. Put differently, the ability to skillfully negotiate the "harshness" of life, as Freud called it, including in one's challenging work situation is a constituent aspect of the art of living the "good life."

Some tips on coping with the narcissistic boss, manager or leader

A narcissistic boss is very challenging to effectively manage, especially for a subordinate. The best way of containing them is to keep your distance, what can be called strategic and tactical avoidance. Lubit has claimed "moving to another position within the company in order to avoid the destructive narcissist manager is generally the best long-term strategy" (2002, p. 137). Moreover, once a subordinate has moved out of the psychologically uninhabitable position, the competent subordinate is more threatening to the narcissistic manager and is someone he wants to undercut or retaliate against, so the subordinate should report to his new superiors verbally and in writing how he and co-workers have been poorly treated [preferably with co-workers since there is strength and protection in numbers (ibid.)].

Savvy subordinates have learned what the triggers are that set a narcissist boss or manager off and do their best to stay away from them. For example, they have learned that gossiping with such people, or other types of casual conversations that are not carefully thought through can go wrong in unanticipated ways later for the subordinate. Borrowing something from a narcissistic boss, or lending him something, is likely to put the subordinate in harm's way. It is best to get written directives from the boss rather than rely on verbal ones since narcissists are prone to self-servingly interpret ambiguous information at the expense of the subordinate. Getting important information in writing reduces the uncertainty and chance that a complaint will be lodged against the subordinate. It's important for the subordinate to carefully document his work to protect himself from possible allegation of failings or wrongdoings on the job. This documentation can be very useful when you have to defend yourself to higher-ups who, in most cases, are psychologically and organizationally allied with superiors rather than subordinates (ibid.).

It should be emphasized that a narcissistic boss is not willing and able to have a reasonable give-and-take discussion about something that is troubling a subordinate. This is in part because they are markedly intolerant of hearing, let alone effectively metabolizing, constructive criticism and taking self-corrective action. Similarly, with their truncated ties to empathy, the narcissistic boss is prone to say nasty and mean things to a subordinate who wants to raise an interpersonal or other problem that implicates the boss. Taking to heart what a narcissistic boss says to or about a subordinate can be psychologically lethal in terms of maintaining emotional equipoise, just as getting into a quarrel or lively discussion with them can be futile, if not dangerous in terms of the narcissist's tendency to engage in punitive retaliation like making the subordinate look bad to superiors and co-workers.

Other sensible advice on how to best manage a narcissistic co-worker (or boss) includes setting clear and consistent boundaries with them. For example, a narcissist co-worker who enters your office and borrows things without your consent needs to be firmly but skillfully held accountable. Likewise, such destructive narcissists frequently expect favors but almost never do them in return, and this should not be taken personally. Co-workers who are prone to give instructions as if they were in fact your superiors need to be effectively confronted. Narcissistic co-workers are also willing and able to steal your good ideas so you had better let your superiors know your ideas in writing to protect yourself before sharing them with co-workers. Finally, if a co-worker tells you that the boss wants you to do something, first request a clarification about what your tasks and responsibilities are from your boss for such co-workers are known "to play fast and loose" with the truth (ibid.).

Most importantly, when dealing with the hostile and degrading words and actions of a destructive narcissistic boss or co-worker, one should keep in mind the self-protective insight embedded in Sartre's explanation of his often misinterpreted statement from *No Exit* mentioned in the first line of this chapter, "hell is other people":

> "Hell is other people" has always been misunderstood. It has been thought that what I meant by that was that our relations with other people are always poisoned, that they are invariably hellish relations. But what I really mean is something totally different. I mean that if relations with someone else are twisted, vitiated [as with the narcissistic boss] then that other person can only be hell. Why? Because … when we think about ourselves, when we try to know ourselves … we use the knowledge of us which other people already have. We judge ourselves with the means other people have and have given

us for judging ourselves. Into whatever I say about myself someone else's judgment always enters. Into whatever I feel within myself someone else's judgment enters. But that does not at all mean that one cannot have relations with other people. It simply brings out the capital importance of all other people for each one of us.

(https://mraybould.wordpress.com)[9]

The "take home" point of Sartre's insight is that when dealing with a destructive narcissist boss, manager, leader or co-worker (or, for that matter, with anyone), the overarching goal is to do the best you can to never align yourself with anyone else's description of yourself. If you relinquish responsibility for your own self-definition and behavior, you will lose your "inner center of gravity" and will be left to the mercy of others' judgments and opinions, and in the case of the narcissistic boss, this leads to an orgy of disorder and interpersonal hell.

Finally, it is worth noting that at least one recognized company, Zappos, an online shoe and clothing shop based in Las Vegas, has implemented the radical idea that employees are more likely to function better without any managers and bosses. Indeed, CEO Tony Hsieh has eliminated all job titles and management positions, replacing it with an operating model called "holacracy," a total system for self-organization (*The Week*, 5/22/15, p. 33; www.holacracy.org). Holacracy is a novel way of running an organization that takes away power from a management hierarchy and distributes it across well-delineated roles that can then be performed autonomously, without the intrusion of a micromanaging boss. Thus, holacracy promotes a more democratic organizational culture compared to the conventional quasi dictatorship, while also encouraging more experimentation and transparency. Rather ironically, in a holacracy, the work is actually more structured than in a traditional company with its top-down command and control approach, but in a markedly different way. With holacracy there is an unambiguous set of rules and processes for how a team divides its work, and defines its roles, with clearly articulated responsibilities and expectations (www.holacracy. org). Whether this "flat management," shared leadership approach that strives to facilitate structure and discipline to a peer-to-peer work context is in the long run going to enhance creativity and performance is still an open question (www. holacracy.org).

The irrational work group

"In individuals, insanity is rare," said Nietzsche in *Beyond Good and Evil*, "but in groups, parties, nations, and epochs, it is the rule" (Christian, 2012, p. 494). While less pithy in his formulation, Freud made a similar point:

Some of [a group's] features—the weakness of intellectual ability, the lack of emotional restraint, the incapacity for moderation and delay, the inclination to exceed every limit in the expression of emotion and to work it off completely in the form of actions—these and similar features ... show an unmistakable picture of a regression of mental activity to an earlier stage such as we are not surprised to find among savages or children.

(1921 [1955], p. 117)

Indeed, given the emotional environment of the work world today with its cutthroat rivalries and competition, the more limited nature of important resources, and the amplified financial accountability (Youssef and Luthans, 2010, p. 285), it is not surprising that there has been an upsurge of the use of team-based working in organizations [for example, one 2001 survey indicated that 72 percent of Fortune 1000 companies use teams (Aamodt, 2007, p. 490)]. Compared to individuals more or less working in isolation, "teams can integrate and link to produce synergies that individuals cannot," often leading to "outstanding productivity and innovation" (Richardson and West, 2010, pp. 235, 236). However, while teams can help streamline inefficient processes, expand and deepen employee participation, improve quality, and create a positive sense of a shared accountability in which employees are both individually responsible but share in rewards and losses (Twenge and Campbell, 2010, p. 30), the fact is that teams also frequently get "off track," sometimes pathologically, and it is this aspect of team functioning and its negative impact on the individual trying to flourish, to create the "good life" in the workplace, on which I will focus.[10]

The psychology of work literature has empirically demonstrated what tends to bring about optimal team or small group functioning in the workplace. As summarized by researchers Richardson and West: 1) teams have an inspiring task and clear objectives; 2) team members are clear about their roles and those of their team colleagues; 3) teams have an autonomy and authority to decide the means of accomplishing their objectives; 4) teams regularly review their performance and how it can be improved; and 5) teams have an excellent team leader who has the skills to develop effective team processes (2010, p. 246).

The above practical guidelines are very helpful for the successful implementation of team-based working, including increasing group cohesion, the building of positive relationships, and the accelerated expansion and deepening of creativity and personal growth (Sole, 2006, p. 805). This being said, when one gets down to the "nuts and bolts" of implementing these five guidelines, one realizes that it is much easier said than done. Individuals working as part of a team or other kind of small group have tremendous resistance to rationally approaching their tasks and collaboratively implementing sensible and realistic procedures to accomplish their goals. There are mostly unconscious, irrational forces at work that tend to undermine, if not obliterate, that wonderful human capacity for combined action of a group of people that is effective and efficient. High levels of intra-team conflict, such as frequent and intense disagreements, tensions and personal frustrations can characterize teams that get "off track." In fact, according to one organizational psychology researcher, "[t]he scientific literature suggests that teams are seldom more effective than individuals" (Aamodt, 2007, p. 495).

Before reviewing the details of some of these destructive processes that impede successful teamwork, I want to summarize what is probably the most important single psychoanalytic theoretical contribution to understanding small group processes, namely, the work of Wilfred R. Bion. Bion's descriptions in his *Experiences in Groups* (1959) of the primitive defenses, object relations, and anxieties that can implode a group's high-level functioning have become "classic" in the psychology of group processes (Kernberg, 1998, pp. 92–93). Moreover, his work on groups is regarded as "a cornerstone of the study of organizational dynamics" (Kets de Vries, 2011, p. 32). This is especially noteworthy as his observations and formulations relate to the sub-specialty of psychotherapy—group psychotherapy, a field that has greatly contributed to the psychoanalytic understanding of both small and large group processes, dynamics and psychopathology. Ironically, group psychotherapy is a field that is currently characterized by "theoretical confusion and contradiction in both theory and practice … [and is] bewildering in its diversity" (Nitsun, 2015, p. 63).

Bion's view of small group behavior

Bion defines his famous basic group assumptions as "the capacity of the individual for instantaneous combination with other individuals in an established pattern of behavior" (1959, p. 160). In other words, basic assumptions are the unconscious group dynamics, the "common, agreed upon, and anonymous obedience prevalent in a group at a given time" (Akhtar, 2009, p. 33). When a group is lodged in a basic assumption, its capacity to work efficiently and effectively is seriously compromised, often leading to more primitive, archaic and infantile modes of behavior that make the realistic business of the team nearly impossible to reasonably engage in. Bion describes three types of basic assumption: dependency, fight-flight, and pairing, though others have formulated fourth, fifth and sixth assumptions, namely "oneness" (Turquet, 1975), further elaborated as "incohesion: aggregation/massification" (Hopper, 2003); "Me-ness" (Bain and Gould, 1996); and "violent destructive aggression" mainly expressed in large groups (Roth, 2013, p. 527). These latter three assumptions have not "caught on" in small group theory the way Bion's three assumptions have, and Nitsun raises the criticism that any conceptualization of basic assumptions tends to create "confusion and overlap … between different versions of assumptions" as well as arbitrary "fixed polarities" that do not do justice to the real-life complexity and fluidity of group process (Nitsun, 2015, p. 243).

The first Bionic assumption, dependency, "is that the group is met in order to be sustained by a leader on whom it depends for nourishment, material and spiritual, and protection" (Bion, 1959, p. 132). This basic assumption thus postulates a "collective belief in a protective deity, leader, or organization that will always provide security for the group" (Akhtar, 2009, p. 33). For example, the group leader may ask a thought-provoking question only to be received by the members with passive silence, as if he had not spoken at all. The leader may be idealized into something of an omnipotent and omniscient god who can perfectly look after his docile children, a role that certain types of overly zealous leaders may be prone to assuming. However, resentment at being dependent on the god-like leader may gradually stimulate in the group members the wish to depose the leader, if not "kill" him off, and then look for a new leader, only to repeat the destructive process (http://achakra.com).

As Kets de Vries points out, groups that are under the sway of the dependency assumption seek out a charismatic leader because, like small children, they feel helpless, inadequate, needy, and are afraid of the external world. In such groups one frequently hears such statements as "What do you want me/us to do"? Or, "I can't take this kind of decision; you'll have to talk to my boss." Moreover, while group cohesiveness and goal directedness may be keen in such groups, for the most part the group is not capable of autonomy, criticality or creativity. Even when the leader has left the group and they can, in principle, independently grow and develop, they tend to reside in a retrospective consciousness, fantasizing about what the long-lost leader/parent would have done in a decision-making situation if he still was the leader of the group. In such instances, the group may fall back on bureaucratic inactivity and apathy and, thus, function without a trace of initiative or innovation (2011, p. 33).

The flight-fight group assumption "is that the group has met to fight something or to run away from it. It is prepared to do either indifferently" (Bion, 1959, p. 138). In other words, the group believes in "the existence of an external enemy who one must vanquish or avoid" (Akhtar, 2009, p. 33). An important characteristic of this group culture is that it puts into sharp focus the individual with "paranoid trends," causing the work world to be divided into those who are loved friends and hated enemies, an "us-versus-them" outlook (Bion, 1959, p. 63; Kets de Vries, 2011, p. 33). As Kets de Vries notes, fight responses are expressed in aggressive behavior against the colleagues, bosses or the self. "Envy, jealousy, competition, elimination, boycotting, sibling rivalry, fighting for a position in the groups and privileged relationships with authority figures" are typical reactions in this group culture. Flight reactions may include avoidance of colleagues, managers and bosses, absenteeism and an overall comportment of having given up caring. Common remarks of such groups are "Let's not give those updated figures to the contracts department; they'll just try to take all the credit," and "This company would be in good shape if it weren't for the so-and-sos who run the place." In addition, there is a lack of embracing of individual responsibility in such groups; rather, there is a marked tendency to project and externalize, blaming others for one's mistakes or for the team's lack of success. In such groups there is an inevitable strengthening of group cohesion and identity and increased dependence on a strong, charismatic leader who self-righteously fosters this "you are either with us, or against us" way of thinking, and further "fires up" group members to adhere to their irrational group mentality (Kets de Vries, 2011, p. 33).

Finally, we come to the pairing group assumption, "the opposite pole to feelings of hatred, destructiveness, and despair" that may exist in fight-flight group cultures, what Bion describes as "the air of the hopeful expectation." The function of the pairing group "is to provide an outlet for feelings centered on ideas of breeding and birth, that is to say for Messianic hope, … a precursor to sexual desire," and "without ever arousing the fear that such feelings will give rise to an event that will demand development" (1959, pp. 136, 143). Thus, the pairing basic assumption expresses "the messianic hope that someone from the future generations will solve the problems of the group" (Akhtar, 2009, p. 33). As Kets de Vries notes, the pairing assumption is a way for an individual group member to connect to a perceived powerful other, a colleague, manager or boss, and assist him in effectively managing his "anxiety, alienation and loneliness." Not only does such a tactic provide a modicum of safety and security, it satisfies the fantasy that by connecting with a powerful other, individual and collective creativity will magically upsurge. This being said, when there is pairing, there is a loss of group integrity in that sub-groups emerge via the splitting up process and create both intra- and inter-group disagreements, including ganging up against, even bullying the designated aggressor, whether they be a colleague, manager or boss. In high-tech companies, for example, where there is a tendency toward individuals maintaining grandiose notions, the pairing assumption leads to an underplaying of feasibility and profitability in favor of co-produced fantasies of creative breakthroughs and innovation. In pairing assumption teams, one typically hears statements like "Leave it to the two of us, we can solve this problem" or "If only the CEO and COO had a better relationship our company would be in really good shape" (Kets de Vries, 2011, pp. 33, 34).

The main thrust of Bion's contribution to the psychology of small group process, including team-based working, is that when the group is under the sway of one of the basic assumptions, it cannot reasonably think, so it becomes "psychotic, albeit temporarily," engaging in "patterns of psychotic behavior" (Bain and Gould, 1996, p. 119; Bion, 1959, p. 165). For example, there are severe impairments in representing, mentalizing, remembering, and acknowledging, mainly because the group's tendencies for direct hallucinatory gratification of early developmental wishes for safety and security have a strong interpretive grip on the group process (Roth, 2013, pp. 535, 527). That is, Bion's brilliant two-tier psychology of the small group shows how the internal mental state of the group, the "group culture," together resonates with particular primordial unconscious anxieties and fantasies that greatly hinder and obstruct the efficient and effective "surface" work of productivity of any type of rationally conceived group function (ibid., p. 526). Bion calls the standard, normative group structures that promote adaptation to reality and are instantiated by the accomplishment of realistic group goals and gratify the members' reasonable needs the "work group culture." As I have suggested, the "work group culture," specifically within a team context, is vulnerable to assault from many perspectives. It is to this subject that I now briefly turn.

A few common problems in team-based working

Trust is perhaps most important for a team to function efficiently, effectively and happily, that firm belief in the reliability, truth, ability and/or strength of one's co-workers and leader. (In teams there is the designated team leader, the facilitator, but in actuality, psychologically speaking, there are often many leaders depending on the issue on the table, the group process and other contextual factors.) Trust—and its sister interpersonal quality, mutual respect—fosters a sense of group psychological safety, an important pre-condition for good teamwork. This emotional and social need for trust is rooted in the human propensity for positive attachments in relationships and a sense of belonging. Without trust between and among team members not much productive work can get accomplished, for mutual trust brings about a team's willingness and ability to venture out of their comfort zone and engage in risk-taking behavior, consider novel venues, and implement helpful interventions that both maintain team cohesion and integrity and advance performance. Trust, especially of those who are different in background and knowledge, is especially relevant in fostering team performance excellence in decision-making. Research has demonstrated that a demographically varied team, one that values diverse perspectives and experiences, is "more creative in their decision-making" (Richardson and West, 2010, pp. 236, 243, 238).[11]

One of the main causes of the absence of trust in a team is the lack of clear communication. Clear communication has been niftily formulated in terms of "The 7 Cs"—clear, concise, concrete, correct, coherent, complete and courteous (www.mindtools.com). Not only is clear communication a pre-condition for developing trust, but it promotes a more far-reaching rapport, that all-important emotional bond and friendly relation between people lodged in trust, mutual liking and a sense that they understand and share each other's concerns. Extrapolating from Erikson's first stage of psychosocial development, when the team leader(s), the symbolic parental presence, does not provide adequate "maternal" care, that is, he operates in a way that is emotionally and practically unreliable, unclear, frustrating or worse, he induces in the group the unconscious proclivity toward pessimism, withdrawal, lack of faith and paranoia (Akhtar, 2009, p. 35).

"If you want to build a ship," said Antoine de Saint-Exupéry, the author of the wonderful novella *The Little Prince*, "don't drum up people together to collect wood and don't assign them tasks and work, but rather teach them to long for the endless immensity of the sea" (thefutureofinnovation.org). Indeed, another major problem in teams is that there is no inspiring task, one that puts forth a noble and ennobling vision that group members can cognitively and emotionally identify with and justify working hard to actualize. As Richardson and West succinctly note, regardless of the particular goals, it is vital that the tasks through which they are accomplished offer "challenge, opportunities for growth, and a sense of self-efficacy." Self-efficacy is an individual's belief in his capacity to implement behaviors required to generate specific performance attainments. High levels of self-efficacy indicate a person's confidence in his capacity to bring to bear control over his own motivation, behavior, and social context. Thus boring and deadening team tasks, the opposite of "flow" or being in the "zone," are lethal to a high-level team performance. Tasks that provide an opportunity for "personal growth, achievement, and recognition" promote performance excellence (Richardson and West, 2010, p. 238). The point is that unless a team member feels that that the work they are engaged in is meaningful and purposeful in terms of their deeply held values, they are unlikely to generate the motivation to work efficiently, effectively and creatively. Research has shown that team members who are "intrinsically motivated," who are propelled by internal rewards, show "more interest, persistence, creativity, and enhanced performance" (ibid., p. 238).

One of the major obstacles in efficient and effective team functioning is lack of clarity about individual roles, responsibilities and goals as the team's work progresses. As the team is a developing group process, one that is context-dependent and setting-specific, each team member must have their role, responsibilities and goals, frequently updated and fine-tuned depending on what is needed and wanted by the group and personally doable. Moreover, this updating must always be guided by principles of fairness, equality and respect for individual autonomy. The more skillful this critical negotiation of the individual's changing role is, and the more the role is tailored to foster personal growth and development, the more likely that the team member will be motivated to work hard and well. When this is happening, the group synergy leads to greater team efficiency and effectiveness, mainly because team members are happier with what they are doing (ibid., p. 239). As Aristotle noted, "Pleasure in the job puts perfection in the work" (classiclit.about.com).

While the above point appears rather obvious, at least theoretically speaking, the fact is that it is enormously difficult to consistently implement a reasonable group process of updating and fine-tuning the individual's role. Team members are often derailed from focusing on realistic and important issues related to increased individual productivity because unresolved conflicts between and among them both before the team has been established and during meetings are at play. In this context, unresolved issues of power, status, prestige and competition, and other neurotic individual needs and wishes, get in the way of making timely and sensible decisions and engaging in a "work group culture" (Kets de Vries, 2011, p. 49).

In "power hoarding" the team is controlled by a few individuals such that those in power are more focused on "winning" than in effective problem-solving while those who are on the losing end or are outside of the power grab become apathetic and/or function in the group as docile bystanders, often keeping their "real" opinions and feelings about important issues private. As a result of this dysfunctional group configuration, premature, ill-conceived and ill-fated decisions may be made by the team. This includes disgruntled team members undermining decisions and their implementation in a variety of overt and covert, conscious and unconscious ways (ibid., p. 50).

In a similar way, status differences in teams may erode group functioning effectiveness. If, for instance, one member is a specialist compared to the other members, his deference-conferred role in decision-making about a particular issue will be lopsided in terms of a more inclusive group process. Lower status team members may begin to question their ability to thoughtfully contribute to the group. They tend to inordinately self-monitor, self-limit and self-censor their behavior in terms of their input in the constructive group process, often leading to premature, poorly thought through agreement among the team members. In addition, sometimes hidden agendas may be enacted among the team, with lower status members being more focused on "looking good" to a senior team member than with engaging in realistic problem-solving and task completion (ibid).

Groupthink and group polarization

Irving Janis, the brilliant originator of the social psychological phenomenon known as "groupthink," began his investigation as part of the American Soldier Project. In his 1972 book, *Victims of Groupthink: A Psychological Study of Foreign-Policy Decisions and Fiascoes*, Janis defined groupthink as "[a] mode of thinking that people engage in when they are deeply involved in a cohesive in-group, when the members' strivings for unanimity override their motivation to realistically appraise alternative courses of action" (pp. 8–9). Groupthink thus involves "a deterioration of mental efficiency, reality testing, and moral judgment." It is rooted in group pressures for conformity, compliance and the avoidance of anxiety and conflict.[12] Groupthink thus shuns opposing perspectives from being articulated and critically assessed and it rejects non-traditional or innovative ideas. As a result of groupthink, premature, ill-conceived and ill-fated decisions are made. For example, Janis describes how groupthink led to disastrous foreign policy decisions such as the failure to expect and foresee the Japanese attack on Pearl Harbor, Hitler's decision to invade the Soviet Union, The Bay of Pigs Invasion debacle, and President Lyndon B. Johnson's ruinous prosecution of the Vietnam War.

While scholars have challenged some of Janis's formulations, and his theory has been further developed (Janis, 1982), many of his insights have stood the test of time. They deserve to be mentioned, for they put into focus some of the dangers of how the average person makes decisions within the small group context.

Janis outlines three conditions of possibility that tend to bring about group-think: 1) a cohesive, like-minded and isolated group is sanctioned and authorized to make decisions; 2) independent and impartial leadership is missing inside or outside the group; and 3) there is pronounced stress on the group decision-making process to satisfy specific goals and objectives. Janis further described six symp-toms of groupthink: 1) "closed-mindedness," where group members are averse to considering alternative points of view; 2) "rationalization," where group members make a great effort to defend and justify both the method and the result of the decision-making process, often deforming and twisting reality in the service of convincing others; 3) "squelching of dissent," those who express contradictory viewpoints are disregarded, criticized or sometimes ostracized; 4) "formation of a group 'mindguard,'" where one self-appointed group member becomes the enforcer of the group's norms and makes sure that others are compliant; 5) "feeling invulnerable," whereby the group members fantasize that they must be correct in what they are deciding given how smart they all are and the information to which they have access; 6) "feeling unanimous," where the group members have the conviction that the whole group has the same opinion. As a result of these six group processes, there is a heavy group-serving, biased processing and evaluation of information alternatives. Moreover, risks are inadequately and insufficiently considered, as are contingency plans, leading to faulty decision-making.

Janis and others have suggested some practical counter-measures to group-think, such as the group leader fostering and encouraging a diversity of view-points, constructive debate and criticism, and the leader withholding his preferred view in the beginning. A group can also seek input from impartial, independent others who are outside of the group and do not have a vested interest in the result. A group can also divide itself into smaller sub-groups to consider other options. All of these tactics work against groupthink. As General George Patton said, "If everyone is thinking alike, someone isn't thinking" (Martin, 2006, p. 34). There are other techniques that are used in group decision-making that, depending on the task characteristics, can work against groupthink and other negative group influences on decision-making, like production blocking and evaluation apprehension. In general, these techniques encourage the generation of alternatives, debate and criticality: brainstorming, nominal group technique, delphi technique and devil's advocacy, and dialectical inquiry (Nelson and Quick, 2008, pp. 240–241).

Group polarization refers to the fact that within decision-making groups there is a tendency, after interaction and discussion, for the group and individuals to take more extreme positions, both in terms of risk-taking and cautiousness. Moreover, research has shown that after discussion, group members who at first opposed a subject become more radically against it, and members who were in support of the subject become more aggressively supportive. What this means for group decision-making is that groups who at the onset have a point of view that veers in a particular direction are more likely to embrace a more extreme perspective after interaction with each other. In the context of war and other comparably dangerous decision-making contexts, this can be catastrophic. For example, if group members are inclined to make riskier decisions in a dangerous context, they are more likely to be supportive of doing so after interacting with other group members (ibid, p. 239).[13] When, for example, soldiers with the same opinion about an enemy spend most of their time interacting with each other, their opinions tend to become considerably stronger and more extreme. Such a polarization effect can have obvious detrimental effects on collective decision-making.

The practical antidote to the worst of these team-destructive group dynamics is to have regular team meetings that promote free, open and constructive critical discussion about realistic issues, though these discussions must also be mindful of the irrational unconscious group processes that may be at play.[14] In addition, the encouragement of "positive, warm experiences and relationships in teams" can help its members to not be capsized by intra-group conflict (Richardson and West, 2010, p. 240). Needless to say, as Bion and his followers have so aptly pointed out, this is a lot easier said than done in light of the powerful hold that the irrational anxieties and archaic wishes have on all small groups. The extent to which team members are self-aware, self-critical, psychologically minded, and emotionally committed to the group's flourishing has an impact on the likelihood that group processes will not become wayward for long periods of time. Perhaps most importantly, as the American author and international management consultant Ken Blanchard noted, "the productivity of a work group seems to depend on how the group members see their own goals in relation to the goals of the organization" (www.leadersbeacon.com). It is to this subject, the psychopathology of organizational life, that I now turn.

The irrational organization

"An organization's ability to learn and translate that learning into action rapidly," said Jack Welch, former chairman and CEO of General Electric, "is the ultimate competitive advantage" (www.damarque.com). While Welch is putting his finger on one of the key elements that make for a successful organization, indeed, during his CEO tenure between 1981 and 2001 General Electric's value increased 4,000 percent, a psychoanalytic gloss on his observation suggests that this is a lot harder to accomplish than it sounds. For as Bion noted, individuals have a conscious and unconscious "hatred of learning by experience," what amounts to "a hatred of a process of development" (1959, pp. 75, 77). One of the important reasons for this is that "experience" is the name we give to our mistakes and mistakes are hugely narcissistically wounding. Learning by "experience" also requires the will and ability to venture into unfamiliar and challenging situations that generate anxiety about one's self-efficacy, another important aspect for maintaining a modicum of narcissistic equilibrium. As is abundantly clear from individual psychoanalytic treatment, most people "do not have much belief in their capacity for learning by experience," that is, neurotic attitudes and behavior are extremely hard to decisively and lastingly modify, and most neurotics know or at least sense this. To put emphasis on this point, Bion comments, "what we learn from history is that we do not learn from history" (ibid., p. 75).

While there is a huge scholarly and popular literature on what promotes organizational success, I want to describe some of the manifestations of anxiety, hostility and other negative emotions toward the organization that can chip away at its constructive, collaborative and creative potential, what Nitsun has called "anti-group" phenomenon. Such disruptive and disintegrative processes cannot only severely compromise an organization's adaptation and survival, but it leaves the individual employee feeling demoralized if not traumatized (Nitsun, 2015, pp. 2, 3). I will briefly comment on two interrelated, interdependent and interactive elements, best viewed as processes, that when they are "off track," can contribute to an individual employee feeling he is working in a "crazy" organization: bad leadership and bad organizational culture, especially lack of support during times of adversity.

Bad leadership

"A fish first rots from the head down," the popular proverb goes. When an organization fails, the ultimate cause is the leadership.[15] I have earlier commented on the tremendous practical psychological difficulties for the employee having to cope with an inordinately narcissistic boss, but there are many other aspects of bad leadership that can make a worker feel horrid, if not unhinged. Put succinctly, leaders have a central role in fostering a "healthy" and flourishing group and organization, one that goes beyond establishing clear and well-formulated goals and evaluating the progress of a team. Most importantly, at least psychoanalytically speaking, leaders "become the emotional center" of an organization, and they "are in the best position to deal with anxieties that develop" (Swogger, 1993, p. 112). While the main qualities of a great leader in the business context are well-researched, for example, such a person displays honesty, good communication skills, a sense of humor, confidence, commitment, a positive attitude, creativity, intuition and an ability to inspire (www.forbes.com), the fact is that great leaders are hard to come by. For example, a 2014 Harvard Business School study found that "half of employees" (20,000 studied from around the world) "don't feel respected by their bosses." This leader behavior had the biggest effect on employees compared to all other outcomes that were measured. That is, "being treated with respect was more important to employees than recognition and appreciation, communicating an inspiring vision, providing useful feedback—even opportunities for learning, growth, and development" (https://hbr.org). This is a dismal research finding, for one would think that a boss giving an employee respect would be axiomatic. This and other disheartening findings, such as the 2013 Gallup Poll State of the American Workplace finding that many employees "complained of 'bosses from hell' who ignored talent and didn't cultivate growth," put into sharp focus what a boss, manager or leader does or doesn't do that can seriously negatively impact job satisfaction (www.nydailynews.com). While there is a vast scholarly literature on leadership describing almost an infinite number of ways leaders can be lousy—psychologists have cited the ballpark figure "that 50% of executives fail and that 60–75% of US managers are incompetent"—I want to mention a few of the more common types of "bosses from hell" that can make employees feel like they are being driven "out of their minds" (https://www.psychologytoday.com).

"Nothing is more difficult, and therefore more precious, than to be able to decide," said Napoleon Bonaparte (Marcus, 2014, p. 199). Indeed, the "laissez-faire leader," as Ronald E. Riggio, a professor of leadership and organizational psychology, calls him, is one that renounces his main leadership responsibility—to make decisions—especially tough ones (https://www.psychologytoday.com). From the perspective of the subordinate, a leader that will not make decisions, or make timely ones, is putting the subordinate in a position analogous to a child waiting for gratification from his parent, in this instance, of direction that never comes, or comes too late. Conversely, such enforced passivity makes the subordinate feel similar frustration to the parent trying to get the toddler to make a "pooh" in the toilet. Indeed, while there are many psychodynamic reasons why a boss may not make decisions, from the perspective of the subordinate who is waiting, it feels like one is up against an anal-retentive character. To be anal-retentive is to need to be in control of all aspects of one's surroundings; in short, such a person "won't let go of his shit," his symbolic "gift" to his parents. He does this to both keep his prized "gift" all for himself while at the same time irritatingly defying his parents' socially sanctioned requests. Needless to say, such a procrastinating boss angers and demoralizes subordinates, fostering a feeling within the organization that it is without a leader. Over time workers simply give up caring. Ironically, in one variation such controlling bosses can be prone to over-manage instead of lead. As the "Great One," hockey icon Wayne Gretzky noted, "Procrastination is one of the most common and deadliest of diseases and its toll on success and happiness [especially among subordinates in an organization] is heavy" (izquotes.com).

Another category of leaders who are likely to greatly upset employees are the "incompetent leaders," a group that includes a wide range of behaviors and personality types that demonstrate seriously defective managerial and leadership skills. For example, such leaders can be markedly rigid, habitually applying the same strategy and tactics regardless of the circumstances, often with unsuccessful outcomes. As Einstein allegedly said, "insanity is doing the same thing over and over again and expecting different results" (White, 2004, p. 36). In other instances incompetent leaders can display very low levels of motivation that lead them to make ill-conceived and ill-fated decisions, in part because they have not put adequate time into studying the details of the problem and in other ways doing what is necessary to make a smart decision. Moreover, they do not actually care about the negative impact of a bad decision on others as long as they are not seriously implicated in the consequences. In another variation, such leaders may also over-delegate making important decisions with little oversight of their subordinates, often creating troubling imbalances in workloads such as over- or under-utilization of individuals or groups. Such bosses mainly do this to avoid taking responsibility for failure that could be attributed to them (https://www.psychologytoday.com; www.citehr.com).

To some extent the fact that there are so many incompetent leaders should not be surprising when we consider the famous managerial "law," The Peter Principle. This is "the observation that in a hierarchy people tend to rise to 'their level of incompetence.' Thus, as people are promoted they become progressively less effective because good performance in one job does not guarantee similar performance in another" (www.businessdictionary.com). According to The Peter Principle, there are two types of managers: those who move up the leadership hierarchy and those who have gone as far as their competence allows them to move. Moreover, once a person enters a job in which they are not competent they tend to stay there for many years or until retirement. In this context, it is inevitable that such poorly qualified leaders will make a high percentage of bad decisions that negatively impact the organization and particular individuals (smallbusiness.chron.com).

The main negative impact on the individual who has an incompetent leader is analogous to a child who has an incompetent parent or teacher, namely, a profound loss of trust that fosters high levels of anxiety. A competent parental caregiver is the "psychological parent," the one who most symbolizes nurturance and stability. If a "good enough mother," as Winnicott famously called the imperfect though competent parent, is devoted to the child, the incompetent boss leaves the subordinate feeling largely adrift, if not abandoned; if the "good enough mother" tries to identify with and understand the child's thoughts and feelings, the incompetent boss is unwilling and unable to do so toward his employees, for he often lacks the listening and communication skills and the patience and empathy. If the "good enough mother" is able to contain the child's assaults and help him psychologically metabolize them, the incompetent boss experiences criticism as an attack that deserves retaliation; if the "good enough mother" almost never fails in meeting the child's developmentally appropriate ego needs for encouragement and support, while at the same time frustrating his inordinate id wishes, the incompetent leader hardly cares about being helpful to his underlings and is overly frustrating of his work-related playful and creative desires, such as "playing" with new ideas or taking risks. Finally, while the "good enough mother" is willing and able to give the child his space to explore the world at his own time and in his own way, the incompetent boss makes little or no effort to give underlings autonomy of thought, feeling and perhaps most importantly, of action (Akhtar, 2009, p. 124).

Riggio describes "toxic leaders" and "evil leaders," the former being the extreme narcissists I described earlier, though there are many variations on such leaders who engage in destructive behavior and display markedly dysfunctional personality characteristics that foster a poisonous work environment. For example, such leaders tend to give yes or no or black and white answers to complex questions, for they are unwilling and unable to think deeply about a problem or consider very far into the future, as they are moving from one crisis to another in which damage control is their only concern. As a result, workers feel unheard, not understood and disrespected; such leaders often selfishly let their personal lives and self-seeking needs and wishes intrude into their work and are not able to properly attend to important matters of underlings who feel ignored and disregarded. Such leaders don't graciously tolerate mistakes or use them for learning purposes like a master teacher; in fact they are prone to humiliate others in a group setting when underlings are found to have erred. In short, such self-centered and egotistical leaders most often leave their organization "worse off than how they found it." Enron executives Andrew Fastow and Jeffrey Skilling are excellent examples of toxic business leaders. Evil business leaders would certainly include Bernard Madoff, the former stockbroker and mastermind of the "swindle of the century" (about $20 billion) who was convicted of fraud. Madoff drastically hurt, if not destroyed, many organizations and individual lives because of his pathological obsession to dishonestly accumulate vast sums of money and power (https://www. psychologytoday.com).

Exactly why so many people tolerate remaining in devaluing and debasing positions with "bosses from hell" is a complex and important question, one that deserves a study of its own. Pragmatically speaking, most reasonable people would probably claim that having a hated job is still better than being unemployed, especially if one has a family to support, given the current challenging job market and harsh economic climate. There are two other psychologically based considerations that no doubt have considerable applicability to many employees staying put when they have to endure a "boss from hell": so-called "commitment effects" and "reflected glory" (Pfeffer and Fong, 2005, p. 377).

Within the context of the individual employee's escalation of cognitive and emotional commitment to a position that one has consciously chosen, there is a pronounced tendency to reconstruct and rationalize their circumstances as being better than they really are. Social psychologist Leon Festinger (1957) famously calls this "cognitive dissonance theory," that is, in circumstances that involve conflicting attitudes, beliefs or behaviors, the feelings of discomfort bring about a modification in one of the attitudes, beliefs or behaviors to diminish the discomfort and reinstate psychic equilibrium. Moreover, this compelling motivation to uphold cognitive consistency can foster irrational and highly maladaptive behavior (www.simplypsychology. org). Research in organizational psychology has demonstrated that people often prefer to continue in their chosen course of action, like staying in a job with an abusive boss, even though it is very disagreeable. Even more strikingly, they persist in an unpleasant course of action when they no longer realistically have to. Such findings are best understood in terms of "self enhancement" theory, "the desire, or observed reality of seeing oneself and by extension one's actions, traits, and attitudes in the most positive light" (Pfeffer and Fong, 2005, pp. 377, 374).

Similarly, individuals may also tolerate horrible bosses because they wish to feel favorably about themselves, that is, they want to increase their self-esteem and enhance their self-concept by associating with "winners." In this scenario, many subordinates are willing and able to sustain a fair amount of mistreatment, even abuse, to "bask" in the "reflected glory" of high-status superiors, which includes self-subjugating, to varying degrees, aspects of their own best interests and painful feelings, at least for significant periods of time. Moreover, if the successful boss is willing to symbolically share some of his success with his subordinates, this can intensify the latter's attachment to the abusive boss (ibid., pp. 377, 378).

There is probably a complex interaction between these and other psychological factors in understanding why employees allow themselves to be subjugated by their bosses. For example, voluntary subjugation to a boss can be simply viewed as a reflection of low self-esteem and a poor self-concept that is typical among those who feel personally and organizationally powerless. Abuse is conceived as self-verifying, including being unconsciously deserved in a way that can easily fuse with an individual's masochistic proclivities. However, such employees may in certain contexts and settings also calculate that short-term mistreatment is worth imagined long-term benefits (ibid., p. 378).

Organizational culture

The American industrialist who revolutionized the automotive industry, Henry Ford, famously described organizational culture at its best: "Coming together is the beginning, keeping together is progress. Working together is success" (www.usdreams.com).[16] Indeed, it is near impossible to have a lasting success-ful organization without a flourishing organizational culture. An organiza-tional culture has been aptly defined as "the values and behaviors that contribute to the unique social and psychological environment of an organiza-tion." Specifically,

> Organizational culture includes an organization's expectations, experi-ences, philosophy, and values that hold it together, and is expressed in its self-image, inner workings, interactions with the outside world, and future expectations. It is based on shared attitudes, beliefs, customs, and written and unwritten rules that have been developed over time and are considered valid.
>
> (www.businessdictionary.com)

Given the broad nature of this definition, there are many aspects of organiza-tional culture that can promote in the employee a strong sense that he inhabits a work place that is very disagreeable, if not maddening. Moreover, since the nature of organizational culture is heavily influenced from above, by those in charge, and leadership style is rooted in personality dynamics in complex interaction with the environment, it is not surprising that there are nearly an infinite number of ways that an organizational culture can turn nasty for an employee.

Kets de Vries aptly describes, for example, certain types or "organizational archetypes," each with its strengths and weaknesses: the "dramatic/cyclothymic, suspicious, compulsive, detached and depressive" (2006, pp. 323–327). Each one of these archetypes creates a set of potentially obnoxious psychological and practical problems for employees that I here briefly describe.

The "dramatic/cyclothymic" leaders are mainly motivated by their inordinate narcissistic need for affirmation from outsiders. They desire to win people over with "flow" or "in the zone" types of experiences; they are prone to superficial thinking and interacting; they tend to be emotionally labile, moving from extremes of elation and depression; they are over-reactive to minor matters; and they have an over-reliance upon intuition, so-called "gut feelings" in their deci-sion-making style that often leads to ill-conceived and ill-fated audaciousness, risk-taking and unpleasant showiness. Moreover, such leaders are too confident that they are the masters of their fate, not properly reckoning with the fact that they have much less control of their lives, and the organizations they lead, than they imagine. In short, says Kets de Vries, dramatic/cyclothymic leaders' decision-making can be summed up as, "We want to get attention from and impress the people who count in the world." English billionaire investor Richard Branson's Virgin Group is an example of a dramatic/cyclothymic organization. Such a CEO powerfully wants to be noticed and applauded, he longs for high-octane excite-ment, and seeks out situations that are characterized by flamboyance and drama (ibid., p. 323).

"Suspicious organizations" are mainly built on what Melanie Klein called paranoid anxiety, a foreboding of being assaulted by "bad objects," which are either "internal, projected internal, or external." Most often, at least according to Klein, this anxiety is projected onto objects (that is, to people), and in another variation, "into" objects in the case of projective identification, as a primitive defense against one's own disavowed destructive impulses, and ultimately, denied self-destructive wishes (Rycroft, 1995, p. 125). In the organizational context, such organizations are characterized by hyper-vigilance against real but most often imagined "enemies." A profound feeling of mistrust and doubt pervades such an organization, especially when something wrong may have happened that has not been adequately explained or dealt with. In light of such organizational suspiciousness, there is a centralization of power and a consolida-tion of influence, one that uses a conservative business strategy combined with unadventurous tactics. As a result, autonomy is discouraged and initiative is muted, and unsuitable and unbending responses from superiors become the norm. The FBI under J. Edgar Hoover, with its secret abuses of government powers, illegal ways of evidence collection, and intimidation of governmental leaders and others who were afraid of retaliations, is a good example of such an organization (Kets de Vries, 2006, p. 323).

This being said, it is worth mentioning that the upsurge of workplace spying has for good reason increased paranoid thinking among workers. For example, a survey from the American Management Association (AMA) reported that no less than 66 percent of US companies monitor their employees' internet use while 43 percent track employee emails. Moreover, not only office workers are in the grip of "Big Brother": in Amazon's warehouses, workers are mandated to carry tablets that record their speed and efficiency as they retrieve merchandise for shoppers; in hospitals, nurses have to wear badges that record how frequently they wash their hands. In other words, within the context of our surveillance society where says an official of the AMA, "privacy in today's workplace is largely illusory," paranoid thought process and behavior is being potentiated (*The Week*, 7/10/15, p. 11).[17]

Similar to the mode of being-in-the-world of an obsessive-compulsive neurotic, a "compulsive organization" can be best understood when we juxtapose it with its opposite way of being, namely, spontaneous, voluntary, free and ego-syntonic (Rycroft, 1995, p. 24). Such maladjusted organizations are characterized by an exaggerated concern about unimportant matters; they tend to be inflexible and structure-bound, excessively exacting about rules, and they apply complicated information systems and highly formalized, painstaking evaluation procedures that are both slow and overbearing while they tend to squash any unprompted and improvisational tendencies. Thus, in a "compulsive organization" the business strategy is overly calculated and focused, motivated by a reliance on one entrenched, deeply rooted concern such as cost-cutting or quality, without adequately reflecting on any other important considerations at play. Moreover, such organizations tend to use a conventional management-hierarchical bureaucratic model, such that an employee's standing, rank and position emanates from their place in the power "pecking order" rather than more important qualitative, performance-based considerations. As a result, instead of emphasizing social connection and collaboration in the workplace, an approach that is lodged in an interactive and dynamic premise about what matters most to workers (e.g., as in self-organizing teams), relationships are largely governed by control and submission. As Kets de Vries further comments, compulsive organizations are characterized by high levels of anxiety in which employees are frequently asking themselves such questions as "Will we do it right?," "Will they do it right?," "Can we let them do it?," and "How will it threaten us?" An example of such a "compulsive organization" that failed miserably was IBM under the leadership of John Akers (ibid., p. 324), between about 1983 and 1993, who was described by CNBC as one of "the worst American CEOs of all time" (www.cnbc.com/id/30502091/page/12, retrieved 6/19/15). Not only did Akers not know his product, as well as being trapped in an antiquated way of thinking about computers that emphasized mainframe when personal computing was beckoning, but he was a terrible procrastinator when it came to making important decisions.

"There is no detachment where there is no pain," said French philosopher Simone Weil, and the same applies to an organization (Martusewicz, 2001, p. 35). A "detached organization" is similar to the one earlier described as run by a "laissez faire" leader and calls to mind the schizoid personality, characterized by a marked unresponsiveness to social relationships and a truncated range of emotional expressiveness (i.e., flat affect) and experience. Psychoanalytically speaking, while such pained people are "overtly detached, self-sufficient, absentminded, uninteresting, asexual and idiosyncratically moral"—for example, the stereotypical "loner" who exudes an attitude of "leave me the fuck alone," covertly, they are "exquisitely sensitive, emotionally needy, acutely vigilant, creative, often perverse, and vulnerable to corruption" (Akhtar, 2009, p. 252). Thus, in such an organization the emotional environment is characterized by a palpable chilliness, a lack of engagement both within and outside the organization, and a leadership that avoids any hands-on involvement with the everyday life of the organization. As a result of such laissez faire leadership, a power vacuum is generated that leads to an upsurge of the use of aggressive or dubious tactics among the leadership, such as psychological intimidation to gain an advantage over one's colleagues while still technically observing the organization's rules. Such gamesmanship, especially among mid- and lower-level executives, permits strategies and tactics that are markedly erratic and wavering. Moreover, since the leadership is generally not responsive to the healthy dependency needs of subordinates, such as for positive connection rooted in acknowledgement of the need for others and letting others need you, leaders at all levels of the "pecking order" tend to fashion their own spheres of influence and control, their little kingdoms, including generating obstacles to the lifeblood of any successful organization, namely, the free and uninterrupted flow of information. The reclusive American business tycoon who probably suffered from obsessive-compulsive disorder, Howard Hughes, is a good example of a detached leader (Kets de Vries, 2006, pp. 324–325).

The influential existential psychologist Rollo May noted that the main problem in clinical depression "is the inability to construct a future" (http://www.scientificamerican.com). Likewise, a "depressive organization" is characterized by its lack of confidence, where employees collectively feel a lack of trust and faith in themselves and their abilities to put things right, or at least make them significantly better. As a result, "depressive organizations" are typically dull, sluggish and stagnant, they discourage new ideas and are unwilling and unable to change, especially regarding implementing sharp change (hence they are often overly bureaucratic and hierarchical), and they tend to be markedly inward looking. Often such organizations are lodged in a retrospective consciousness which makes effective decision-making nearly impossible; they avoid adventure, they are locked into shrinking and outdated markets, they lack any *esprit de corps* and sense of healthy competition, and their leadership is characterized by indifference. Many governmental organizations are depressive in character, and not surprisingly, so was the Walt Disney Company after the death of its charismatic founder (Kets de Vries, 2006, p. 325).[18]

To be a subordinate in any of these neurotic organizations can be markedly destructive to one's vocational identity. Perhaps the best one can say is that by being knowledgeable of the limitations, strengths and dynamics of these fundamentally flawed organizations one can protect oneself to some degree from their worst aspects. For example, a greater mindfulness of the limitations of each type of organizational culture can help one better understand some of the more troubling aspects of the behavior of its leaders and colleagues in both individual and group contexts, which is more likely to foster adaptive responses to them. Moreover, such knowledge and awareness helps the subordinate to craft psychological "safe zones" where one can function more creatively and productively while staying out of harm's way. If one is a leader in such an organization, greater awareness and knowledge of the dynamics of the neurotic aspects of one's organization is the first critical step in changing the organizational culture for the better. Such a "positive culture," as it is often described, is one in which "professionalism, high achievement and team-building is concentrated," such that employees will be more likely to happily work at a higher level (yourbusiness. azcentral.com).

Conclusion

The prominent Canadian psychoanalyst and organizational psychologist Elliott Jaques noted before he died in 2003 that "The system [i.e., the current organizational structure] we have now is much more crushing to the individual" (http://www.nytimes.com). Indeed, what I have tried to suggest in this chapter is that there are many irrational and in other ways deleterious individual, group and organizational processes operative in a typical workplace that, when not individually and collectively properly attended to, tend to undermine an average worker's sense of autonomy, integration and humanity. To again quote Jaques, one of the key cohesive elements that binds "individuals into institutionalized human association is that of defense against psychotic anxiety." While it would be incorrect to say that an institution or organization is inevitably, and generally speaking, "psychotic," as I have suggested, there are group relationships that show psychotic aspects such as "unreality, splitting, hostility, suspicion," and other expressions of seriously "maladaptive" and maladjusted behavior (Jaques, 1974, p. 279).

Indeed, there is considerable research-based evidence that in today's workplaces there are many risk factors for significant mental health problems. For example, a landmark Johns Hopkins study from 1990 summarized recently in the *New York Times* reported that lawyers were "3.6 times as likely as non-lawyers to suffer from depression, putting them at greater risk than people in any other occupation." More recently, in December 2014, a Yale Law School study found that "70 percent of its students were affected by mental health issues," suggesting that lawyers may be more susceptible to mental health problems for a variety of complex reasons related to the nature of their everyday work and practice (http://well. blogs.nytimes.com).

More generally, as industrial and organizational psychologist Jay C. Thomas[19] noted, "modern organization design, with its flat hierarchies, team emphasis, goal setting, fast pace, accountability, the need for flexibility and continual change, and high-stress conditions," puts severe demands on the interpersonal skills, coping techniques, and initiative of a typical employee, too often prompting one to declare, "This job is driving me crazy" (2004, pp. 5, 6). Researchers have found a number of risk factors that tend to foster troubling mental health problems in the workplace, factors that have been clustered into nine categories (Stewart *et al.*, 2004, p. 333) that, to a large extent, conceptually and practically, dynamically co-mingle with many of the psychoanalytically oriented formulations described throughout this chapter.

For example, the risk factor category of "organizational function and culture," such as an inadequate problem-solving environment, inadequate communication, and an unsupportive culture, negatively impacts on the mental health of employees. In the category of "role in the organization," risk factors included role ambiguity, role conflict, and high responsibility for others. In "career development," career uncertainty, career plateau, inadequate salary, and fear of job loss were correlated with compromised mental health. In "decision latitude/control," the paucity of decision-making and the paucity of control over work negatively impacted psychological adjustment. Likewise, in the category of "interpersonal relationships at work" such as the degree of social or physical isolation; troubled relationships with bosses, managers and leaders; relational conflict in all of its varieties or violence; and lack of social support, especially during challenging times, were significant risk factors. The category of "home/work interface," which connotes the disparate and contradictory demands of work and home, inadequate social or practical encouragement and support at home, and dual career difficulties, all negatively impacted on mental health. "Task design," which refers to problems around poorly defined work, uncertainty of work, lack of variety or abbreviated work cycles, and over exposure to demanding people, clients, or customers, were also important risk factors. "Workload," whether too much or too little, lack of control over the pacing and speed of work, and time pressure or unreasonable deadlines also compromised mental health. The final category of aggravating factors for employees to maintain their psychological equipoise was "work schedule," such as shift work and working long, unsociable hours (ibid).

In light of the above-described mental health risk factors it is a near "miracle" that anyone is able to psychologically survive at work;[20] and yet, despite some previously cited dismal statistics about the lack of job satisfaction in the United States (and other parts of the western world), the fact is that there are some people who are able to flourish while on the job. While I have provided a plausible account in Chapter 3 for the job satisfaction of this group of resourceful and inventive people, one that emphasizes "work as the created birthplace of the transcendent," I want to reiterate that the capacity to flourish on the job, at least in terms of the individual, depends on one's emotional self-mastery, especially "emotional creativity." While working in an organization that is animated by "strengths-based" and "positive" organizational psychology principles is most likely to bring out the best in workers and lead to higher levels of job satisfaction, the fact is that what probably matters most on the personal level is "emotional creativity." By this I mean the robust capacity for "novel, effective and authentic" receptiveness, responsiveness and responsibility, an openness, curiosity and imagination that promotes what Nietzsche called "spiritualization of the passions," a process of greater "self-realization and expansion" and increased "vitality, connectedness and meaningfulness" (Averill, 2009, p. 255). To the extent that one can conceive of one's work in broadly aesthetic terms, as analogous to fashioning a work of art or as an imaginative undertaking that draws from personality qualities like "playfulness, creativity, sense of humor, ego-strength, and self-actualization" (Javerill-creativdadcursos.com), while at the same time shielding oneself from the destructive aspects of one's job, the more likely that one has mastered the art of living the "good life" in the workplace. One should never forget that from the point of view of individual freedom, a worker, like anyone else, is capable of psychologically nurturing something in one's fantasy and imagination, a kind of creative visualization, which one has to live without in objective reality. Such "life longings," as they have been called in the psychology of wisdom literature, may serve as the best defense against situations characterized by unattainability, failure and loss (Scheibe *et al.*, 2009, p. 179).

Notes

1 Depending on how you define and conceptualize the murky terms of boss, manager and leader, there are differences and similarities. For example, managers tend to focus on process while leaders focus more on generating imaginative ideas (Zaleznik, 1991, p. 109). As the late leadership scholar Ralph Stogdill noted, "there are almost as many definitions of leadership as there are persons who have attempted to define the concept" (Kets de Vries and Miller, 1985, p. 584). In this chapter I treat all of these organizational roles as roughly equivalent in terms of being people who have authority over employees, and when this authority becomes hard-going, or even worse, abusive, it presents serious adaptational difficulties for subordinates in terms of flourishing on the job.

2 Narcissism as a personality trait is conceptualized along a continuum in psychoanalytic theory, for example, from normal or healthy narcissism to the narcissistic personality disorder. The latter is a rare character disorder that affects less than 1 percent of the general population (Campbell *et al.*, 2005, p. 1359).

3 In my discussion of narcissism in the workplace I am liberally drawing from Kernberg (1979, 1998).

4 I am paraphrasing Goethe who made this very point: "Hatred is active, and envy passive dislike; there is but one step from envy to hate" (www.whale.to).

5 Research has indicated that those people in "high powered roles," even temporarily, tend to show "brain activity consistent with lower empathy." This may be due to the fact that "they have less incentive to interact with others." In other words, narcissists (and psychopaths) are, in fact, able to feel empathy, but they choose not to (Cameron *et al.*, 2015, p. 12). Another research stream indicates that among low-skilled workers on a professional path, it is not the traditional markers of success, such as education, industry experience and employer recommendations that most matter, but rather "optimism and empathy" (Davidson, 2016, p. 43).

6 Dissociation and splitting are hard to distinguish; in the clinical psychoanalytic literature most analysts have not bothered to do so, though some have described dissociation more in terms of impacting "processes" while splitting impacts "structures" (Zaleznik, 1991, p. 102). For the most part, such hard to pin down notions are used interchangeably in the psychoanalytic literature.

7 In a well publicized quest for the "perfect team" (i.e., "Project Aristotle") Google researchers have re-discovered what capable managers have known for many years as have psychoanalysts, namely, that the best performing teams and groups are composed of members who empathically listen to one another and show responsiveness to feelings and needs within a secure and trusting context (Duhigg, 2016, p. 75).

8 A process of employee performance appraisal that includes multisource anonymous evaluations from superiors, subordinates, peers and self-evaluation, and sometimes from customers or clients who an employee has interacted with. While most Fortune 500 companies have embraced such an approach, there is little empirical data to support its efficacy (Schultz and Schultz, 2006, pp. 147, 148).

9 This explanatory quote is taken from a talk Sartre gave that preceded a recording of the play issued in 1965.

10 Teams, called "quality circles" in the 1970s, have been conceptualized as somewhat different from "groups" and "committees." While there is some confusion in the literature about what constitutes a "work team," one serviceable definition is "a collection of three or more individuals who interact intensively to provide an organizational product, plan, decision, or service." To make matters even more complicated, there are "work teams," "parallel teams," "project teams," "management teams," "crews" and "virtual teams," each somewhat different in their characteristics and dynamics (Aamodt, 2007, pp. 491, 493, 494).

11 I have liberally drawn from Richardson and West's (2010) excellent review article in this section.

12 A revised edition of this book came out in 1982; see pp. 174–175 in particular.

13 There are two main theoretical explanations for group polarization, one based on social comparison theory and the other on a persuasive arguments theory (also known as informational influence theory). See Moscovici and Zavalloni (1969) and Van Swol (2009), respectively.

14 Research has shown that many employees find most meetings boring, useless and greatly dislike them. One study reported in the *New York Times* calculated that in the US over $37 billion is wasted in "unproductive meetings." See Heffernan (2016, pp. 29, 30).

15 Of course, well-intentioned bosses, supervisors and leaders have their own set of anxieties, fears and challenges to becoming the best they can become in their critical roles in an organization. However, understanding in detail what personality and other factors impair their effectiveness is beyond the scope of this book. One very good, psychoanalytically informed investigation of organizational leadership is Kets de Vries (2006).

16 It is noteworthy that there are signs that in today's workplace there is a lack of "collaborative, innovative social space" as indicated by the fact that about 62 percent

of professionals surveyed say they typically eat lunch at their desks, what has been called "desktop dining." That is, eating alone is a way, for instance, to answer e-mails and catch up on to-do's or go on Facebook rather than hang out and bond with colleagues. In fact, about a quarter of so-called millennial wage earners preferred to eat alone so they could multitask more effectively. However, work performance and satisfaction tends to be correlated with eating with colleagues, which is typical in say fire houses where there is a strong sense of fellowship (Wollan, 2016, pp. 54, 50).

17 Most recently, in Silicon Valley, Slack, the hugely popular office collaboration app has over 2.3 million daily active users. Companies as diverse as Salesforce, eBay and HBO use this platform to assist widespread teams of workers to communicate more quickly and efficiently, through group chat rooms and one-to-one instant messages rather than email or conference calls. However, "Slack workplaces are environments of total surveillance," said one technical expert. That is, the software keeps all your conversations, including your private messages, forever, unless they are deleted. If a company is sued, an employee's messages can be used and they are subject to government subpoena (*The Week*, 3/25/16, p. 20).

18 Kets de Vries points out that each of these organizational archetypes has its advantages, at least before it begins to implode. For example, a "dramatic/cyclothymic" organizational culture tends to generate "entrepreneurial initiative;" a "suspicious organization" can spot unreasonable risks to proposed business ventures; "compulsive organizations" can be efficient, strategically focused and have precise internal organizational controls; a "detached organization" is able to exploit the points of view of a wide range of contributors from different levels in the "pecking order" as they fashion business strategy; and the "depressive organization" is characterized by a marked "consistency of internal processes" (2006, p. 326). As is almost always the case when discussing organizational processes, they have both enabling and constraining elements.

19 Thomas is paraphrasing from the research of Miller (1998).

20 Research data has found that in France "between 300 and 400 employees each year commit suicide, the cause of which is attributed to working conditions." This is quite likely an underestimation of the problem (Amado, 2013, p. 13).

References

Aamodt, M. G. (2007). *Industrial/Organizational Psychology: An Applied Approach* (6th ed.). Belmont, CA: Wadsworth.

Akhtar, S. (2009). *Comprehensive Dictionary of Psychoanalysis.* London: Karnac.

Amado, G. (2013). Psychic imprisonment and its release within organizations and working relationships. In: L. Vanisina (Ed.), *Humanness in Organizations. A Psychodynamic Contribution* (pp. 7–28). London: Karnac.

Averill, J. R. (2009). Emotional Creativity: Toward "Spiritualizing the Passions." In: C. R. Snyder and S. J. Lopez (Eds.), *Oxford Handbook of Positive Psychology* (pp. 249–257). Oxford: Oxford University Press.

Bain, A. and Gould, L. J. (1996). The Fifth Assumption. *Free Associations*, 6:1, no. 37, 1–20.

Bion, W. R. (1959). *Experiences in Groups.* New York: Ballantine Books.

Cameron, D., Inzlicht, M. and Cunningham, W. A. (2015). Empathy is Actually a Choice. *New York Times*, Sunday Review, 7/12/15, p. 12.

Campbell, W. K., Bush, C. P., Brunell, A. B. and Shelton, J. (2005). Understanding the Social Costs of Narcissism: The Case of the Tragedy of the Commons. *Personality and Social Psychology Bulletin, 31*, 1358–1368.

Christian, J. (2012). *Philosophy: An Introduction to the Art of Wondering*. Boston, MA: Wadsworth.

Colman, A. M. (2009). *Oxford Dictionary of Psychology*. Oxford: Oxford University Press.

Davidson, A. (2016). Cleaning Up. *The New York Times Magazine*, 2/28/16, p. 43.

Doonan, S. (2015). Viewpoint. *The Week*, 4/3/15, p. 10.

Duhigg, C. (2016) Group Study. *The New York Times Magazine*, 2/28/16, p. 75.

Emerson, R. W. (1984). *Emerson in His Journals*. Joel Porte (Ed.). Cambridge, MA: Belknap Press.

Festinger, L. (1957). *A Theory of Cognitive Dissonance*. Redwood City, CA: Stanford University Press.

Freud, S. (1921) [1955]. Group Psychology and the Analysis of the Ego. In: J. Strachey (Ed. and Trans.), *The Standard Edition of the Complete Psychological Works of Sigmund Freud*, Vol. 18 (pp. 65–143). London: Hogarth Press.

Frew, J. (2004). Motivating and Leading Dysfunctional Employees. In: J. C. Thomas and M. Hersen (Eds.), *Psychopathology in the Workplace. Recognition and Adaptation* (pp. 293–311). New York: Brunner-Routledge.

Friedman, T. (2015). Contain and Amplify. *The New York Times OP-ED*, 5/27/15, p. A23.

Fromm, E. (1947). *Man for Himself. An Inquiry into the Psychology of Ethics*. Oxford: Routledge.

Gambrill, E. (2004). Social Skills Deficits. In: J. C. Thomas and M. Hersen (Eds.), *Psychopathology in the Workplace. Recognition and Adaptation* (pp. 243–257). New York: Brunner-Routledge.

Gould, L. J. (1993). Contemporary Perspectives on Personal and Organizational Authority: The Self in a System of Work Relationships. In: L. Hirschhorn and C. K. Barnett (Eds.), *The Psychodynamics of Organizations* (pp. 49–63). Philadelphia, PA: Temple University Press.

Heffernan, V. (2016). Meet is Murder. In *New York Times Magazine*, 2/28/16, pp. 29, 30.

Hopper, E. (2003). *Traumatic Experience in the Unconscious Life of Groups: The Fourth Basic Assumption: Incohesion: Aggregation/Massification or (ba) I:A/M International Library of Group Analysis* (Book #23). London: Jessica Kingsley.

Hugo, V. (1901) [1907]. *Intellectual Autobiography (Postscriptum)*. L. O'Rourke (Trans.). New York: Funk and Wagnalls Company.

Huntley, H. L. (1997). How Does "God-Talk" Speak to the Workplace: An Essay on the Theology of Work. In D. P. Bloch and L. J. Richmond (Eds.), *Connections Between Spirit and Work in Career Development: New Approaches and Practical Perspectives* (pp. 115–136). Palo Alto, CA: Davies-Black Publishing.

Janis, I. (1972). *Victims of Groupthink: A Psychological Study of Foreign-Policy Decisions and Fiascoes*. Boston, MA: Houghton Mifflin.

Janis, I. (1982). *Groupthink: Psychological Studies of Policy Decisions and Fiascoes* (2nd ed.). New York: Houghton Mifflin.

Jaques, E. (1974). Social Systems as Defense Against Persecutory and Depressive Anxiety. In: G. S. Gabbard, J. J. Hartmann and R. D. Mann (Eds.), *Analysis of Groups* (pp. 277–299). San Francisco, CA: Jossey-Bass.

Judge, T. A., LePine, J. A. and Rich, B. L. (2006). Loving Yourself Abundantly: Relationship of the Narcissistic Personality to Self- and Other Perceptions of Workplace Deviance, Leadership, and Task and Contextual Performance. *Journal of Applied Psychology*, 91:4, 762–776.

Kernberg, O. F. (1979). Regression in Organizational Leadership. *Psychiatry*, *42*, 24–39.

Kernberg, O. F. (1998). *Ideology, Conflict, and Leadership in Groups and Organizations.* New Haven, CT: Yale University Press.

Kets de Vries, M. F. R. (1991). On Becoming a CEO: Transference and the Addictiveness of Power. In M. F. R. Kets de Vries and Associates (Eds.), *Organizations on the Couch: Clinical Perspectives on Organizational Behavior and Change* (pp. 120–139). San Francisco, CA: Jossey-Bass.

Kets de Vries, M. F. R. (2006). *The Leader on the Couch: A Clinical Approach to Changing People and Organizations.* San Francisco, CA: Jossey-Bass.

Kets de Vries, M. F. R. (2011). *Reflections on Groups and Organizations.* San Francisco, CA: Jossey-Bass.

Kets de Vries, M. F. R. and Miller, D. (1985). Narcissism and Leadership: An Object Relations Perspective. *Human Relations, 38*:6, 583–601.

Krantz, J. and Gilmore, T. N. (1991). Understanding the Dynamics Between Consulting Teams and Client Systems. In: M. F. R. Kets de Vries *et al.* (Eds.), *Organizations on the Couch: Clinical Perspectives on Organizational Behavior and Change* (pp. 307–330). San Francisco, CA: Jossey-Bass.

Labier, D. (1984). Irrational Behavior in Bureaucracy. In: M. F. R. Kets de Vries (Ed.), *The Irrational Executive: Psychoanalytic Explorations in Management* (pp. 3–37). New York: International Universities Press.

Lapierre, L. (1991). Exploring the Dynamics of Leadership. In: M. F. R. Kets de Vries and Associates (Eds.), *Organizations on the Couch: Clinical Perspectives on Organizational Behavior and Change* (pp. 69–93). San Francisco, CA: Jossey-Bass.

Lubit, R. (2002). The Long-Term Organizational Impact of Destructively Narcissistic Managers. *Academy of Management Executive, 16*:1, 127–138.

Lunbeck, E. (2014). *The Americanization of Narcissism.* Cambridge, MA: Harvard University Press.

Maccoby, M. (1984). The Corporate Climber Has to Find His Heart. In: M. F. R. Kets de Vries (Ed.), *The Irrational Executive: Psychoanalytic Explorations in Management* (pp. 96–111). New York: International Universities Press.

Marcus, P. (2014). *They Shall Beat Their Swords Into Plowshares: Military Strategy, Psychoanalysis and The Art of Living.* Milwaukee, WI: Marquette University Press.

Martin, S. W. (2006). *Heavy Hitter Sales Wisdom.* Hoboken, NJ: John Wiley and Sons.

Martusewicz, R. A. (2001). *Seeking Passage: Post-Structuralism, Pedagogy, Ethics.* New York: Teachers College Press, Columbia University.

Miller, C. C. (2016). About Face. In: *The New York Times Book Magazine*, 2/28/16, p. 35.

Miller, D. (1998). Workplaces. In: R. Jenkins and T. B. Ustun (Eds.), *Preventing Mental Illness: Mental Health Promotion in Primary Care* (pp. 343–351). Chichester, UK: Wiley.

Moore, B. E. and Fine, B. D. (Eds.). (1990). *Psychoanalytic Terms & Concepts.* New Haven, CT: The American Psychoanalytic Association and Yale University Press.

Moscovici, S. and Zavalloni, M. (1969). The Group as a Polarizer of Attitudes. *Journal of Personality and Social Psychology, 12*, 125–135.

Nelson, D. L. and Quick, J. C. (2008). *Understanding Organizational Behavior* (3rd ed.). Mason, OH: South Western Cengage Learning.

Nitsun, M. (2015). *Beyond the Anti-Group: Survival and Transformation.* East Sussex, UK: Routledge.

Penney, L. M. and Spector, P. E. (2002). Narcissism and Counterproductive Work Behavior: Do Bigger Egos Mean Bigger Problems? *International Journal of Selection and Assessment, 10*:1/2, 126–134.

Person, E. S., Cooper, A. M. and Gabbard, G. O. (Eds.). (2005). *Textbook of Psychoanalysis*. Washington, DC: American Psychiatric Association Publishing.

Pfeffer, J. and Fong, C. T. (2005). Building Organization Theory from First Principles: The Self-Enhancement Motive and Understanding Power and Influence. *Organization Science, 16*:4, 372–388.

Ratcliffe, S. (2011). *Oxford Treasury of Sayings and Quotations*. Oxford: Oxford University Press.

Richardson, J. and West, M. A. (2010). Dream Teams: A Positive Psychology of Team Working. In P. A. Linley, S. Harrington and N. Garcea (Eds.), *Oxford Handbook of Positive Psychology and Work* (pp. 235–249). Oxford: Oxford University Press.

Roth, B. (2013). Bion, Basic Assumptions, and Violence: A Corrective Reappraisal. *International Journal of Group Psychotherapy, 63*, 525–543.

Rycroft, C. (1995). *A Critical Dictionary of Psychoanalysis* (2nd ed.). London: Penguin.

Scheibe, S., Kunzmann, U. and Baltes, P. B. (2009). New Territories of Positive Life-Span Development: Wisdom and Life Longings. In: S. L. Lopez and C. R. Snyder (Eds.), *Oxford Handbook of Positive Psychology* (pp. 171–183). Oxford: Oxford University Press.

Schultz, D. and Schultz, S. E. (Eds.). (2006). *Psychology and Work Today*. Saddle River, NJ: Pearson/Prentice Hall.

Sole, K. (2006). Eight Suggestions from the Small-Group Conflict Trenches. In: M. Deutsch, P. T. Coleman and E. C. Marcus (Eds.), *The Handbook of Conflict Resolution: Theory and Practice* (pp. 805–821). New York: Jossey-Bass.

Stewart, C., Ward, T. and Purvis, M. (2004). Promoting Mental Health in the Workplace. In: J. C. Thomas and M. Hersen (Eds.), Psychopathology in the Workplace: Recognition and Adaptation (pp. 329–343). New York: Brunner-Routledge.

Stolorow, R. (1975). Toward a functional definition of narcissism. In: A. P. Morrison (Ed.), *Essential Papers on Narcissism* (pp. 97–209). New York: New York University Press.

Swogger, Jr., G. (1993). Group Self-Esteem and Group Performance. In: L. Hirschhorn and C. K. Barnett (Eds.), *The Psychodynamics of Organizations* (pp. 99–116). Philadelphia, PA: Temple University Press.

Thomas, J. C. (2004). Introduction. In: J. C. Thomas and M. Hersen (Eds.), *Psychopathology in the Workplace: Recognition and Adaptation* (pp. 3–8). New York: Brunner-Routledge.

Turquet, P. (1975). Threats to identity in the large group. In: L. Kreeger (Ed.), *The Large Group: Dynamics and Therapy* (pp. 57–86). London: Constable.

Twenge, J. M. and Campbell, S. M. (2010). Generation Me and the Changing World of Work. In P. A. Linley, S. Harrington and N. Garcea (Eds.), *Oxford Handbook of Positive Psychology and Work* (pp. 25–35). Oxford: Oxford University Press.

Van Swol, L. M. (2009). Extreme Members and Group Polarization. *Social Influence, 4*:3, 185–199.

Week, The. (2015, May 22). The Fatal Flaw of a Company without Bosses. p. 33.

Week, The. (2015, July 10). The Rise of Workplace Spying. p. 11.

Week, The. (2016, March 25). Apps. How Slack is Changing Work. p. 20.

Week, The. (2016, September 23). Crossing the boss. p. 6.

White, R. (2004). *Living an Extraordinary Life: Unlocking Your Potential for Success, Joy and Fulfillment.* Denver, CO: Balance Point International.

Winnicott, D. (1953). Transitional Objects and Transitional Phenomena. *International Journal of Psychoanalysis, 34,* 89–97.

Wollan, M. (2016). Failure to lunch. The lamentable rise of desktop dining. *The New York Times Magazine,* 2/28/18, pp. 54, 50.

Youssef, C. M. and Luthans, F. (2010). An Integrated Model of Psychological Capital in the Workplace. In P. A. Linley, S. Harrington and N. Garcea (Eds.), *Oxford Handbook of Positive Psychology and Work* (pp. 277–288). Oxford: Oxford University Press.

Zaleznik, A. (1984). Management and Disappointment. In M. F. R. Kets de Vries (Ed.), *The Irrational Executive: Psychoanalytic Explorations in Management* (pp. 224–246). New York: International Universities Press.

Zaleznik, A. (1991). Leading and Managing: Understanding the Difference. In M. F. R. Kets de Vries and Associates (Eds.), *Organizations on the Couch: Clinical Perspectives on Organizational Behavior and Change* (pp. 97–119). San Francisco, CA: Jossey-Bass.

Web sources

classiclit.about.com › … › Aristotle, retrieved 5/3/15.

izquotes.com/quote/158222, retrieved 3/2/15.

izquotes.com/quote/75728, retrieved 5/12/15.

Javerill-creativdadcursos.com, retrieved 5/29/15.

smallbusiness.chron.com › … › Organizations, retrieved 5/13/15.

thefutureofinnovation.org/contributions/…/the_future_of_innovation_up…, retrieved 4/30/15.

yourbusiness.azcentral.com/poor-company-culture-affect-employees-4410, retrieved 5/25/15.

http://achakra.com/2013/11/30/wilfred-bion-group-dynamics-the-basic-assumptions-from-wikipedia/, retrieved 4/27/15.

http://well.blogs.nytimes.com/2015/05/12/lawyers-with-lowest-pay-report-more-happiness/?_r=0, retrieved 5/28/15.

http://www.nytimes.com/2003/03/17/obituaries/17JAQU.html, retrieved 5/26/15.

http://www.scientificamerican.com/section/mind-matters/, retrieved 5/22/15.

https://hbr.org/…/half-of-employees-dont-feel-r…, retrieved 5/8/15.

https://mraybould.wordpress.com/2009/01/page/2/, retrieved 4/3/15.

https://www.psychologytoday.com/blog/cutting-edge-leadership/200904/bosses-hell-typology-bad-leaders, retrieved 5/12/15.

www.businessdictionary.com/definition/organizational-culture.ht…, retrieved 5/14/15.

www.businessdictionary.com/definition/Peter-principle.html, retrieved 5/13/15.

www.citehr.com › Business & Services Market Area, retrieved 5/11/15.

www.cnbc.com/id/30502091/page/12, retrieved 6/19/15.

www.damarque.com › Intangible Capital, retrieved 5/5/15.

www.forbes.com/sites/…/top-10-qualities-that-make-a-great-lea…, retrieved 5/8/15.

www.gallup.com/poll/…/workers-least-happy-work-stress-pay.asp…, retrieved 2/13/15.

www.glassmanpsyd.com/the-importance-of-boundaries/, retrieved 3/25/15.

www.heightcelebs.com/2014/11/hugh-grant-quotes/, retrieved 3/16/15.

www.holacracy.org/, retrieved 6/20/15.

www.holacracy.org/how-it-works/, retrieved 6/20/15.

www.izquotes.com/quote/158222, retrieved 3/2/15.

www.leadersbeacon.com/, retrieved 5/5/15.

www.mindtools.com › Communication Skills, retrieved 4/29/15.

www.nydailynews.com/.../70-u-s-workers-hate-job-poll-article-1.13812…, retrieved 5/9/15.

www.reformtaoism.org/Zhuangzi_Translations/watson_26-30.php, retrieved 3/23/15.

www.refspace.com/quotes/Sigmund_Freud/Q8130, retrieved 3/26/15.

www.simplypsychology.org › Social Psychology › Attitudes, retrieved 5/15/15.

www.unitedearth.com.au/spinoza.html, retrieved 3/20/15.

www.usatoday.com/story/.../americans-hate-jobs.../2457089/, retrieved 3/13/15.

www.usdreams.com/FordW19.html, retrieved 5/19/15.

www.whale.to/a/goethe_q.html, retrieved 6/1/15.

Chapter 6

The crucial role of emotions in facilitating organizational change

In today's complicated and topsy-turvy work environment, including "the world-wide economic crisis, the globalization of business, the rise of new technologies and the deep demographic shifts" (hbr.org), businesses and other organizations constantly have to adapt to new challenges, both in terms of changing the way they function and their basic business model.[1] They have to change their design for the successful operation of their business, identify revenue sources, customer bases, products, and details of financing. "Strategic change," as it is called in organizational psychology, "the qualitative change in the firm's philosophy or core perspective/identity," is a radically destabilizing organizational change, for it cuts into an organization's "core identity," usually within the context of dwindling organizational resources and temporal pressures. "Core identity" is the "enduring, and distinctive characteristics of the organization that all members feel proud of and have personally identified with" (Huy, 2012, p. 811). Such large-scale, planned organizational changes include mergers and acquisitions, downsizing, organizational restructuring and significantly altering the organizational culture (Liu and Perrewe, 2005, p. 264). Strategic changes often cause high levels of stress and tension to the change agents, the leadership, and even more so to the change recipients—the employees—who are required to learn new operating procedures and skills and orient themselves to a new, or at least significantly modified, "core identity." Indeed, it is largely the negative emotional impact of strategic initiatives, especially the intense fear and anxiety about the unpredictable future, that lead to change failures. Some researchers have claimed "that as many as seventy percent of change initiatives fail to achieve their intended goals" (Higgs, 2010, p. 67).[2] This dismal statistic is connected to the intrinsic conservatism of individual and organizational life that resists change. Even more important is the tremendous difficulty that, on the one hand, change agents and change recipients have in effectively reckoning with the "frustration, anger and fear" among other self-undermining affects associated with large-scale changes, and, on the other, in collaboratively co-creating "positive workplaces," those characterized by efficacy, hope, optimism and resiliency (Luthans and Youssef, 2009, p. 579). As business professors Liu and Perrewe note, "not being able to induce and manage the content and intensity of the emotions evoked by change events serve as a key reason why some change programs fail" (2005, p. 263). For example, Amado reports a troubling 2007 study that investigated 1,000 directors of 40 companies to assess 2,200 industrial projects in a range of sectors. The findings showed "that 85% of the failures of such programmes are due to organizational silence: things left unsaid, unresolved conflict, and the cult of Internet communication" (2013, p. 17). The study recommended that leadership and employees should start talking to each other in emotionally honest and meaningful ways. Such organizations are *not* what Peter Senge famously called in his "systems thinking" best-seller, *The Fifth Discipline*, "learning organizations." That is, they are not organizations where everyone continually expands and deepens their capacity to create the results they most desire, "where new and expansive patterns of thinking are nurtured, where collective aspiration is set free, and where people are continually learning how to learn together" (Senge, 2006, p. 124).[3] As Senge further notes, at the heart of the learning organization is adequately resolving the daunting emotionally driven human conflict that "we both fear and seek change" (ibid., p. 3). Viewing systems collectively involves "a multifaceted journey of thinking and feeling," (ibid., p. 144) and the success of this journey mainly depends on the "quality of relationships people develop" (ibid., p. 356). Moreover, research has found that in many contexts emotions "influence behavior independently of cognition." For example, "emotional reactions to risky situations," such as decision-making during strategic change, "often diverge from cognitive assessment of those risks." In addition, "when such divergence exists emotional reactions often drive behavior" (Huy, 2005, p. 8). Also worth noting is that the often described discrepancy between what people say and do, such as in customer purchasing behavior or team relations, has been found to be mainly unconsciously driven. Marketing experts like Gerald Zaltman of Harvard Business School noted that "[u]nconscious thoughts [and emotions] are the most accurate predictors of what people will actually do" and this is hardly accessible in a typical focus group (Roberto, 2011, p. 323). Thus, regardless of one's theoretical perspective, there is a consensus in the scholarly literature that emotions and their dispersions, dysfunctions and pathologies have a powerful role in facilitating successful organizational change and learning. However, ironically, "thoughtful management of employees' emotions during strategic change is little understood and even less systematically practiced in organizations" (Huy, 2012, p. 814).[4] In fact, one IBM-sponsored survey from 2010 of 1,500 chief executives found that "many leaders expressed doubt or lack of confidence in their own ability to lead through times of complexity" (Mueller *et al.*, 2011, p. 497), while another survey done in 1997 of 500 corporations during restructuring and other changes reported that 70% of respondents "stated that they did not have the knowledge to address [organizational] cultural issues" (Aamodt, 2010, p. 523).

In this chapter I take up two key interrelated, interdependent and interactive questions pertinent to the problem of how to creatively and effectively respond to strategic change: What can leadership do to bring about successful change in an organization, especially in terms of addressing the conscious and unconscious emotional needs and aspirations of the ultimate facilitators of innovative organizational change, the employees? How can the average employee more effectively metabolize and positively respond to the many emotional and other challenges that are associated with strategic change? The art of living the "good life" in the workplace requires a robust capacity to adapt to change and to effectively engage in what is called "organizational" or "institutional learning": the "organization-wide continuous process that enhances its collective ability to accept, make sense of, and respond to internal and external change" (www.businessdictionary.com). As Senge further noted, the process of institutional change occurs when management teams shift "their shared mental models of the company, their markets, and their competitors" (2006, p. 81). Indeed, effectively engaging in these fear and anxiety-generating, stress-inducing change processes requires a re-fashioning of one's way of being in the workplace in terms of one's identity, relationships and purpose (Schlossberg, 2009).

To unpack all of this requires that we draw from a variety of vast scholarly literatures, such as leadership/management studies, organizational psychology and psychoanalysis, and some of this complex and disparate material may not be familiar to the non-specialist. Therefore, in this effort of integration, I have summarized and synthesized the best of their respective insights so that the non-specialist can not only become familiar with this intriguing material, but benefit from the chapter. I beg the reader's patience, and ask that you "hang in there."

What makes strategic change so difficult?

As the great American economist John Kenneth Galbraith quipped, "Faced with the choice between changing one's mind and proving there is no need to, almost everybody gets busy with the proof" (Kets de Vries, 2011, p. 172). There are many reasons why individuals and groups resist change in the organizational context. Reviewing some of the typical reasons frequently given is a good point of entry into the main focus of this chapter: What can leadership and employees do, largely in the emotional realm,[5] to co-create the conditions of possibility to bring about successful strategic change?

Terror of surprises and of the unknown

To be ambushed, a surprise attack by people lying in wait in a concealed position, is one of the worst fears that people have. Indeed, the American poet laureate and novelist, James Dickey, captured the terror of suddenly being set upon from behind in his wonderful drama thriller, *Deliverance*. An ambush, and even certain kinds of less menacing surprises, probably stimulates unconscious anxiety of being physically assaulted, and as Dickey grippingly depicted, of being anally raped. In the context of an organization, it is well known that the less workers know about a planned change, especially if it is viewed as negative in nature, the more afraid they become. Moreover, informed employees are usually happier on their job than when they are kept in the dark. This is because not knowing the details of a planned change and its likely impact tends to evoke individual phantasmagoric imaginings that destructively circulate in the organization, often morphing into rumors that undermine the effectiveness of any planned change. Individuals will only be on board when they strongly feel that the risks of maintaining the status quo are greater than the imagined risks of moving in a new direction (www.torbenrick.eu). If the need for change is not convincingly put forth by change agents, especially to those employees who view the status quo as working effectively, resistance is inevitable.

Loss of job safety or status in the organization

If employees, co-workers or managers (as opposed to top executives) believe that administrative, technological or other structural changes will be self-destructive in terms of how they are situated in the organization, that is, if they believe that their role will be made superfluous or downwardly modified, they will resist change, or in the extreme, quit their job. For example, when a company proclaims that it will be restructuring or downsizing, employees may feel that they will lose their jobs or be forced into a new position they do not want within the company. Such a disempowering approach generates the feeling of being out of control of one's destiny, and this high-anxiety context will most often be a basis for strong resistance to change.

Lack of reward systems

Most people are motivated to make long-term changes in an organization by the perceived rewards for doing so. Simply put, when the benefits and rewards for making a change are not judged as sufficient, individuals tend to resist the change. Such rewards can be external, like pay increases, bonuses and benefits, or internal, such as increased status and power. The fact is that all of us have been raised in a reward/punishment regime of power as children, and the psychological traction that this parentally originating process has on our adult outlook and behavior is immense. American economist Emily Oster has aptly made this point as it relates to understanding motivation in the workplace: "The basic idea that incentives can be used to motivate behavior is a powerful one. It works for employees, and it has a clear place in parenting, as anyone who has tried to potty-train a recalcitrant toddler with sticker rewards knows" (lexbook.net). Psychoanalytically speaking, the point is that in many instances, like children, adults are motivated in the workplace from having internalized a dependency-oriented, transference-based "learning for love" principle, rather than a more self-governing and autonomous "love of learning" one.[6]

Atmosphere of mistrust

Trust, the firm belief in the integrity, ability, or character of a change agent, is essential for effective organizational change. When employees feel that their leadership cannot capably implement and manage change, there is increased resistance, this being a form of self-protection. Similarly, change agents need to be able to trust change recipients. For example, if a manager has developed trust over an extended period of time from his work team, the employees are much more likely to embrace rather than reject any implemented changes. And if the manager has helped to cultivate trustworthiness, that is, dependability and reliability in the performance of team members, he too will be more willing and able to effectively respond to their evolving needs during the change process, which contributes to the success of a planned change.

Peer group pressures

If a planned change does not consider the fact that humans are group-oriented social beings, the change agents are going to run into intense resistance from change recipients. Peer group pressure, the influence that people who belong to a specific group can have on members of the group, is a particularly salient social dynamic during strategic change. Employees will resist any change that undermines the best interests of their group by, for example, shielding co-workers from being put in harm's way. Similarly, managers will go out of their way to shield their team or workgroup from any threatening change.

Politics within the organization

Organizational politics, the pursuit of individual agendas and self-interest in an organization without regard to their effect on the organization's efforts to achieve its goals, is a pervasive dynamic that needs to be attended to during strategic change. For example, some employees will vigorously resist any planned change in order to demonstrate that the change was ill conceived from the start, thus showing that the particular change agent is not competent. There are a variety of ways that employees can resist change for the sake of self-promotion and self-aggrandizement. "Negative politics" include the application of subversive methods to advance a personal agenda which compromises organizational objectives, siphons energy away from those objectives and compromises the best interests, collaboration and job satisfaction of other employees. Such tactics include "filtering or distortion of information, non-cooperation, allocating blame, reprisals, dishonesty, obstructionism and threats" (toolkit.smallbiz.nsw.gov.au). As Senge points out, in today's organizations, teams are the "fundamental learning unit," and frequently they are inclined "to spend their time fighting for turf, avoiding anything that will make them look bad personally and pretending that everyone is behind the team's collective strategy—maintaining the appearance of a cohesive team" (2006, pp. 10, 24; Hackman, 2002). Needless to say, when such destructive politically motivated behavior is in ascendance during planned change, the likelihood of implementing a successful change is in serious jeopardy. It is for this reason that organizational leaders need to engage in constructive political behavior that can assist in strengthening commitment, buy-in, and mutual comprehension pertaining to strategic plans, such as coalition formation, lobbying, alliance building and advocacy. Such efforts especially require the skillful use of powers of persuasion, a psychological tool of leadership that can be a process of negotiation and collaboration (including nudging, pushing and shaping) rather than commanding control, or worse, heavy-handed manipulation (Roberto, 2011, pp. 195, 211, 318, 217; Conger and Kanungo, 1987).

To summarize, while the above list of frequent reasons given for why organizational change is resisted is not comprehensive, it should be clear that resistance to change usually involves the following psychological considerations in whole or combination:

1. If the rationale for the change is not clear. Ambiguity concerning costs, equipment or jobs can precipitate adverse reactions among employees.
2. If those affected by the change have not been conferred with regarding the change and it is presented to them as an accomplished fact.
3. If the change portends to modify well-established, satisfying patterns of working relationships between employees.
4. If the communication regarding the change, such as its purpose, scope, timetables and personnel has been ill conceived and deficient. Employees need to be aware of what is going on, most importantly when their jobs may be impacted. Informed employees almost always have greater job satisfaction than uninformed ones.
5. If the benefits and rewards for implementing the change are not judged as sufficient by employees for the difficulties endured.
6. If the change threatens jobs, or undermines power and status in an organization (Higgs, 2010, p. 73).

On the face of it, the above summary appears to be fairly obvious in terms of what *not* to do when planning change, and yet for the most part, most strategic change initiatives do not succeed. Indeed, as Freud pointed out, there is deep resistance to personality/character change even if it promises relief from extreme psychic suffering. The great Anglo-American poet W. H. Auden beautifully expressed this human tendency to maintain our delusionary convictions when there is the threat of an implementation of a new order of things: "We would rather be ruined than changed / We would rather die in our dread / Than climb the cross of the moment / And let our illusions die" (Roberto, 2011, p. 87).[7] Thus, it is vital to explore what emotional processes organizational leadership needs to promote to create the conditions of possibility for successful strategic change. It is to this subject that I now turn.

Effective leadership and strategic change

As Malcolm Higgs, professor of human resource management and human behavior, noted in his thoughtful 2010 review article [based on his co-authored, research-based book with Deborah Rowland, *Sustaining Change. Leadership that Works* (2008)], while there is "vast and confusing" (Rowland and Higgs, 2008, p. 62) scholarly literature on leadership,[8] some of which deals with the leader's contribution to the successful change process, for the most part, strategic, intent-led, top-down change has been greatly under-researched: "The behavior of leaders in a change context per se has been an area which is lacking empirical support." Moreover, Higgs claims, "there is relatively little research into what leads to successful change" in the organizational context (2010, pp. 68–69).[9] "High-magnitude" complex change—what Rowland and Higgs call strategic change—that involves leading change in the performance and functioning of a whole organization, including relinquishing former attachments and behaviors and moving in the direction of a new and improved way of operating, demands skillfully crafted alignment, dedication and energy of many individuals working synergistically together. This means viewing the change process less in terms of being driven by a charismatic "'heroic' leadership," a kind of "lone genius" or "corporate savior" (Roberto, 2011, pp. 21, 78) at the apex of the organization, than an "'engaging' leadership framework," one that is a "collective leadership" with the entire top management team acting as a shepherding coalition (Rowland and Higgs, 2008, pp. 3, 21, 66, 280; Roberto, 2011, pp. 45, 106). To make matters even more complicated and confusing, professors of strategy and management Kim and Mauborgne have noted that the majority of so-called strategic "plans don't contain a strategy," rather they are "a smorgasbord of tactics that individually make sense but collectively don't add up to a unified, clear direction that sets a company apart" (2005, p. 82). Given the limited, murky nature of our knowledge of the conceptual and practical linkages among the behaviors of leaders, models of change, and the effectiveness of change, much of what can be said about what constitutes a positive emotional context for bringing about change success is preliminary and suggestive (Higgs, 2010, p. 69).

A great leader is like a "good-enough" mother

In *The Fifth Discipline*, Senge quotes approvingly from his late colleague William O'Brien, the pioneering developer of "vision-driven, value-guided" organizational culture at The Hanover Insurance Company: "The primary determinant of the outcome of an intervention is the inner state of the intervenor," the change initiator (Senge, 2006, p. 372).[10] Indeed, O'Brien put his finger on probably the most important aspect of change leadership, namely, whether the change agent personifies in his mode of being, the valuative attachments that I believe are roughly equivalent to those associated with being a "good enough" mother or caregiver.[11] A "good enough" mother is psychoanalyst Donald Winnicott's famous evocative term for the "ideal" mother in terms of what is realistically possible as she tries to raise a healthy, happy, effective and creative child. Such a mother, though not perfect, is passionately dedicated to her child's best interests, she attempts to comprehend his "inner world" by being accurately empathically attuned to his emotions, she survives his aggressive incursions, she hardly ever fails in support- ing the child's ego-based requirements though often frustrates his id-based desires, and is willing and able to leave him on his own when he appears to need autonomous expression (Akhtar, 2009, p. 124; Winnicott, 1960 [1965]). Similarly, says Senge, like a "good enough" mother, the great organizational leader, has the deep "desire to serve," and when necessary, to unhesitatingly sacrifice for the best interests of those he leads. It is this heartfelt desire to serve, whether one's children, students, or in our context, one's employees and colleagues, that is "the core motivation for great leaders," especially during the change process when the going gets tough. Like a "good enough" mother, such "servant leaders" as they have been called, view the "growth of people" as their central concern; there is, says O'Brien, an "almost sacredness of their responsibil- ity for the lives of so many people" (Senge, 2006, p. 329). Kernberg notes that "it is the leader's job to protect individuals from poor working conditions, from arbitrariness in job assignment, from risks connected with the work, regardless of the impact of these measures on work efficiency" (1998, p. 119). Rowland and Higgs also noted in their research that those leaders who were "humble, modest and enabling," who engaged in "a less ego-centric" style of leadership, one that de-emphasized the leader's position, role, power and their abilities (the "Shaping leadership factor"), were much better suited to creating an organization that could change and move effectively into the future: "Are you serving yourself, or the organisation around you?" a leader should constantly ask himself (Rowland and Higgs, 2008, pp. 93, 85, 167). An example of this approach at its best was described by David Garvin, a professor of business administration at Harvard Business School, who investigated the remarkable turnaround at Serengeti Eyewear, a small entrepreneurial division within Corning (a company that specializes in glass, ceramics and optical physics products), that sold high-end, premium, technology-oriented sunglasses. The business was in deep financial trouble and Corning executives wanted to close down the division. However, Saki Mustafa, one of the entrepreneurial leaders, resisted the closure and convinced top leadership to let him try and turnaround the failing company. He increased sales four times in the first two years, and gross margin increased six times. Over a five-year period he increased sales and gross margin by three times. When asked the secret of his amazing leadership-driven turnaround he said, "I regard myself not just as a business manager, but as a surrogate father for our employees. I say to our employees: You worry about your work. I'll worry about you. I am a friend, and I get a lot of pleasure out of it" (Roberto, 2011, p. 56).[12] This leadership behavior should be contrasted with certain types of negative lead- ers, like the narcissistically motivated, charismatic type who is driven by his wish for followers to regress and personally identify with him as a father (or in the case of a woman, a mother). By inducing a regressive response such a leader is able to exert power and control over his followers rather than help them to internalize the values and beliefs that promote sociality and individual autonomy and benefit the organization (ibid., p. 77).

If a change agent ideally views himself as a parental-like "grower of people" (Senge, 2006, p. 329), it implies that he is motivated by deep feeling—call it love— best conceived of by the great ethical philosopher Emmanuel Levin as a "responsibility for the other," a lived mode of comportment that is characterized by "being for the other." Like a "good enough" mother, this often means putting the needs and desires of the child, or in the workplace, of employees and colleagues, before "being for oneself," or at least on the same footing. Senge quotes his colleague, Humberto Maturana, the prominent Chilean biologist, cybernetics theoretician and self-help author, who gave a powerful talk to engineers "about love as the recognition of the other as a legitimate other—and the 'emotion that expands intelligence.'" That is, as one strengthens and deepens one's way of relating to the other, as one becomes more other-directed, other-regarding and other-serving, "the quality of thinking improves." It becomes more creative and innovative, and this capacity positively ripples through the change process just as it does in any learning organization during less turbulent times (ibid., pp. 271, 280).[13] As Winnicott notes, it is precisely the "good enough" mother's capacity to generate a "holding environment," a "total environmental provision," as he called it, that leads to the child's growth and development (1960 [1965], p. 43). Thus, when the mother/leader is willing and able to create and maintain the psychological circumstances that constitute a facilitative context of such positive emotions like trust, acceptance, safety and containment of emotions (especially the metabolising/processing of aggressive projections), then the child and employee will be more willing and able to change, learn and grow (Akhtar, 2009, p. 130).

One final aspect of this "good enough" mother/great leader analogy that should be emphasized pertains to Winnicott's observation that the "good enough" mother is attuned to the aspirations and fears of the child's emotional world, and strives to be properly responsive, containing and supportive. As Elliot points out, the mother does this mainly by a "mirroring" process, in which her dedication, care, and competent hands-on parenting allows the child "to find himself reflected in the mother's face" (Rycroft, 1995, p. 104), in the gleam of her eyes. In this way, the child gradually develops a robust sense of self, one that is marked by self-cohesion, self-continuity and self-esteem. Winnicott notes that the more attuned the mirroring, the greater the likelihood that the child will be capable of being spontaneous, alive and autonomous. Most importantly as it relates to change leadership, it is the imagination, what Winnicott describes in terms of "transitional space," "the intermediate area of experience" between the mother and the child, that is key for the creative development of the child's self. The psychic space between the mother and the child is infused with growth and inventive potential only when the mother gives the child the opportunity and encouragement to explore, experiment and create. The teddy bear, for example, is typically provided to a child as a thing meant for play and comforting attachment. If the mother does not behave intrusively or controllingly, the teddy bear can eventually become unconsciously endowed by the child's own imagination as something new and original. As Elliot further notes, this is the radically creative potential of transitional space, "taking something that seems determined by family, culture or economics and turning it into something else, something more inventive, magical or personally meaningful" (2014, pp. 68–69). In the context of the workplace both during and after strategic change, to the extent that the change leadership can "mirror" employees like a "good enough" mother does at her best, he is likely over time to generate the emotional context for employees to be not only more adaptive, but also creative and innovative.

"Changing leadership" practices and behaviors

As any psychoanalyst will tell you, as in any kind of serious educational experience, including the bailiwick of psychoanalytic treatment, "education to reality," the process of helping an analysand change something that matters to him or her is infused with ambiguity, uncertainty and especially suffering. Indeed, this "negative capability," the capacity to remain in doubt and creatively work with not knowing by continuing to inquire and interrogate, is what allows for learning and development, painful as it may be (Rowland and Higgs, 2008, pp. 253, 327). As the French philosopher Jean-François Lyotard evocatively put it, "All education is inhuman, because it does not happen without constraint and terror" (Britzman, 2003, p. 21). That is, for Freud, since all efforts at deep personal change are emotionally super-charged, a process that is characterized by conscious and unconscious obstacles, such as conflict, but also "misunderstandings, accidents, mistakes, and refusals," the change process is anything but straight, direct and undeviating (Britzman, 2011, p. 19). As the saying goes, "God writes straight with crooked lines," meaning that the road to actualizing Beauty, Truth and Goodness in one's personal life is circuitous, unclear and paradoxical, as it involves human interpretation and judgment every step of the way, a process that is notoriously "messy" (and frightening). With this insight in mind, it is not surprising that organizational change researchers have noted that, to a large extent, the linkages between how change is approached and its success in varying organizational contexts depends on how one views the notion of change in general. When change is conceived as programmatic, linear, sequential and predictable, the change initiatives usually are not successful in most contexts. However, when change is conceived as a "complex responsive process," one that is "messier, less planned and informal," and this awareness is woven into the change process, the success of the change initiative is much more likely (Higgs, 2010, p. 70; Rowland and Higgs, 2008, p. 29). In short, change is hardly "a straightforward top down" process and effective leadership emanates from different sources (Carnall, 2008, p. ix).

Rowland and Higgs (2008; Higgs, 2010) describe four change leadership types; however, they note that the most effective leaders implement all four approaches depending on the circumstances. That is, they engage in "'multi-hit' interventions." Such leaders "stood head and shoulders above the rest in their ability to implement high magnitude change" (ibid., pp. 319, 132). While it is unlikely that a leader will have all of the traits contained in each type, to be a good leader you require many of them. Moreover, these are ideal types and therefore leaders are equally likely to have a combination of the four types of leaders.

The "Attractor" type is emotionally in tune with employees in a way that powerfully conveys the intentions and goals of the organization. He fashions "a magnetic pull" or energy in the organization via a "shared vision of change," one that "aligns and propels change" (i.e., people "buy into" the vision). This is not "magnetism" that centers around the leader (ibid., pp. 194, 117, 131), or what has been called a "Negative" charismatic leader. The Negative leader comports himself from a personalized power frame of reference, one that aims to get others dedicated to him as an individual, rather than to his ideas, concepts, product or strategy (Roberto, 2011, p. 309). In contrast, the Attractor leader is realistic and links patterns and themes to a wider movement and uses these linkages to fashion a compelling narrative, a "meta story" (Rowland and Higgs, 2008, p. 151) that is meaningful and appealing to the organization. This involves generating the conceptual context for seeing how seemingly disparate things are part of an integrated whole and weaving the narrative into smart organizational decisions. The Attractor is notably other-directed, other-regarding and other-serving; the best interests of the organization and community come before his personal career advancement. Such a leader is not abstract or a generalizer in how he leads; rather he uses his well-honed skills in a nuanced, "nuts and bolts" manner that is always context-dependent and setting-specific. The "dark side" of the Attractor is that such a practice can become ultra leader-centric, and not focused on the larger organization and effort. Such undermining behavior is often connected to the leader's inordinate narcissistic needs for affirmation, control and the like (ibid., pp. 166, 85).

The "Edge-and-Tension" type is a "straight talker," that is, he describes so-called "reality" frankly, truthfully and honestly. Such a leader is steady during challenging and stormy times, he does not flee from difficult situations while he holds others accountable for their actions. The Edge-and-Tension type is willing and able to interrogate and challenge what is taken to be the self-evident and accepted operating assumptions and models, even being a gadfly when necessary. He alters the system's capacity to function to its potential by focusing attention on the difficult issues that get in the way of movement and improved performance, and by doing so, he generates an atmosphere of increased trust and receptivity (ibid., pp. 173, 184). He has high standards and keeps upwardly adjusting those standards in a reasonable manner with an eye to bringing out the best in employees. The Edge-and-Tension type finds and keeps the best employees, for he believes that high quality people are what drive excellence. The "dark side" of this leadership practice is that his well-intentioned efforts to enhance people's performance may begin to rely less on vision and persuasion and more on fear-inducing tactics like intimidation, and in its extreme, bullying (ibid., pp. 200–201).

The "Container" type acts as a benign authority figure, one that generates reasonable rules, protocols and boundaries[14] so that employees are clear about expectations, organizational values and acceptable behaviors (e.g., "how things are done around here"). Such a leader is self-confident and stance-taking, especially in trying circumstances; they are "non-anxious, affirming and resolute while still being able to acknowledge their own issues and anxiety to others" (ibid., p. 208). He potentiates in others a sense of trust, assurance and ownership, in part by creating a sense of safety for others to say and do daring things and have frank discussions about tough issues. He does this mainly by exhibiting accurate empathy and effective communication and listening skills. For example, the Container type does not take on a team's anxiety himself, or attempt to smooth it over; rather, he tries to make the anxiety visible and is open about it in the "here and now" (ibid., p. 216). The Container type also tends to skillfully generate alignment in key structures, systems and personnel at the top of the leadership hierarchy that fosters the perception of a modicum of consistency and constancy in the change approach. The "dark side" of the Container type is that he can create unhelpful dependencies, a form of "over containment," and like a parent that is overprotective, he can engage in rescuing behavior that is disempowering to others and undermines autonomy, which causes the organization to operate in a more childish or regressive manner (ibid., p. 235).

Lastly, the "Creates-Movement" type is excellent at creating the conditions of possibility for trust among employees and colleagues, allowing them to go to different and better places, to be more creative and innovative. Such a leader encourages employees to move out of their comfort zones, role modeling this capacity by not hesitating to be vulnerable, open and responsive, the psychological pre-conditions for inventive and novel thinking. The Creates-Movement type is "here and now" oriented and crosses accepted, conventional patterns of thought and behavior to generate movement and growth. He is a "systems thinker" who aspires to bring about deep, structural changes and not simply troubleshoot. Such a leader also generates the time and space, including focusing on its physical qualities, for transforming and improving face-to-face and other encounters. At its best, when practiced mindfully, the Creates-Movement type is able to transform psychological space and generate movement towards the organization's larger purpose. He can quicken change, bring on critical learning, and foster "special moments" (ibid., p. 274). The "dark side" of this leadership practice is that it can feel self-serving, indulgent and rather emotionally manipulative to others, even "cult-like," just as its anxiety-generating and destabilizing aspects can feel "weird and spooky." For example, such a leader's efforts at exposing others' psychological vulnerability can be regarded as narcissistically-based, arrogant attempts to show that one is omnipotent and "in control," rather than authentic and helpful to reveal sites of anxiety in the organization that need to be addressed and resolved.

According to Rowland and Higgs, the results of their research indicated that the skillful combination of these leadership practices explained about half of the variance in the success of change. They also reported that conventional leader-centric behaviors, such as mainly focusing on what is flawed or "broken" and needs shoring up or "fixing," were associated with failed change initiatives. Therefore, they argue, we should be educating leaders to engage all the above-described practice behaviors in order to succeed in leading change. In this view, the emphasis should be on embracing a conception of change as less tradition-ally leader-centric, less a matter of "doing change to" employees, to a more "contextually complex" notion, one of "doing change with" them (Higgs, 2010, pp. 79, 73). Senge put this point similarly when he famously noted, "People don't resist change. They resist being changed" (www.gurteen.com). This centrally involves conceiving of change not mainly from a deficit model, as a question of implementing reactionary interventions to solve problems, reduce dysfunction, and surmount obstacles that frustrate goal achievement, but rather, from the perspective of "a focused mindfulness"[15] on strengths and positive psychological capital that already exist within the organizational system (Sekerka and Frederickson, 2010, p. 82). As Higgs aptly quipped, "To make change happen successfully, lead less and change more" (watercoolernewsletter.com; Rowland and Higgs, 2008, p. 57).

Positive emotions and change

What, then, can leadership do to create "positive emotional climates" (Sekerka and Frederickson, 2010, p. 81) to bring about success change during the change process, especially during the highly disruptive and destabilizing circumstances of strategic change?

While Frederickson's positive psychology-based "broaden-and-build" theory mainly deals with less distressing change contexts—what she describes as the "purposive evolution" of "strength-based organizational development and change process" (ibid.)—and not with the more upsetting effects to sense-making (the way a person gives meaning and organization to his experience)[16] and sense-giving of strategic change (Huy, 2012, p. 811, 812), it is a useful conceptual framework for what leadership can do to support employees during the emotion-ally challenging experiences of strategic change. Frederickson focuses on the role of "positive" emotions, like joy, interest, contentment and love (2001, p. 219), and the character strengths, like optimism, hope, efficacy and resilience (Sekerka et al., 2010, p. 170), in terms of fathoming what leaders and employees can do to better relate to each other to generate novel and helpful relationships that make the change process less traumatic and more successful. "Transformative cooperation" is Frederickson's term to describe this critical organizational process, "a specific type of change initiated by people who pool their knowledge, skills, and passion to collectively conceptualize and construct a novel and dynamic future." It is through transformative cooperation that organizations generate "upward spirals of growth and development" (ibid., p. 171).[17] Indeed, research findings lodged in broaden-and-build theory have suggested that positive emotions can favorably contribute to strategic change initiatives. For example, positive emotions strengthen leadership resilience to adversity, increase flexible and creative thinking and enhance relational skills, all of which can magnify the effectiveness of a change agent's interventions (Huy, 2012, p. 814). Moreover, emotional dedication to the change process gives change agents the staying power, hope and optimism to press on in long-term change efforts, and tends to lessen early anguish and premature abandonment of their dedication to change because of initial unsatisfactory results (ibid.). Broaden-and-build theory puts forth that positive emotions "serve to broaden an individual's momentary thought-action repertoire, which, in turn, over time, has the effect of building that individual's physical, intellectual and social resources" (Sekerka and Frederickson, 2010, p. 83). While negative emotions such as anxiety, anger and depression tend to narrow and blunt one's thought–action repertoire and reduce it to a survivalist mindset (e.g., "flight" in the case of anxiety, "fight" in the case of anger, and inertia in the case of depression), positive emotions broaden one's momentary thought–action repertoire, which then build lasting and sustaining personal resources. Says Frederickson, "Joy sparks the urge to play, interest sparks the urge to explore, contentment sparks the urge to savor and integrate, and love sparks a recurring cycle of each of these urges within safe, close relationships" (2004, p. 1367).[18]

While acknowledging that the form and function of negative and positive emotions are phenomenologically different and complementary in human behavior, meaning they both have to be reckoned with on their own terms on the individual and organizational level, Frederickson asserts that positive emotions deepen a person's capacity to create ideas, diversify the range of alternatives for actions, and enhance overall subjective well-being. Also worth noting is that positive emotions can counteract the ill-fated behavioral implications of negative emotions in that they help a person better cope with difficulties and tough times. For example, while anxiety usually leads to avoidance or escapist behavior and sadness and depression lead to inactivity and withdrawal, a sense of security predicts engagement and outgoingness, and joy stimulates an individual's playfulness and improvisation. Such positive emotions broaden a person's cast of mind and strengthen social connections, and these capacities are helpful during strategic change (Liu and Perrewe, 2005, p. 265).

The main idea here as it relates to how to better manage individual and organizational change is that rather than primarily concentrating on the impact of negative reactions among employees and how to modify them, an emphasis that reflects a survivalist outlook, the focus should also be on positive emotions that favorably impact on individual and organizational outcomes. As Sekerka and Frederickson aptly note about broaden-and-build theory,

> individual benefits of positive emotions extend beyond simply feeling good at a given moment. Positive emotions and their associated cognitions and

behaviors are not simply-end-states: rather than merely signaling optimal functioning, they help to generate both individual and organizational growth, and enduring improvements in performance over time.

(2010, p. 84)

An example of the advantage of optimal functioning may be augmented with mindful decision-making, which may help accomplish performance objectives "with moral fortitude" (ibid.). "Positive affective disposition" (being cheerful and optimistic) has been correlated longitudinally with higher income and job satisfaction and less of a chance of future unemployment. A positive affective disposition has been connected to motivational processes that assist employees to anticipate success and be more likely to effectively deal with challenges and problems. Research has suggested that employees with a positive affective disposition tend to accomplish more and generate a "higher" quality of social milieu and increased fellowship due to the advantages of organizational performance. The "take home" point is that work environments that generate and support positive experiences and the associated emotions may be the vehicles to accomplish efficient and effective organizational performance-related outcomes (ibid.), including during the strategic change process when the familiar norms of the workplace are disrupted and transformed.

While Frederickson's research suggests how important "positive emotional climates" are for employees to flourish on the job, including in some change contexts, it is the research of Nguyen Huy on strategic intent-led, top-down change that shows how organizations can develop helpful "routines" ["emotion-based dynamic capabilities"] (2005, p. 6) that deal constructively with employees' emotions, in addition to managing the many "challenges that organization leaders face in perceiving and managing employees' collective emotions" (Huy, 2012, p. 811; 1999; 2002; 2005).[19]

Though most people can appreciate the wisdom of Carl Jung's observation in *Modern Man in Search of a Soul* (1933 [2005], p. 240), "We cannot change anything unless we accept it, condemnation does not liberate, it oppresses," there is a marked proclivity to resist personal and collective change, especially within the organizational context. As I have suggested, strategic change in particular produces anxiety and other negative emotions, and these troubling feeling states, as well as positive emotions supportive of change, need to be dealt with by leadership or the change initiative is less likely to be successful. In particular, organizational leaders must accurately perceive the wide range of emotions of employees and be willing and able to manage them in a helpful and productive manner. While Huy notes that accurately perceiving emotions in individuals is an important element of well-developed managerial social intelligence, he does not adequately indicate how accurately perceiving emotions operates. Such a capacity relates to what social psychologists have called affective and cognitive empathy, which reflects that while there are individual differences, in general people are intrinsically empathic.

Affective empathy is the human tendency to experience emotion in response to others' emotional experiences, while cognitive empathy is the human inclination to see things from another person's perspective. In psychoanalytic language, such empathy is not easy to accomplish, for it involves both being able to put yourself inside the other, without losing yourself, while at the same time being able to put the other in yourself, without eradicating the other's difference and otherness. Precisely how a self's ego is supple enough to embrace the other into its experience without necessarily having to project anything upon or into the other is not clear, nor is it agreed upon by most psychoanalytic and social psychological theoreticians on empathy (Marcus, 2008, pp. 58, 140). This being said, research shows that perceptual accuracy to employees' emotional displays, that is, accurate cognitive and affective empathy, is linked to effectiveness in managing interpersonal relationships in numerous occupations and organizational roles. For instance, studies have indicated that when managers have high recognition of emotional display among employees, employees are more inclined to regard such interpersonally skilled managers as transformational leaders (Huy, 2012, p. 813). Transformational leadership is a desirable form of leadership in which the leader effectively identifies the required change, generates an inspirational vision to guide and navigate the change, and implements the change with the commitment of the participants of the group (www.businessdictionary.com).

Equally important to managing the emotional "nuts and bolts" of strategic change is the leader's capacity to accurately perceive group emotions because they impact a wide range of important group outcomes. As I have suggested in Chapter 5, group emotions in work teams can often be diverse, contradictory, conflicted and highly irrational among its members, leading to a part of the group aligning with the strategic change initiative while the other part may be against it, creating a treacherous emotional terrain for leadership to effectively negotiate.[20] Huy mentions the more important mechanisms that generate collective emotions. For example, employees can collectively have indistinguishable interpretations of the leadership motivation that guides a strategic change announcement, employees may have had identical past experiences that led them to view the costs and benefits of the strategic change to their teams similarly, and their likeminded work identities, such as their identification with the organizational culture, will lead them to experience the strategic change as something to embrace or fear. These and other group dynamics help generate the group emotions that leadership has to astutely reckon with to bring about successful strategic change, especially given the fact that there are often different sub-group assemblages within a team or business unit that have different collective emotions (Huy, 2012, p. 813).

"Emotional contagion" and "emotional aperture" are other mechanisms that tend to promote the dispersal of common emotions within group contexts, mechanisms that have a bearing on how leadership positively deals with strategic change. Emotional contagion refers to the human susceptibility to "catching," somewhat like a cold, the emotions of others. It is the tendency to automatically feel and express those emotions that are similar to and influenced by those of others. Such consciously induced, unconscious mimicry and synchronization focuses on the vocalizations, postures and movements of others. Emotional contagion impacts group processes such as cohesiveness, morale, rapport and performance and this has bearing on the cluster of shared emotions in a range of organizational contexts, including during strategic change.

The transfer of moods in a team can be dire if a leader grossly mishandles an interpersonal situation with a team member during the change process, setting off a "ripple effect" of frustration and anger throughout the team and sometimes beyond it (asq.sagepub.com). Likewise, the group phenomenon of "pluralistic ignorance" is important here, namely, the idea that if employees look to colleagues and notice they are not worried or even concerned, then those employees may inaccurately conclude that there is no compelling reason to be worried or concerned (Roberto, 2011, p. 400). In contrast, some have argued that team leaders may briefly induce collective feelings of frustration or anger when teams have been beaten by a competitor or have not achieved their goals. In other circumstances, leaders may desire to evoke feelings of genuine fear in order to get teams to realistically grasp organizational realities and embrace why a change effort is vital to the organization. Given that employees are extremely attuned to their leaders' feeling states, leaders can significantly influence employee moods, and therefore, via the mechanism of emotional contagion, their attitudes and performance (executiveeducation.wharton. upenn.edu).

Emotional aperture is the ability to discern the constituent aspects of emotional experiences in a group context. It is comparable to how a camera's aperture setting can be regulated to increase field depth, and therefore draws into focus not only one nearby person, but also others dispersed across an extended landscape. Emotional aperture thus "involves adjusting your focus from the emotional experiences of a single individual to the broader emotional composition of a collective" (www.jeffreysanchezburks.com). Huy notes an example of emotional aperture during strategic change. After the announcement of an upcoming change in an organization's strategic direction, about three-quarters of the marketing group may feel optimistic and hopeful, whereas the other quarter may feel anxiety and fear. Four months down the road, the amount of group members that feel optimistic and hopeful may decrease, while the amount of people feeling anxiety and fear may substantially increase. The skillful leader would use emotional aperture to be able to effectively differentiate not only the single-dominant group emotion, but also notice the shifts in the emotional composition of the group, a holistic mindfulness to the emotional circumstances of the group (Huy, 2012, p. 813). Needless to say, if a manager misses how the collective emotions are dispersed he is likely to make poor decisions during the strategic change process, especially in judging how best to calibrate the change and continuity balance (what to change and what to keep the same), this being a critical dynamic in any change success. Indeed, any change leadership must continuously keep a close eye on the organization as a complex, living system that is in transition. That is, he must simultaneously balance the forces of adaptation, novelty and experimentation and those of stability, structure and order, what has been metaphorically called living on the "edge of chaos" (Rowland and Higgs, 2008, p. 25) by physicist/entrepreneur J. Doyne Farmer. It is essential that managers be mindful of their own work and circumstances to implement setting-specific "emotion-management actions with particular work groups" and "calibrate these actions according to their employees' work and personal conditions" (Huy, 2005, p. 10).

Skillful "emotional balancing" and "emotional capability" by managers

"Emotional balancing" pertains to emotionally reckoning with two different groups within an organization, change agents and change recipients. According to Huy, it is effective emotional balancing by leadership that tends to provoke positive organizational adaptation while at the same time reducing dysfunction, especially the extremes that are associated with strategic change—chaos and inertia. Too much and too rapid a change creates anxiety-driven disorder and confusion, while too little and too slow a change creates depression-driven apathy and inactivity (ibid., p. 814). Emotional balancing is "a group-level process juxtaposing emotion-related organizational actions intended to drive change while fostering a sense of continuity among a group of employees" (Huy, 2012, p. 814). From an organizational point of view, emotional balancing has two interrelated aspects. First, the change agent must be emotionally dedicated, both willing and able to fully support change programs and efforts. Second, middle managers must be willing and able to be attuned to their employees' emotional best interests, especially as the employees construe them, which includes the personal meanings and implications that change has for them in their work and private lives. Such a practice has been labeled as "bounded emotionality," the acknowledgment "of the inseparability of private and work feelings and consciously attending to them" (Huy, 2005, p. 13). This emotional balancing requires that different managers assume different roles at different times, and along with emotionally user-friendly, supportive procedures, resources and training, the totality of the organization's emotional skillfulness fosters the "enabling emotional climate," for example, the "positive affective disposition" described by Frederickson earlier that tends to bring about useful strategic change. Huy's research showed that the aggregate of skillful emotional balancing by managers brought about two crucial outcomes during successful strategic change, the "development of new skills" (what changed) and "operational continuity" (what stayed the same). It is a well-known observation in the organizational change literature that to the extent that change recipients both perceive and experience past and future events as more or less continuous, the less the change is perceived and experienced as being of a distressingly high magnitude with all of the negative consequences to individual and organizational functioning (ibid., pp. 814–816).

"Emotional capability" is "the organizational ability to recognize, monitor, discriminate, and attend to emotions of employees at both the individual and collective level" (ibid., p. 815). Rather than rely on the virtuoso relational skills of individual managers, conceiving the organizational system as a living, dynamic whole develops the routines and resources for potentiating actions that are rooted in the accumulated knowledge and skills shown in context-dependent, setting-specific situations to effectively manage the range of emotions associated with strategic change. In other words, an organization's emotional capability to effectively manage strategic change can be more than the sum of the individual skillfulness of its managers.[21] Huy summarizes the "emotional dynamics" that his research suggests significantly impact three critical processes associated with strategic change: "receptivity," the range of diverse responses that constitute a willingness to accept change; "collective mobilization," motivating clusters of the organization to engage in joint action and actualize common change goals, and "organizational learning," acquiring new skills and competencies via the goal-action-outcome learning feedback loop, "feedback mechanisms linking receptivity to mobilization" (ibid.; Huy, 1999, pp. 328–329, 331).

Huy's processes of successful organizational change

Empathy and organizational heedfulness

Empathy and organizational heedfulness on the part of managers and leaders is vital during successfully implemented strategic change. As I have said, accurate cognitive and affective empathy between managers and employees throughout the relationship and decision-making matrix of an organization benefits everyone, including performance outcomes and productivity. This being said, research has suggested that the next generation of leaders and employees may find such empathic immersion challenging. One study found there has been "a steep decline in empathy [40%], as measured by standard psychological tests, among college students of the smartphone generation" (Franzen, 2015, p. 22). From an organizational point of view, leadership can communicate to its employees that how they feel and what they emotionally need and want matters to the leadership and will generate a helpful response from them. Organizations that have developed sensitivity training and coaching opportunities for managers (especially the change agents) and employees, as well as anxiety-decreasing support structures like informal communication forums, self-help groups, counseling services, and single- and double-loop learning intercessions (a learning style that is problem solving versus one that reconceptualizes and reframes goals and values), can be of assistance in helping employees come to terms with the shifting circumstances, realities and personal distress connected to strategic change. Leadership can further reduce anxiety and boost morale by being mindful of the timing, pacing and sequencing of different aspects of the change process, always keeping in mind what can be done to maintain a modicum of emotional stability for those who are going through the major changes in their familiar job routines.

Sympathy and the dynamics of reconciliation

Huy describes sympathy and the dynamics of reconciliation as another aspect of what is psychologically optimal to bring about a successfully implemented change initiative. Sympathy is a forerunner of empathy, the less psychologically demanding ego response to another person going through strategic change, and therefore should be distinguished. Where empathy is a "feeling into" moment between two people, of first cognitively viewing someone's else's circumstances from his point of view, and then affectively sharing his feelings, whether positive or negative, sympathy is more of a "feeling with" moment, of commiserating with a person's challenging circumstances. Typically, a person can empathize when they have personally felt what the other person is feeling, like having a life-threatening disease or trying to lose weight. Sympathy is rooted more in under-standing and compassion for what the person has experienced. It typically prompts an urge to offer comfort and assurance. Where a psychopath can empa-thize with his victim, such as drawing him into his manipulative web, he in no way can sympathize with him. Thus, while empathy requires having a self with a more flexible ego, one that is willing and able to get inside another person's way of thinking and feeling without losing himself, sympathy is an expression of a self's ego that is guided mainly by emotionally animated "moral" values, such as Levinasian "responsibility for the other." On an organizational level, leadership expressions of sympathy assist in increasing employee receptivity to change (Huy, 2005, p. 11).

Huy is suggesting that during the strategic change process it is essential that the change-initiators sympathize with the change recipients, which involves creating the psychological space on the individual, group and organizational level for employees to grieve the loss of their prior organizational culture, those "core" values that animated their sense of belonging, informed their self-concept and bolstered their self-esteem, the psychological basis of their voca-tional identity. Moreover, given that in many instances one's vocational identity is a central part of one's personal identity, the cluster of thoughts, feelings and actions that constitute who we feel we essentially are as a complete person, the mourning process is a powerfully upsetting experience (Kets de Vries, 2011, p. 143).

To the extent that employees effectively engage in the emotional process of "reconciliation," as Huy calls the mourning process, of working through their sense of separation and loss from their past sense-making and sense-giving work routines and values that compose their narrative of self-identity, they are more likely to be open and responsive to the difficulties and sacrifices associated with strategic change. One must never overlook the fact that at the extreme, to relinquish all aspects of one's organizational identity is unconsciously equated with annihilation and nothingness. As French poet Anatole France said, "All changes, even the most longed for, have their melancholy; for what we leave behind us is a part of ourselves; we must die to one life before we can enter another" (Lee, 1999, p. 36). If leadership does not properly allow a mourning process among employees, the typical signs of incomplete mourning are often generated, such as overt and/or covert frustration, anger, depression, and greatly reduced spontaneity and creative energy (Huy, 2005, p. 16).

What needs to be emphasized is that while mourning, psychoanalytically speaking, is a normative analogue to depression, it is not just a response to the actual losses in the external world. Think, for example, about a colleague, unconsciously regarded like a "family member," who has been laid off in a company's downsizing, or of the big and small losses in one's source of security and/or self-esteem, like job role, status or power. Mourning also involves the loss of the "internal object." Internal objects are those imagined phantoms that are responded to as if they were real that have been ambivalently invested (Rycroft, 1995, pp. 106, 113). It is this aspect of the mourning process that makes "complete" mourning so difficult, the ability to psychologically move beyond the loss, even though it often demands a fair bit of denial and idealization of the lost object during the middle phases of the mourning process. Without adequate mourning of this experience of oneself in relation to the lost internal object, whether of a colleague or a vocational identity, it is near impossible to move forward, let alone replace the lost object with a new one. While Freud believed that mourning involved a replacing of the lost object with a new object as the sign of "complete" mourning, most psychoanalysts acknowledge the lost object is rarely thoroughly relinquished, though it attains a lesser, or at least different, emotional meaning to the mourner as time passes. As Volkan notes, some individuals develop "linking phenomena," ways of denying or reversing the negative impact of the loss of a laid off colleague or one's vocational identity. Such linking phenomena are "'a token of triumph' over loss" (1972, p. 220). In the workplace this includes the symbolically important ways of replacing a colleague or one's vocational identity with a gratifying fantasy or behavior that permits the mourner to feel as if he is emotionally reconnected with what was lost (and the robust self-esteem that went with it). Such fantasies and behaviors give the mourner a sense that the better time before the loss has been frozen and/or the current harsher reality has been magically reversed, eliminating, if only briefly, the distress of the loss. Organizations that patiently and skillfully use their resources to give employees the time and space to mourn the loss of their "cherished values" associated with the organizational culture can greatly reduce the negative impact of the strategic change process on employees. For example, in one instance change managers designed mourning rituals that were implemented prior to the closing of employees' beloved work sites. They employed heritage and succession rituals and last suppers served by managers, fostering a sense in employees that they were valued and respected by their leaders (Huy, 2005, p. 15). Also worth remembering is that survey data has shown that "social support from coworkers was the most important coping resource for employees who were not laid off" (Schultz and Schultz, 2006, p. 265).

Hope and the dynamic of encouragement

Hope and the dynamic of encouragement is what an organization's leadership can do to generate hope processes in employees undergoing strategic change. Hope, as philosopher Gabriel Marcel noted, is best conceived as "hoping," that is, the phenomenology of hope reveals that it is not simply a fixed idea that one possesses in one's head, but rather it is a process-driven, emergent, and renewable psychological and behavioral activity that tends to upsurge in particular challenging contexts, in "extreme" situations of imprisonment; indeed, poorly implemented strategic change can often feel like a near-obliterating form of imprisonment to change recipients (Marcus, 2013a, pp. 59–60). The assumption, says Huy, is that "the higher the degree of encouragement" (e.g., support, praise, incentive) "to elicit hope among all employees the higher the posited degree of collective mobilization for strategic change" (2012, p. 816). Such interventions include creating meaningful and appealing change goals; fashioning small victories to renew self-confidence; regular and upbeat interactions between change agents and change recipients; inspiring rituals such as stirring speeches and award ceremonies that honor achievement; and putting forth a convincing, if not irresistible, strategic vision. Such compelling signals, symbols, rituals and metaphors help shape a facilitating environment that increases the internal motivation of employees (Roberto, 2011, p. 177).

Authenticity and the dynamics of display freedom

Touched upon earlier, authenticity and the dynamics of display freedom is yet another crucial process that must be part of any successful strategic change. To the extent that change recipients believe that they cannot feel and say what they want about what is occurring in the workplace throughout the change process, especially during its more trying transition points, the more they will feel privately imprisoned and afraid. As a result of this internal condition, change recipients will be prone to imposter-like behavior (e.g., emotional phoniness and pseudo-compliance), risk-aversion, cynicism, learning inhibitions or blocks, and other aggressive forms of resistance to the change process. Thus, to the extent that emotional display freedom exists, of both negative and positive feelings, and that they are properly metabolized and responded to by leadership, the greater the likelihood that maximum organizational learning during strategic change will take place (Huy, 2012, p. 817). Authenticity on the part of leadership facilitates an atmosphere of transparency and trust in an organization. Without employees feeling they can trust their bosses, any well-intentioned emotional-management intervention is useless (Huy, 2005, p. 11).

Fun and the dynamic of playfulness

Fun and the dynamic of playfulness is important during the change process because it puts into sharp focus the obvious though often overlooked fact that the happier an employee feels the more exploratory and creative he tends to be. By playfulness I mean, "when one engages in personally motivating and challenging activities" (Huy, 2012, p. 818). For example, as Einstein noted, sustained "combinatory play seems to be the essential feature in productive thought," the kind of creative thinking that often leads not only to better adaptation during the change process but also innovation (www.brainpickings.org). Experientially, such playfulness means that activities are done for the utter pleasure of doing them. If an employee feels calm, he is capable of being more spontaneous and is prone to improvising, permitting a situation to take him where it will. Playfulness not only minimizes stress, it altogether brightens the totality of circumstances that one feels one is in, and thus it promotes greater and stronger connections with colleagues and leadership. Such a context of playfulness and "deep fun" has obvious beneficial impact on how change recipients experience the worst aspects of strategic change. What is true on a personal level is also true on an organizational level, especially during strategic change—namely that leadership has to cultivate an emotional environment in which playfulness is woven into the typical workday so it facilitates organizational creativity and innovation (Huy, 2005, p. 11; Amabile and Kramer, 2011).[22] As British philosopher Alan W. Watts aptly noted: "This is the real secret of life—to be completely engaged with what you are doing in the here and now. And instead of calling it work, realize it is play" (vimeo.com).

Love and the dynamics of identification

Finally, there is love and the dynamics of identification, the extent that employees are emotionally attached to an organization. The more that it is identified with it, the greater the likelihood employees will be willing to engage in organizational learning during the strategic change. Huy believes that the main psychological mechanism that accounts for emotional attachment to an organization is identification, described as a process analogous to "falling in love," and defined as "the collective behavior whereby organizational members express their deep attachment to salient organizational characteristics" (2012, p. 818). Organizational memory, "the collective ability to store and retrieve knowledge and information," is an important aspect of this emotional attachment to an organization (www.knowledge-management-tools.net).[23] The greater the extent to which organizational memory, the social glue of a thriving organization—unofficial and unrecorded experiences, insights, knowledge and skills obtained over years that are transmitted to new employees through meetings, training courses and mentor-protégé relationships—is disrupted or destroyed by downsizing, regular layoffs, unmanaged employee attritions, etc., the less likely it is that organizational learning during strategic change will occur (www.businessdictionary.com).

Although identification has its role in emotional attachments, "falling in love," whether in a personal or organizational context, is a much more psychologically complex process than Huy describes, especially, as when following Freud, we consider the multifarious nature of subjective identifications that are accessible in fantasy (Elliot, 2014, p. 49). However, identification does help illuminate how a person "brings into the psyche less concrete and more role-oriented aspects of significant others in relationship to oneself." Moreover, such "identifications do not feel like a foreign body in the self [like an "introject"] and are more likely to be ego-syntonic and in harmony with the individual's self-image" (Akhtar, 2009, p. 150). What this way of defining identification means for strategic change is that over time members in a work team develop strong emotional connections to each other and if these relationships are disrupted by the strategic change then, typically, anxiety is generated leading to a wide range of defensive reactions that are meant to blunt if not resist the change initiative. Organizationally speaking, employee attachment helps limit large turnover of key, highly valued personnel (Huy, 2005, p. 11).

Summary

While the above-described practices sound straightforward, they are "easier said than done." For, as Winnicott quipped, "The unconscious [with its "delicious indeterminacy" (Elliot, 2014, p. 81)] may be a nuisance for those who like everything tidy and simple, but it cannot be left out of account by planners and thinkers" of change (Britzman, 2003, p. 97). That is, while change researchers have pointed out that all of these leadership practices can, to some extent, be trained and learned, they are undeniably dependent on the hard-to-pin-down personality capacities, self-awareness and insight, values and beliefs, and relational skillfulness of the change initiator, his individualized way of "being-in-the-world." For example, researchers agree there is no "common set of traits that distinguish high performing leaders from others that don't perform well," and there is no "set of universal leadership traits" (Roberto, 2011, pp. 31, 35). It is for this reason that most change initiatives fail, for such change leadership is not only hard to find or learn, but it requires a near perfect "match" or "fit" between the change initiators and the change recipients. Only where there is an alignment between the leader's style (less his personality and more his behavior) and the contextual demands that he is reckoning with (such as the culture and environment in which leaders and employees work), what is called "situational leadership" (ibid., pp. 401, 37),[24] can leaders and employees co-produce successful high-magnitude change, learning and growth. What the change recipient can do to help this process along, including maintaining his own autonomy, integration and humanity amidst the harsher aspects of the strategic change process, is our final topic.

Tips for employees to emotionally "manage" strategic change

The art of living the "good life" within the context of high-magnitude organizational change requires the same finely-tuned, critical, self-reflective capacities and introspective skills that one has hopefully developed in everyday life in which one feels as if one is being "disciplined." Discipline, "a mechanism of power which regulates the behavior of individuals in the social body," is used by leaders and managers to "make individuals," to control and use employees as if they were objects. This is accomplished by regulating the way space is organized, such as with architecture; time, such as with timetables; and an individual's activities and behavior, such as drills, posture and movement. Discipline is enforced with the assistance of multifaceted surveillance systems (www.michel-foucault.com; Nehamas, 1993, p. 33). Such "normalization" processes, as Foucault called them, are rooted in the notion that there is a principle of "correct" functioning that is based on accepted scientific knowledge, such as the empirical findings reported in the human resource, organizational, vocational and positive psychology literatures about what constitutes "successful" strategic change and how to produce it.

Thus, for Foucault, the average employee must continually engage in a reflexive process of discerning and facing those limiting conditions imposed by leaders and managers that subjectify him (roughly, what one identifies with and absorbs into oneself from the organizational culture), especially those negative practices that undermine his autonomy and freedom to authentically invent himself in the workplace. Following Foucault, the concept of freedom that I am putting forth is a "revolt" within those dominating practices that leaders and managers intentionally and unintentionally levy on employees during the strategic change process. That is, the "real" employee freedom is the ability to "identify and change those procedures or forms through which our stories become true, because we can question and modify those systems which make [only] particular kinds of action possible" (Rajchman, 1985, p. 122). This "consciousness of freedom," as Bruno Bettelheim called it, entails dissolving or changing those anonymous, depersonalizing, conformist practices that constitute our conception of ourselves and that we take to be self-evident and true within the context of the organization going through strategic change. Such autonomy means having the freedom to participate in the project of inventing, improvising and creating whom one can be, what Bettelheim called a "higher integration." Such autonomy is necessary to resist the negative aspects of strategic change, including its often impersonal bureaucratic practices, invasive surveillance, the seductive appeal of ultimately dehumanizing technologies, and a "bottom line" organizational morality that values financial profit above all else, even if it "cuts into" people and hurts them (Marcus, 1999, p. 184).

While Foucault stressed that the way we think is unavoidably enmeshed in practical power relations because it is intimately connected to action and larger economic, social and political forces [e.g., personal identity and social structure are always intertwining, power is thus a relationship between individuals, groups and institutions (Elliot, 2014, pp. 52, 90)], it is difficult to facilitate new power relations, let alone ones that decisively promote individual autonomy, integration and humanity. Resistance is therefore best viewed not as something that resides external to power relations, but rather, it is a potentiality that is internal to it. As Foucault noted, power always fosters its own resistances. In this view, resistance is an agonistic struggle and strategic contest, a form of combat that calls to mind engaging in a judo match or playing a chess game. Such "soft" power can be used by the employee to engage in oppositional behavior that is in his best interests (at least as he construes it) and those of fellow employees who feel that leadership is acting in a manner that is disrespectful and unfavorable to the most important facilitators of all organizational change, the employees. There is a whole stream of studies in the sociology of work that describes "the hidden underside of work," those patterns "of covert defiance, subterfuge, and restriction of output" that are meant to counteract an oppressive leadership/management regime that aggressively controls the efforts of employees. Vallas further notes that even a lowly worker finds and creates "ways of neutralizing, disrupting, or renegotiating leadership regimes to their own advantage" (2012, pp. 15, 16).[25] For example, his research on pulp and paper manufacturing plants in the southern US showed that when manual workers had to cope with machine superintendents who were insufficiently respectful of the workers' knowledge and dignity, they developed "authority contests" in which workers taught their supervisors significant lessons about the meaning of reciprocity and respect. Machines were prone to run "in the ditch" for entire shifts as workers tried to change their supervisors' obnoxious behavior, or, if required, "to inflict moral injuries on their supervisors' careers" (ibid., p. 16). Another subtle tactic with which less powerful employees can control leadership's self-serving and objectionable behavior is spoiling their reputation by gossiping, which has been shown to act as a corrective to those leaders who do not want to lose their authority and favorable reputation—in short, their power (Lammers *et al.*, 2010, p. 743; Marcus, 2010, pp. 81–98).

Within the context of a complex organization, especially one going through strategic change, it is difficult for the individual to systemically change how things are done, to bring about structural modifications in the way the organizational change process is crafted by executive leadership. The average employee is, therefore, often left embracing a constantly questioning, critical orientation to that which he takes for granted as "true" and self-evident in the workplace, as it relates to maintaining his positively viewed autonomous sense of self. In this way, he can loosen the grip of his current normalizing and conformist interpretations of reality perpetuated by leadership—of himself and his organization. By getting a better understanding of how he and the organization got to where they are, the personal and social costs of such understandings, and that things used to be otherwise (e.g., recalling the good aspects of the organizational culture before the change, and reflecting on those "positive" organizations that have humanely and successfully gone through such change), he can show leadership, and himself, how things can be done differently. That is, he is more promoting of individual and group well-being during the strategic change process. Such an attitude and behavior skillfully challenges the present situation, and suggests what can be done by leaders to make things better, especially according to a "responsibility for the other" moral calculus, one that that is mainly other-directed, other-regarding and other-serving as it pertains to employees who have to withstand the worst of the change. In psychoanalytic language, what this boils down to is the employee's capacity to creatively "use aggression in the service of self-definition," this being "a *sine qua non* of healthy working." If psychologically "surviving," let alone flourishing, in the workplace during strategic change is what matters, then aggression and its derivative, anger, has to be sublimated in the service of self-protection and self-actualization (Axelrod, 1999, pp. 113, 4, 9).

Practices of the self

There have been many worthwhile publications that have suggested some of the common "practices" or "technologies of the self," to use Foucault's terms, that employees have used to resist the harsher aspects of strategic change, especially the upsurge of fear and anxiety that it generates in nearly all employees. Being able to fashion a robust, resilient sense of self, including implementing effective and self-enhancing interventions during the change, is what constitutes the art of living the "good life" in an organization that is in high-magnitude transition.

While detailing all of this is beyond the scope of this chapter, I offer suggestions for how creative and resourceful employees manage their fear and anxiety associated with such change (www.bizcoachinfo.com).

1) Face the reality of change. Internally work against one's defensive denial and other neurotic defenses against one's fear of what is "objectively" threatening about change, what is based on the realistic, "rational" perception of imminent danger (admittedly a personal judgment). This is to be distinguished from what is "subjectively" threatening, based on unrealistic, anxiety-inducing "irrational" fear. The unwillingness or inability to acknowledge these different types of reactions to change is a fertile psychological breeding ground for serious problems in adaptation to the totality of circumstances one is in. Writing down one's fears and anxieties, making them feel objectified, can make them more emotionally manageable. Well-developed, critical, self-reflective and introspective skills are crucial here, especially as Freud pointed out, so-called reality is internally represented via fantasy and imagination, which inevitably includes psychic creations and distortions (Elliot, 2014, p. 67).

2) Accept your fears by engaging in self-talk that affirms that fear and anxiety are what you are feeling in the here and now (do not dodge your experienced emotions). Most importantly, label your fears and anxiety without censuring self-judgment, without personal condemnation.

3) Draw from your support system, like a significant other, friends, trusted colleagues, and a psychotherapist, to reduce fear and anxiety. Do not be reticent

to reach out for help from others, as fear and anxiety are almost always reduced when one feels that one is not alone. Research has shown that engaging in prosocial practices, behavior that is geared to shield and/or advance the best interests of others such as helping colleagues, promotes a positive identity and flourishing at work, including during the change process (Dutton *et al.*, 2011).

4) When you are not working and are relaxed (relaxation being essential), bracket time to analyze your "external" and "internal" circumstances with an eye to problem-solving.

5) Avoid imagining catastrophic scenarios. Instead, concentrate on likely near-future "real" problems and work on feasible solutions.

6) Avoid asking yourself anxiety-inducing "what if" questions, such as, What if my work is not appreciated, or suppose management does not listen to what I am expressing or requesting? Remaining in the present "reality" as opposed to the phantasmagorically conceived future is what counts most.

7) Find and create effective ways to communicate to leaders, managers and colleagues by first assimilating the organization's vision for change and learning the "soft skills," like how to speak and write effectively to get your fear and anxiety-reducing points across to reduce them. Avoid paying heed to the rumor mill—such talk at the water cooler can be lethal.

8) Develop optimism, for it is a valuable resource in engaging in the destabilizing and stressful perspective-shifting that comes with strategic change. This can be done by cultivating the art of tragicomic humor—seeing the tragic in the comic and the comic in the tragic—an important tool for managing the worst aspects of the change process (Marcus, 2013a).

9) Learn from your history that you have successfully managed other crises in your career and life, and therefore tell yourself you can again prevail. Remind yourself that unless you are being tortured or executed, there is always an "escape" from your dire situation, even if it means a purely mental one: "No matter how terrifying a given system may be, there always remain the possibilities of resistance, disobedience, and oppositional groupings" (Foucault, 1984, p. 245).

10) Practice the "Principle of Contrary Action," that is, do your job differently each time, or at least frequently, as this will help cultivate an open and flexible mind, something that will both serve your adaptation and be favorably noticeable to leadership.

11) Volunteer to be an agent of change and to assist leadership in implementing it. This will ultimately reduce one's fear and anxiety since one has essentially forced oneself to reckon with, and master, one's objective fear and subjugate one's subjective demons. It also is self-empowering as it allows one to have some input on the larger change process and influence on the decision-makers.

12) Reduce stress through other activities that you find pleasurable outside the workplace. Rigorous exercise is particularly valuable, for it has been shown to reduce anxiety and depression. The key is not to let the "work self" become the "whole self," with all of the deleterious effects to self-esteem, self-concept and behavior that come along with feeling "under siege."

13) Become a "go-to" person, that is, analyze your strengths and limitations concerning the change process and create improvement goals that are coordinated with what leadership needs and wants. This will help reduce one's fear and anxiety and favorably impress leadership, which can be beneficial to oneself and one's likeminded colleagues.

It is hard to dispute the advice of the above suggestions for better managing the fear and anxiety generated by negative organizational processes that threaten one's autonomy, integration and humanity. However, as with the practices of leadership described earlier, these "technologies of the self," what employees can do to personally transform themselves, are much easier to suggest and to describe in theory, than to successfully implement in the topsy-turvy, high-stress, everyday environment of a transitioning organization. Perhaps one should take comfort in the quip by the great American novelist Henry Miller: "The man who looks for security, even in the mind, is like a man who would chop off his limbs in order to have artificial ones which will give him no pain or trouble" (1949 [1994], p. 339).

Final comment

I have argued that effective organizational leadership during strategic change is less about the individual capabilities of a charismatic leader who drives change, and more about his and the leadership team's ability to mobilize the dynamic capability of the change recipients, the employees, in a collaborative effort at transformation, one that "sticks" (Roberto and Levesque, 2005; Sawyer, 2007). Such "adaptive leadership," as Heifetz (1998) has called it, is willing and able to engage in the following practices: 1) To clearly and astutely delineate the key challenges and opportunities an organization faces. 2) While he and his team are pressing employees to face the gravity of the challenges and opportunities, which can be anxiety-producing, they are also mindful of modulating and dosing the levels of stress and tension that the organization goes through to avoid dysfunctional and pathological responses. 3) Keep employees concentrated on the crucial issues and curb their tendencies to scapegoat others, blame the nature of assignments, engage in sabotaging behavior, or in other ways get distracted from what really matters. 4) Give the work back to employees (e.g., they authorize greater responsibility for idea generation, problem-solving and taking on difficult challenges) in a way that employees can comfortably manage, that is, at a rate they can effectively perform well with. 5) Shield and encourage the voices of leadership that do not have formal authority or are lower on the leadership hierarchy, those employees who have significant data and information, often informally collected, who are also able to raise hard questions and challenge the status quo and can generate new ways of seeing and doing. Such dissenting voices often stimulate "bottom up" change, using their hands-on knowledge of the dynamics of organizational culture and functioning to facilitate learning. It is through these and other leadership practices described earlier that a positive working environment, including during decision-making processes, is generated, one that will help an organization to transform itself in a favorable manner (Roberto, 2011, pp. 14, 15).[26]

Most importantly, I have stressed that leadership has to be acutely sensitive to the totality of emotional circumstances that influence, by both promoting and impairing, the emotional well-being and best interests of employees during the entire change process. This requires leadership to have well-developed forms of attunement, such as emotional and social intelligence, as well as other psychological skills throughout the change process as they try to co-produce with employees the conditions of possibility for transformation. While rationalistic, conscious and cognitive factors are important in this process, being attuned to unconscious feeling and desire matters as much, if not more (Elliot, 2014, pp. 35, 156). As Ruti aptly put this point, "Rational and self-reflexive psychic states are obviously an achievement of a very high order, but if we are to remain capable of growth they need to be continuously replenished by the unruly energies of the unconscious" (2008, p. 79).

As for employees, what is most important for them during the change process is to conceptualize their overall experience in terms of how to maintain their autonomy, integration and humanity, especially during its harsh phases. This entails developing "technologies of the self," the variety of open-ended ways that employees constitute their identities in the workplace in a creative and constructive fashion (i.e., they find/create their "own" unique voice). This symbolic project simultaneously involves identifying those forms of power that constrain, limit or repress personalized modes of self-expression and finding workable and effective ways to counteract them. In short, employees must engage both the positive and negative forms of identity formation as they are expressed within the broader power dynamics operating within the organization and beyond. This emancipatory strategy of actively engaged self-construction and reconstruction requires considerable self-awareness, self-mastery and relational skillfulness (Elliot, 2014, pp. 50, 110, 220, 186).

Finally, and most importantly, for an organization to flourish during and after the change process, a "win-win" outcome for leaders and employees, there must be a very good "fit" between change initiators and change recipients from the onset of the change process to its culminating point. This "fit" needs to be continually adjusted and regrooved within the totality of circumstances of the change process. While we know a lot about how to foster such alignments, the fact is that successful, high-magnitude organizational change is ultimately rooted in an existential "leap of faith." The decision to act only on currently available data and analysis in circumstances where the outcome is uncertain involves the irrational faith and trust in a set of mysterious processes that gloriously come together in a moment of what feels like utter serendipity. Indeed, Steve Jobs seems to have had a similar view when he said, "You can't connect the dots looking forward; you can only connect them looking backwards. So you have to trust that the dots will somehow connect in your future. You have to trust in something—your gut, destiny, life, karma, whatever. This approach has never let me down, and it has made all the difference in my life" (www.movemequotes.com).

Notes

1 Paraphrasing Richard Sennett's wonderful book *The Corrosion of Character*, Elliott notes that while in the past the workplace was characterized by "rigid, hierarchical organizations," such that self-discipline formed the durability and resilience of the self, in recent times we reside in "a brave new economy of corporate re-engineering, inovation and risk." In our era this brings about a more fragmented and splintered self-experience. Indeed, the fact that the conditions of work are typically characterized by "networking, short-term teamwork and instant self-reinvention" tends to support Sennett's claim (Elliot, 2014, pp. 139, 165).

2 As organizational theorist Henry Chesbrough noted, "Most innovations fail. And companies that don't innovate die" (2003, p. xvii).

3 See Garvin (2000) for another useful book on organizational learning.

4 Some scholars make a sharp distinction between leadership, which is focused on "change and transformation," and management, which is focused on "consistency and order." These designations are hard to empirically distinguish as they often co-mingle. Thus, there is no scholarly consensus about what constitutes the "real world" similarities and differences between leaders and managers (Roberto, 2011, p. 29).

5 While I believe that the human being is best understood as "being-in-the-world," as an indivisible unity of feeling, thought and action, for the purposes of this chapter, I will mainly discuss organizational change and learning from the point of view of emotions and their cognitive and behavioral implications.

6 Britzman (2011, p. 81) correctly points out a paradoxical quality of transference in the educational context, that while there cannot be any learning without the transference (e.g., idealization of knowledge, and/or authority, such as one's teacher), the transference, however, can be an impediment to learning in that it leads to a lack of critical reflection or the ill-conceived unconscious infantile quest for absolute knowledge.

7 One is reminded of Freud's similar observation made in his essay *Humour*: "The ego refuses to be distressed by the provocations of reality, to let itself be compelled to suffer. It insists that it cannot be affected by the traumas of the external world; it shows, in fact, that such traumas are no more than occasions for it to gain pleasure" (1927 [1961], p. 162).

8 A few very good books on change leadership are Heath and Heath (2010), Collins (2001), Heifetz (1998) and Kotter (1996).

9 Much of the change leadership literature was influenced by social psychologist Kurt Lewin's theorizing regarding how organizational change happens: "Unfreezing," being willing and able to change, "changing," developing new ways of doing things, and "freezing," institutionalizing changes. As Lewin noted, "If you want to understand something, try and change it." Drawing from Lewin, leadership scholar John Kotter (1996) has developed an eight-step model for leading transformation (Roberto, 2011, p. 98, 99; Lewin, 1958).

10 The late Harvard psychologist, Richard J. Hackman, one of the great investigators on teams noted, "effective leaders set the organizational stage for great team performances" (Roberto, 2011, p. 286).

11 Senge uses the master "teacher" as the ideal model for the leader in a "learning organization," though I think the image of the "good enough mother" cuts deeper in terms of the need for the leader to be exquisitely sensitive and supportive of the inner world and material needs of employees. Hackman (2002) also uses a parenting metaphor to articulate how best to lead teams.

12 The question of whether Musafti's leadership style would be effective in larger companies in size, scale and scope has been debated. Indeed, Musafti's uniquely contoured, relationship-based approach would be hard to effectively implement in a bigger organization, one whose culture and employee make-up would be different and probably less responsive to his interventions (Roberto, 2011, p. 57).

13 For a detailed discussion of Levinas's views on maternity, the personification of being for the other before oneself, a mode of comportment in which there is an abundance of compassion and forgiveness, see Marcus (2008, pp. 112–116).

14 Kernberg notes that the breakdown of boundary control is the most troubling symptom of the breakdown in the control function in an organization (1998, p. 95).

15 Mindfulness is a Buddhist term that suggests that one should go below the surface level of your moment-to-moment experience, which is often clouded and distorted by troubling emotions, to view the "truth" of what is actually going on. In everyday life, mindfulness aids a person in clearly seeing what needs to be done, what a person is capable of doing, and how a decision connects to the larger "truths" and valuative attachments of life. Mindfulness can be cultivated through the practice of mindfulness meditation (dharmawisdom.org).

16 Following sociologist Anthony Giddens, sense-making is a process that includes both certainty and anxiety, that permits a person "to read," to make sense of "cultural life and its textured flow in social action" (Elliot, 2014, p. 45).

17 Frederickson's theory has been thoughtfully criticized by Kjell (www.positivepsychology.org.uk) and Wilkinson (2013).

18 In her best-selling book, Frederickson (2009) mentions the ten most common positive emotions: joy, gratitude, serenity, interest, hope, pride, amusement, inspiration, awe and love.

19 I have mainly relied on Huy (2012) in this section as this is the most up-to-date and succinct statement of his important research findings.

20 Leadership, especially for managers, is fundamentally about negotiating and building coalitions. In fact, it is their "way of life" (Roberto, 2011, p. 246; Lax and Sebenius, 1987).

21 Different managers also have widely differing skill sets and this must be taken into account and orchestrated by leaders.

22 The earlier-mentioned survey of 1,500 chief executives identified "'creativity, the ability to generate novel and useful solutions, as the most important leadership competency for the successful organization of the future" (Mueller *et al.*, 2011, p. 494). It is also worth noting that over 20 years of research on incentives and motivation indicate that financially rewarding employees for higher productivity, so-called "performance pay," only is effective for routine tasks. When it comes to creative jobs, a *Harvard Business Review* article concluded that "where innovative, nonstandard solutions are needed," performance pay of CEOs and other executives can actually diminish performance (*The Week*, 2016, p. 34).

23 Fashioning a viable self has been made considerably harder given that most working people complain of "information overload" in Western society (Elliot, 2014, p. 3).

24 There are other "contingency models" of leadership effectiveness that assert that successful leadership is context-dependent and setting-specific, such as the Least Preferred Coworker Model, the Path-Goal Model and Normative Decision Theory (Roberto, 2011, pp. 50–52).

25 Vallas notes that such resistance to oppressive leadership/management practices also takes place in non-manufacturing contexts, since all workplaces have "'backstage' regions" as Goffman called them. These "unmanaged spaces" are where unhappy employees "outwit management and sidestep its practices" (2012, pp. 17, 59, 16).

26 In some decision-making contexts, such as a tough situation that requires a timely decision, the top executive needs to be willing and able to courageously make the decision on his own. Change leadership demands both top- and bottom-down capabilities. Also worth mentioning is that those leaders who are guiding programmatic change have to be mindful of what happens after the change and transformation in terms of leadership succession and its impact on organizational functioning. Succession planning, preparing the next generation of leadership ("growing leaders," to call to mind my "good enough" mother/leader metaphor), is a topic that has become

increasingly important since leadership turnover of CEOs and senior executives has greatly increased in the global economy (i.e., the end of job-for-life employment). Many organizations botch this process (Roberto, 2011, p. 385).

References

Aamodt, M. G. (2010). *Industrial/Organizational Psychology: An Applied Approach* (6th ed.). Belmont, CA: Wadsworth.

Amabile, T. and Kramer, S. (2011). *The Progress Principle*. Boston, MA: Harvard Business School Press.

Amado, G. (2013). Psychic imprisonment and its release within organisations and working relationships. In: L. Vansina (Ed.), *Humanness in Organisations: A Psychodynamic Contribution* (pp. 7–28). London: Karnac.

Akhtar, S. (2009). *Comprehensive Dictionary of Psychoanalysis*. London: Karnac.

Axelrod, S. D. (1999). *Work and the Evolving Self. Theoretical and Clinical Considerations*. Hillsdale, NJ: Analytic Press.

Britzman, D. P. (2003). *After Education: Anna Freud, Melanie Klein, and Psychoanalytic Histories of Learning*. Albany, NY: State University of New York Press.

Britzman, D. P. (2011). *Freud and Education*. New York: Routledge.

Carnall, C. A. (2008). Foreword. In: D. Rowland and M. Higgs (Eds.), *Sustaining Change: Leadership that Works* (pp. vii–x). Southampton, UK: Jossey-Bass.

Chesbrough, H. (2003). *Open Innovation. The New Imperative for Creating and Profiting from Technology*. Cambridge, MA: Harvard Business School Press.

Collins, J. (2001). *Good to Great*. New York: Harper Business.

Conger, J. A. and Kanungo, R. N. (1987). Toward a Behavioral Theory of Charismatic Leadership in Organizational Settings. *Academy of Management Review, 12*:4, 637–647.

Dutton, J. E., Roberts, L. M. and Bednar, J. (2011). Prosocial Practices, Positive Identity, and Flourishing at Work. In: S. I. Donaldson, M. Czikszentmihalyi and J. Nakamura (Eds.), *Applied Positive Psychology: Improving Everyday Life, Health, Schools, Work, and Society* (pp. 155–170). New York: Routledge.

Elliot, A. (2014). *Concepts of the Self*. Cambridge, UK: Polity Press.

Foucault, M. (1984). Space, Knowledge, and Power. In: P. Rabinow (Ed.), *The Foucault Reader* (pp. 239–256). New York: Pantheon.

Franzen, J. (2015, Oct. 4). *New York Times Book Review*.

Frederickson, B. L. (2001). The Role of Positive Emotions in Positive Psychology. *American Psychologist, 56*:3, 218–226.

Frederickson, B. L. (2004). The Broaden-and-Build Theory of Positive Emotions. *Transactions of the Royal Society of London, Biological Science, 359*:1449, 1367–1378. doi:10.1098/rstb.2004.1512

Frederickson, B. L. (2009). *Positivity. Top-Notch Research Reveals 3-to-1 Ratio that Will Change Your Life*. New York: Harmony.

Freud, S. (1927) [1961]. Humour. In: J. Strachey (Ed. and Trans.), *The Standard Edition of the Complete Psychological Works of Sigmund Freud*, Vol. 21 (pp. 161–166). London: Hogarth Press.

Garvin, D. (2000). *Learning in Action*. Boston, MA: Harvard Business School Press.

Hackman, R. J. (2002). *Leading Teams: Setting the Stage for Great Performances*. Boston, MA: HBS Press.

Heath, C. and Heath, D. (2010). *Switch: How to Change Things When Change Is Hard*. New York: Crown Business.

Heifetz, R. (1998). *Leadership without Easy Answers*. Cambridge, MA: Harvard University Press.

Higgs, M. (2010). Change and its Leadership: The Role of Positive Emotions. In: P. A. Linley, S. Harrington and N. Garcea (Eds.), *Oxford Handbook of Positive Psychology and Work* (pp. 67–80). Oxford: Oxford University Press.

Huy, Q. N. (1999). Emotional Capability, Emotional Intelligence, and Radical Change. *Academy of Management Review*, 24:2, 325–345.

Huy, Q. N. (2002). Emotional Balancing or Organizational Continuity and Radical Change: The Contribution of Middle Managers. *Administrative Science Quarterly*, 47:1, 31–36.

Huy, Q. N. (2005). An Emotional-Based View of Strategic Renewal. In G. Szulanski, J. Potac and Y. Doz (Eds.), *Strategy Process: Advances in Strategic Management* (pp. 3–37). New York: Elsevier.

Huy, Q. N. (2012). Emotions and Strategic Change. In K. Cameron and G. Spreitzer (Eds.), *Oxford Handbook of Positive Organizational Scholarship* (pp. 811–824). New York: Oxford University Press.

Jung, C. (1933) [2005]. *Modern Man in Search of a Soul*. Oxford: Routledge.

Kernberg, O. F. (1998). *Ideology, Conflict, and Leadership in Groups and Organizations*. New Haven, CT: Yale University Press.

Kets de Vries, M. F. R. (2011). *Reflections on Groups and Organizations*. San Francisco, CA: Jossey-Bass.

Kim, W. C. and Mauborgne, R. (2005). *Blue Ocean Strategy. How to Create Uncontested Market Space and Make the Competition Irrelevant*. Cambridge, MA: Harvard Business School.

Kotter, J. (1996). *Leading Change*. Boston, MA: Harvard University Press.

Lammers, J., Stapel, D. A. and Galinsky, A. D. (2010). Power Increases Hypocrisy: Moralizing in Reasoning, Immorality in Behavior. *Psychological Science*, 21:5, 737–744.

Lax, D. and Sebenius, J. (1987). *The Manager as Negotiator*. New York: Free Press.

Lee, W. M. L. (1999). *An Introduction to Multicultural Counseling*. New York: Routledge.

Lewin, K. (1958). Group Decision and Social Change. In E. E. Maccoby, T. M. Newcomb and E. L. Hartley (Eds.), *Readings in Social Psychology* (pp. 97–211). New York: Holt, Rinehart & Winston.

Liu, Y. and Perrewe, P. L. (2005). Another Look at the Role of Emotion. A Process Model. *Human Resource Management Review*, 15, 263–290.

Luthans, F. and Youssef, C. M. (2009). Positive Workplaces. In: S. J. Lopez and C. R. Snyder (Eds.), *Oxford Handbook of Positive Psychology* (2nd ed., pp. 579–588). Oxford: Oxford University Press.

Marcus, P. (1999). *Autonomy in the Extreme Situation: Bruno Bettelheim, the Nazi Concentration Camps and the Mass Society*. Westport, CT: Praeger.

Marcus, P. (2008). *Being for the Other: Emmanuel Levinas, Ethical Living and Psychoanalysis*. Milwaukee, WI: Marquette University Press.

Marcus, P. (2010). *In Search of the Good Life: Emmanuel Levinas, Psychoanalysis and the Art of Living*. London: Karnac.

Marcus, P. (2013a). *How to Laugh Your Way Through Life: A Psychoanalyst's Advice*. London: Karnac.

Marcus, P. (2013b). *In Search of the Spiritual: Gabriel Marcel, Psychoanalysis, and the Sacred*. London: Karnac.

Miller, H. (1949) [1994]. *Sexus: The Rosy Crucifixion I*. New York: Grove Press.

Mueller, J. S., Goncalo, J. A. and Kamdar, D. (2011). Recognizing Creative Leadership: Can Creative Expression Negatively Relate to Perceptions of Leadership Potential? *Journal of Experimental Social Psychology*, *47*, 494–498.

Nehamas, A. (1993, Feb. 15). "Subject and Object." *The New Republic*, pp. 27–35.

Rajchman, J. (1985). *Michel Foucault: The Freedom of Philosophy*. New York: Columbia University Press.

Roberto, M. A. (2011). *Transformational Leadership: How Leaders Change Teams, Companies, and Organizations*. Chantilly, VA: Transcript Book, The Great Courses.

Roberto, M. and Levesque, L. (2005). The Art of Making Change Initiative Stick. *MIT Sloan Management Review*, *46*:4, 53–59.

Rowland, D. and Higgs, M. (2008). *Sustaining Change: Leadership that Works*. Southampton, UK: Jossey-Bass.

Ruti, M. (2008). *A World of Fragile Things: Psychoanalysis and the Art of Living*. Albany, NY: State University of New York Press.

Rycroft, C. (1995). *A Critical Dictionary of Psychoanalysis* (2nd ed.). London: Penguin.

Sawyer, K. (2007). *Group Genius: The Creative Power of Collaboration*. New York: Perseus Books Group.

Schlossberg, N. K. (2009). *Revitalizing Retirement: Reshaping Your Identity, Relationships, and Purpose*. Washington, DC: American Psychological Association.

Schultz, D. and Schultz, S. E. (Eds.). (2006). *Psychology and Work Today*. Saddle River, NJ: Pearson/Prentice Hall.

Sekerka, L. E. and Frederickson, B. L. (2010). Working Positively Toward Transformative Cooperation. In: P. A. Linley, S. Harrington and N. Garcea (Eds.), *Oxford Handbook of Positive Psychology and Work* (pp. 81–94). Oxford: Oxford University Press.

Sekerka, L. E., Vacharkulksemsuk, T. and Frederickson, B. L. (2010). Positive Emotions: Broadening and Building Upward Spirals of Sustainable Enterprise. In: P. A. Linley, S. Harrington and N. Garcea (Eds.), *Oxford Handbook of Positive Psychology and Work* (pp. 168–177). Oxford: Oxford University Press.

Senge, P. M. (2006). *The Fifth Discpline: The Art & Practice of the Learning Organization* (Revised and Updated). New York: Doubleday.

Vallas, S. P. (2012). *Work*. Cambridge, UK: Polity Press.

Volkan, V. D. (1972). The Linking Objects of Pathological Mourners. *Archives of General Psychiatry*, *27*, 215–221.

Week, The (2016, March 11). Performance Pay Is Dangerous. p. 34.

Wilkinson, W. (2013). Barbara Frederickson's Bestselling "Positivity" Is Trashed by a New Study. www.thedailybeast.com.

Winnicott, D. (1960) [1965]. Ego-Distortion in Terms of True and False Self. In *The Maturational Process and Facilitating Environment* (pp. 140–152). New York: International Universities Press.

Web sources

asq.sagepub.com/content/47/4/644.abstract, retrieved 9/24/15.

dharmawisdom.org/teachings/articles/decision-time#sthash.77nSIsHE.dpuf, retrieved 9/21/15.

executiveeducation.wharton.upenn.edu/thought-leadership/wharton-at-work/2011/02/emotional-contagion#sthash.yIwImvkj.dpuf, retrieved 9/24/15.

hbr.org/…/how-to-bounce-back-from-ad…, retrieved 8/13/15.

lexbook.net/en/recalcitrant *The* basic idea *that* incentive, retrieved 8/14/15.

toolkit.smallbiz.nsw.gov.au/part/8/41/198, retrieved 8/14/15.

vimeo.com › BuildASoil › Videos, retrieved 10/3/15.

watercoolernewsletter.com/leading-change-successfully/, retrieved 9/11/15.

www.bizcoachinfo.com/archives/13642, retrieved 10/15/15.

www.brainpickings.org/2013/08/14/how-einstein-thought-combinatorial-creativity/, retrieved 10/3/15.

www.businessdictionary.com/definition/organizational-learning.html, retrieved 8/12/15.

www.businessdictionary.com/definition/organizational-memory.html#ixzz3nPZ73hul, retrieved 10/2/15.

www.businessdictionary.com/definition/transformational-leadership.html, retrieved 9/23/15.

www.gurteen.com/gurteen/gurteen.nsf/id/X001B71A6/, retrieved 9/24/15.

www.jeffreysanchezburks.com/blog/emotional-aperture/, retrieved 9/23/15.

www.knowledge-management-tools.net/organizational-memory-and-knowledge.html#ixzz3nPXgsIJL, retrieved 10/2/15.

www.michel-foucault.com/concepts/, retrieved 10/16/15.

www.movemequotes.com/top-10-steve-jobs-quotes/#sthash.tnD4H67h.dpuf, retrieved 10/21/15.

www.positivepsychology.org.uk/...theory/positive-emotions/118-the-ben..., retrieved 9/15/15.

www.torbenrick.eu › Change Management, retrieved 8/13/15.

Chapter 7

When to call it quits: retirement

"Retirement," said French author Simone de Beauvoir, "may be looked upon either as a prolonged holiday or as a rejection, a being thrown on to the scrap-heap" (1996, p. 263). Indeed, a depressed Freud seemed to view himself as in the latter category. Fifteen years before he died in 1939, he wrote in a letter to his colleague and friend Max Eitingon, "I am no longer the same man. In reality, I am tired and in need of rest, can scarcely get through my six hours of analytic work, and however cannot think of doing anything else. The right thing to do would be to give up all work and obligations and wait in a quiet corner for the natural end" (Schur, 1972, p. 377).

While de Beauvoir is aptly describing the extremes of how some people experience retirement, the fact is that for most people, as with any important identity-altering decision—and in western society, one's personal identity is connected more to work than to any other aspect of life (Schlossberg, 2009, p. 99)—our life before and after retirement is much less "black and white." Rather, the retirement transition lands us in the "gray zone," the experiential realm of heightened ambivalence and ambiguity as we struggle to maintain our autonomy, integration and humanity. Surveys have suggested that more than 60 percent of retirees "un-retire" and carry on in some type of paid employment, and then "re-retire" or "semi-retire" in the future (Milne, 2013, p. 2). In the US, research has found that more people are choosing "phased retirement" rather than "cold turkey with-drawal from the workforce" (*The Week*, 9/18/15, p. 33).[1] Moreover, retirement is almost always enmeshed with the physical and psychosocial effects of the aging process. Retirement usually takes place in the later years (age 62 is the United States' earliest legal eligibility, though many people delay it for financially advantageous reasons), and this means it is intimately connected to profound changes associated with the phase of life sometimes called "late adulthood" (roughly age 65 and over), which includes changes in the way one looks, "empty nest" syndrome, female and male menopause, economic shifts, the death of parents, and chronic health problems (Kloep and Hendry, 2007, p. 742). These and other changes, especially increased life expectancy in part due to better healthcare [in about 20 years it is estimated that every third person will be over age 60 in the western world (Junkers, 2013b, p. 95)], require a significant re-fashioning of one's identity, relationships, and sense of purpose (Schlossberg, 2009). The great Roman lyric poet, Horace, put this point just right when he said, "We rarely find anyone who can say he has lived a happy life, and who, content with his life, can retire from the world like a satisfied guest" (1863, p. 143). Research has indicated that about one third of mental health services in the UK's National Health Service are used by people of age 65, many of whom are retirees (Milne, 2013, p. 4). Similar findings are reported in the United States (www.nimh.nih.gov).

Indeed, deciding when to retire is undoubtedly one of the most important decisions one makes during a lifetime (Knoll, 2011, p. 1), and even more important is how one constructs a flourishing existence during this psychologically challenging life- and identity-altering transition. As Milne noted, while the average person in western society will live out the last third of their lives in retirement, "we are in a position of having limited high-quality scientific information to guide retirement specifically" (2013, pp. 4, 8–9). In fact, the scholarly psychological literature on retirement is in a state of near conceptual disarray in which even basic terms are yet to be coined. As one counseling psychologist and retirement expert recently noted, "Today it's no longer clear what constitutes retirement" (Is it a phase or a stage? Is it one single event or a process?), as even "the term retirement is being retired, or at least redefined" (Schlossberg, 2009, p. 6; Milne, 2013, p. 2). Thus, however one defines and characterizes the murky notion of retirement, and as is so often the case with the art of living the "good life," a successful transition out of the fulltime work force centrally involves the capacity to adapt to change. This requires considerable creative and skillful improvisation along with lots of "guts, grit and gumption." Indeed, what Bette Davis famously said about the aging process, "old age ain't no place for sissies," can also be applied to the retirement transition that usually accompanies it (www.quotegarden.com). Most importantly, similar to old age, retirement involves "having a world," or one's pre-retirement way of life, "losing a world," leaving the fulltime workforce, and "replacing a world,"[2] creating a satisfying way of life in retirement. It is to these topics that I now turn.

"Having a world"

The Retirement Decision

The great Spanish cellist Pablo Casals said what many people feel who are beginning to seriously contemplate retirement: "To retire is to begin to die" (m.imdb. com). That is, it is undeniable that for most people who have had a reasonably satisfying work life and are at least minimally reflective, fulltime retirement means reckoning with one's vulnerability, finitude and mortality in an unusually striking manner. As Freud showed, all forms of mourning start with an awareness of the reality of loss. Such reflection on loss is decidedly "up front and personal," at least compared to when one is younger and fully engaged in one's career and family, and there is still a trace of omnipotence and illusion animating one's outlook.

When viewed in its totality, retirement as a process can thus be conceptualized as an individual's struggle to maximize growth, development and learning amidst a wide range of personal losses. Exactly why a particular person at a particular time decides to retire is of course a matter of understanding their idiosyncratic trajectory; however, there seems to be some fairly common behavioral and psychological aspects of the retirement decision (Knoll, 2011).[3]

On a "surface" level, typically individuals often retire within the context of a cluster of emotionally infused practical considerations such as layoffs, declining health, caring for ill family members, unhappiness with one's career, and the wish to have the freedom to engage in enjoyable interests and hobbies. While these surface reasons for retirement are not to be minimized, quite often embedded in a person's motivation to leave the fulltime workforce is the amorphous, lurking and unavoidable sense that "the time may indeed be right." As the wise Hebrew philosopher-poet Ecclesiastes famously said, coming to terms with time, being able to judge the right moment at which to do something, is a constituent aspect of the art of living the "good life": there is "a time to plant and a time to uproot ... a time to keep and a time to cast off" (Marcus, 2003, p. 123). Indeed, the capacity to endure intense separation anxiety is a prerequisite for creative and productive adaptation to reality. Moreover, we must be able to say farewell to the old to make internal room for the new.[4]

For the most part, research into the retirement decision has focused on the effects of health and economic status. Unsurprisingly, research has confirmed "that individuals in poor health, or whose loved ones are suffering from negative health conditions, retire earlier than those in better health." Moreover, those individuals who benefit from a higher socioeconomic status usually work longer than those with a lower socioeconomic status (Knoll, 2011, p. 1). Not surprisingly, retirees who are healthy and financially well-off tend to fare psychologically better than those who are unhealthy and poor. Similarly, if one was expecting to retire with a healthy spouse or partner and this does not happen, chances are one's satisfaction with the retirement transition will be lower. Also worth mentioning is the rather troubling fact that research has shown that despite the existential importance of the retirement decision, many future retirees do not contemplate the decision for very long. In fact, their decisions could be reasonably described as somewhat impulsive and short-sighted. For example, about 22 percent of those surveyed in 2008 said they initially began to consider the retirement decision merely six months before they actually departed from their jobs, while another 22 percent spent only one year thinking about the decision. This reported lack of "deep" thinking about the retirement decision, including the potentially misleading cognitive tendency to mainly focus on the positive aspects of retirement, often means that future retirees do not properly plan, including financially, for worst case scenarios, such as a spouse getting terminally ill (ibid., pp. 7, 8). As Freud and his followers have noted, in general, human beings are neurotically inclined to avoid sensible consequential thinking compared to seeking immediate gratification of their wishes. Moreover, this infantile pleasure-seeking tendency has a stronger interpretive grip on their outlook and behavior compared to anxiously contemplating potentially bad, let alone catastrophic, scenarios. Having the maturity and courage to counteract these infantile tendencies of avoidance and denial in favor of realistically facing the immediate or potential harshness of life and steadfastly persevering is probably what Shakespeare meant when he wrote in King Lear, "ripeness is all."

Given that the decision to retire is context-dependent, setting-specific, and heavily influenced by one's personality, coping skills and general outlook, individuals have to evaluate their retirement alternatives from their unique personal perspectives that include trying to delineate possible gains and losses as a basis for predicting future adjustment and happiness (ibid., pp. 3, 4). While discussing the details of the psychology of decision-making as it relates to retirement is beyond the scope of this chapter, it is worth discussing some typical cognitive biases, or in psychoanalytic parlance, ego deficiencies, that can negatively impact the retirement decision.

To begin with, there is the problem of how one "frames" retirement. To "frame" a problem boils down to how one defines and conceptualizes it. It centrally involves asking smart questions rooted in the conviction that decisively shaping the conceptual context of a decision will determine its personal meaning. In other words, how one defines and conceptualizes retirement will enable or constrain how effectively one responds to the challenges associated with this phase of the life cycle. If one's angle of vision on retirement is gloomy, for instance, viewing it as the "beginning of the end" rather than as the beginning of something new, as an opportunity to further grow and develop without the encumbrances of fulltime work, then how one feels about retirement will be very different. The issue of "framing" retirement sounds pretty straightforward, especially if we mistakenly assume that people's behaviors are governed by conscious rationality; however, as I have argued in Chapter 2, decision-making, especially about "high stakes" issues, is significantly influenced by unconscious processes, often obscure ones that are lodged in one's early childhood history. This is why reasonably "framing" retirement is often such hardgoing for many people—they do not know what they "really" psychologically need, want, or can comfortably manage and realistically achieve once they leave fulltime work.

One of the other problems associated with accurately predicting what life will be like after retirement is called "impact bias." When a person thinks about an emotionally tinged event such as retirement, there is a tendency to over-estimate how strongly he will feel, the duration of the feeling, and other elements that impact him. This cognitive tendency operates in both negative and positive events. In their six studies, Gilbert and colleagues (1998), the originators of the concept of "impact bias," demonstrated that participants overestimated the duration of their affective responses to rejection by a prospective employer, the failure to achieve tenure, an electoral defeat, negative personality feedback, the dissolution of a romantic relationship, and an account of a child's death. The "impact bias" suggests that there is a tendency to not remember that other events in one's life, in addition to the capacity to recover from trauma, will diminish the impact of these distressing feelings brought on by ego-bruising setbacks. Gilbert and colleagues called this ability to recover one's psychological set point the "psychological immune system." It denotes the way that we unconsciously, psychologically combat distressing feelings and, therefore, recover from trauma more quickly than we might otherwise do. The upshot of "impact bias" when one is considering retirement is that one should think at least twice when reflecting on potential emotional response to retirement and remember that one will be better able to psychologically manage than expected (changingminds.org).

The related concept of "affective" or "hedonic" "forecasting," the ability to predict how one will feel in the future, also critically impacts the retirement decision-making context. Research has shown that we are generally awful at judging what will make us happy, and we have great difficulty seeing through or beyond the filter of the here and now. That is, "our feelings in the present blind us to how we'll make decisions in the future, when we might be feeling very differently" (https://www.psychologytoday.com). There are many reasons for this tendency to inaccurately predict future happiness, such as "imprecise" and unrealistic "mental simulations of future events" (i.e., internal models or mental representations of the outside world that allow us to "preview" and "prefeel" the imagined future). We are governed in our decision-making behavior by "exaggerated expectations" (Knoll, 2011, p. 5; Gilbert and Wilson, 2009, pp. 1351, 1352), overstated prospects that are often interwoven with conscious and unconscious fantasies that lead to ill-conceived and ill-fated decisions about the retirement transition. Drawing from the research on social cognition of Gilbert and Wilson (2009), Knoll indicates that what makes these "mental simulations of future events" so problematic is that they are unrepresentative, essentialized, abbreviated and decontextualized.

By "unrepresentative" it is meant that the simulations are fashioned from past memories of events that do not necessarily reflect in what way future events will play out. Moreover, individuals tend to recall most intensely the best and the worst elements of an event, as well as the final moments, thus neglecting the times that were more typical and average or pleasantly ordinary.

Mental simulations are also "essentialized," that is, they only include the main aspects of the event while excluding the minor details. While the totality of an individual's experience with an event considers major and minor elements that are regarded as both positive and negative, in "mental simulation of future events" it is mainly the major events that are considered. Therefore, the major, episodically negative events that are included in mental simulations of retirement are less likely to be modulated by smaller, potentially positive elements that could animate the actual experience of retirement so that it is not so troubling. Likewise, such essentialized mental simulations may gear individuals to focus on the major elements of departing from the workforce, such as greatly increased amounts of leisure time, without including the smaller details, for example, having retired friends with which one can spend this newly obtained leisure time.

"Mental simulations of future events" are also "abbreviated," that is, they are unavoidably "shorter than the actual event being simulated," as they represent only a few, select moments of future events (Knoll, 2011, p. 5; Gilbert and Wilson, 2009, p. 1353). In addition, abbreviated prospections generally include symbolizations of the earliest moments of the event being considered. For instance, an individual may fantasize about Labor Day, and the fact that in retirement he will not have to return to work like most other people after the summer is over. In other words, when mentally simulating how retirement might play out, a potential retiree is prone to consider only the earlier phase of retirement and consider much less so, if at all, the lasting effects of retiring early, in particular, the reduced financial benefits for themselves and their spouse.

Lastly, "mental simulations of the future" are "decontextualized," that is, the contextual elements that exist at the time an individual mentally simulates a prospective event are quite likely not to exist at the time the event actually happens. When the contexts in which prospections are created and events experienced are not equivalent, mental simulations are prone to markedly differ from actual experiences. For instance, when prospective retirees are considering whether to depart from the workforce, they most often do not have nearly as much free time to manage on their own as they would in retirement. Thus, the context in which potential retirees mentally simulate the future may lack anticipation of feelings like tedium and monotony that some experience in retirement.

Gilbert and colleagues' important research about decision-making, including as it applies to retirement, is in sync with longstanding cherished insights from ancient religious wisdom and spirituality: namely, the greater the congruence between one's expectations and one's fate, the greater the happiness will be in retirement. In a sense, this is a self-empowering insight in terms of achieving artful retirement. As Gilbert and Ebert have noted, "We make decisions as though our future satisfaction depended entirely on the immutable, intrinsic properties of events we are about to experience and take little account of our ability to reshape our view of things." In other words, "if life [i.e., retirement] is an apple, then its sweetness depends as much on the taster as the tasted. If we overlook the fact, we risk missing the best fruit on the tree" (2002, p. 512).

"Losing a world"

The retirement transition is centrally concerned with adequately coming to terms with one's real and imagined losses, such as to one's identity, relationships and purpose. Indeed, as Schlossberg has noted, there are retirees who long "for their former role, power and prestige," those disgruntled people who have not relinquished the infantile narcissistic wish "to hold center stage" (2009, p. 91). Such people unconsciously equate the loss of being center stage with the loss of parental

love and adoration, and therefore they experience a painful loss of self-idealiza-
tion. In order to better understand the psychology of loss and resilience as it
relates to the retirement transition, it is useful to consider these challenges within
the larger context of human development and the life cycle. There is probably no
better psychological way of doing this than to briefly consider Erikson's final two
stages of his famous "Eight Ages of Man," each with its own "ego crisis" or
psychosocial conflict that needs to be resolved: "mature adulthood" with its crisis
of "generativity vs. stagnation," and "old age," with its crisis of "ego integrity vs.
despair" (1963, pp. 268–269). Since the retirement transition usually takes place
somewhere amidst these two psychosocial stages, Erikson's framework can assist
us in understanding how one's altered, if not diminished, sense of identity, relationships and purpose can best be reckoned with and transformed into a life-affirming
"encore."

"Generativity vs. stagnation" is "primarily concerned in establishing and guiding the next generation" (ibid., p. 267). This, of course, includes having one's
own ego and libidinally invested children, but that alone does not constitute
generativity. In addition, generativity refers to the capacity to project and extend
oneself, and Erikson means quite literally so, to give oneself with the fullness of
one's whole being to the future. The gist of generativity, then, is the capacity to
go beyond one's immediate self-related concerns in favor of a perspective of
future generations. Put differently, ideally in this stage of development there is a
noticeable shift from a "being for oneself" existential orientation in which self-
indulgence and self-satisfaction is the paramount focus, to one that is mainly
"being for the other." That is, to a productive and creative way of being that is
other-directed, other-regarding, and other-serving toward one's own offspring,
and by extension, to all those children anywhere, including those who will come
after one dies. Psychoanalyst Andre Green suggests the power of this motive
when he wrote, "for the artist [the generative adult] the preservation of his work
[what good he leaves behind] is more important than the preservation of his life"
(Junkers, 2013a, p. 4). According to Erikson, the "ego strength" or "virtue" that
the generative adult develops is "Care": "The widening concern for what has
been generated by love, necessity, or accident; it overcomes the ambivalence
adhering to irreversible obligation" (1964, p. 131). Moreover, care includes the
self-awareness that one "needs to be needed [i.e., the honor to need the young],[5]
and maturity needs guidance as well as encouragement from what has been
produced and must be taken care of" (Erikson, 1963, pp. 266–267). It is important to note that Erikson was not simply referring to work connected to those one
has personally created, but for the life-affirming works of all of humanity.

For Erikson, the distinguishing aspect of adult generativity is what he calls the
"generational." The generational is a "ritualization," a persistent pattern of behavior typical of a specific society that acts as a socializing and directing mechanism.
This includes, for example, "the parental, the teaching, and the curative," that is,
the transmission of the best of humanistic values. The gist of the generational is
to be willing and able to use one's authority with a strong belief that one knows

"what one is doing," and to obtain support from the range of formalized cultural images of accepted authority, for example, God, kings, and one's own parents, that one is, in fact, "doing it right" (Monte, 1980, pp. 244, 257).

If retirement occurs during this stage of the life cycle, ideally it means that the retiree has fashioned the deep capacity to nurture and benevolently direct the generation to come. He regards himself as a conveyor of society's cherished principles, standards, morals and customs. As we have seen, for Erikson this is easier said than done, for there is always the danger of what he calls "authoritism" (a "ritualism," stereotypical and robot-like behavior such as functioning strictly according to the letter and not the spirit of the law), a reflection of "stagnation," the unwillingness and inability to find value and significance in directing and assisting the future generation in life-affirming activities. This can be rooted in inordinate envy, a feeling that reflects a negative self-appraisal and fury toward those younger who are viewed as much better off. "Authoritism" is the use of power for self-serving benefits rather than in the assistance of others. In contrast, the high-level psychological capacity of generativity requires the willingness and ability for "care," including to promote the next generation's autonomy, to encourage their growth and development, and support them in their pursuits and interests. Also included in this psychological capacity is caring for our planet, for animals and plants, and embracing an outlook that is geared toward strengthening worthwhile public structures through such "for the other" behavior as charitable work and volunteerism.

If retirement takes place during mature adulthood, where the ego-crisis is "generativity vs. stagnation," in which the emerging ego strength is "care" rather than remaining indifferent or self-preoccupied, and the "ritualization" is "generational" rather than the "ritualism" of "authoritism," one is most likely to fare pretty well psychologically when one leaves fulltime work. This includes reckoning with the final stage of the life cycle, "old age," where the ego-crisis is "ego-integrity vs. despair."

According to Erikson, the sensibility that composes ego integrity is roughly what is meant by "serenity in old age" (Rycroft, 1995, p. 45), a kind of "disinterested interest" in which life is enjoyed as an end in itself, rather than for any benefits that it bestows on the individual. It is the adult counterpart of the trust that the well looked-after infant has toward his mother or primary caregiver. Erikson has succinctly described "ego integrity":

> It is the ego's accrued assurance of its proclivity for order and meaning. It is a post-narcissistic love of the human ego—not of the self—as an experience which conveys some world order and spiritual sense, no matter how dearly paid for. It is the acceptance of one's one and only life cycle as something that had to be and that, by necessity, permitted of no substitutions: it thus means a new, a different love of one's parents [i.e., an acceptance of their limitations and strengths]. It is a comradeship with the ordering ways of distant times and different pursuits as expressed in the simple products and sayings of such times and pursuits.
>
> (1963, p. 268)

In terms of the retirement transition, what is most relevant about "ego integrity" is that such a person consciously or unconsciously feels that his life was "the accidental coincidence of but one life cycle with but one segment of history." Moreover, in a certain sense he grasps that the way his life, including his career, was lived had to be what it was, and perhaps most importantly, it is self-judged as essentially gratifying (ibid.). As a result of this benevolent self-appraisal, he is not angry or regretful that he has somehow irrevocably missed out in his life, a reflection that Erikson subsumes under the category of "despair." Most importantly, as Erikson notes, if the old-aged person does not successfully resolve the previous seven stages of the life cycle, his self-experience is infiltrated by a pervasive terror of dying. That is, Erikson is affirming the insight that only a person who has not authentically lived is afraid of dying. Such a fear of death implies that the person is unwilling and unable to accept the course of his life, his life cycle, "as the ultimate of life," and the only meaning that living entails (Erikson, 1963, p. 269; Monte, 1980, p. 258). Rather, he despairs about how his life has played out and feels it was essentially a "vanity of vanities," to again quote Ecclesiastes. Ironically, while such a person feels his life has been a fundamentally meaningless and unsatisfying enterprise, he nevertheless desperately clings to it, experiencing it as "a thousand little disgusts" that do not coalesce into one big remorse (Erikson, 1963, p. 269). One only has to consider the many grumpy elderly retirees who have made health concerns the center of their universe. Such people spend vast amounts of time, effort and money running to doctors, often unnecessarily, and worrying and troubling about their health at the expense of more creative, productive and potentiating endeavors. One can easily spot such an unhappy retiree, for almost always his conversation focuses mainly on one leitmotif: being sick, having been sick, or getting sick. Such is what Erikson means by one's life becoming the sum total of a thousand petty miseries, a feeling that is driven by the internal sense that one is essentially "finished" being a significant person in the world. As Schlossberg noted, "If you feel that you are appreciated and that you matter, you have the potential for a happy retirement" (2009, p. 18).

When an old-aged person has acquired the capacity to face vulnerability, finitude and mortality with courage and integrity, he has acquired the ego strength or virtue called "wisdom": "detached concern with life itself, in the face of death itself." Such a person has the ability to embrace harsh reality with an attitude of resignation without despair: "of facing the period of relative helplessness which marks the end as it marked the beginning" (Erikson, 1964, pp. 133, 134). The word "integral" is Erikson's "ritualization" for the capacity to assimilate the seven previous stages of the life cycle into an overall affirmation that justifies the authenticity of the life that one has lived, it is "'a patrimony of the soul', the seal of moral paternity of himself" (1963, p. 258). In contrast, there is the "ritualism" of "sapientism," the pretense of wisdom. Wisdom thus means that the significant accomplishments of the prior seven stages have been integrated into the self-awareness that "new ideas, new meanings, new persons have been personally created" (Monte, 1980, p. 258). It is this awareness that gives the old-aged person a "glimpse of immortality" (Marcus, 2015, p. 206) in that he believes that his creations in the realms of love and work will live on after him to the benefit of future generations. With such a final synthesis and consolidation of the self, mercifully, "death loses its sting" (Erikson, 1963, p. 268). Finally, says Erikson, as if having gone full circle, the old-aged person develops a new appreciation and liking for what was childlike, especially for what is creatively playful. It is this development that is often expressed in the retiree's enjoyment and adoration of grandchildren and, by extension, though on a lesser register, delighting in the playfulness, enchantment and hopefulness of all children. As Winnicott noted, one of the important goals of a successful analysis is precisely to develop the sensibility we equate with what is childlike. The aim of analysis is to transform "the patient from a state of not being able to play into a state of being able to play." The crucial reason for this, says Winnicott, is that it is "in playing and only in playing that the individual child or adult is able to be creative and to use the whole personality, and it is only being creative that the individual discovers the self" (1971, p. 10). Not unsurprisingly, Erikson and Winnicott's insights are in sync with ancient spiritual wisdom, at least if we give the words from Aristophanes' lampooning play, *The Clouds*, a positive spin: "The old are in a second childhood." Rather than view old age as a second childhood because of a reduction of one's mental capacities, one can regard it as an opportunity to travel lighter, to embrace a freer, flowing and unrestrained way of being associated with childhood at its best.

Losing one's world in retirement

As sociologist Anthony Giddens pointed out, to fashion a world that one feels safe and secure in, where one is not threatened by death anxiety (the background of "unsafety" that we all must contend with), requires more than simply a set of propositional beliefs or insights. Rather, the most important constituent element necessary for fashioning a world is engaged activity, what Giddens calls routines. By routinization Giddens means "[t]he habitual, taken-for-granted character of the vast bulk of the activities of day-to-day social life" (1984, p. 376). For most people, these routines encompass one's work, family life, communal associations and all aspects of one's everyday social existence. The importance of routine is that it "is vital to the psychological mechanisms whereby a sense of trust or onto-logical security [a feeling of order and continuity in relationship to one's experi-ences] is sustained in the daily activities of social life" and it "is integral to the continuity of the personality of the agent, as he or she moves along the paths of daily activities" (ibid., p. 60). Routines foster a sense of autonomy and integra-tion; it is through them that one experiences the world as a place that can be controlled and understood and, most importantly, effective decisions and inter-vention can be made. Moreover, there is a deep generalized affective involvement in the routines of daily life that ties one to routines. Routine allows one to move smoothly and comfortably in the world without being overwhelmed by death anxiety. Routinization also minimizes the unconscious sources of anxiety. It is the canalization, management and avoidance of such primal tensions and diffuse anxiety that Giddens says is one of the main motives of human behavior. Moreover, routines, like any ongoing social practices, by definition have meanings embedded in them, in particular the beliefs and values that constitute the "self" (Marcus, 1999, pp. 75–76).

Given the extreme importance of routines, it is no wonder that for most retirees, leaving the fulltime workforce means leaving the round of routines and activities that they have spent most of their time doing on a typical weekday in their adult life. It is a huge challenge in terms of reconfiguring a workable identity, relationships and purpose. However, as researchers have pointed out, in many instances those nearing retirement, with its many real and symbolic losses, embrace a "head-in-the-sand" approach to this most challenging stage of the life cycle.

Identity

One of the biggest losses in retirement in terms of identity is how one relates to time. When one is younger and focusing on building a family and career, there is a denial of the passage of time; it is experienced as unambivalently propulsive and unambiguously limitless. Psychoanalytically speaking, one might say that in this context time is "unconsciously experienced as the unlimited availability of a vital elixir," as the forever nurturing and stabilizing "good maternal breast" (Junkers, 2013c, p. 25). This is compared to the unsettling experience of temporality in mature adulthood, and even more so in old age, that "time is running out,"[6] that one has to somehow survive the frustrating and rapidly depleting "bad maternal breast." Even Erikson and his wife were prone to disavow the passage of time. As Joan Erikson wrote, "Although at age eighty we began to acknowledge our elderly status, I believe we never faced its challenges realistically until we were close to ninety … we had still taken the years ahead for granted" (Milne, 2013, p. 33). Put succinctly, retirement that takes place in the stages of "mature adulthood" and "old age" demands relinquishing omnipotent thought and demands acknowledging the historical nature of one's unique life. Moreover, it requires relinquishing infantile "fantasies of immortal objects and the hunt for an ideal object." Contending with such psychic losses, with this painful self-awareness of the irreversibility of lived time and the sorrow over life's transience is the psychological context for an individual to grieve and mourn (Teising, 2013, p. 47). As Freud pointed out, only when one has faced the reality of such losses can one begin to transcend them by drawing from one's repository of internalized "good objects" that serves as something like a psychic "safe haven." In terms of retirement, this means using one's ego strengths or virtues in the service of creating a world of meanings that include a new sense of personal effectiveness and significance.

Another aspect of losing one's identity in retirement in mature adulthood and old age is the perceived negative changes in one's body, "a site of perception, of projection and expression" (ibid, p. 49). As Freud famously noted in *The Ego and the Id*, "the ego is first and foremost a bodily ego," emphasizing the somatocentric origins and nature of child and adult self-experience. That is, the body ego, the aspect of the ego which emanates from the self's self-perception, and one's body image—one's self representation of one's own body—are important considerations in terms of feeling securely, safely and happily lodged "in one's own skin" and in the outside world. When this is not the case, as in eating and body dysmorphic disorders, there is considerable psychological suffering. In retirement, when the body discernibly gives way to the gradual ravages of lived time, one's wellbeing is compromised, as is one's narcissistic equilibrium and the unconscious view of the self in which it is lodged. One has to come to terms with the radical inconsistency between the imagined and/or wished for body, especially one's earlier, more robust psychosexual self-concept,[7] and the "real" body, the diminished one that one inhabits. As Teising further notes, "the loss of physical or mental abilities, such as hearing loss or restrictions in movement, can be seen as a grave humiliation,"[8] such that it can foster an avoidance of going out and engaging in productive activities and satisfying interpersonal relationships (ibid).

It is a well-known observation that when one is without their familiar world of meaning—their social position, prestige and power to command—without a sense of the world as orderly, stable, continuous and comprehensible, one is less likely to be able to sustain a narrative of self-identity (i.e., the story one tells oneself about one's life).[9] In other words, when the security of a person's being is seriously threatened, their sense of self can be markedly compromised, even shattered (Weinstein, 1980, pp. 6, 16). For many retirees, when these props of work life on which their self-esteem, self-concept and sense of identity rested no longer exist, they feel like a deflated balloon, narcissistically assaulted, if not humiliated. This is especially the case if their role-status was heavily ego-invested, equated with an Oedipal victory or satisfied feelings of grandiosity and omnipotence (Eizirik, 2013, p. 129). As philosopher Richard Rorty noted, when the story one has been telling oneself about life, the narrative which constituted self-identity, is no longer viable, especially if one's career identity was taken away through an unexpected layoff, firing or being involuntarily "squeezed out" or "retired," one's self and world have been rendered almost completely meaningless, cutting deeply into one's motivation to carry on (1989, p. 179). This scenario is one of the reasons some retirees get depressed, since depression is associated with a lack of self-efficacy, feeling unable to exert control over one's own motivation, behavior, and social environment. Such retirees can feel helpless, hopeless and hapless to put things right as they conceive of it or to reinvent themselves by creating new storylines in their different role-status.

Relationships

Retirement in mature adulthood, and even more so in old age, is characterized by two paradoxical shifts that significantly impact the nature of friendship patterns.

On the one hand, escalating health problems, decreased mobility, and diminishing energy lessen possibilities for interacting with friends and the vigor the retiree has to dedicate to them. On the other hand, with retirement there is a lessening of social and familial obligations that, at least in principle, increases the free time the individual can use to expand and deepen existing friendships and to cultivate new ones (http://www.encyclopedia.com, retrieved 7/6/15). For many retirees, however, trying to create a workable balance within the context of this paradox is no small accomplishment. This is especially the case if one's friends are involved in assisting raising grandchildren or are simply deeply engaged in their children's and grandchildren's lives, which makes them unavailable to meaningfully interact with. As Schlossberg has summarized it, researchers have shown that in the United States, most people over age 60 do not move to a different part of the country because they prefer to stay close to their family and friends. However, between 1985 and 2004, "the size of intimate circles and number of 'close confidantes' decreased significantly and there has been a shift away from ties in the neighborhood; voluntary associations; community; and kin, especially spouses." What this finding suggests is that there is a downward societal trend toward a typical person's degree of felt and actual connection to his community and to voluntary groups (Schlossberg, 2009, p. 60). Given that human beings are "hard-wired" for attachment, sociability, empathy and affection, this trend often leads to a diminished sense of happiness. One only has to consider an important finding reported by researchers from the University of Scotland who studied the records of more than 50,000 married couples in 2010. They found "that 40 percent of men and 26 percent of women died within three years of their partner." Tellingly, these researchers concluded that there was, indeed, "powerful evidence" that regardless of other explanations related to illnesses, accidents and suicides, it was the death of the spouse that was mainly responsible for this correlation (Milne, 2013, p. 79). For most people, the death of a beloved spouse or partner is a traumatic loss, one that subverts their identity, taints their outlook, truncates how they express themselves, and greatly complicates, if not mars, the reactions evoked in others (Keltner, 2015, p. 10). The problems of fear, isolation and loneliness after the death of a spouse are often especially prominent.

The "take home" point about friendship patterns in retirement is that for a variety of reasons there can often be a troubling diminishment in the quality and quantity of meaningful friendship.[10] Rather than having regular and easy access to one's beloved "old friends," one is left trying to create new friendships which are often experienced as superficial "time fillers" that are not entirely satisfying. With the diminution of one's identity and friendship patterns, retirees often experience their lives as lacking an overall sense of vital purpose.

Purpose

As I have indicated, for many fulltime working men and, increasingly, women, work life provides an all-important sense of being, what Ernest Becker described as a locus of primary value in a world of meaning; in other words, having the heartfelt sense that one's life is significant and really matters. Consider the interesting finding from the psychology of regret research of Morrison and Roese. In their 2011 study they analyzed data from a telephone survey of 370 adult Americans. Subjects were requested to describe in detail one regret, including the context in which the regret occurred and whether the regret was due to an action or inaction. Among their interesting findings was that about 34 percent of men reported having work-oriented regrets versus 27 percent of women reporting similar regrets (Morrison and Roese, 2011). Thus, it is no surprise that when an important affect-integrating, meaning-giving and action-guiding structure like one's work is removed it can be a shock to one's existence, as the horizons of one's life are beginning to close (Civitarese and Ferro, 2013, p. xvii), which evokes feelings of grief and mourning.

"Replacing a world"

Simone de Beauvoir noted in her masterpiece, *The Coming of Age*, the antidote to the extreme psychosocial challenges of retirement in old age: "There is only one solution if old age is not to be an absurd parody of our former life, and that is to go on pursuing ends that give our existence a meaning, devotion to individuals, to groups or to causes, social, political, intellectual or creative work" (1996, p. 540). What de Beauvoir is claiming is perfectly in sync with the best of social theory. It is a well-known observation that in order to maintain one's autonomy, integration and humanity in challenging if not harsh circumstances (and retirement can certainly feel this way), one needs a consistent set of self-transcending values and strong beliefs in which one believes and to which one adheres. What a consistent set of values and beliefs provides is a coherent narrative of self-identity that gives the retiree the ability to make sense out of their challenging or harsh situation, give direction to their life, and strengthen their autonomy and integration. As Giddens pointed out, it is through a coherent narrative of self-identity that an individual has a feeling of biographical continuity that he is able to grasp reflexively and, to a greater or lesser degree, communicate to other people. A narrative, says Giddens, allows the person to have regular interaction with others in the day-to-day world and to integrate events that occur in the external world and sort them into the ongoing "story" about the self. Moreover, according to Giddens, a person with a coherent narrative of self-identity is also better able to establish a "protective cocoon" which "filters out," in the practical conduct of day-to-day life, many of the dangers and primal anxieties that often threaten the integrity of the self. For such a person, ontological security is more securely anchored. Finally, through a narrative of self-identity the individual is better able to accept that integrity as worthwhile. There is adequate self-regard to sustain a sense of the self as "alive"—within the scope of reflexive control, rather than having the inert quality of things in the object world. In other words, it is through a coherent narrative of self-identity that a person is able to feel a greater sense of integration and personhood (Giddens, 1991, pp. 52–54). As Freud pointed out, to fashion a revised narrative of self-identity that has life-affirming storylines first requires adequately mourning the "lost object," in this case one's work life (e.g., career identity, relationships, purpose), until such time that it is more or less comfortably lodged into the self, as one of the important objects that make up one's nurturing and stabilizing internal world (Eizirik, 2013, p. 128). As Melanie Klein noted, somewhat paradoxically, the process of properly mourning "lost objects" actually expands and deepens one's relationship to them, leading to an upsurge of love and trust for them, rather than hating and feeling persecuted by them.

It is within this theoretical context that we can understand retirees who are better able to replace their prior world of meaning that was rooted in their fulltime work life with something else that is viable. By a replacement world I mean a new set of routines—both attitudinal (i.e., a revised narrative of self-identity) and behavioral—that helps to give a degree of order and direction to one's life in retirement. A replacement world also typically involves a new reference group— a group whose beliefs, attitudes and behaviors provides a standard against which individuals compare and orient themselves to the demanding circumstances of retirement (e.g., the retirement community, friends who have retired). A replacement world also involves a new set of roles—different behaviors displayed in connection with the individual's new, inferior social position in the context of normative society (yes, old retirees are often looked down upon as "out to pasture"). When a revised or new narrative of self-identity is lodged in one's self-transcending values and strong beliefs, it provides the retiree with a sense of greater control, self-esteem and ontological security, thus helping one to press on in the struggle to survive intact, if not flourish, during the trying phase of retirement. This being said, it should be noted that survey research has shown "that the majority of retirees feel comfortable about their retirement"; they report "happiness, emotional wellbeing, and life satisfaction" (Milne, 2013, p. 7). This finding is perhaps best understood within the context of the psychology of old age: a rather surprising sociological finding from a national study of 20,000 individuals from ages 18 to 88 between 1972 and 2004 shows that "older individuals were the happiest" (Schlossberg, 2009, p. 200).

Some pragmatic tips for reinventing oneself in retirement

If the central problem in retirement is conceptualized as how to replace one's "old world," the identity, relationships and purpose that was lodged in fulltime work, with a "new world," one that gives one a sense of autonomy, integration and humanity, then the art of living the "good life" in retirement means fashioning a round of routines and activities that draw from the strengths and creativity of one's personality as it interacts with the totality of circumstances one is in. There are hundreds of good practical books on how to cope with retirement, books that provide the "nuts and bolts" on how to reconfigure and reinvigorate one's identity, relationships and purpose. Schlossberg (2009), for example, has aptly described the various retirement paths that retirees typically take.

A "Continuer" maintains identification with prior work, home and volunteer life. That is, they carry on using their familiar skills, interests and activities, though they contour them to retirement. Such people have the benefit of sustaining their identity as they gradually rather than abruptly change their self-conception and the way they comport themselves to the social world. For instance, former President Jimmy Carter continues to have a positive impact on people by maintaining his role as a courier for peace, authoring books and being vigorously involved in the Carter Center in Atlanta. The positive aspect of being a Continuer is the calm of maintaining an unsurprising life, one that is lodged in prior routines and predictable activities that have been satisfying. However, if a retiree is too focused on doing what they have always done, they may lose out on other satisfying opportunities or prospects that may have not been accessible when engaged in fulltime work.

An "Easy Glider" disengages "from his past and take[s] each day as it comes" (ibid., p. 148). For example, one may occupy oneself one day by visiting a good friend, the next day going on an outing to a museum, botanical garden or on a shopping spree, and the next day meandering in one's old neighborhood. In other words, Easy Gliders thoroughly enjoy being "footloose and fancy free," doing whatever feels right in the here and now. While such retirees tend to feel tranquil as they have almost no stress or pressure, the downside is that once they have dabbled in various activities for a while, the consequence of having a lot of free time, they can feel bored stiff, a feeling of *ennui* if not *anomie*, that can create the conditions of possibility for serious undermining of their sense of being a significant person in the world.

The "Adventurer" travels "in new directions" (ibid., p. 149). They view retirement as the context for generating bold modifications in their lives. While they may have retired from one career, they have now re-tooled, like going back to school or training, and embarked on another career. The positive side of being an Adventurer is that one can address key regrets and misgivings, and, in effect, pursue "the road not taken," which includes the fantasized bliss that they imagine they missed out on. Such engaged activity can feel utterly invigorating and inventive. However, if the adventure does not pan out the way one imagined and wanted, it can be a terrible let down, and one is again face-to-face with a more severe version of the unsettling problem of figuring out what one wants, and can realistically accomplish, in retirement.

The "Searchers" have disengaged "from the main activities of their past but have not yet found the 'right' path" (ibid, p. 151). One type of Searcher is seeking a permanent place to reside, a new niche, while the other type enjoys the process of exploration. They delight in the possibility of continuously seeking out different kinds of opportunities, venues and experiences. The path of either type of Searcher can be tempting because it provides the hope of satisfying opportunities, including those that can significantly increase one's happiness. This is especially the case for Searchers who enjoy the process of exploration itself. This being said, the disadvantage in this path is that Searchers can become drifters and dilettantes, constantly exploring and seeking out exciting options and never actually settling into something in depth that feels purposeful and satisfying.

"Involved Spectators," are still ego-invested in their prior work. While they have relinquished the role-status of being a major player, they compensate by searching for ways to re-connect to the people, ideas and activities that made their work satisfying. This retirement path provides the chance to remain attentive to and knowledgeable about their professional field; however, the downside is that by inserting themselves in their prior work world they can remain too lodged in a retrospective consciousness. This can lead to an ego-bruising mindfulness that one is no longer a player in the work world that one so loved, and one's former friends and associates view him as largely irrelevant if not a "has-been."

Finally, Schlossberg mentions the "Retreater." Such retirees regard the effort to actively engage in anything beyond their everyday necessary routines as demanding too much energy output. One group of retreaters have abandoned the search for ways to replace the sense of purpose and meaning they felt while working, while others may just require some "time out" to think through and clarify how to navigate their new stage of life with all the demanding changes that retirement typically involves. Retreating for a short period of time can be a helpful "way to clear your head and relax before searching for your next commitment" (ibid, p. 153). However, some retreaters wind up feeling as if they are in an "endless thicket" of confusion and distress once they retire. For example, they long for their workplace friends and have been unable or unwilling to generate new meaningful friendships. In this context, the fact of no longer being part of their prior fulltime work life is a severe narcissistic injury. As Joseph Sandler and his colleagues have pointed out, such people not only feel they have lost their "love object," their work life, but they have lost something that was vital to their narcissistic integrity, their sense of well-being, for which their work life was responsible (Mendelson, 1974, p. 99). This assault on one's self-esteem and self-concept can lead to a withdrawal from friends, family and previously satisfying activities. Such retirees have essentially become clinically depressed, spending inordinate amounts of time alone at home doing fairly mindless activities like watching television, surfing the internet, or engaging in other escapist behavior meant to further numb them from their painful grief and mourning over their lost work world and sense of well-being. Retirees who fall into this rut often require a professional therapeutic intervention.

Final reflection

The art of living the "good life" in retirement requires considerable perspective-shifting and behavioral changes in terms of sustaining a viable identity, relationships and purpose. This is a process that is best conceived as taking place over a number of years rather than a one-off decision. Enhanced willpower and robust emotional and moral muscle are vital to a successful retirement, including the ability to positively re-frame the past in terms of the present challenging circumstances (Milne, 2013, pp. 21, 56). Retirement also requires a deepening capacity for suffering (e.g., to endure multiple losses) and transforming that suffering into practical wisdom, that is, into skillfully implemented, purposeful everyday living. This includes drawing from powerful unconscious resources, such as adaptive defenses, but also those wonderful affect-integrating, meaning-giving and action-guiding psychic potentials that can help a retiree maintain probably the most important element that constitutes being human at its best: personal dignity. Moreover, it is maintaining and affirming personal dignity, developing the internal ability to sustain self-respect while relinquishing self-importance (Schlossberg, 2009, p. 145), which is the prerequisite for flourishing in retirement. As existential psychologist Rollo May noted, "Joy, rather than happiness, is the goal of life, for joy is the emotion which accompanies our fulfilling our natures as human beings. It is based on the experience of one's identity as a being of worth and dignity" (www.entheos.com).

While the subject of personal dignity is an enormously complicated psychological and philosophical one, in this conclusion I simply suggest why maintaining a sense of personal dignity is so important to flourishing amidst a phase of the life cycle in which one's self-respect and self-pride can feel seriously challenged, if not assaulted. As I have emphasized throughout this chapter, depending on the totality of circumstances, for most people retirement is experienced as a narcissistic injury, at least to some degree; that is, it evokes painful, child-based feelings of being unvalued, unwanted and unloved (Mendelson, 1974, p. 170).

One of the great philosophical contributors to understanding personal dignity, including its pragmatic implications for retirement, was Christian Socratic philosopher Gabriel Marcel (1889–1973).[11] In Marcel's view, the problem of maintaining dignity is best construed in terms of two interrelated concrete questions that preoccupied him throughout his work life: how "to be a man" and how "to remain men" within our contemporary western social context (Marcel, 1963, p. 124). That is, how to maintain one's autonomy, integration and humanity amidst the dehumanizing and depersonalizing "mass society." In Marcel's view, the mass society reflected our "broken world" with its technomania (especially in our computer-driven Information Age), its atomization, collectivization, pervasive anonymous bureaucracy, over-reliance on so-called experts, its totalitarian potential, and even worse, its nuclear self-destructive possibility.

Marcel's main conclusion, which is hard to disagree with, is that human beings long for "fullness," for a rich individual and communal existence that is affirmed through such universal values as love, peace, beauty, justice and truth. These God-given values, as Marcel, the Christian believer, conceives them, are the counterpoint to our "broken world" of the mass society that is characterized by selfishness, alienation, and the atomist perspective (Anderson, 2006, pp. 120, 141). Atomism views the social system as merely an aggregate of individuals in which the whole is the sum of its parts. In other words, if we comprehend individuals then we know all that is necessary about the social system. This is compared to holism, which regards the social system as more than the aggregate of individuals who take part in them, but rather, as a network of statuses and roles that animate and limit a person's experience and overall behavior (Johnson, 1995, p. 14). This "psychologisation" and "individualisation" of the social realm has a perverse aspect to it, for it works against a thorough study of the underlying toxic societal processes (e.g., political and economic) that have led to the atomization in the first place, thus creating the illusion of having solved the individual and communal problem (Amado, 2013, pp. 14, 205). Manifestations of these dehumanizing and depersonalizing tendencies associated with mass society are prevalent in the fact that so many older retirees feel like they have been put "out to pasture," that they are "has-beens," "finished" as significant participants in life, as well as in the "warehousing" of elderly poor retirees in inadequate nursing homes, assisted living and other such isolating facilities. What is necessary, says Marcel, on both the individual and communal level is the "restoration of the sacred," which above all else means honoring the inherent dignity of all human beings, without exception (Anderson, 2006, pp. 120, 141).

Marcel further indicates that dignity is not about the respect or honor that a high rank or position is shown, what he calls a "decorative conception of dignity" or "affected dignity" (Marcel, 1963, pp. 128, 134).[12] Such a form of so-called dignity is "tissue-thin" in terms of expressing and maintaining one's autonomy, integration and humanity. Rather, dignity is associated with the "side of weakness," with the persecuted and oppressed, with compassion (ibid., p. 134) and empathy for the suffering of others, including a desire to provide concrete help. Marcel thus relates dignity to a kind of courage, to that quality of mind and heart that resists "all forms of tyranny," including those "that operate behind a screen of democratic phraseology" or rely on the disciplinary discourses of experts and external authority for direction. Dignity requires a modicum of courage in that a person does what he thinks he should do even though it requires great effort and sacrifice and often involves opposing the homogenizing norms of mass society. Dignity, then, for Marcel is the "remarkable ... fact that within us something builds up to resist this disintegration and downward course" that all forms of tyranny—political, social, economic, and, I would add, personal—personify. This includes the resistance to the dehumanizing and depersonalizing forces that are often in ascendance when one is an elderly retiree, especially a poor one where resources to prop up resilience are extremely limited. As Marcel further notes, "We can affirm with absolute certainty ... that there is within the human creature as we know him something that protests against the sort of rape or violation of which he is the victim" (Marcel, 2001a, p. 33). Such resistance and protest is not based on the mere "affirmation of the self" and its pretensions, but, in addition, and more profoundly, "on a stronger consciousness of the living tie which unites all men" (1963, p. 135)—that is, embracing the valuative attachment that we all have an essential moral worth that ought to be always respected. Dignity is intimately connected to conscience, to that internal sense of what is right and wrong that governs one's thoughts and actions, urging one to do right rather than wrong despite the negative personal costs. Such dignity is powerfully expressed and reinforced through other-directed, other-regarding and other-serving behavior, for it is lodged in a self-conception that positively "extends to other people, the planet and beyond" (Csikszentmihalyi and Nakamura, 2005, p. 240).

Marcel strongly links his notion of dignity to the concept of integrity, evidenced in a person possessing and steadfastly adhering to high moral principles. In everyday life, integrity is manifested in terms of living one's life according to one's cherished values; moreover, to the extent that one does so, one tends to feel greater self-respect. In retirement, for example, this means maintaining one's "inner center of gravity" amidst all of the indignities associated with the loss of role-status, power and the like. Maintaining integrity and dignity are indissolubly connected (ibid., p. 162), and for the retiree it is these qualities that are the basis for the profound sense of having lived a complete, meaningful and satisfying life.

Marcel's main concern was that because of the erosion of such meaning-giving traditional self-understandings as being a "child of God," a person having a divine-like nature that above all else deserves human respect, the average person has become estranged from himself, riddled by uncertainty and anxiety about his self-identity and his future. This is especially the case in the Information Age in which individuals must respond efficiently and effectively "to the fragmented, dispersed, attenuated, globalized situations in which they increasingly find themselves" (Krantz, 2005, p. 64). Such a "metaphysical uneasiness" (Marcel, 2001a, p. 35) is a deeply unsettling feeling-state that is especially sharp in the elderly retiree who may be unable (and unwilling) to cope with the impersonal set of competencies (e.g., those based on equating the human with a computer to be loaded and downloaded) and flexibility that characterize our turbulent surroundings (Vansina, 2013, p. xxii). Such "metaphysical uneasiness" reflects our contemporary "broken world" in which the urge to self-transcendence (e.g., being for the other before oneself) is hardly recognized, let alone affirmed. The defining feature of this loss of ontological "weight" to human existence is that individual "dignity and sacredness," and the sense of gratitude and humility that underlies it, is substituted with an all-pervasive societal value of function and functionality—that is, with the belief that the intended function of something should determine its significance, importance and meaning, that practical and utilitarian concerns should take priority over moral and esthetic ones (Keen, 1967, p. 9). Thus, man is valued in our society, including his self-valuing, largely in terms of the work he efficiently performs and the functions that he effectively satisfies. This observation speaks volumes about the possible negative psychological impact of retirement for the retiree whose very existence flies in the face of this powerful norm. The idealization of technology (as opposed to the sensible use of technology that Marcel appreciated and endorsed), with its over-valuation of scientific and functional thinking, and the egolatry and narcissism that it exalts, becomes the governing calculus of everyday living. Gone is the sense, Marcel says, that we are God's highly fallible human creatures, humble, grateful, serving (not servile!), devoted to using our "gifts" in a joyful, meaning-saturated, communal and responsible-for-the-other manner. As Keen further summarizes, such a functional outlook often leads to a sense of hopelessness and the belief that life is pointless and human values are worthless. Such an outlook can be searing to one's sense of dignity in retirement, especially if one has reduced one's inner life to one narcissistic theme like worrying about one's health and longevity.

> The results of such a [functional] way of thinking are disastrous for human dignity. As the capacity to love, to admire, and to hope dries up, the functional man loses the ability, and even the desire, to transcend his situation of alienation and captivity. His world loses its mysterious character, it becomes "purely natural", and all things are explained by reference to the categories of cause and effect. With the eclipse of mystery goes the atrophy of the sense of wonder.
>
> (ibid., p. 11)

It is a well-known observation that the capacity for wonder tends to get muted as one gets older. A degree of cynicism and gloominess can take hold. This is especially the case in those who have retired in late adulthood and old age, and often feel marginal to the pulse and activities of mainstream society, or even worse, they feel "finished" as significant contributors to life. The art of living the "good life" in retirement demands that one vigorously resists such an outlook. Marc Chagall has aptly put his finger on the connection between maintaining dignity and being able to wonder: "The dignity of the artist [the retiree] lies in his duty of keeping awake the sense of wonder in the world. In this long vigil he often has to vary his methods of stimulation; but in this long vigil he is also himself striving against a continual tendency to sleep" (www.history ofpainters.com). The "tendency to sleep" is precisely the metaphor for what is most debilitating in retirement—the proclivity to dampen one's enthusiasm to embrace life without reserve. This often involves shutting oneself down by re-grooving one's everyday life into the same old minimalist and dreary routines and activities that provide a sense of safety and security at the expense of living more creatively and productively. Where Ecclesiastes famously opined, "there is nothing new under the sun," the life-affirming retiree must say, "there is nothing old under the sun."

For Marcel, it is the spirit of abstraction, dealing with ideas rather than events, that is the root cause of the estrangement, nihilism and violent potential of modern man, which includes the situation of the typical retiree (Marcel, 2008, p. 1). Marcel defines the spirit of abstraction as follows: "As soon as we accord to any category, isolated from all other categories, an arbitrary primacy, we are victims of the spirit of abstraction" (ibid., p. 116). Marcel does understand and appreciate the usefulness of abstraction, just as he appreciates and understands the usefulness of technology, but what he is against is the deleterious, dangerous effect of excessive abstraction, especially as it plays out in everyday relations with others. Abstraction is a consequence of forgetting, disregarding and not honoring the concrete reality from which the abstraction is derived. For example, forgetting that an elderly patient diagnosed as psychotic is a unique individual with a painful family history that drove him into his psychosis is not reducible to his medical ascription; disavowing that the enemy a soldier is ordered to kill is a thinking, feeling person, perhaps with a partner and children; that a thing of nature, like a daffodil, is more than, and different from, its scientifically described structure and characteristics (Keen, 1967, pp. 13–14). And finally, perhaps worst of all, especially for the elderly retiree, there is the danger that our personal way of self-defining and self-fashioning may become mainly animated by the alienating spirit of abstraction. According to Marcel, "it is pretty certain … that we are tending to become bureaucrats, and not only in our outward behavior, but in our relations with ourselves. This is as much as to say that between ourselves and existence we are interposing thicker and thicker screens" (Marcel, 2001a, p. 91). This includes the associated poisonous and corrupting emotions that give one a sense of living in an everyday fogginess, as if something is obscuring and confusing a situation or one's thought processes. For Marcel, it is this spirit of abstraction that is at the root of so much dehumanization and violence that characterizes our "broken world" at its worst, as in totalitarianism where the human is reduced to a destroyable object, evidenced in Nazi and other forms of industrialized mass killing. Moreover, according to Marcel, such a life attitude, mindlessly governed by the spirit of abstraction, is the basis for the less extreme, but still very toxic, everyday loss of appreciation for, and affirmation of, the dignity and sacredness of all human beings and the physical environment. This is especially exemplified in our truncated, if not dehumanized and dehumanizing, everyday relations with others, as is manifested in common discourtesy and unkindness, and our disrespectful attitude toward our physical environment. The worst aspects of the spirit of abstraction is also manifest in "elder abuse," a term that refers "to any knowing, intentional, or negligent act by a caregiver or any other person that causes harm or a serious risk of harm to a vulnerable adult" (www.aoa.gov). Indeed, the increase in the reported neglect, exploitation (e.g., financial), emotional (and sometimes physical or sexual) abuse, and abandonment of the elderly strongly speaks to this point. This increase in elder abuse includes the number of elders who self-neglect and self-abuse, a good example of how this spirit of abstraction can operate in relationship to oneself (www.ncea.aoa.gov).

The "take home" point of this Marcellian-inspired reflection on dignity as it applies to retirement is this: one must resist being determined by external forces, one must maintain one's "inner center of gravity," that inviolate, untouchable and autonomous sense of self-worth and innocence, that constitutes selfhood at its best. As Terrence Des Pres noted, "Dignity, in this case, appears as a self-conscious, self-determining faculty whose function is to insist upon the recognition of itself *as such*" (1976, p. 73). The individual who cannot generate a creative and productive life after retirement is unable to integrate post-work experiences into a narrative of self-identity, an ongoing story of the self. Such a failure of the imagination and practical living is experienced as nothing short of humiliation—a radical subversion of self-identity and self-esteem, with the whole range of dire psychological consequences described earlier.

Thus, what the retiree needs to do is to engage in a "practice of the self" that involves honest and searching self-interrogation such that the conditions of possibility for generating a different form of apprehension and attunement come into being. One needs to ask and re-ask oneself a series of important questions, not just the "usual suspects" like, "Why do I exist rather than not?" but also, "Have I the right to be, am I worthy of being?" In addition to asking, "What do I hope for, what do I desire to be happy?" one must ask, "What must I do?" (Marcus, 2010, p. 239). In other words, what other-directed, other-regarding and other-serving actions ought I commit? Indeed, many retirees intuitively grasp this summoning call as they engage in self-transcendent activities like mentoring, grandparenthood, environmental conservation and civic life (Csikszentmihalyi and Nakamura, 2005, p. 238).

Both Marcel and Freud deeply honored the principle that a person's identity, a sense of ethical personhood, was not a luxury that one can tamper with, treat lightly or disregard, but, rather, it must *necessarily* be protected, defended and nurtured, until one's last breath (Meyers, 2003, p. 23). As Marcel poignantly suggests, which strongly applies to the elderly retiree, it is precisely this interminable struggle to maintain one's inner moral center of gravity in the face of the ambiguities, contradictions, ambivalences, fears and downright harshness, if not painfulness of life, that gives human existence its "tragic dignity" (Marcel, 1964, p. 238). Indeed, whether a retiree or still working, the self-awareness of the tragic dignity of life entails proclaiming to oneself again and again what the English poet William Ernst Henley famously wrote in *Invictus*, "My head is bloody, but unbowed."

Notes

1 The renowned English sociologist, Anthony Giddens, claimed "I'm sure retirement will be abolished as a notion within a relatively short time as is already happening in the US. There will be more mobility in and out of the labour force at different ages and people will have all sorts of different relationships to work" (1998, p. 107).

2 For a description and analysis of the paradigm of "having, losing and replacing a world," specifically as it applies to inmates in the Nazi concentration camps, see Marcus, 1999.

3 I have liberally drawn from Knoll (2011) in my discussion in this section.

4 This is easier said than done, for individuals tenaciously cling to their internal objects even when they are self-undermining, if not self-destructive.

5 For some individuals it is precisely the fear of greater-than-before dependency that makes retirement in old age so difficult. Often it is the unconscious fear of helplessness and immobility that is the root cause of their aversion to dependency.

6 Civitarese and Ferro (2013, p. xi) note the importance of reckoning with temporality as a crucial aspect of self-fashioning. For example, sickness can be experienced as "time fragmented" while old age can be experienced as "time pressing."

7 Even actor Jack Nicholson has had to come to grips with this: at age 73 he said in an interview, "I've struck bio-gravity … I can't hit on women in public anymore. I didn't decide this; it just doesn't feel right … that makes me sad … but I also think a lot of improvements in my character have come through ageing and the diminishing of powers" (Milne, 2013, p. 132).

8 For some individuals, physical diminution in old age can also stir up infantile annihilation anxieties, adding to the experienced horror of their ordeal.

9 This involves being able to metabolize and assimilate the emotionally significant events in one's life into the narrative.

10 There are of course differences in how men and women typically manage their friends in retirement, a subject that is beyond the scope of this chapter.

11 I have liberally drawn from my study of Marcel's work in this section (Marcus, 2013, pp. 135–141).

12 Aristotle had a similar point of view when he said, "Dignity consists not in possessing honors, but in the consciousness that we deserve them" (izquotes.com).

References

Amado, G. (2013). Psychic imprisonment and its release within organisations and working relationships. In: L. Vansina (Ed.), *Humanness in Organisations: A Psychodynamic Contribution* (pp. 7–28). London: Karnac.

Anderson, T. C. (2006). *A Commentary on Gabriele Marcel's Mystery of Being*. Milwaukee, WI: Marquette University Press.

de Beauvoir, S. (1996). *The Coming of Age*. P. O'Brien (Trans.). New York: Norton.

Civitarese, G. and Ferro, A. (2013). Prologue: Mourning and the Empty Couch: A Conversation between Analysts. In: G. Junkers (Ed.), *The Empty Couch: The Taboo of Ageing and Retirement in Psychoanalysis* (pp. xv–xxv). London: Routledge.

Csikszentmihalyi, M. and Nakamura, J. (2005). The Role of Emotions in the Development of Wisdom. In: R. J. Sternberg and J. Jordan (Eds.), *A Handbook of Wisdom: Psychological Perspectives* (pp. 220–242). Cambridge, UK: Cambridge University Press.

Des Pres, T. (1976). *The Survivor: The Anatomy of Life in the Death Camps*. New York: Pocket.

Eizirik, C. L. (2013). Giving Up an Important Role in Psychoanalytic Organizations. In: G. Junkers (Ed.), *The Empty Couch: The Taboo of Ageing and Retirement in Psychoanalysis* (pp. 119–129). London: Routledge.

Erikson, E. H. (1963). *Childhood and Society* (2nd ed.). New York: W. W. Norton & Company.

Erikson, E. H. (1964). *Insight and Responsibility*. New York: W. W. Norton & Company.

Giddens, A. (1984). *The Constitution of Society*. Berkeley, CA: University of California Press.

Giddens, A. (1991). *Modernity and Self-Identity*. Stanford, CA: Stanford University Press.

Gilbert, D. T. and Ebert, J. E. (2002). Decisions and Revisions: The Affective Forecasting of Changeable Outcomes. *Journal of Personality and Social Psychology*, 82(4), 503–514.

Gilbert, D. T., Pinel, E. C., Wilson, T. D., Blumberg, S. J. and Wheatley, T. P. (1998). Immune neglect: A source of durability bias in affective forecasting. *Journal of Personality and Social Psychology*, 175, 617–638.

Gilbert, D. T. and Wilson, T. D. (2009). Prospective Experiencing of the Future. *Science*, 317(5843), 1351–1354.

Horace. (1863). *The Works of Horace, Translated Literally*. C. Smart (Trans.). New York: Harper & Brothers.

Johnson, A. G. (1995). *The Blackwell Dictionary of Sociology: A User's Guide to Sociological Language*. Oxford: Blackwell.

Junkers, G. (2013a). The Ageing Psychoanalyst: Thoughts on Preparing for a Life Without the Couch. In: G. Junkers (Ed.), *The Empty Couch: The Taboo of Ageing and Retirement in Psychoanalysis* (pp. 3–6). London: Routledge.

Junkers, G. (Ed.). (2013b). Containing Psychoanalysis: The Analytic Institution. In: G. Junkers (Ed.), *The Empty Couch: The Taboo of Ageing and Retirement in Psychoanalysis* (pp. 95–100). London: Routledge.

Junkers, G. (2013c). Later, Perhaps … Transience and Its Significance for the Psychoanalyst. In: G. Junkers (Ed.), *The Empty Couch: The Taboo of Ageing and Retirement in Psychoanalysis* (pp. 17–31). London: Routledge.

Keen, S. (1967). *Gabriel Marcel*. Richmond, VA: John Knox Press.

Keltner, D. (2015). The Science of "Inside Out." *New York Times*, Sunday Review, 7/5/15, p. 10.

Kloep, M. and Hendry, L. B. (2007). Retirement: A New Beginning. *The Psychologist*, 20 (December), 742–745.

Knoll, M. A. Z. (2011). Behavioral and Psychological Aspects of the Retirement Decision. *Social Security Bulletin*, *71*(4), 1–13.

Krantz, J. (2005). Approaching Twenty-First Century, Information-Based Organizations. In: R. J. Sternberg and J. Jordan (Eds.), *A Handbook of Wisdom: Psychological Perspectives* (pp. 51–69). Cambridge, UK: Cambridge University Press.

Marcel, G. (1963). *The Existential Background of Human Dignity*. Cambridge, MA: Harvard University Press.

Marcel, G. (1964). *Creative Fidelity*. R. Rosthal (Trans.). New York: Farrar, Straus and Giroux.

Marcel, G. (2001a). *The Mystery of Being: Volume I: Reflection and Mystery*. South Bend, IN: St. Augustine Press.

Marcel, G. (2008). *Man Against Mass Society*. South Bend, IN: St. Augustine's Press.

Marcus, P. (1999). *Autonomy in the Extreme Situation: Bruno Bettelheim, the Nazi Concentration Camps and the Mass Society*. Westport, CT: Praeger.

Marcus, P. (2003). *Ancient Religious Wisdom, Spirituality, and Psychoanalysis*. Westport, CT: Praeger.

Marcus, P. (2010). *In Search of the Good Life: Emmanuel Levinas, Psychoanalysis and the Art of Living*. London: Karnac.

Marcus, P. (2013). *In Search of the Spiritual: Gabriel Marcel, Psychoanalysis, and the Sacred*. London: Karnac.

Marcus, P. (2015). *Creating Heaven on Earth: The Psychology of Experiencing Immortality in Everyday Life*. London: Karnac.

Mendelson, M. (1974). *Psychoanalytic Concepts of Depression* (2nd ed.). Flushing, NY: Spectrum Publications.

Meyers, D. G. (2003). Jean Améry: On Being a Jewish Victim. In: S. L. Kremer (Ed.), *Holocaust Literature: An Encyclopedia of Writers and Their Work* (pp. 20–23). New York: Routledge.

Milne, D. (2013). *The Psychology of Retirement: Coping with the Transition from Work*. West Sussex, UK: Wiley-Blackwell.

Monte, C. F. (1980). *Beneath the Mask: An Introduction to Theories of Personality* (2nd ed.). New York: Holt, Rinehart and Winston.

Morrison, M. and Roese, N. K. (2011). Regrets of the Typical American: Findings from a Nationally Representative Sample. *Social Psychological and Personality and Science*, 2(6), 576–583.

Rorty, R. (1989). *Contingency, Irony, and Solidarity*. Cambridge, UK: Cambridge University Press.

Rycroft, C. (1995). *A Critical Dictionary of Psychoanalysis* (2nd ed.). London: Penguin.

Schlossberg, N. K. (2009). *Revitalizing Retirement: Reshaping Your Identity, Relationships, and Purpose*. Washington, DC: American Psychological Association.

Schur, M. (1972). *Freud Living and Dying*. London: Hogarth Press.

Teising, M. (2013). Narcissistic Challenges for Ageing Analysts. In: G. Junkers (Ed.), *The Empty Couch: The Taboo of Ageing and Retirement in Psychoanalysis* (pp. 46–52). London: Routledge.

Vansina, L. (2013). General introduction. In: L. Vansina (Ed.), *Humanness in Organisations: A Psychodynamic Contribution* (pp. xv–xxvii). London: Karnac.

Week, The (2015, September 18). No Need to Retire All At Once. p. 33.

Weinstein, F. (1980). *The Dynamics of Nazism*. New York: Academic Press.

Winnicott, D. W. (1971). *Playing and Reality*. London: Tavistock.

Web sources

changingminds.org/explanations/theories/impact_bias.htm, retrieved 6/18/15.

izquotes.com/quote/280972, retrieved 7/13/15.

m.imdb.com/name/nm0142829/quotes, retrieved 6/16/15.

www.aoa.gov/AoA.../elder.../whatisEA.aspx, retrieved 7/14/15.

www.encyclopedia.com. "Friendship." International Encyclopedia of Marriage and Family, retrieved 7/6/15.

www.entheos.com/quotes/by_topic/Rollo+May, retrieved 7/10/15.

www.historyofpainters.com/chagall.htm, retrieved 7/13/15.

www.ncea.aoa.gov/Library/Data/index.aspx, retrieved 7/14/15.

www.nimh.nih.gov/health/.../use-of-m..., retrieved 6/18/15.

www.psychologytoday.com/.../affective-foreca..., retrieved 6/18/15.

www.quotegarden.com/age.html, retrieved 6/16/15.

References

Aamodt, M. G. (2010). *Industrial/Organizational Psychology: An Applied Approach* (6th ed.). Belmont, CA: Wadsworth.

Aaron, S. (1986). *Stage Fright: Its Role in Acting*. Chicago, IL: The University of Chicago Press.

Ainsworth, M. D. and Bowlby, J. (1965). *Child Care and the Growth of Love*. London: Penguin Books.

Akhtar, S. (2009). *Comprehensive Dictionary of Psychoanalysis*. London: Karnac.

Albion, M. (2006). Foreword. In: L. Kang (Ed.), *Passion at Work: How to Find Work You Love and Live the Time of Your Life*. Upper Saddle River, NJ: Prentice Hall.

Allen, D. A. (2014). *How to Quit Anything in 5 Simple Steps: Break the Chains that Bind You*. Bloomington, IN: Balboa Press.

Amabile, T. and Kramer, S. (2011). *The Progress Principle*. Boston, MA: Harvard Business School Press.

Amado, G. (2013). Psychic imprisonment and its release within organisations and working relationships. In: L. Vansina (Ed.), *Humanness in Organisations: A Psychodynamic Contribution* (pp. 7–28). London: Karnac.

Anderson, T. C. (2006). *A Commentary on Gabriele Marcel's Mystery of Being*. Milwaukee, WI: Marquette University Press.

Arnold, J. and Cohen, L. (2013). Careers in Organizations. In: W. B. Walsh, M. L. Savickas and P. J. Hartung (Eds.), *Handbook of Vocational Psychology: Theory, Research, and Practice* (pp. 273–304). New York: Routledge.

Averill, J. R. (2009). Emotional Creativity: Toward "Spiritualizing the Passions." In: S. L. Lopez and C. R. Snyder (Eds.), *Oxford Handbook of Positive Psychology* (pp. 249–258). Oxford: Oxford University Press.

Axelrod, S. D. (1999). *Work and the Evolving Self. Theoretical and Clinical Considerations*. Hillsdale, NJ: Analytic Press.

Bain, A. and Gould, L. J. (1996). The Fifth Assumption. *Free Associations*, 6:1, no. 37, 1–20.

Bakker, A. B., Demerouti, E. and Burke, R. (2009). Workaholism and Relationship Quality: A Spillover-Crossover Perspective. *Journal of Occupational Health Psychology*, *14*:1, 23–33.

Barnes, B. (1983). *T.S. Kuhn and Social Sciences*. New York: Columbia University Press.

de Beauvoir, S. (1996). *The Coming of Age*. P. O'Brien (Trans.). New York: Norton.

Becker, E. (1969). *Angel in Armor: Post Freudian Perspectives on the Nature of Man*. New York: George Braziller.

Bauman, Z. (2003). *Liquid Love*. Cambridge, UK: Polity Press

Bellah, R. N., Madsen, R., Sullivan, W. M., Swidler, A. and Tipton, S. M. (1986). *Habits of the Heart: Individualism and Commitment in American Life*. New York: Harper & Row.

Berg, J. M., Grant, A. G. and Johnson, V. (2010). When Callings are Calling: Crafting Work and Leisure in Pursuit of Unanswered Occupational Callings. *Organization Science*, *21*:5, 973–994.

Bergler, E. (1949). On Acting and Stage Fright. *Psychiatric Quarterly Supplement*, *23*, 313–319.

Bergler, E. (1950). *The Writer and Psychoanalysis*. Garden City, NY: Doubleday & Company.

Bergler, E. (1955). Unconscious Mechanisms in "Writer's Block." *Psychoanalytic Review*, *42*, 160–167.

Bergmann, M. V. (1997). Creative Work, Work Inhibitions and their Relation to Internal Objects. In: C. W. Socarides and S. Kramer (Eds.), *Work and Its Inhibitions: Psychoanalytic Essays* (pp. 191–207). Madison, CT: International Universities Press.

Bibring, E. (1941). The Conception of the Repletion Compulsion. *Psychoanalytic Quarterly*, *12*, 486–519.

Bion, W. R. (1959). *Experiences in Groups*. New York: Ballantine Books.

Blair, S. E. E. (2013). Foreword. In: L. Nicholls, J. C. Piergrossi, C. de Sena Gibertoni and M. A. Daniel (Eds.), *Psychoanalytic Thinking in Occupational Therapy: Symbolic, Relational and Transformational* (pp. ix–x). London: Wiley Blackwell.

Blum, H. P. (1997). Psychoanalysis and Playful Work. In: C. W. Socarides and S. Kramer (Eds.), *Work and Its Inhibitions: Psychoanalytic Essays* (pp. 19–34). Madison, CT: International Universities Press.

Blustein, D. L., Prezioso, M. S. and Schultheiss, D. P. (1995). Attachment Theory and Career Development: Current Status and Future Directions. *The Counseling Psychologist*, *23*:3, 416–432.

Bonebright, C. A., Clay, D. and Ankenmann, R. D. (2000). The Relationship of Workaholism with Work-Life Conflict, Life Satisfaction, and Purpose of Life. *Journal of Counseling Psychology*, *47*:4, 469–477.

Bordin, E. S. (1987). The 1986 Leona Tyler Award Address: Aim and Trajectory. *The Counseling Psychologist*, *15*, 358–367.

Bordin, E. S., Nachman, B. and Segal, S. J. (1963). An Articulated Framework for Vocational Development. *Journal of Counseling Psychology*, *10*:2, 107–116.

Bright, J. E. H., Pryor, R. G. L., Wilkenfeld, S. and Earl, J. (2005). The Role of Social Context and Serendipitous Events in Career Decision Making. *Journal for Educational and Vocational Guidance*, *5*, 19–36.

Brill, A. A. (1949). *Basic Principles of Psychoanalysis*. Garden City, NY: Garden City Books.

Britton, R. (1994). Publication Anxiety: Conflict Between Communication and Affiliation. *International Journal of Psychoanalysis*, *75*, 1213–1224.

Britzman, D. P. (2003). *After Education: Anna Freud, Melanie Klein, and Psychoanalytic Histories of Learning*. Albany, NY: State University of New York Press.

Britzman, D. P. (2006). *After Education: Anna Freud, Melanie Klein, and Psychoanaytic Histories of Learning*. Albany, NY: State University of New York Press.

Britzman, D. P. (2011). *Freud and Education*. New York: Routledge.

Bruce, M. A. G. and Borg, B. (2002). *Frames of Reference in Psychosocial Occupational Therapy*. Thorofare, NJ: Slack.

Burke, R. J. and Matthiesen, S. (2004). Short Communication: Workaholism among Norwegian Journalists: Antecedents and Consequences. *Stress and Health*, *20*, 301–308.

Butler, S. (1903) [2004]. *The Way of All Flesh*. Garden City, NY: Dover.

Cain, S. (1979). *Gabriel Marcel*. South Bend, IN: Regnery/Gateway.

Cain, S. (1995). *Gabriel Marcel's Theory of Religious Experience*. New York: Peter Lang.

Cameron, D., Inzlicht, M. and Cunningham, W. A. (2015). Empathy is Actually a Choice. *New York Times*, Sunday Review, 7/12/15, p. 12.

Campbell, W. K., Bush, C. P., Brunell, A. B. and Shelton, J. (2005). Understanding the Social Costs of Narcissism: The Case of the Tragedy of the Commons. *Personality and Social Psychology Bulletin*, *31*, 1358–1368.

Carnall, C. A. (2008). Foreword. In: D. Rowland and M. Higgs (Eds.), *Sustaining Change: Leadership that Works* (pp. vii–x). Southampton, UK: Jossey-Bass.

Carroll, S. T. (2013). Addressing Religion and Spirituality in the Workplace. In: K. I. Pergament (Ed.), *APA Handbook of Psychology, Religion, and Spirituality, Volume 2* (pp. 595–612). Washington, DC: American Psychological Association.

Cascio, W. F. (2010). The Changing World of Work. In: P. A. Linley, S. Harrington and N. Garcea (Eds.), *Oxford Handbook of Positive Psychology and Work* (pp. 13–23). Oxford: Oxford University Press.

Casement, P. (1991). *Learning from the Patient*. New York: Guilford.

Chang, R. (2015). Resolving to Create a New You. *New York Times Sunday Review*, 1/4/15, p. 7.

Chesbrough, H. (2003). *Open Innovation. The New Imperative for Creating and Profiting from Technology*. Cambridge, MA: Harvard Business School Press.

Christian, J. (2012). *Philosophy: An Introduction to the Art of Wondering*. Boston, MA: Wadsworth.

Civitarese, G. and Ferro, A. (2013). Prologue: Mourning and the Empty Couch: A Conversation between Analysts. In: G. Junkers (Ed.), *The Empty Couch: The Taboo of Ageing and Retirement in Psychoanalysis* (pp. xv–xxv). London: Routledge.

Clark, M. A., Lelchook, A. M. and Taylor, M. L. (2010). Beyond the Big Five: How Narcissism, Perfectionism, and Dispositional Affect Relate to Workaholism. *Personality and Individual Differences*, *48*, 786–791.

Collins, J. (2001). *Good to Great*. New York: Harper Business.

Colman, A. M. (2009). *Oxford Dictionary of Psychology*. Oxford: Oxford University Press.

Conger, J. A. and Kanungo, R. N. (1987). Toward a Behavioral Theory of Charismatic Leadership in Organizational Settings. *Academy of Management Review*, *12*:4, 637–647.

Csikszentmihalyi, M. and Nakamura, J. (2005). The Role of Emotions in the Development of Wisdom. In: R. J. Sternberg and J. Jordan (Eds.), *A Handbook of Wisdom: Psychological Perspectives* (pp. 220–242). Cambridge, UK: Cambridge University Press.

De Vos, A. and Sorens, N. (2008). Protean Attitude and Career Success: The Mediating Role of Self-management. *Journal of Vocational Behavior*, *73*, 449–456.

Dejours, C. (2015a). Introduction. In: C. Dejours (Ed.), *Psychopathology of Work: Clinical Observations* (pp. xiii–xviii). C. Williamson (Trans.). London: Karnac.

Dejours, C. (2015b). Madness and Work: From Aetiological Analysis to Theoretical Contradictions (A Case of *Status Asthmaticus*). In: C. Dejours (Ed.), *Psychopathology of Work: Clinical Observations* (pp. 1–19). C. Williamson (Trans.). London: Karnac.

Des Pres, T. (1976). *The Survivor: The Anatomy of Life in the Death Camps*. New York: Pocket.

Dewey, J. (1916). *Democracy and Education: An Introduction to the Philosophy of Education*. New York: Macmillan.

Dik, B. J. and Duffy, R. D. (2009). Calling and Vocation at Work: Definitions and Prospects for Research and Practice. *The Counseling Psychologist*, *37*:3, 424–450.

Dominus, S. Parent Companies. In: *The New York Times Magazine*, 2/28/16, p. 48.

Doonan, S. (2015). Viewpoint. *The Week*, 4/3/15, p. 10.

Duhigg, C. (2016) Group Study. *The New York Times Magazine*, 2/28/16, p. 75.

Dutton, J. E., Roberts, L. M. and Bednar, J. (2011). Prosocial Practices, Positive Identity, and Flourishing at Work. In: S. I. Donaldson, M. Csikszentmihalyi and J. Nakamura (Eds.), *Applied Positive Psychology: Improving Everyday Life, Health, Schools, Work, and Society* (pp. 155–170). New York: Routledge.

Elliott, A. (2003). Slavoj Zizek. In: A. Elliott and L. Ray (Eds.), *Key Contemporary Social Theorists* (pp. 273–378). Malden, MA: Blackwell Publishers

Eizirik, C. L. (2013). Giving Up an Important Role in Psychoanalytic Organizations. In: G. Junkers (Ed.), *The Empty Couch: The Taboo of Ageing and Retirement in Psychoanalysis* (pp. 119–129). London: Routledge.

Eliot, G. (1882). *Wit and Wisdom of George Eliot*. Boston, MA: Roberts Brothers.

Elliot, A. (2014). *Concepts of the Self*. Cambridge, UK: Polity Press.

El-Sawad, A. (2005). Becoming a "Lifer"? Unlocking Career through Metaphor. *Journal of Occupational and Organizational Psychology*, *78*, 23–41.

Emerson, R. W. (1984). *Emerson in His Journals*. Joel Porte (Ed.). Cambridge, MA: Belknap Press.

Erikson, E. H. (1950). *Childhood and Society*. New York: Norton.

Erikson, E. H. (1956). The Problem of Ego Identity. *Journal of the American Psychoanalytical Association*, *4*, 56–121.

Erikson, E. H. (1959). *Identity and the Life Cycle: Selected Papers* (Psychological Issues, Vol. 1, No. 1, Monograph 1). New York: International Universities Press.

Erikson, E. H. (1962). *Young Man Luther: A Study in Psychoanalysis and History*. New York: W.W. Norton.

Erikson, E. H. (1963). *Childhood and Society* (2nd ed.). New York: W.W. Norton & Company.

Erikson, E. H. (1964). *Insight and Responsibility*. New York: W.W. Norton.

Erikson, E. H. (1970). *Gandhi's Truth: On the Origins of Militant Nonviolence*. New York: W.W. Norton.

Erikson, E. H. (1974). *Dimensions of a New Identity: Jefferson Lectures, 1973*. New York: W.W. Norton.

Erikson, E. H. (1977). *Toys and Reasons*. New York: Norton.

Fadiman, C. and Brand, A. (Eds.). (1985). *Bartlett's Book of Anecdotes*. New York: Little, Brown & Co.

Farrington, C. (2014). *Failing at School: Lessons for Redesigning Urban High Schools*. New York: Teacher's College Press.

Fenichel, O. (1945). *The Psychoanalytic Theory of Neurosis*. New York: W.W. Norton.

Ferenczi, S. (1919) [1980]. *Sunday Neurosis: Further Contributions to the Theory and Technique of Psychoanalysis* (pp. 174–177). J. I. Suttie (Trans.). New York: Brunner/Mazel.

Ferro, A. and Civitarese, G. (2013). Foreword. In: G. Junkers (Ed.), *The Empty Couch: The Taboo of Ageing and Retirement in Psychoanalysis* (pp. x–xi). London: Routledge.

Festinger, L. (1957). *A Theory of Cognitive Dissonance*. Redwood City, CA: Stanford University Press.

Fineman, S. (1993). *Emotion in Organizations*. Newbury Park, CA: Sage.

Flugel, J. C. (1938). Stage Fright and Anal Eroticism. *British Journal of Medical Psychology, 17,* 189–196.

Foucault, M. (1984). Space, Knowledge, and Power. In: P. Rabinow (Ed.), *The Foucault Reader* (pp. 239–256). New York: Pantheon.

Foucault, M. (1989). The Ethics of the Concern for Self as a Practice of Freedom. In: S. Lotringer (Ed.), *Foucault Live: Collected Interviews, 1961–1984* (pp. 432–449). New York: Semiotexte.

Frankl, V. E. (1963). *Man's Search for Meaning. An Introduction to Logotherapy.* I. Lasch (Trans.). New York: Pocket Books.

Franklin, B. (1840). *The Works of Benjamin Franklin* (Vol. 8). J. Sparks (Ed.). Boston, MA: Hilliard Gray and Company.

Franzen, J. (2015, Oct. 4). *New York Times Book Review.*

Frederickson, B. L. (2001). The Role of Positive Emotions in Positive Psychology. *American Psychologist, 56:*3, 218–226.

Frederickson, B. L. (2004). The Broaden-and-Build Theory of Positive Emotions. *Transactions of the Royal Society of London, Biological Science, 359:*1449, 1367–1378. doi:10.1098/rstb.2004.1512

Frederickson, B. L. (2009). *Positivity. Top-Notch Research Reveals 3-to-1 Ratio that Will Change Your Life.* New York: Harmony.

Freud, S. (1908) [1959]. On the Sexual Theories of Children. In: J. Strachey (Ed. and Trans.), *The Standard Edition of the Complete Psychological Works of Sigmund Freud,* Vol. 9 (pp. 205–226). London: Hogarth Press.

Freud, S. (1910) [1963]. *Psychoanalysis and Faith: The Letters of Sigmund Freud and Oskar Pfister.* H. Meng and E. L. Feder (Eds.). E. Mosbacher (Trans.). London: Hogarth Press.

Freud, S. (1914) [1957]. On Narcissism: An Introduction. In: J. Strachey (Ed. and Trans.), *The Standard Edition of the Complete Psychological Works of Sigmund Freud,* Vol. XIV (pp. 67–102). London: Hogarth Press.

Freud, S. (1916–1917) [1961]. Introductory Lectures on Psycho-Analysis. In: J. Strachey (Ed. and Trans.), *The Standard Edition of the Complete Psychological Works of Sigmund Freud,* Vol. 15 and 16. London: Hogarth Press.

Freud, S. (1920) [1964]. *Beyond the Pleasure Principle.* In: J. Strachey (Ed. and Trans.), *The Standard Edition of the Complete Psychological Works of Sigmund Freud,* Vol. 18 (pp. 3–66). London: Hogarth Press.

Freud, S. (1921) [1955]. Group Psychology and the Analysis of the Ego. In: J. Strachey (Ed. and Trans.), *The Standard Edition of the Complete Psychological Works of Sigmund Freud,* Vol. 18 (pp. 65–143). London: Hogarth Press.

Freud, S. (1923) [1955]. The Ego and the Id. In: J. Strachey (Ed. and Trans.), *The Standard Edition of the Complete Psychological Works of Sigmund Freud,* Vol. 17 (pp. 3–68). London: Hogarth Press.

Freud, S. (1925) [1957]. Some Character-Types Met with in Psycho-analytic Work. In: J. Strachey (Ed. and Trans.), *The Standard Edition of the Complete Psychological Works of Sigmund Freud,* Vol. 14 (pp. 311–333). London: Hogarth Press.

Freud, S. (1926) [1959]. *The Question of Lay Analysis.* In: J. Strachey (Ed. and Trans.), *The Standard Edition of the Complete Psychological Works of Sigmund Freud,* Vol. 20 (pp. 179–249). London: Hogarth Press.

Freud, S. (1927) [1961]. Humour. In: J. Strachey (Ed. and Trans.), *The Standard Edition of the Complete Psychological Works of Sigmund Freud,* Vol. 21 (pp. 161–166). London: Hogarth Press.

Freud, S. (1927) [1961]. The Future of Illusion. In: J. Strachey (Ed. and Trans.), *The Standard Edition of the Complete Psychological Works of Sigmund Freud*, Vol. 21 (pp. 5–56). London: Hogarth Press.

Freud, S. (1930) [1961]. *Civilization and Its Discontents*. In: J. Strachey (Ed. and Trans.), *The Standard Edition of the Complete Psychological Works of Sigmund Freud*, Vol. 21 (pp. 57–145). London: Hogarth Press.

Freud, S. (1974). *The Freud/Jung Letters*. W. McGuire (Ed.). Princeton, NJ: Princeton University Press.

Freud, S. (1985). *The Complete Letters of Sigmund Freud to Wilhelm Fliess*: 1887–1904. J. Masson (Ed.). Cambridge, MA: Harvard University Press.

Freundlich, D. (1968). Narcissism and Exhibitionism in the Performance of Classical Music. *Psychiatric Quarterly Supplement, 42*, 1–13.

Frew, J. (2004). Motivating and Leading Dysfunctional Employees. In: J. C. Thomas and M. Hersen (Eds.), *Psychopathology in the Workplace. Recognition and Adaptation* (pp. 293–311). New York: Brunner-Routledge.

Friedman, T. (2015). Contain and Amplify. *The New York Times OP-ED*, 5/27/15, p. A23.

Fromm, E. (1947). *Man for Himself: An Inquiry into the Psychiatry of Ethics*. New York: Fawcett.

Furman, E. (1997). Child's Work: Developmental Aspects of the Capacity to Work and Enjoy It. In: C. W. Socarides and S. Kramer (Eds.), *Work and Its Inhibitions: Psychoanalytic Essays* (pp. 3–17). Madison, CT: International Universities Press.

Gabbard, G. O. (1979). Stage Fright. *The International Journal of Psychoanalysis, 60*, 383–392.

Gabbard, G. O. (1983). Further Contributions to the Understanding of Stage Fright: Narcissistic Issues. *Journal of the American Psychoanalytic Association, 31*, 423–441.

Gabbard, G. O. (1997). The Vicissitudes of Shame in Stage Fright. In: C. W. Socarides and S. Kramer (Eds.), *Work and Its Inhibitions: Psychoanalytic Essays* (pp. 209–220). Madison, CT: International Universities Press.

Galinsky, M. D. (1962). Personality Development and Vocational Choice of Clinical Psychologists and Physicists. *Journal of Counseling Psychology, 13*, 89–92.

Galinsky, M. D. and Fast, I. (1966). Vocational Choice as a Focus of the Identity Search. *Journal of Counseling Psychology, 13*:1, 89–92.

Gallagher, K. T. (1962). *The Philosophy of Gabriel Marcel*. New York: Fordham University Press.

Gambrill, E. (2004). Social Skills Deficits. In: J. C. Thomas and M. Hersen (Eds.), *Psychopathology in the Workplace. Recognition and Adaptation* (pp. 243–257). New York: Brunner-Routledge.

Garvin, D. (2000). *Learning in Action*. Boston, MA: Harvard Business School Press.

Gay, P. (1988). *Freud: A Life for Our Time*. New York: Norton.

Gedo, J. E. (1997). In Praise of Leisure. In: C. W. Socarides and S. Kramer (Eds.), *Work and Its Inhibitions: Psychoanalytic Essays* (pp. 133–141). Madison, CT: International Universities Press.

Giddens, A. (1984). *The Constitution of Society*. Berkeley, CA: University of California Press.

Giddens, A. (1991). *Modernity and Self-Identity*. Stanford, CA: Stanford University Press.

Giddens, A. and Pierson, C. (1998). *Conversations with Anthony Giddens. Making Sense of Modernity*. Stanford, CA: Stanford University Press.

Gilbert, D. L. (1981). *Oxygen and Living Processes: An Interdisciplinary Approach.* Berlin: Springer-Verlag.

Gilbert, D. T. and Ebert, J. E. (2002). Decisions and Revisions: The Affective Forecasting of Changeable Outcomes. *Journal of Personality and Social Psychology*, 82(4), 503–514.

Gilbert, D. T., Pinel, E. C., Wilson, T. D., Blumberg, S. J. and Wheatley, T. P. (1998). Immune Neglect: A Source of Durability Bias in Affective Forecasting. *Journal of Personality and Social Psychology*, *175*, 617–638.

Gilbert, D. T. and Wilson, T. D. (2009). Prospective Experiencing of the Future. *Science*, *317*(5843), 1351–1354.

Gilovich, T. and Savitsky, K. (1999). The Spotlight Effect and the Illusion of Transparency: Egocentric Assessments of How We Are Seen by Others. *Current Directions in Psychological Science*, *8*, 165–168.

Gould, L. J. (1993). Contemporary Perspectives on Personal and Organizational Authority: The Self in a System of Work Relationships. In: L. Hirschhorn and C. K. Barnett (Eds.), *The Psychodynamics of Organizations* (pp. 49–63). Philadelphia, PA: Temple University Press.

Grant, A. M. and Berg, J. M. (2011). Prosocial Motivation at Work: When, Why, and How Making a Difference Makes a Difference. In: K. Cameron and G. Spreitzer (Eds.), *Oxford Handbook of Positive Organizational Scholarship* (pp. 28–44). New York: Oxford University Press.

Guindon, M. and Hanna, F. (2002). Coincidence, Happenstance, Serendipity, Fate, or the Hand of God: Case Studies in Synchronicity. *The Career Development Quarterly*, *50*, 195–208.

Gysbers, N. C., Heppner, M. J. and Johnston, J. A. (2009). *Career Counseling. Contexts, Processes, and Techniques.* Alexandria, VA: American Counseling Association.

Hackman, R. J. (2002). *Leading Teams: Setting the Stage for Great Performances.* Boston, MA: HBS Press.

Hadot, P. (1997). *Philosophy as a Way of Life.* Oxford: Blackwell.

Hall, D. T. and Chandler, D. E. (2005). Psychological Success: When the Career is a Calling. *Journal of Organizational Behavior*, *26*, 155–176.

Hardy, G. E. and Barkham, M. (1994). The Relationship between Interpersonal Attachment Styles and Work Difficulties. *Human Relations*, *47*:3, 263–281.

Hartung, P. J., Porfeli, E. J. and Vondracek, F. W. (2005). Child Vocational Development: A Review and Reconsideration. *Journal of Vocational Behavior*, *66*, 385–419.

Hartung, P. J., Walsh, W. B. and Savickas, M. L. (2013). Introduction: Stability and Change in Vocational Psychology. In: W. B. Walsh, M. L. Savickas and P. J. Hartung (Eds.), *Handbook of Vocational Psychology: Theory, Research, and Practice* (pp. xi–xvi). New York: Routledge.

Hayes, D. (1975). The Archetypal Nature of Stage Fright. *Art Psychotherapy*, *2*, 279–291.

Hazan, C. and Shaver, P. R. (1990). Love and Work: An Attachment Theory Perspective. *Journal of Personality and Social Psychology*, *19*:2, 270–280.

Heath, C. and Heath, D. (2010). *Switch: How to Change Things When Change is Hard.* New York: Crown Business.

Heath, C. and Heath, D. (2013). *Decisive. How to Make Better Choices in Life and Work.* New York: Crown Business.

Heffernan, V. (2016). Meet is Murder. In *New York Times Magazine*, 2/28/16 (p. 30).

Heifetz, R. (1998). *Leadership without Easy Answers.* Cambridge, MA: Harvard University Press.

Helmreich, J. and Marcus, P. (2008). *Warring Parents, Wounded Children and the Wretched World of Child Custody: Cautionary Tales*. Westport, CT: Praeger.

Hendrik, I. (1943). Work and the Pleasure Principle. *Psychoanalytic Quarterly*, *12*, 311–329.

Hesse, M. (1980). The Exploratory Function of Metaphor. In: M. Hesse, *Revolutions and Reconstructions in Philosophy of Science*. Bloomington: Indiana University Press. Quoted in R. Rorty (1989), *Contingency, Irony, and Solidarity*. New York: Cambridge University Press.

Higgs, M. (2010). Change and its Leadership: The Role of Positive Emotions. In: P. A. Linley, S. Harrington and N. Garcea (Eds.), *Oxford Handbook of Positive Psychology and Work* (pp. 67–80). Oxford: Oxford University Press.

Hirschhorn, L. (1988). *The Workplace Within: Psychodynamics of Organizational Life*. Cambridge, MA: The MIT Press.

Hodgson, J. and Richards, E. (1974). *Improvisation*. New York: Grove Weidenfeld.

Hopper, E. (2003). *Traumatic Experience in the Unconscious Life of Groups: The Fourth Basic Assumption: Incohesion: Aggregation/Massification or (ba) I:A/M International Library of Group Analysis* (Book #23). London: Jessica Kingsley.

Horace. (1863). *The Works of Horace, Translated Literally*. C. Smart (Trans.). New York: Harper & Brothers.

Hugo, V. (1901) [1907]. *Intellectual Autobiography (Postscriptum)*. L. O'Rourke (Trans.). New York: Funk and Wagnalls Company.

Huntley, H. L. (1997). How Does "God-Talk" Speak to the Workplace: An Essay on the Theology of Work. In D. P. Bloch and L. J. Richmond (Eds.), *Connections Between Spirit and Work in Career Development: New Approaches and Practical Perspectives* (pp. 115–136). Palo Alto, CA: Davies-Black Publishing.

Huy, Q. N. (1999). Emotional Capability, Emotional Intelligence, and Radical Change. *Academy of Management Review*, *24*:2, 325–345.

Huy, Q. N. (2002). Emotional Balancing or Organizational Continuity and Radical Change: The Contribution of Middle Managers. *Administrative Science Quarterly*, *47*:1, 31–36.

Huy, Q. N. (2005). An Emotional-Based View of Strategic Renewal. In G. Szulanski, J. Potac and Y. Doz (Eds.), *Strategy Process: Advances in Strategic Management* (pp. 3–37). New York: Elsevier.

Huy, Q. N. (2012). Emotions and Strategic Change. In K. Cameron and G. Spreitzer (Eds.), *Oxford Handbook of Positive Organizational Scholarship* (pp. 811–824). New York: Oxford University Press.

Inkson, K., Gunz, H., Ganesh, S. and Roper, J. (2012). Boundaryless Careers: Bringing Back Boundaries. *Organizational Studies*, *33*:3, 323–340.

Inman, L. D. (1997). A Room of One's Own Revisited. In: C. W. Socarides and S. Kramer (Eds.), *Work and Its Inhibitions: Psychoanalytic Essays* (pp. 115–131). Madison, WI: International Universities Press.

Jacques, E. (1960). Disturbances in the Capacity to Work. *International Journal of Psycho-Analysis*, *41*, 357–367.

Janis, I. (1972). *Victims of Groupthink: A Psychological Study of Foreign-Policy Decisions and Fiascoes*. Boston, MA: Houghton Mifflin.

Janis, I. (1982). *Groupthink: Psychological Studies of Policy Decisions and Fiascoes* (2nd ed.). New York: Houghton Mifflin.

Jaques, E. (1974). Social Systems as Defense Against Persecutory and Depressive Anxiety. In: G. S. Gabbard, J. J. Hartmann and R. D. Mann (Eds.), *Analysis of Groups* (pp. 277–299). San Francisco: Jossey-Bass.

Johnson, A. G. (1995). *The Blackwell Dictionary of Sociology: A User's Guide to Sociological Language*. Oxford: Oxford University Press.

Jones, E. (1953–1957). *The Life and Work of Sigmund Freud* (3 vols.). New York: Basic Books.

Judge, T. A., LePine, J. A. and Rich, B. L. (2006). Loving Yourself Abundantly: Relationship of the Narcissistic Personality to Self- and Other Perceptions of Workplace Deviance, Leadership, and Task and Contextual Performance. *Journal of Applied Psychology*, *91*:4, 762–776.

Jung, C. [1933] (2005). *Modern Man in Search of a Soul*. Oxford: Routledge.

Jung, C. G. (1966). *Two Essays on Analytical Psychology*. London: Routledge & Keegan Paul.

Jung, G. C. (1917). *The Psychology of the Unconscious*. B. M. Hinkle (Trans.). New York: Moffat, Yard and Company.

Junkers, G. (2013a). The Ageing Psychoanalyst: Thoughts on Preparing for a Life Without the Couch. In: G. Junkers (Ed.), *The Empty Couch: The Taboo of Ageing and Retirement in Psychoanalysis* (pp. 3–6). London: Routledge.

Junkers, G. (Ed.). (2013b). Containing Psychoanalysis: The Analytic Institution. In: G. Junkers (Ed.), *The Empty Couch: The Taboo of Ageing and Retirement in Psychoanalysis* (pp. 95–100). London: Routledge.

Junkers, G. (2013c). Later, Perhaps… Transience and Its Significance for the Psychoanalyst. In: G. Junkers (Ed.), *The Empty Couch: The Taboo of Ageing and Retirement in Psychoanalysis* (pp. 17–31). London: Routledge.

Kaplan, D. M. (1969). On Stage Fright. *The Drama Review*, *14*:1, 60–83.

Kaplan, L. J. (1995). *Adolescence: The Farewell to Childhood*. New York: Touchstone Books.

Kashdan, T. B. and Silva, P. J. (2009). Curiosity and Interest: The Benefits of Thriving on Novelty and Challenge. In S. J. Lopez and C. R. Snyder (Eds.), *Oxford Handbook of Positive Psychology* (2nd ed., pp. 367–374). Oxford: Oxford University Press.

Keen, S. (1967). *Gabriel Marcel*. Richmond, VA: John Knox Press.

Keltner, D. (2015). The Science of 'Inside Out.'" *New York Times*, Sunday Review, 7/5/15, p. 10.

Kernberg, O. (1979). Regression in Organizational Leadership. *Psychiatry*, *42*, 24–39.

Kernberg, O. F. (1998). *Ideology, Conflict, and Leadership in Groups and Organizations*. New Haven, CT: Yale University Press.

Kets de Vries, M. F. R. (1991). On Becoming a CEO: Transference and the Addictiveness of Power. In M. F. R. Kets de Vries *et al.* (Eds.), *Organizations on the Couch: Clinical Perspectives on Organizational Behavior and Change* (pp. 120–139). San Francisco: Jossey-Bass.

Kets de Vries, M. F. R. (1993). Alexithymia in Organizational Life: The Organizational Man Revisited. In: L. Hirschhorn and C. K. Barnett (Eds.), *The Psychodynamics of Organizations* (pp. 203–218). Philadelphia, PA: Temple University Press.

Kets de Vries, M. F. R. (2006). *The Leader on the Couch: A Clinical Approach to Changing People and Organizations*. San Francisco, CA: Jossey-Bass.

Kets de Vries, M. F. R. (2010). *Reflections on Leadership and Career Development: On the Couch with Manfred Kets de Vries*. West Sussex, UK: Jossey-Bass.

Kets de Vries, M. F. R. (2011). *Reflections on Groups and Organizations*. San Francisco, CA: Jossey Bass.

Kets de Vries, M. F. R. and Miller, D. (1985). Narcissism and Leadership: An Object Relations Perspective. *Human Relations*, *38*:6, 583–601.

Kieffer, C. C. (2004). Selfobjects, Oedipal Objects, and Mutual Recognition: A Self-Psychological Reappraisal of the Female "Oedipal Victory." *Annual of Psychoanalysis*, *32*, 69–80.

Kim, W. C. and Mauborgne, R. (2005). *Blue Ocean Strategy. How to Create Uncontested Market Space and Make the Competition Irrelevant*. Cambridge, MA: Harvard Business School.

Kjell, O. The Beneficial and Potentially Problematic Effects of Positive Emotions. www.positivepsychology.org.uk/...theory/positive-emotions/118-the-ben..., retrieved 9/15/15.

Kloep, M. and Hendry, L. B. (2007). Retirement: A New Beginning. *The Psychologist*, 20 (December), 742–745.

Knoll, M. A. Z. (2011). Behavioral and Psychological Aspects of the Retirement Decision. *Social Security Bulletin*, 71(4) 1–13.

Kotb, H. (2014). *Ten Years Later: Six People Who Faced Adversity and Transformed Their Lives*. New York: Simon and Schuster.

Kotter, J. (1996). *Leading Change*. Boston, MA: Harvard University Press.

Kramer, P. D. (2014). Why Doctors Need Stories. *The New York Times*, Sunday Review, 10/19/14, pp. 1, 7.

Krantz, J. (2005). Approaching Twenty-First Century, Information-Based Organizations. In: R. J. Sternberg and J. Jordan (Eds.), *A Handbook of Wisdom: Psychological Perspectives* (pp. 51–69). Cambridge, UK: Cambridge University Press.

Krantz, J. and Gilmore, T. N. (1991). Understanding the Dynamics Between Consulting Teams and Client Systems. In: M. F. R. Kets de Vries *et al.* (Eds.), *Organizations on the Couch: Clinical Perspectives on Organizational Behavior and Change* (pp. 307–330). San Francisco, CA: Jossey-Bass.

Krieshok, T. S., Black, M. D. and McKay, R. A. (2009). Career Decision Making: The Limits of Rationality and the Abundance of Non-Conscious Processes. *Journal of Vocational Behavior*, *75*, 275–290.

Labier, D. (1984). Irrational Behavior in Bureaucracy. In: M. F. R. Kets de Vries (Ed.), *The Irrational Executive: Psychoanalytic Explorations in Management* (pp. 3–37). New York: International Universities Press.

Lammers, J., Stapel, D. A. and Galinsky, A. D. (2010). Power Increases Hypocrisy: Moralizing in Reasoning, Immorality in Behavior. *Psychological Science*, *21*:5, 737–744.

Lantos, B. (1943). Work and the Instincts. *International Journal of Psychoanalysis*, *24*, 114–119.

Lantos, B. (1952). Metapsychological Consideration on the Concept of Work. *International Journal of Psychoanalysis*, *33*, 439–443.

Lapierre, L. (1991). Exploring the Dynamics of Leadership. In: M. F. R. Kets de Vries *et al.* (Eds.), *Organizations on the Couch: Clinical Perspectives on Organizational Behavior and Change* (pp. 69–93). San Francisco, CA: Jossey-Bass.

Lapierre, L. (1993). Mourning, Potency, and Power in Management. In: L. Hirschhorn and C. K. Barnett (Eds.), *The Psychodynamics of Organizations* (pp. 19–32). Philadelphia, PA: Temple University Press.

Laplanche, J. and Pontalis, J.-B. (1973). *The Language of Psycho-Analysis*. D. Nicholson-Smith (Trans.). New York: Norton.

Lax, D. and Sebenius, J. (1987). *The Manager as Negotiator*. New York: Free Press.

Leader, Z. (1991). *Writer's Block*. Baltimore, MD: John Hopkins University Press.

Lechte, J. (2003). Julia Kristeva. In: A. Elliott and L. Ray (Eds.), *Key Contemporary Social Theorists* (pp. 183–189). Malden, MA: Blackwell Publishers.

Lee, W. M. L. (1999). *An Introduction to Multicultural Counseling*. New York: Routledge.

Levi, P. (1996). *Survival in Auschwitz*. New York: Touchstone.

Levinas, E. (1989). *Difficult Freedom: Essays on Judaism*. S. Hand (Ed.). Baltimore, MD: The Johns Hopkins University Press.

Levine, H. (1997). Men at Work: Work, Ego and Identity in the Analysis of Adult Men. In: C. W. Socarides and S. Kramer (Eds.), *Work and Its Inhibitions: Psychoanalytic Essays* (pp. 143–157). Madison, CT: International Universities Press.

Levy, K. (1949). The Eternal Dilettante. In. K. R. Eissler (Ed.), *Searchlights on Delinquency* (pp. 65–76). New York: International Universities Press.

Levy, S. T., Seelig, B. J. and Inderbitzin, L. B. (1995). On Those Wrecked by Success: A Clinical Inquiry. *The Psychoanalytic Quarterly*, *64*, 639–657.

Lewin, K. (1958). Group Decision and Social Change. In E. E. Maccoby, T. M. Newcomb and E. L. Hartley (Eds.), *Readings in Social Psychology* (pp. 97–211). New York: Holt, Rinehart & Winston.

Lifton, R. J. (1976). *The Life of the Self: Toward a New Psychology*. New York: Basic Books.

Lilius, J. M., Kanov, J., Dutton, J. E., Warline, M. C. and Maitlis, S. (2012). Compassion Revealed: What We Know About Compassion at Work (and Where We Need to Know More). In: K. S. Cameron and G. M. Spreitzer (Eds.), *The Oxford Handbook of Positive Organizational Scholarship* (pp. 273–287). Oxford: Oxford University Press.

Liu, Y. and Perrewe, P. L. (2005). Another Look at the Role of Emotion. A Process Model. *Human Resource Management Review*, *15*, 263–290.

Loewald, H. W. (1971). Some Considerations on Repetition and Repletion Compulsion. *International Journal of Psychoanalysis*, *52*, 59–65.

Lopez, F. G. (2009). Adult Attachment Security: The Relational Scaffolding of Positive Psychology. In S. J. Lopez and C. R. Snyder (Eds.), *Oxford Handbook of Positive Psychology* (2nd ed., pp. 405–415). Oxford: Oxford University Press.

Lorand, S. (1950). *Clinical Studies in Psychoanalysis*. New York: International Universities Press.

Lubit, R. (2002). The Long-Term Organizational Impact of Destructively Narcissistic Managers. *Academy of Management Executive*, *16*:1, 127–138.

Lunbeck, E. (2014). *The Americanization of Narcissism*. Cambridge, MA: Harvard University Press.

Luthans, F. and Youssef, C. M. (2009). Positive Workplaces. In: S. J. Lopez and C. R Snyder (Eds.), *Oxford Handbook of Positive Psychology* (2nd ed., pp. 579–588). Oxford: Oxford University Press.

Maccoby, M. (1984). The Corporate Climber Has to Find His Heart. In: M. F. R. Kets de Vries (Ed.), *The Irrational Executive: Psychoanalytic Explorations in Management* (pp. 96–111). New York: International Universities Press.

Mahony, P. J. (1997). Freud: Man at Work. In: C. W. Socarides and S. Kramer (Eds.), *Work and Its Inhibitions: Psychoanalytic Essays* (pp. 79–98). Madison, CT: International Universities Press.

Malach-Pines, A. and Yalfe-Yanai, O. (2001). Unconscious Determinants of Career Choice and Burnout: Theoretical Model and Counseling Strategy. *Journal of Employment Counseling*, *38*, 170–184.

Marcel, G. (1952). *Metaphysical Journal*. B. Wall (Trans.). Chicago, IL: Henry Regnery Company.

Marcel, G. (1963). *The Existential Background of Human Dignity*. Cambridge, MA: Harvard University Press.

Marcel, G. (1964). *Creative Fidelity*. R. Rosthal (Trans.). New York: Farrar, Straus and Giroux.

Marcel, G. (1965). *Homo Viator: Introduction to a Metaphysic of Hope*. E. Crauford (Trans.). New York: Harper & Row.

Marcel, G. (1967). *Searchings*. New York: Newman Press.

Marcel, G. (1973). *Tragic Wisdom and Beyond*. Evanston, IL: Northwestern University Press.

Marcel, G. (1984). Reply to Otto Friedrich Bollnow. In A. Schilpp and L. E. Hahn (Eds.), *The Philosophy of Gabriel Marcel* (pp. 200–203). La Salle, IL: Open Court.

Marcel, G. (1995). *The Philosophy of Existentialism*. New York: Carol Publishing Group.

Marcel, G. (2001a). *The Mystery of Being: Volume I: Reflection and Mystery*. South Bend, IN: St. Augustine Press.

Marcel, G. (2001b). *The Mystery of Being: Volume 2: Faith and Reality*. South Bend, IN: St. Augustine Press.

Marcel, G. (2005). *Music and Philosophy*. S. Maddux and R. E. Wood (Trans.). Milwaukee, WI: Marquette University Press.

Marcel, G. (2008). *Man Against Mass Society*. South Bend, IN: St. Augustine's Press.

Marcus, P. (1999). *Autonomy in the Extreme Situation: Bruno Bettelheim, the Nazi Concentration Camps and the Mass Society*. Westport, CT: Praeger.

Marcus, P. (2003). *Ancient Religious Wisdom, Spirituality, and Psychoanalysis*. Westport, CT: Praeger.

Marcus, P. (2008). *Being for the Other: Emmanuel Levinas, Ethical Living and Psychoanalysis*. Milwaukee, WI: Marquette Univesity Press.

Marcus, P. (2010). *In Search of the Good Life: Emmanuel Levinas, Psychoanalysis and the Art of Living*. London: Karnac.

Marcus, P. (2013a). *How to Laugh Your Way Through Life: A Psychoanalyst's Advice*. London: Karnac.

Marcus, P. (2013b). *In Search of the Spiritual: Gabriel Marcel, Psychoanalysis, and the Sacred*. London: Karnac.

Marcus, P. (2014). *They Shall Beat Their Swords Into Plowshares: Military Strategy, Psychoanalysis and the Art of Living*. Milwaukee, WI: Marquette University Press.

Marcus, P. (2015). *Creating Heaven on Earth: The Psychology of Experiencing Immortality in Everyday Life*. London: Karnac.

Marcus, P., with Marcus, G. (2011). *Theater as Life: Practical Wisdom from Great Acting Teachers, Actors and Actresses*. Milwaukee, WI: Marquette University Press.

Marianetti, O. and Passmore, J. (2010). Mindfulness at Work: Paying Attention to Enhance Well-Being and Performance. In: P. A. Linley, S. Harrington and N. Garcea (Eds.), *Oxford Handbook of Positive Psychology and Work* (pp. 189–200). Oxford: Oxford University Press.

Martin, S. W. (2006). *Heavy Hitter Sales Wisdom*. Hoboken, NJ: John Wiley & Sons.

Martusewicz, R. A. (2001). *Seeking Passage: Post–Structuralism, Pedagogy, Ethics*. New York: Teachers College Press, Columbia University.

McDougall, J. (1989). The Dead Father: Early Psychic Trauma and Its Relationship in Sexual Functioning and Creative Activity. *International Journal of Psycho-Analysis*, 70, 205–219.

Meissner, W. W. (1997). The Self and the Principle of Work. In: C. W. Socarides and S. Kramer (Eds.), *Work and Its Inhibitions: Psychoanalytic Essays* (pp. 35–60). Madison, WI: International Universities Press.

Meissner, W. W. (2003). *The Ethical Dimension to Psychoanalysis: A Dialogue*. Albany, NY: State University of New York Press.

Mendelson, M. (1974). *Psychoanalytic Concepts of Depression* (2nd ed.). Flushing, NY: Spectrum Publications.

Menninger, K. A. (1942). Work as Sublimation. *Bulletin of the Menninger Foundation*, 6:6, 170–182.

Meyers, D. G. (2003). Jean Améry: On Being a Jewish Victim. In: S. L. Kremer (Ed.), *Holocaust Literature: An Encyclopedia of Writers and Their Work* (pp. 20–23). New York: Routledge.

Miceli, V. P. (1965). *Ascent to Being: Gabriel Marcel's Philosophy of Communion*. New York: Desclee.

Miller, C. C. (2016). About Face. In *The New York Times Book Magazine*, 2/28/16, 35.

Miller, D. (1998). Workplaces. In: R. Jenkins and T. B. Ustun (Eds.), *Preventing Mental Illness: Mental Health Promotion in Primary Care* (pp. 343–351). Chichester, UK: Wiley.

Miller, H. (1994) [1949]. *Sexus: The Rosy Crucifixion I*. New York: Grove Press.

Milne, D. (2013). *The Psychology of Retirement: Coping with the Transition from Work*. West Sussex, UK: Wiley-Blackwell.

Monte, C. F. (1980). *Beneath the Mask: An Introduction to Theories of Personality* (2nd ed.). New York: Holt, Rinehart and Winston.

Moore, B. E. and Fine, V. D. (Eds.) (1990). *Psychoanalytic Terms and Concepts*. New Haven, CT: American Psychoanalytic Association and Yale University Press.

Morrison, M. and Roese, N. K. (2011). Regrets of the Typical American: Findings from a Nationally Representative Sample. *Social Psychological and Personality and Science*, 2(6), 576–583.

Moscovici, S. and Zavalloni, M. (1969). The Group as a Polarizer of Attitudes. *Journal of Personality and Social Psychology*, 12, 125–135.

Mueller, J. S., Goncalo, J. A. and Kamdar, D. (2011). Recognizing Creative Leadership: Can Creative Expression Negatively Relate to Perceptions of Leadership Potential? *Journal of Experimental Social Psychology*, 47, 494–498.

Muller, J. P. (1995). *Beyond the Psychoanalytic Dyad: Developmental Semiotics in Freud, Peirce and Lacan*. New York: Routledge.

Munley, P. M. (1977). Erikson's Theory of Psychosocial Development and Career Development. *Journal of Vocational Behavior*, 10, 261–269.

Nachman, B. (1960). Childhood Experiences and Vocational Choice in Law, Dentistry and Social Work. *Journal of Counseling Psychology*, 7, 243–250.

Nakamura, J. and Csikszentmihalyi, M. (2009). Flow Theory and Research. In: S. L. Lopez and C. R. Snyder (Eds.), *Oxford Handbook of Positive Psychology* (pp. 195–206). Oxford: Oxford University Press.

Neff, W. S. (1965). Psychoanalytic Conceptions of the Meaning of Work. *Psychiatry*, 28:4, 324–333.

Nehamas, A. (1993, Feb. 15). "Subject and Object." *The New Republic*, pp. 27–35.

Nelson, D. L. and Quick, J. C. (2008). *Understanding Organizational Behavior* (3rd ed.). Mason, OH: South Western Cengage Learning.

Ng, T. W. H. and Feldman, D. C. (2008). Long Work Hours: A Social Identity Perspective on Meta-Analysis Data. *Journal of Organizational Behavior*, 29, 850–880.

Ng, T. W. H., Sorensen, K. L. and Feldman, D. C. (2007). Dimensions, Antecedents and Consequences of Workaholism: A Conceptual Integration and Extension. *Journal of Organizational Behavior*, 28, 111–136.

Nicholls, L. (2007). A Psychoanalytic Discourse in Occupational Therapy. In: J. Creek and A. Lawson-Porter (Eds.), *Contemporary Issues in Occupational Therapy* (pp. 55–86). Chichester, UK: John Wiley & Sons, Ltd.

Nitsun, M. (2015). *Beyond the Anti-Group: Survival and Transformation*. East Sussex, UK: Routledge.

Oates, W. E. (1971). *Confessions of a Workaholic: The Facts about Work Addiction*. New York: World Pub. Co.

Obholzer, A. and Roberts, V. Z. (Eds.). (1994). *The Unconscious at Work: Individual and Organizational Stress in the Human Services*. East Sussex, UK: Routledge.

Olinick, S. L. (1997). On Writer's Block: For Whom Does One Write or Not Write? In: C. W. Socarides and S. Kramer (Eds.), *Work and Its Inhibitions: Psychoanalytic Essays* (pp. 183–190). Madison, CT: International Universities Press.

Osipow, S. H. (1983). *Theories of Career Development* (3rd ed.). Englewood Cliffs, NJ: Prentice-Hall.

Parsons, F. (1909). *Choosing a Vocation*. Boston, MA: Houghton-Mifflin.

Penney, L. M. and Spector, P. E. (2002). Narcissism and Counterproductive Work Behavior: Do Bigger Egos Mean Bigger Problems? *International Journal of Selection and Assessment*, *10*:1/2, 126–134.

Person, E. S., Cooper, A. M. and Gabbard, G. O. (Eds.). (2005). *Textbook of Psychoanalysis*. Washington, DC: American Psychiatric Publishing.

Peterson, C. (2009). Foreword. In: S. L. Lopez and C. R. Snyder (Eds.), *Oxford Handbook of Positive Psychology* (pp. xiii–xiv). Oxford: Oxford University Press.

Pfeffer, J. and Fong, C. T. (2005). Building Organization Theory from First Principles: The Self-Enhancement Motive and Understanding Power and Influence. *Organization Science*, *16*:4, 372–388.

Popper, N. (2016). Stocks and Bots. *The New York Times Magazine*, 2/28/16, pp. 59, 62.

Porfeli, E. J., Lee, B. and Vondracek, F. W. (2013). Identity Development and Careers in Adolescents and Emerging Adults: Content, Process, and Structure. In: W. B. Walsh, M. L. Savickas and P. J. Hartung (Eds.), *Handbook of Vocational Psychology: Theory, Research, and Practice* (pp. 133–153). New York: Routledge.

Porfeli, E. J. and Skorikov, V. B. (2010). Specific and Diversive Career Exploration During Late Adolescence. *Journal of Career Assessment*, *18*:1, 46–58.

Porter, G. (1996). Organizational Impact of Workaholism: Suggestions for Researching the Negative Outcomes of Excessive Work. *Journal of Organizational Health Psychology*, *1*:1, 70–84.

Pruyser, P. W. (1980). Work: Curse or Blessing. *Bulletin of the Menninger Clinic*, *44*:1, 59–73.

Rajchman, J. (1985). *Michel Foucault: The Freedom of Philosophy*. New York: Columbia University Press.

Ratcliffe, S. (2011). *Oxford Treasury of Sayings and Quotations*. Oxford: Oxford University Press.

Reik, T. (1983). *Listening with the Third Ear*. New York: Farrar, Straus and Giroux.

Rhoads, J. M. (1977). Overwork. *Journal of the American Medical Association*, *237*:24, 2615–2618.

Richardson, J. and West, M. A. (2010). Dream Teams: A Positive Psychology of Team Working. In P. A. Linley, S. Harrington and N. Garcea (Eds.), *Oxford Handbook of Positive Psychology and Work* (pp. 235–249). Oxford: Oxford University Press.

Robbins, S. B. and Patton, M. J. (1985). Self-Psychology and Career Development: Construction of the Superiority and Gold Instability Scales. *Journal of Counseling Psychology,* 32:2, 221–231.

Roberto, M. A. (2011). *Transformational Leadership: How Leaders Change Teams, Companies, and Organizations.* Chantilly, VA: Transcript Book, The Great Courses.

Roberto, M. and Levesque, L. (2005). The Art of Making Change Initiative Stick. *MIT Sloan Management Review, 46*:4, 53–59.

Roberts, B. W. (2009). Back to the Future: Personality and Assessment and Personality Development. *Journal of Research in Personality, 43*, 137–145.

Roberts, L. M. and Creary, S. J. (2012). Positive Identity Construction: Insight from Classical and Contemporary Theoretical Perspectives. In K. S. Cameron and G. M. Spreitzer (Eds.), *The Oxford Handbook of Positive Organizational Scholarship* (pp. 70–83). Oxford: Oxford University Press.

Roe, A. (1956). *The Psychology of Occupations.* New York: John Wiley & Sons.

Rorty, R. (1989). *Contingency, Irony, and Solidarity.* Cambridge, UK: Cambridge University Press.

Rorty, R. (1990). *Objectivity, Relativism, and Truth.* New York: Cambridge University Press.

Rosso, B. D., Dekas, K. H. and Wrzesniewski, A. (2010). On the Meaning of Work: A Theoretical Integration and Review. *Research in Organizational Behavior, 30*, 91–127.

Roth, B. (2013). Bion, Basic Assumptions, and Violence: A Corrective Reappraisal. *International Journal of Group Psychotherapy, 63*, 525–543.

Rothbard, N. P. and Patil, S. V. (2012). Being There: Work Engagement and Positive Organizational Scholarship. In K. S. Cameron and G. M. Spreitzer (Eds.), *The Oxford Handbook of Positive Organizational Scholarship* (pp. 56–68). Oxford: Oxford University Press.

Rottinghaus, P. J. and Miller, A. D. (2013). Convergence of Personality Frameworks Within Vocational Psychology. In: W. B. Walsh, M. L. Savickas and P. J. Hartung (Eds.), *Handbook of Vocational Psychology: Theory, Research, and Practice* (pp. 105–131). New York: Routledge.

Rounds, J. B. and Tracey, T. J. (1990). From Trait-and-Factor to Person-Environment Fit Counseling: Theory and Process. In: W. B. Walsh and S. H. Osipow (Eds.), *Career Counseling: Contemporary Topics in Vocational Psychology* (pp. 1–44). Hillsdale, NJ: Lawrence Erlbaum Associates.

Rowland, D. and Higgs, M. (2008). *Sustaining Change: Leadership that Works.* Southampton, UK: Jossey-Bass.

Ruti, M. (2008). *A World of Fragile Things: Psychoanalysis and the Art of Living.* Albany, NY: State University of New York Press.

Rycroft, C. (1995). *A Critical Dictionary of Psychoanalysis* (2nd ed.). London: Penguin.

Safirstein, S. L. (1962). Stage Fright in a Musician. *American Journal of Psychoanalysis,* 22, 15–42.

Savickas, M. L. (2001). Toward a Comprehensive Theory of Career Development: Dispositions, Concerns, and Narratives. In F. T. L. Leon and A. Barak (Eds.), *Contemporary Modes in Vocational Psychology: A Volume in Honor of Samuel H. Osipow* (pp. 295–320). Mahwah, NJ: Lawrence Erlbaum.

Savickas, M. L. (2011). *Career Counseling*. Washington, DC: American Psychological Association.

Savickas, M. L. (2012). Life Design: A Paradigm for Career Intervention in the 21st Century. *Journal of Counseling & Development, 90*, 13–18.

Sawyer, K. (2007). *Group Genius: The Creative Power of Collaboration*. New York: Perseus Books Group.

Schafer, R. (1983). *The Analytic Attitude*. New York: Basic Books.

Scheibe, S., Kunzmann, U. and Baltes, P. B. (2009). New Territories of Positive Life-Span Development: Wisdom and Life Longings. In: S. L. Lopez and C. R. Snyder (Eds.), *Oxford Handbook of Positive Psychology* (pp. 171–183). Oxford: Oxford University Press.

Schlossberg, N. K. (2009). *Revitalizing Retirement: Reshaping Your Identity, Relationships, and Purpose*. Washington, DC: American Psychological Association.

Schultheiss, D. E. P., Kress, H. M., Manzi, A. J. and Glassock, J. M. J. (2001). Relational Influences in Career Development: A Qualitative Inquiry. *The Counseling Psychologist, 29*, 216–241.

Schultz, D. and Schultz, S. E. (Eds.). (2006). *Psychology and Work Today*. Saddle River, NJ: Pearson/Prentice Hall.

Schumacher, E. F. (1979). *Good Work*. New York: Harper & Row.

Schur, M. (1972). *Freud Living and Dying*. London: Hogarth Press.

Schwartz, H. S. (1982). Job Involvement as Obsession-Compulsion. *Academy of Management Review, 7:3*, 429–432.

Schwartz, H. S. (1993). On the Psychodynamics of Organizational Totalitarianism. In: L. Hirschhorn and C. K. Barnett (Eds.), *The Psychodynamics of Organizations* (pp. 237–250). Philadelphia, PA: Temple University Press.

Scott, D. J. and Church, T. (2001). Separation/Attachment Theory and Career Decidedness and Commitment: Effects of Parental Divorce. *Journal of Vocational Behavior, 58*, 328–347.

Seelig, B. J. and Rosof, L. S. (2001). Normal and Pathological Altruism. *Journal of the American Psychoanalytic Association, 49*, 933–959.

Segal, H. (1977). *The Work of Hanna Segal: A Kleinian Approach to Clinical Practice*. London: Free Association Books/Maresfield Library.

Segal, S. and Szabo, R. (1964). Identification in Two Vocations: Accountants and Creative Writers. *Personnel and Guidance Journal, 43*, 252–255.

Sekerka, L. E. and Frederickson, B. L. (2010). Working Positively Toward Transformative Cooperation. In: P. A. Linley, S. Harrington and N. Garcea (Eds.), *Oxford Handbook of Positive Psychology and Work* (pp. 81–94). Oxford: Oxford University Press.

Sekerka, L. E., Vacharkulksemsuk, T. and Frederickson, B. L. (2010). Positive Emotions: Broadening and Building Upward Spirals of Sustainable Enterprise. In: P. A. Linley, S. Harrington and N. Garcea (Eds.), *Oxford Handbook of Positive Psychology and Work* (pp. 168–177). Oxford: Oxford University Press.

Senge, P. M. (2006). *The Fifth Discpline: The Art & Practice of the Learning Organization* (Revised and Updated). New York: Doubleday.

Sennett, R. (1998). *The Corrosion of Character: the Personal Consequences of Work in the New Capitalism*. New York: Norton.

Sennett, R. (2006). *The Culture of the New Capitalism*. New Haven, CT: Yale University Press.

Shafer, R. (1984). The Pursuit of Failure and the Idealization of Unhappiness. *American Psychologist, 39*:4, 398–405.

Silver, C. B. and Spilerman, S. (1990). Psychoanalytic Perspectives on Occupational Choice and Attainment. *Research in Social Stratification and Mobility, 9*, 181–214.

Simmonds, J. G. and Southcott, J. E. (2012). Stage Fright and Joy: Performers in Relations to the Troupe, Audience and Beyond. *International Journal of Applied Psychoanalytic Studies, 9*:4, 318–329.

Socarides, C. W. and Kramer, S. (Eds.). (1997). Editors' Introduction and Overview. In: C. W. Socarides and S. Kramer (Eds.), *Work and Its Inhibitions: Psychoanalytic Essays* (pp. xiii–xxii). Madison, CT: International Universities Press.

Sole, K. (2006). Eight Suggestions from the Small-Group Conflict Trenches. In: M. Deutsch, P. T. Coleman and E. C. Marcus (Eds.), *The Handbook of Conflict Resolution: Theory and Practice* (pp. 805–821). New York: Jossey Bass.

Spolin, V. (1986). *Theater Games for the Classroom: A Teacher's Handbook*. Evanston, IL: Northwestern University Press.

Spolin, V. (1999). *Improvisation for the Theater: A Handbook of Teaching and Directing Techniques* (3rd ed.). Evanston, IL: Northwestern University Press.

Stairs, M. and Galpin, M. (2010). Positive Engagement: From Employee Engagement to Workplace Happiness. In: P. A. Linley, S. Harrington and N. Garcea (Eds.), *Oxford Handbook of Positive Psychology and Work* (pp. 155–172). Oxford: Oxford University Press.

Stewart, C., Ward, T. and Purvis, M. (2004). Promoting Mental Health in the Workplace. In: J. C. Thomas and M. Hersen (Eds.), Psychopathology in the Workplace: Recognition and Adaptation (pp. 329–343). New York: Brunner-Routledge.

Stolorow, R. (1975). Toward a functional definition of narcissism. In: A. P. Morrison (Ed.), *Essential Papers on Narcissism* (pp. 97–209). New York: New York University Press.

Super, D. E. (1990). A Life-Span, Life-Space Approach to Career Development. In D. Brown and L. Brooks (Eds.), *Career Choice and Development: Applying Contemporary Approaches to Practice* (2nd ed., pp. 197–261). San Francisco, CA: Jossey-Bass.

Swogger, Jr., G. (1993). Group Self-Esteem and Group Performance. In: L. Hirschhorn and C. K. Barnett (Eds.), *The Psychodynamics of Organizations* (pp. 99–116). Philadelphia, PA: Temple University Press.

Szekely, L. (1950). Success, Success Neurosis and the Self. *British Journal of Medical Psychology, 33*, 45–51.

Tapio, R. (Ed.). (2014). *The Forbes Quote Bible: Inspiring, Eye-Opening and Motivational Words for Success*. Forbes Media (Kindle).

Teising, M. (2013). Narcissistic Challenges for Ageing Analysts. In: G. Junkers (Ed.), *The Empty Couch: The Taboo of Ageing and Retirement in Psychoanalysis* (pp. 46–52). London: Routledge.

Thomas, D. A. (1993). Mentoring and Irrationality: The Role of Racial Tensions. In: L. Hirschhorn and C. K. Barnett (Eds.), *The Psychodynamics of Organizations* (pp. 191–202). Philadelphia, PA: Temple University Press.

Thomas, J. C. (2004). Introduction. In: J. C. Thomas and M. Hersen (Eds.), *Psychopathology in the Workplace: Recognition and Adaptation* (pp. 3–8). New York: Brunner-Routledge.

Thomas, J. C. and Hersen, M. (Eds.). (2004). *Psychopathology in the Workplace: Recognition and Adaptation*. New York: Brunner-Routledge.

Tuch, R. H. (1995). On the Capacity to be Creative: A Psychoanalytic Exploration of Writer's Block. *Progress in Self Psychology*, *11*, 243–257.

Turquet, P. (1975). Threats to identity in the large group. In: L. Kreeger (Ed.), *The Large Group: Dynamics and Therapy* (pp. 57–86). London: Constable.

Twenge, J. M. and Campbell, S. M. (2010). Generation Me and the Changing World of Work. In P. A. Linley, S. Harrington and N. Garcea (Eds.), *Oxford Handbook of Positive Psychology and Work* (pp. 25–35). Oxford: Oxford University Press.

Tzu, C. (1965). *The Way of Chuang Tzu*. T. Merton (Trans.). New York: New Directions.

Vallas, S. P. (2012). *Work*. Cambridge, UK: Polity Press.

Van Swol, L. M. (2009). Extreme Members and Group Polarization. *Social Influence*, *4*:3, 185–199.

Vansina, L. (2013). General introduction. In: L. Vansina (Ed.), *Humanness in Organisations: A Psychodynamic Contribution* (pp. xv–xxvii). London: Karnac.

Volkan, V. D. (1972). The Linking Objects of Pathological Mourners. *Archives of General Psychiatry*, *27*: 215–221.

Walker, A. (1994). *Everyday Use*. B. T. Christian (ed.). New Brunswick, NJ: Rutgers University Press.

Walsh, W. B., Savickas, M. L. and Hartung, P. J. (Eds.). (2013). *Handbook of Vocational Psychology: Theory, Research, and Practice*. New York: Routledge.

Watkins, E. C., Jr. and Savickas, M. L. (1990). Psychodynamic Career Counseling. In: W. B. Walsh and S. H. Osipow (Eds.), *Career Counseling: Contemporary Topics in Vocational Psychology* (pp. 79–116). Hillsdale, NJ: Lawrence Erlbaum Associates.

Week, The. (2015, May 22). The Fatal Flaw of a Company Without Bosses. p. 33.

Week, The. (2015, July 10). The Rise of Workplace Spying. p. 11.

Week, The. (2015, September 18). No Need to Retire All At Once. p. 33.

Week, The. (2016, March 11). Performance Pay is Dangerous. p. 34.

Week, The. (2016, March 25). Apps. How Slack is Changing Work. p. 20.

Weinstein, F. (1980). *The Dynamics of Nazism*. New York: Academic Press.

Whiston, S. C. and Keller, B. K. (2004). The Influences of the Family of Origin on Career Development: A Review and Analysis. *The Counseling Psychologist*, *32*, 493–567.

White, R. (2004). *Living an Extraordinary Life: Unlocking Your Potential for Success, Joy and Fulfillment*. Denver, CO: Balance Point International.

Wilkinson, W. (2013). Barbara Frederickson's Bestselling "Positivity" Is Trashed by a New Study. www.thedailybeast.com/articles/2013/08/16/barbara-fredrickson-s-bestselling-positivity-is-trashed-by-a-new-study.html, retrieved 9/23/15.

Winnicott, D. (1953). Transitional Objects and Transitional Phenomena. *International Journal of Psychoanalysis*, *34*, 89–97.

Winnicott, D. (1965) [1960]. Ego-Distortion in Terms of True and False Self. In *The Maturational Process and Facilitating Environment* (pp. 140–152). New York: International Universities Press.

Winnicott, D. (1971). *Playing and Reality*. London: Tavistock.

Wolf, E. (1997). A Self Psychological Perspective of Work and Its Inhibitions. In: C. W. Socarides and S. Kramer (Eds.), *Work and Its Inhibitions: Psychoanalytic Essays* (pp. 99–114). Madison, CT: International Universities Press.

Wollan, M. (2016) Failure to Lunch. The Lamentable Rise of Desktop Dining. *The New York Times Magazine*, 2/28/16, pp. 54, 50.

Woolf, V. (2007). *Selected Works of Virginia Woolf*. Hertfordshire, UK: Wordsworth Editions.

Wooten, P. and Cameron, K. S. (2010). Enablers of a Positive Strategy: Positively Deviant Leadership. In: P. A. Linley, S. Harrington and N. Garcea (Eds.), *Oxford Handbook of Positive Psychology and Work* (pp. 53–65). Oxford: Oxford University Press.

Wordsworth, W. (1888). *The Complete Poetical Works*. London: Macmillan and Co.; Bartleby.com, 1999. www.bartleby.com/145/.

Wrzesniewski, A. (2012). Callings. In K. S. Cameron and G. M. Spreitzer (Eds.), *The Oxford Handbook of Positive Organizational Scholarship* (pp. 45–55). Oxford: Oxford University Press.

Wrzesniewski, A. and Dutton, J. E. (2001). Crafting a Job: Revisioning Employees as Active Crafters of Their Work. *Academy of Management Review*, *25*:2, 179–201.

Yearley, L. (1983). The Perfected Person in the Radical Chuang Tzu. In: V. H. Mair (Ed.), *Experimental Essays in Chuang Tzu* (pp. 125–139). Honolulu, HI: University of Honolulu Press.

Youssef, C. M. and Luthans, F. (2010). An Integrated Model of Psychological Capital in The Workplace. In P. A. Linley, S. Harrington and N. Garcea (Eds.), *Oxford Handbook of Positive Psychology and Work* (pp. 277–288). Oxford: Oxford University Press.

Zaleznik, A. (1984). Management and Disappointment. In M. F. R. Kets de Vries (Ed.), *The Irrational Executive: Psychoanalytic Explorations in Management* (pp. 224–246). New York: International Universities Press.

Zaleznik, A. (1991). Leading and Managing: Understanding the Difference. In M. F. R. Kets de Vries and Associates (Eds.), *Organizations on the Couch: Clinical Perspectives on Organizational Behavior and Change* (pp. 97–119). San Francisco, CA: Jossey-Bass.

Web resources

asq.sagepub.com/content/47/4/644.abstract, retrieved 9/24/15.

changingminds.org/explanations/theories/impact_bias.htm, retrieved 6/18/15.

classiclit.about.com › … › Aristotle, retrieved 5/3/15.

dharmawisdom.org/teachings/articles/decision-time#sthash.77nSIsHE.dpuf, retrieved 9/21/15.

executiveeducation.wharton.upenn.edu/thought-leadership/wharton-at-work/2011/02/emotional-contagion#sthash.yIwImvkj.dpuf, retrieved 9/24/15.

hbr.org/…/how-to-bounce-back-from-ad…, retrieved 8/13/15.

http://achakra.com/2013/11/30/wilfred-bion-group-dynamics-the-basic-assumptions-from-wikipedia/, retrieved 4/27/15.

http://well.blogs.nytimes.com/2015/05/12/lawyers-with-lowest-pay-report-more-happiness/?_r=0, retrieved 5/28/15.

http://www.nytimes.com/2003/03/17/obituaries/17JAQU.html, retrieved 5/26/15.

http://www.scientificamerican.com/section/mind-matters/, retrieved 5/22/15.

https://hbr.org/…/half-of-employees-dont-feel-r…, retrieved 5/8/15.

https://mraybould.wordpress.com/2009/01/page/2/, retrieved 4/3/15.

https://resurrectionwaltz2013.wordpress.com/category/r-m…/page/24/, retrieved 10/29/14.

https://www.psychologytoday.com/blog/cutting-edge-leadership/200904/bosses-hell-typology-bad-leaders, retrieved 5/12/15.

izquotes.com/quote/280972, retrieved 7/13/15.

izquotes.com/quote/75728, retrieved 5/12/15.

Javerill-creativdadcursos.com, retrieved 5/29/15.
lareviewofbooks.org/review/a-man-apart, retrieved 10/27/14.
lexbook.net/en/recalcitrant *The* basic idea *that* incentive, retrieved 8/14/15.
m.imdb.com/name/nm0000059/quotes, retrieved 1/5/15.
m.imdb.com/name/nm0142829/quotes, retrieved 6/16/15.
smallbusiness.chron.com › ... › Organizations, retrieved 5/13/15.
thefutureofinnovation.org/contributions/.../the_future_of_innovation_up..., retrieved 4/30/15.
toolkit.smallbiz.nsw.gov.au/part/8/41/198, retrieved 8/14/15.
vimeo.com › BuildASoil › Videos, retrieved 10/3/15.
watercoolernewsletter.com/leading-change-successfully/, retrieved 9/11/15.
www.africanamericanquotes.org/martin-luther-king-jr..html, retrieved 12/19/14.
www.aoa.gov/AoA.../elder.../whatisEA.aspx, retrieved 7/14/15.
www.articles.chicagotribune.com/.../9001210747_1_humpty-..., retrieved 2/9/15.
www.backstage.com/.../study-shows-stage-fright-is-common..., retrieved 1/23/15.
www.bancroft.berkeley.edu/.../mtatplay/wor..., retrieved 11/28/14.
www.bizcoachinfo.com/archives/13642, retrieved 10/15/15.
www.bostonglobe.com/ideas/...playfulness.../story.html, retrieved 11/28/14.
www.brainpickings.org/2013/08/14/how-einstein-thought-combinatorial-creativity/,
    retrieved 10/3/15.
www.businessdictionary.com/definition/organizational-culture.ht..., retrieved 5/14/15.
www.businessdictionary.com/definition/organizational-learning.html, retrieved 8/12/15.
www.businessdictionary.com/definition/organizational-memory.html#ixzz3nPZ73hul,
    retrieved 10/2/15.
www.businessdictionary.com/definition/Peter-principle.html, retrieved 5/13/15.
www.businessdictionary.com/definition/transformational-leadership.html, retrieved 9/23/15.
www.careerwisdom.net.au/career-quotes/, retrieved 12/2/14.
www.catholicbible101.com/motherteresaquotes.htm, retrieved 12/23/14.
www.cbn.com/.../spontaneous-50-ways-t..., retrieved 1/28/15.
www.centria.wordpress.com/2009/11/16/dr-seuss-today, retrieved 12/10/14.
www.citehr.com › Business & Services Market Area, retrieved 5/11/15.
www.civilrightsdefence.org.nz/tuhoe/mlk.html, retrieved 12/21/14.
www.cnbc.com/id/30502091/page/12, retrieved 6/19/15.
www.cnn.com/2014/10/02/world/heroes-reveal/, retrieved 12/21/14.
www.damarque.com › Intangible Capital, retrieved 5/5/15.
www.encyclopedia.com › ... › International Dictionary of Psychoanalysis, retrieved
    12/22/14.
www.encyclopedia.com. "Friendship." International Encyclopedia of Marriage and
    Family. 2003.
www.entheos.com/quotes/by_topic/Rollo+May, retrieved 7/10/15.
www.examiner.com/.../lady-gaga-quotes-outrageous-witty-intelligent-ins..., retrieved
    12/2/14.
www.fcs.txstate.edu/cdc/, retrieved 12/2/14.
www.forbes.com/.../12-great-quotes-from-gandhi-on-his-birthday..., retrieved 12/25/14.
www.forbes.com/.../2013/05/28/inspirational-quotes/5, retrieved 12/14/14.
www.forbes.com/.../another-humorous-view-on-the-fear-of-publi..., retrieved 1/26/15.
www.forbes.com/.../quotes-sayings-proverbs-thoughts-about-wom..., retrieved 2/13/15.
www.forbes.com/sites/.../top-10-qualities-that-make-a-great-lea..., retrieved 5/8/15.
www.gallup.com/poll/.../workers-least-happy-work-stress-pay.asp..., retrieved 2/13/15.

www.glassmanpsyd.com/the-importance-of-boundaries/, retrieved 3/25/15.

www.glass-quotes.com/quote/24185.html, retrieved 2/18/15.

www.goodreads.com/author/show/1143744.Edmund_Bergler, retrieved 2/15/15.

www.gurteen.com/gurteen/gurteen.nsf/id/X001B71A6/, retrieved 9/24/15.

www.heightcelebs.com/2014/11/hugh-grant-quotes/, retrieved 3/16/15.

www.historyofpainters.com/chagall.htm, retrieved 7/13/15.

www.holacracy.org/, retrieved 6/20/15.

www.holacracy.org/how-it-works/, retrieved 6/20/15.

www.huffingtonpost.com/.../famous-writers-share-h..., retrieved 2/16/15.

www.inkorkeys.wordpress.com/2014/.../what-authors-say-about-writers-block/, retrieved 2/4/15.

www.inspirational-quotations.com/success-quotes.html, retrieved 8/20/14.

www.ivcc.edu/jbeyer/.../Vonnegut.ht...izquotes.com/quote/191292, retrieved 2/6/15.

www.izquotes.com/quote/158222, retrieved 3/2/15.

www.izquotes.com/quote/226584, retrieved 12/24/14.

www.izquotes.com/quote/4378, retrieved 12/9/14.

www.jeffreysanchezburks.com/blog/emotional-aperture/, retrieved 9/23/15.

www.jungseattle.org/f10/f10long.html, retrieved 12/9/14.

www.katherinepreston.com/the-importance-spontaniety/#sthash.Hj4dRKcW.dpuf, retrieved 1/28/15.

www.keepinspiring.me/helping-others-quotes/, retrieved 12/29/14.

www.knowledge-management-tools.net/organizational-memory-and-knowledge.html#ixzz3nPXgsIJL, retrieved 10/2/15.

www.leadersbeacon.com/, retrieved 5/5/15.

www.lep.utm.edu/marcel/, retrieved 12/29/14.

www.michel-foucault.com/concepts/, retrieved 10/16/15.

www.mindtools.com › Communication Skills, retrieved 4/29/15.

www.movemequotes.com/top-10-steve-jobs-quotes/#sthash.tnD4H67h.dpuf, retrieved 10/21/15.

www.movemequotes.com/top-25-work-ethic-quotes/, retrieved 12/29/14.

www.ncea.aoa.gov/Library/Data/index.aspx, retrieved 7/14/15.

www.news.stanford.edu/news/2005/june15/jobs-061505.html, retrieved 12/2/14.

www.nimh.nih.gov/health/.../use-of-m..., retrieved 6/18/15.

www.notable-quotes.com/n/nietzsche_friedrich.html, retrieved 12/9/14.

www.nydailynews.com/.../70-u-s-workers-hate-job-poll-article-1.13812..., retrieved 5/9/15.

www.nytimes.com/.../books-of-the-times-books-of-..., retrieved 2/11/15.

www.nytimes.com/.../in-picking-up-an-inside-view, retrieved 12/20/14.

www.nytimes.com/2006/10/20/arts/.../20goul.html?..., retrieved 1/22/15.

www.nytimes.com/books/98/.../gibran-secrets.html, retrieved 12/3/14.

www.nytimes.com/learning/.../onthisday/.../0615.ht..., retrieved 11/26/14.

www.orwell.ru › Library › Essays › Wiw › English, retrieved 2/4/15.

www.oxfordreference.com/view/10.1093/acref/...001.../q-oro-00002544, retrieved 10/20/14.

www.panicattacktreatmentreviews.com/celebrities-social-anxiety-disorder-agor..., retrieved 1/20/15.

www.pbs.org/marktwain/learnmore/writings_tom.html, retrieved 11/28/14.

www.poemhunter.com/quotations/famous.asp?people..., retrieved 2/6/15.

www.positivepsychology.org.uk/...theory/positive-emotions/118-the-ben..., retrieved 9/15/15.

www.psychologytoday.com/.../affective-foreca..., retrieved 6/18/15.

www.psychologytoday.com/.../fighting-stage-fright, retrieved 1/22/15.

www.quoteauthors.com/quotes/alan-watts-quotes.html, retrieved 12/26/14.

www.quotegarden.com/age.html, retrieved 6/16/15.

www.quoteinvestigator.com/2010/06/09/twain-speech/, retrieved 1/23/15.

www.quotes.net/quote/1914, retrieved 2/19/15.

www.quoteworld.org › Mark Twain, retrieved 11/2/14.

www.quoteworld.org › Pablo Picasso, retrieved 12/20/14.

www.quoteworld.org/quotes/4132, retrieved 12/14/14.

www.rebellesociety.com › troublemakers, retrieved 12/24/14.

www.reformtaoism.org/Zhuangzi_Translations/watson_26-30.php, retrieved 3/23/15.

www.refspace.com/quotes/Sigmund_Freud/Q8130, retrieved 3/26/15.

www.riverbankoftruth.com/2013/03/14/leave-it-alone-by-alan-watts, retrieved 12/2/14.

www.seattleplaytherapy.com/play-therapy, retrieved 12/9/14.

www.simplypsychology.org › Social Psychology › Attitudes, retrieved 5/15/15.

www.snpp.com/episodes/8F24.html, retrieved 12/10/14.

www.theatromathia.gr/theaterland/impro_en.html, retrieved 2/19/15.

www.theguardian.com › Arts › Music › Lady Gaga, retrieved 12/2/14.

www.thewritepractice.com/hemingway-quotes/, retrieved 2/11/15.

www.torbenrick.eu › Change Management, retrieved 8/13/15.

www.trainingindustry.com/.../does-today's-market-dictate-your-need-for..., retrieved 2/14/15.

www.uky.edu/~eushe2/Bandura/BanEncy.html, retrieved 2/18/15.

www.unitedearth.com.au/spinoza.html, retrieved 3/20/15.

www.usatoday.com/story/.../americans-hate-jobs.../2457089/, retrieved 3/13/15.

www.usdreams.com/FordW19.html, retrieved 5/19/15.

www.values.com/.../3113-these-are-days-when-no-one-should-rely-undu..., retrieved 2/2/15.

www.vatican.va/.../ns_lit_doc_20031019_madre-teresa_en.html, retrieved 12/18/14.

www.whale.to/a/goethe_q.html, retrieved 6/1/15.

www.wheelercentre.com/dailies/post/a0cf1a03c5e2/, retrieved 2/15/15.

www.worldofquotes.com/author/Walter+Benjamin/1/index.html, retrieved 2/2/15.

www.zimbio.com/Evan+Esar+Quotes, retrieved 12/24/14.

www.zquotes.com/quote/127300, retrieved 2/19/15.

www.zquotes.com/quote/191277, retrieved 2/19/15.

yourbusiness.azcentral.com/poor-company-culture-affect-employees-4410, retrieved 5/25/15.

Index

Added to a page number 'n' denotes a note.